Postdigital Sc

CW01642208

This series is a new, international book series dedicated to postdigital science and education. It brings together a rapidly growing community of authors and the currently highly scattered body of research. The series complements the Postdigital Science and Education Journal and together they provide a complete, whole-rounded service to researchers working in the field. The book series covers a wide range of topics within postdigital science and education, including learning and data analytics, digital humanities, (digital) learning, teaching and assessment, educational technology and philosophy of education.

We no longer live in a world where digital technology and media are separate, virtual, 'other' to a 'natural' human and social life. Book series engaged with technology and education tend to view the research field as concerned with the 'effects' of digital media and other technologies on the existing activities of teaching and learning in education. This still assumes a clear division between an authentic educational practice and the imposition of an external, and novel, technology. The rapid growth of research and books and articles dealing with education and research in and for the postdigital age calls for a different approach that is no longer based on a division but rather on an integration of education and technology. This book series meets that need.

This book series

- Fills the gap in the scholarly community as the first academic book series in postdigital science and education
- Explicitly focuses on postdigital themes and research approaches
- Forms a hub for a growing body of scholarship in the field
- Enables communication, dissemination, and community building for researchers, authors, and students

More information about this series at http://www.springer.com/series/16439

Alison MacKenzie • Jennifer Rose • Ibrar Bhatt
Editors

The Epistemology of Deceit in a Postdigital Era

Dupery by Design

Springer

Editors
Alison MacKenzie
School of Social Sciences Education and Social Work
Queen's University Belfast
Belfast, United Kingdom

Jennifer Rose
School of Social Sciences Education and Social Work
Queen's University Belfast
Belfast, United Kingdom

Ibrar Bhatt
School of Social Sciences Education and Social Work
Queen's University Belfast
Belfast, United Kingdom

ISSN 2662-5326 ISSN 2662-5334 (electronic)
Postdigital Science and Education
ISBN 978-3-030-72156-5 ISBN 978-3-030-72154-1 (eBook)
https://doi.org/10.1007/978-3-030-72154-1

This Springer imprint is published by the registered company Springer Nature Switzerland AG
The registered company address is: Gewerbestrasse 11, 6330 Cham, Switzerland

Series Editor's Preface

Less than five minutes after I sat at my desk to write this Series Editor's Preface for *The Epistemology of Deceit in a Postdigital Era: Dupery by Design*, I received an email from my dear friend and colleague, Michael Peters. Michael sent me Peter Webster's recently published book, *The Edited Collection: Pasts, Present and Futures* (2020), and asked: What do you think? As I welcomed the opportunity to procrastinate and started reading, I was taken aback. Already in the abstract, Webster puts forward a set of disturbing claims:

> Edited collections are widely supposed to contain lesser work than scholarly journals; to be incoherent as volumes, no more than the sum of their parts; and to be less visible to potential readers once published. It is also often taken as axiomatic that those who make decisions in relation to hiring, promotion, tenure and funding agree. To publish in or edit an essay collection is thought to risk being penalised for the format before even a word is read. (Webster 2020)

Webster provides a convincing set of sources which indicate that this attitude towards the edited book is indeed quite widespread. While he takes pains to argue the opposite, the very fact that (seemingly many) people look down at the edited book opens a myriad questions. What is the distinct value of the edited book? And what is our responsibility, as scholars and academic editors, towards the edited book?

Arguably, a useful way to examine the value of the edited book is to compare it with its closest cousin: the journal special issue. Edited books and special issues both have a clear theme and scope; journal articles and book chapters are roughly of the same length; and review processes, at least in the Postdigital Science and Education publishing ecosystem, are the same (double-blind peer review). According to Webster, however, journal special issues are slightly more impersonal, while the edited collection is fundamentally more conversational in nature.

> Born themselves often from ongoing interactions among groups of scholars, edited collections often display those conversations, with all the elements of consonance and dissonance that are entailed. In their turn, these volumes often become points of reference in the continuing conversations within the discipline. (Webster 2020: 13)

The Postdigital Science and Education community is well aware that 'my words and ideas in this article are not just mine: they are an amalgam of all encounters with colleagues, friends, and people known and unknown that have passed through my professional and personal life' (Jandrić 2020: 179; see also Mañero 2020). Epistemically, this is why the edited book has an important place in postdigital research based on the concept of (postdigital) dialogue (Jandrić et al. 2019), and the dialectics between we-think, we-learn, we-act, and we-feel (Jandrić 2019; Jandrić and Hayes 2020). Pragmatically, this is why this Preface emphasises the genre: postdigital research cannot be done in isolation from political economy.

This book was borne from our shared feeling that the world needs a serious conversation about truth, lies, and epistemology. In 2019, Alison MacKenzie and Ibrar Bhatt published the Special Issue of *Postdigital Science and Education* titled 'Lies, Bullshit and Fake News Online: Should We Be Worried?'[1] In 2021, it is my honour to present Alison MacKenzie, Ibrar Bhatt, and Jennifer Rose's edited book *The Epistemology of Deceit in a Postdigital Era: Dupery by Design*. For those who want to compare journal special issues and edited books, this is an exemplary case study.

So, what is the distinct value of this edited book? 'Lies, Bullshit and Fake News Online: Should We Be Worried?' is a set of distinct voices gathered around a common theme, with an odd loose connection. *The Epistemology of Deceit in a Postdigital Era: Dupery by Design* is more compact; the chapters are in deeper conversation with each other. One can clearly see an emerging community of scholars who have already made significant contributions in the field, and will surely continue to do so in the future. The journal special issue is a clowder of cats; the edited book is a pack of dogs. Both are equally important, but each brings about its own distinct value.

And what is our responsibility, as scholars and academic editors, towards the edited book? If you have mice, get a cat; if you are afraid of burglars, get a dog. Ideally, the choice of genre should follow the nature of the examined question. However, the choice of genre often emerges from our personal preferences: some people like cats, other people like dogs, and some of us equally like both. Whatever our choice, we need to remember that well-behaved dog owners will never allow their pets to chase cats, and well-behaved cat owners will never allow their cats to molest dogs. 'Special issue people' and 'edited book people' do not need to love each other, but their genres of choice do deserve equal respect.

In the following pages, Alison MacKenzie, Ibrar Bhatt, and Jennifer Rose have provided us with the simplest proof for this argument – they have produced a valuable edited book which presents years of diverse scholarly dialogues culminating in a coherent whole. This is why *The Epistemology of Deceit in a Postdigital Era:*

[1] See https://link.springer.com/journal/42438/volumes-and-issues/2-1. Accessed 12 January 2021.

Dupery by Design is more than the sum of its parts, and this is why it will be an unavoidable steppingstone for further research in the field.

Zagreb, Croatia Petar Jandrić

References

Jandrić, P. (2019). We-Think, We-Learn, We-Act: the Trialectic of Postdigital Collective Intelligence. *Postdigital Science and Education, 1*(2), 257–279. https://doi.org/10.1007/s42438-019-00055-w.

Jandrić, P. (2020). The Postdigital Challenge of Pandemic Education. *Journal of Contemporary Educational Studies, 71*(4), 176–189.

Jandrić, P., & Hayes, S. (2020). Postdigital We-Learn. *Studies in Philosophy of Education, 39*(3), 285–297. https://doi.org/10.1007/s11217-020-09711-2.

Jandrić, P.; Ryberg, T.; Knox, J.; Lacković, N.; Hayes, S.; Suoranta, J.; Smith, M.; Steketee, A.; Peters, M. A.; McLaren, P.; Ford, D. R.; Asher, G.; McGregor, C.; Stewart, G.; Williamson, B., & Gibbons, A. (2019). Postdigital Dialogue. *Postdigital Science and Education, 1*(1), 163–189. https://doi.org/10.1007/s42438-018-0011-x.

Mañero, J. (2020). Review of Peter McLaren and Petar Jandrić (2020). Postdigital Dialogues on Critical Pedagogy, Liberation Theology and Information Technology. *Postdigital Science and Education*. https://doi.org/10.1007/s42438-020-00191-8.

Webster, P. (2020). *The Edited Collection: Pasts, Present and Futures*. Cambridge, UK: Cambridge University Press.

Foreword: Lying, Politics, Government

In *Lying in Politics* (1971), Hannah Arendt, commenting on the Pentagon Papers, reflects on the fundamental relationship between lying and politics. She explains the nature of political action in the context of lying with surprising consequences that run against modern intuitions and threaten to change our understanding of the history of politics. She provides an account of political imagination that draws connections between 'the ability to lie, the deliberate denial of factual truth, and the capacity to change facts, the ability to act'. Arendt maintains that 'facts need testimony' and 'no factual statement can ever be beyond doubt'. She continues:

> It is this fragility that makes deception so easy up to a point, and so tempting. It never comes into a conflict with reason, because things could indeed have been as the liar maintains they were; lies are often much more plausible, more appealing to reason, than reality, since the liar has the great advantage of knowing beforehand what the audience wishes or expects to hear. He has prepared his story for public consumption with a careful eye to making it credible, whereas reality has the disconcerting habit of confronting us with the unexpected for which we were not prepared. (Arendt 1971)

What Arendt's analysis prepares us for is the deliberate intentionality of the lie in politics and its resistance to truth. Rarely is there a knock-down argument or evidential proof that can be advanced quickly and efficiently to counter false claims. The office of the president also carries with it a stamp of authority where only a few brave people are willing to publicly contradict an announcement from the White House which grips the imagination like an announcement from God himself.

The combination of systematic lying, a veritable torrent of seemingly endless lies, delivered directly through Twitter rather than traditional news media comes close to defining the style of Trump's presidency. He has been massively successful judged by his 32 million Twitter followers and the 74 million Americans that voted for him. It's interesting to discover how many voted for him despite their knowledge of his lying and his lying style.

I cannot think of a more important topic than the topic of this edited collection that focuses on the 'epistemology of deceit in a postdigital era' just as Donald Trump leaves the US presidency and Joe Biden becomes the 46th President. The collection is a reflection on the 4 years of Trump's presidency who came to office already having developed his political style and apparatus of systematic deceit and Big Lies delivered directly to his 32 million core Twitter followers. Trump's 'big lie' conspiracy style of government began with casting aspersion on Obama's birth certificate in the 'birther movement', a conspiracy that claimed Obama was ineligible to be president because he was born in Kenya. It was a deliberate untruth that was designed to cast doubt on his citizenship, his racial origin and his religious convictions. The conspiracy suggested also that Obama's birth certificate was a forgery. Commentators have suggested that this was part of a racist slur against Obama's status as a black man. It was raised by Trump, then businessman and television personality, many times during Obama's election campaign going back as early as 2008. Twenty-five per cent of Americans, especially Republicans, believed that Obama was not born in the United States and was therefore not eligible to run for president.[1]

The 'birther movement', based on a lie, was the forerunner of many lies and conspiracies against Trump's political rivals, both Democrat and Conservative. This false narrative carefully crafted to capture the network of negative belief that was grafted onto a set of historical we-they prejudices, required the active and deliberate work of the architects of the lie, who craft the lie and then disseminate it in the right channels. I tried to draw attention to the viral nature of the post-truth era with my colleagues Sharon Rider, Mats Hyvönen and Tina Besley in the Springer collection *Post-Truth, Fake News: Viral Modernity & Higher Education.*[2] The viral nature of post-truth media, along with its virulent anti-democratic sentiments, served to fire-up the collective imagination of white supremacists, 'Patriot' movements, neo-nazi organisations and QAnon supporters, all of whom had their worst festering fears confirmed by Trump's tweets.

The conspiracy of the 'birther movement' was followed by a range of other major types which could be chanted and tweeted time and again. Climate change was another target of conspiracy, with a president in league with the oil and gas billionaires. As early as 2012, Trump suggested that climate change was 'a very expensive hoax' perpetrated by the Chinese government. Trump tweeted: 'The concept of global warming was created by and for the Chinese in order to make U.S. manufacturing non-competitive' (see Matthews 2017). There followed a large number of conspiracies that fired-up MAGA supporters who were incited by Trump and radicalised by conservative and far-right social media.

Claims that voter fraud in the 2016 election cost him the popular vote.
Questions that childhood vaccines cause autism.
Claims that Obama had wiretapped Trump's phone.
Claims that 3000 people didn't die in Puerto Rico after Hurricane Maria and that Democrats inflated the death toll.
Claims that windmills cause cancer.
Claims that the Clintons killed Jeffrey Epstein.

[1] https://en.wikipedia.org/wiki/Barack_Obama_citizenship_conspiracy_theories. Accessed 15 January 2021.

[2] https://link.springer.com/book/10.1007/978-981-10-8013-5. Accessed 15 January 2021.

Claims that former vice president Joe Biden was corrupt in his dealings with Ukraine during the Obama administration.
Claims that a cybersecurity company named Crowdstrike framed Russia for election interference.
Claims that the Ukraine may be hiding Hillary Clinton's missing emails.
Claims about voter fraud.
Claims about the stolen election.[3]

The Washington Post reports that Trump made 30,573 misleading claims during his presidency, with more than half in the final year.[4] The production of the lie is not a casual process but the result of a carefully crafted political strategy engaging a team of political workers.

Trumpology is a carefully constructed litany of lies and conspiracies where evidence is irrelevant to his supporters because these lies confirm his supporters' worst fears. They already 'knew' – their network beliefs were primed to accept these lies because they exonerated their worldview and gave life to their seething hatreds, acerbating and deepening racist and paranoid fears.[5]

The viral nature of conspiracy thinking is a subject we explored in 'A viral theory of post-truth' (Peters et al. 2020), drawing on Gregory Bateson's (1972) insight that '[t]here is an ecology of bad ideas, just as there is an ecology of weeds, and it is characteristic of the system that basic error propagates itself'. As we argued in that paper: 'Viral information and viral media have developed a special link between the way that information behaves in digital networks and the role that information plays as a messaging system in genomic biology'.

What is encouraging about this collection of chapters is that they help to rectify the historical imbalance in epistemology that favours the focus on knowledge and truth claims to begin to examine more carefully *The Epistemology of Deceit in a Postdigital Era: Dupery by Design*. My congratulations to the editors – Alison MacKenzie, Jennifer Rose and Ibrar Bhatt – who have done us philosophers, educators and social scientists a major service by linking epistemological questions to lies, manipulation and deceit, to post-truth and fake news, to dupery and democracy, and to questions of digital literacy and critical pedagogy. The collection is a major theoretical step forward in understanding the 'ecology of lies' where the propagation of falsehoods and government by conspiracy are inherent in the two-party system of American democracy in 'the era of digital reason' (Peters and Jandrić 2015).

Trump lost the election but he will be back, working to build his party and his white militia. American politics shows the historical deep divisions that were one of the main causes of the civil war. This division has barely faded. It has given birth to American fascism, which is not about to disappear any time soon. If anything, under

[3] 24 outlandish conspiracy theories Donald Trump has floated over the years.

[4] https://www.washingtonpost.com/politics/how-fact-checker-tracked-trump-claims/2021/01/23/ad04b69a-5c1d-11eb-a976-bad6431e03e2_story.html. Accessed 15 January 2021.

[5] https://en.wikipedia.org/wiki/Category:Conspiracy_theories_promoted_by_Donald_Trump; https://www.factcheck.org/2020/10/trumps-long-history-with-conspiracy-theories/. Accessed 15 January 2021.

Trump, whether impeached or not, fascism has hardened into American desolation. In these circumstances, *Dupery by Design* will become ever more important.

Beijing, People's Republic of China Michael A. Peters

References

Arendt, H. (1971). Lying in politics: Reflections on the Pentagon papers. The New York Review of Books, 18 November. https://www.nybooks.com/articles/1971/11/18/lying-in-politics-reflections-on-the-pentagon-pape/. Accessed 26 January 2021.

Bateson, G. (1972). *Steps Towards an Ecology of Mind.* New York: Ballantine.

Matthews, D. (2017). Donald Trump has tweeted climate change skepticism 115 times. Here's all of it. Vox, 1 June. https://www.vox.com/policy-and-politics/2017/6/1/15726472/trump-tweets-global-warming-paris-climate-agreement. Accessed 26 January 2021.

Peters, M. A., & Jandrić, P. (2015). Philosophy of education in the age of digital reason. *Review of Contemporary Philosophy, 14,* 161–182.

Peters, M. A., Rider, S., Hyvönen, M., & Besley, T. (Eds.). (2018). *Post-Truth, Fake News: Viral Modernity & Higher Education.* Singapore: Springer.

Peters, M., McLaren, P. & Jandrić, P. (2020). A viral theory of post-truth. *Educational Philosophy and Theory*. https://doi.org/10.1080/00131857.2020.1750090.

Wikipedia (2021a). Barack Obama citizenship conspiracy theories. https://en.wikipedia.org/wiki/Barack_Obama_citizenship_conspiracy_theories. Accessed 26 January 2021.

Wikipedia (2021b). Category: Conspiracy theories promoted by Donald Trump. https://en.wikipedia.org/wiki/Category:Conspiracy_theories_promoted_by_Donald_Trump. Accessed 26 January 2021.

Zeballos-Roig, J., Haltiwanger, J., & Kranz, M. (2019). 24 outlandish conspiracy theories Donald Trump has floated over the years. Business Insider, 9 October. https://www.businessinsider.com/donald-trump-conspiracy-theories-2016-5?r=AU&IR=T. Accessed 26 January 2021.

In plain truth, lying is an accursed vice. We are not men, nor have other tie upon one another, but by our word … If falsehood had, like truth, but one face only, we should be upon better terms; for we should then take for certain the contrary to what the liar says: but the reverse of truth has a hundred thousand forms, and a field indefinite, without bound or limit. The Pythagoreans make good to be certain and finite, and evil, infinite and uncertain. There are a thousand ways to miss the white, there is only one to hit it. For my own part, I have this vice in so great horror, that I am not sure I could prevail with my conscience to secure myself from the most manifest and extreme danger by an impudent and solemn lie. An ancient father says 'that a dog we know is better company than a man whose language we do not understand.'

Chapter IX, Of Liars, Essays of Michel de Montaigne (1877)

Telling the truth is, therefore, something which must be learnt. This will sound very shocking to anyone who thinks it must all depend on moral character and that if this is blameless, the rest is child's play. But the simple fact is that the ethical cannot be detached from reality, and consequently continual progress in learning to appreciate reality is a necessary ingredient in ethical action.

Dietrich Bonhoeffer, What is Meant by Telling the Truth? (1965)

Acknowledgements

Our greatest thanks go to Petar Jandrić, the series editor. His drive, enthusiasm, patience, kindness, and encouragement are deeply appreciated by us all. How he finds the time to do all he does is beyond us. We have learned a great deal from him – editing a book is not like editing a special issue or a journal, and he has introduced us to a new set of skills. It is an honour to be part of the Postdigital Science and Education community and to contribute to the book series.

We would also like to thank our contributors. 2020 was an 'unprecedented' year, one that was almost entirely shaped by Covid-19: we lived through lockdowns, restrictions, working from home, home schooling, quarantine, travel bans, not seeing family, friends, and colleagues – save on Zoom, Teams and Skype – and watched in dismay as the virus ran out of control or reacted in admiration at those countries whose leaders kept the virus under control. We are now waiting for our 'jabs' and to be released from our homes.

Our contributors rose above these challenges to write the chapters you will read in this collection. We give them our heartfelt thanks.

Our thanks are also owed to Ian Thatcher and Jonathan McDonald for their insights and support.

Introduction: The Genesis of *Dupery by Design*

In 2018, Ibrar and Alison began collaborating on a paper on algorithms and ignorance that was eventually published as 'Just Google it! Digital literacy and the epistemology of ignorance' (Bhatt and MacKenzie 2019) in the journal *Teaching in Higher Education: Critical Perspectives.* It was a serendipitous decision (Ibrar invited Alison); Alison had very little experience of empirical research and was as ignorant of the operations of Google and other platforms as those surveyed in the research. As it turned out, we started writing on these issues at a very propitious time. Interest in the nature of political messages on social media and concerns over how platforms were being used to manipulate voters and harvest personal data without the knowledge of their users intensified as a result of Brexit[1] in the UK in 2016 and the Presidential elections of 2016 and 2020 in the United States. Lies, manipulation, and deceit are not new, as we discussed in a commentary (MacKenzie and Bhatt 2020a) and subsequent article (MacKenzie and Bhatt 2020b) in a special issue of *Postdigital Science in Education*, 'Lies, Bullshit and Fake News Online: Should We Be Worried?'.[2] However, these events placed these phenomena squarely onto the international agenda, with strategic online disinformation campaigns and computational propaganda, in which governments and private actors make cynical use of algorithms and big data to manipulate public opinion at scale, now prevalent in more than 80 countries – and counting (Bradshaw et al. 2021).

The 2020 US presidential election notoriously culminated in the storming of Congress on Capitol Hill on 6 January 2020 by supporters of Trump, determined to 'Stop the Steal'. The attack on democracy was 'unprecedented' in modern US history. Trump's language, his disdain for political norms and the gravity of the office, and his repeated false claims about fake news and the stolen election on social and

[1] A portmanteau of the words 'British' and 'exit' to refer to the UK's decision in a 23 June 2016 referendum to leave the European Union (EU).

[2] See https://link.springer.com/journal/42438/volumes-and-issues/2-1. Accessed 15 January 2021.

mass media were blamed for the 6 January insurrection. In the UK, the Brexit disinformation campaigns continue to reverberate and divide so-called Remainers (supporters of European Union membership) and Brexiteers (supporters of leaving the European Union).

As we write this, Twitter has banned Trump permanently from its platform; Reddit has banned the subreddit group 'r//DonaldTrump'; Google no longer hosts Parler; Apple has suspended it from its App Store; Amazon has ceased providing Parler with cloud services; and Facebook has banned Trump from posting on his accounts until the transition of power to President-elect Joe Biden is complete. Other media platforms and services have sought to distance themselves from Trump. These actions also seem 'unprecedented' – and welcome to many concerned with the degradation of social and political discourse.

These 'unprecedented' moves have inevitably raised concerns about the risks to free speech. It is not the job, it is claimed, of online platforms to determine who has the right to speech, or what the limits of free speech are, even if that free speech is odious, inciteful, or spreads lies. This is complex moral and political territory because free speech, in liberal democracies at least, is highly contentious because it is valued, even by autocrats (on their terms, of course). Therefore, any limits placed on such speech will be controversial and will place us on the slippery slope towards tyranny and censorship. (One rarely hears the opposite effects, that unfettered speech can lead to anarchy, violence, and, ultimately, tyranny.)

What is 'free' speech? What are the limits, if any, of free speech? At what point do we intervene to say that free speech is so harmful that it risks undermining democracy, the health of the nation, and the wellbeing of individuals, and so must be constrained? As events in the United States and the UK have demonstrably shown, free speech is volatile and contentious because it occurs in contexts of competing, if not antagonistic, values. Whatever one's views on where the limits lie, few states permit unfettered free speech (most countries will have libel, defamation, hate, and child pornography laws, for example). Few would argue that it is absolute: it cannot be. The reasons should be obvious: illegitimately unfettered free speech would corrode other entitlements such as privacy, security, bodily integrity and health, and life. Depending on the intensity, hate and libellous speech may also degrade, humiliate, and undermine the dignity of persons. The contentious question is: should platforms censure elected officials by removing their tweets and posts, or accounts? (Facebook and Twitter do, in fact, remove harmful content and political figures who foment hate.)

What motivated our research was the scale, speed, amplification, and quality of 'information' that spread across social media, particularly the harms of deceit on individuals and the polity. It seemed to us that another 'unprecedented' feature of our social media lives that spills over into mass media and thence into our personal lives, is the effect of deceit on our ability to engage in practical reasoning: our plans of action, goals, decisions, aspirations; on theoretical reasoning: what we should and ought to do; what it means to undertake one course of action as opposed to another. If any one entity seemed to show the hazards of deceit, it was social media.

In 2016, 'post-truth' was Oxford dictionary's word of the year. Perhaps the most widely used word in 2020 was 'unprecedented'. These words point to situations, events, and actions that are unrivalled, unequalled, and unmatched, not because deceit is new, or that leaders making grabs for power is unusual; rather, it seems to be the sheer scale, the sheer hubris, the sheer ruthlessness by which bad speech and its parasitic vices proliferate across media and clamour for our fractured attention. We decided to explore these issues through the philosophical lens of epistemology, more precisely, epistemic vices such as lies, malinformation, disinformation, wilful and insouciant ignorance. However, as we argued (MacKenzie and Bhatt 2020a, b; MacKenzie et al. 2020), determining what is true and truthful is rarely easy or without controversy.

As the collection of chapters gathered in this book will attest, social media, while a valuable and indispensable common good, is also the handmaiden of deception and a critical threat to democracy as a result of sustained manipulation of public opinion (Bradshaw et al. 2021). Technology enables humans to learn false, misleading, inaccurate information, corrupting not only the nature of information, but also social relations by increasing xenophobia (as seen throughout Covid-19, for example), generating new concerns about rights and freedoms, and implicitly supporting the resurgence and escalation of corrupted beliefs in and about politics. The debasement of public and online discourse has led to violent political riots (in the United States and India, for example).

The proliferation of fake news, lies, and deceit on digital media worldwide, and its connection to human and animal harm, is surely sound evidence for the need for a postdigital understanding of these disturbing phenomena. A postdigital understanding aims to rupture previously established ways of thinking, and to spotlight the entanglement of digitality in our everyday actions and interactions which are driven by what we know or presume to know. Digital technology and media are no longer separate or virtual entities but are life shaping and determining forms that exercise remarkable power and influence almost every aspect of our lives: social, political, economic, and biological (see Jandrić et al. 2018 for a literature review on meanings and effects of the postdigital). The extensive and pervasive power affects our capacities to reason, evaluate, deliberate, and analyse information, as many of the chapters in this collection will demonstrate.

This led us to the idea of *Dupery*. To what extent is the design and infrastructure of digital platforms an enabler in the current problem of what is true and truthful; fake or real; informative or misinformative? If dupery is sometimes 'by design' in that humans can, and often do, spread misinformation with intent to cause harm, then is the very 'design' of a social media platform also to be implicated in the current problems we face? Yes. When looked at through a postdigital lens, technologies and social media platforms in particular, via their infrastructural logics, create both new norms for discourse, radically alter a priori notions of 'public sphere', and enable new forms of power and inequality to exist.

As our contributors in this collection demonstrate in their highly diverse ways, deception is a pervasive feature of human interactions. While the reasons for understanding why people deceive and how they deceive are complex, lacking a (consensual) unified understanding, what is increasingly clear is that the Enlightenment legacy, the Anthropocene, and the binary nature of understanding that governs past and present ways of being human, reasoning, and knowing, are no longer adequate for capturing and explaining the complexity that comes with a post-digital understanding.

Organisation of the Book

The book is organised into four parts: (1) Epistemology of Deceit; (2) Dupery, Politics, and Democracy; (3) Discourse and Digital Literacy; and (4) Towards a Critical Pedagogy.

Part 1: Epistemology of Deceit

The three chapters in 'Part 1: Epistemology of Deceit' are concerned with the threats to democratic processes posed by deceit, engagement in bad faith politics, and the rejection of the intrinsic value of truth.

In Chapter 1, MacKenzie and Bhatt draw on Machiavelli's statecraft to explore whether deceit should form part of the armoury of government, and argue emphatically that it should not. Bad faith in politics and on social media can have profound impacts on the polity and public discourse. They argue that platforms which create systems that favour deceit over truth, and which manipulate public opinion to pursue profit, erode trust, increase polarisation, threaten democratic processes, and destabilise democracy, as they discuss in the context of the UK and the United States. Ethical conduct, such as truthtelling, they argue, is critical to democracy and positive human relations.

Jennifer Rose, in Chapter 2, argues that false beliefs arise out of a commitment to truth as the sole epistemic aim for justifying one's belief. Belief in the absoluteness and cohesiveness of truth, and 'truthlings', fortifies trust in manipulated but emulated truth in digitised realities; consequently, deception is enabled, and false beliefs transpire. Resultantly, coinciding with the goals of truth, she argues that education ought to include the value of understanding as an epistemic aim to help reduce postdigital deception.

In Chapter 3, Jake Wright begins his analysis of epistemic nihilism by reference to the 2020 US presidential election and accusations that it was fraudulent. As he reports, liberal democracies depend on good faith engagement wherein citizens stand up for the values of fair and equal participation. Violation of those norms by repeated assertions of fraudulence, the practices of trolling, bullshitting, and vexatious litigation undermine democratic institutions. These phenomena represent what Wright terms 'epistemic nihilism' whereby truth, as a necessary condition for achieving one's good faith aims, is rejected because it is not valuable to the speaker.

Epistemic nihilism is a form of cheating because the nihilist expects his interlocutor to engage in good faith practices that he has rejected, so serving the nihilist an unfair advantage with respect to what is true.

Part 2: Dupery, Politics, and Democracy

Grouped together in this part of the book are four chapters which examine the impact and consequences of dupery, fake news, and information disorders on democracy, liberal democratic institutions, human rights, and the invisibility of animal welfare.

Tess Maginess in Chapter 4 examines how dupery weaponises and infects language, the degradation of which conveys how language betokens that there is something rotten in the State. Words that were once considered progressive and inclusive, such as 'radical' and 'liberal', are now terms of contempt and abuse, designed by the Alt Right and populists to Other the opponent. Concomitant with debasing language, the Populist has to be pretend to be real, to be of the people, and to be distinct from the elite from which they came. This pretence has the effect, Maginess argues, of manipulating the body politic and creating confusion about who or what is real, all the while exploiting the epidemic of resentment.

In Chapter 5, Selman Özdan takes a very different approach to fake news and what one should do about it. Here Özdan examines whether legal remedies against the circulation and publication of fake news are compatible with international human rights law and its criteria. Taking Singapore as his case study, he argues that legal sanctions against the flow of fake news could violate international human rights such as the right to freedom of expression and opinion. Özdan suggests that before forbidding or criminalising expressions and opinions, the danger and risks posed by fake news and disinformation should be clearly defined.

In Chapter 6, Benjamin Green takes up the notion digital nationalism to understand the Trump-dominated authoritarian 'fake news' media ecosystem. US digital nationalism is an authoritarian technic governed by political institutions which promote partisan misinformation to indoctrinate the masses, supported by rightist media. By taking a fake news approach, the aim is to undermine the public's understanding of First Amendment freedoms, protecting the freedoms of his allies, while impinging on and criminalising the freedoms of those who challenge Trump's disinformation and fake news, such as Black Lives Matter.

The chapters hitherto have focused on how fake news, disinformation, infodemics, and the like undermine democratic processes, institutions, and individual freedoms. Absent are analyses which examine the consequences of fake news on animals. In Chapter 7, Victoria O'Sullivan undertakes a project of mourning for our non-human kin that are invisibilised through absence and omission from information. Like the practices of mis- and dis-information, practices that omit the interests and experiences of animals are constitutive, O'Sullivan argues, of untruthfulness, in that the 'anthropocentric noise disorder', which privileges human interests, obscures the trauma of other animals.

Part 3: Discourse and Digital Literacy

This part presents four chapters which collectively problematise discourse and digital literacy and their relationship to epistemologies of deceit. During the last two decades, much of society that previously had little or no acquaintance with digital media have now come to deploy them as part of their regular communicative repertoire. The contributors to this section reveal how processes of discourse and practices of digital literacy are best understood as embedded in social and material networks, and incorporated into platform users' engagement with the world, rather than simply in terms of technologies and their 'affordances'.

Jennifer Saul, in Chapter 8, addresses the question of whether those who are in positions of knowledge are obligated to correct misinformation and oppressive speech online, particularly on social media. The discoursal features of social media, particularly its algorithmic amplification, Saul argues, necessitate a fundamental rethink of what counter-speech actually entails.

In Chapter 9, Albin Wagener argues that our postdigital age is one of hypernarrativity, an interweaving network of discourse where truth becomes marketable via political and ideological actors, echoing similar arguments made by MacKenzie and Bhatt in Chapter 1.

Mike Hajimichael, in Chapter 10, presents an analysis of the discourse of widely circulated yet misinformative memes concerning refugees in the European Union. This is followed by an important media literacy intervention which sought to educate young users about critical media literacy in current times.

Finally, Jialei Jiang and Matthew Vetter's chapter presents a feminist new materialist perspective to examining Wikipedia's systemic biases and inequalities in content coverage. They argue that a sociomaterial sensitivity to agency can help better understand how inequality and misinformation can emerge, allowing us to then attend to the systemic biases within a platform like Wikipedia.

Part 4: Towards a Critical Pedagogy

This final part is comprised of four chapters which connect education, technology, and deception to raise pedagogical questions about the goals and purposes of education, education structures, and uses of technology.

In Chapter 12, Peter McLaren and Petar Jandrić address the ongoing concerns of hegemonic transnational capitalism and its role in sustaining injustice, oppression, and deception. Connecting the political landscape with an educational critical revolutionary praxis, the authors argue for a scallywag pedagogy that focuses on socialist alternatives to capitalism, and a curriculum of liberation focused on action.

Christine Sinclair, in Chapter 13, addresses the question of what we can learn from dupers and deceivers' deceptive practices. She reveals specific tricks of duperation used by magicians, hoaxers, hackers, con artists, and academics who use deceit as an educational tool. She argues that tricks of duperation can exploit human psychology and that while technology can offer solutions to expose deception it can also amplify deception by allowing deceit and creating new subcultures of deceptive practice. She raises a question about ethics and whether education should teach students, not only how not to be deceived, but how to deceive.

In Chapter 14 Shane Ralston discusses the digital age of online teaching and its role in engendering student deception and online cheating. Ralston argues that online education lacks safeguards and penalties for online cheating. Previously established safeguards against student cheating, such as proctoring, and lack of penalisation for cheating encourages student to cheat in online education.

In the final Chapter 15, Eamon Costello and Prajakta Girme draw on the methodological device of speculative fiction, including the donning of human skins, to explore education as posthuman practice. Their unique and highly creative approach challenges the hegemony of the university by exposing how deception is embedded into datafication practices.

References

Bhatt, I., & MacKenzie, A. (2019). 'Just Google it': Digital Literacy and the Epistemology of Ignorance. *Teaching in Higher Education, 24*(3), 302–317. https://doi.org/10.1080/13562517.2018.1547276.

Bradshaw, S., Bailey, H., & Howard, P. N. (2021). Industrialized Disinformation: 2020 Global Inventory of Organised Social Media Manipulation. Working Paper 2021.1. Oxford, UK: Project on Computational Propaganda. https://comprop.oii.ox.ac.uk/research/posts/industrialized-disinformation/. Accessed 16 January 2020.

Jandrić, P., Knox, J., Besley, T., Ryberg, T., Suoranta, J., & Hayes, S. (2018). Postdigital Science and Education. *Educational Philosophy and Theory, 50*(10), 893–899. https://doi.org/10.1080/00131857.2018.1454000.

MacKenzie, A., Rose, J., & Bhatt, I. (2020). Dupery by Design: The Epistemology of Deceit in a Postdigital Era. *Postdigital Science and Education*. https://doi.org/10.1007/s42438-020-00114-7.

Mackenzie, A., & Bhatt, I. (2020a). Lies, Bullshit and Fake News: Some Epistemological Concerns. *Postdigital Science and Education*, *2*(1), 9–13. https://doi.org/10.1007/s42438-018-0025-4.

Mackenzie, A., & Bhatt, I. (2020b). Opposing the Power of Lies, Bullshit and Fake News: The Value of Truth. *Postdigital Science and Education*, *2*(1), 217–232. https://doi.org/10.1007/s42438-019-00087-2.

Contents

About the Editors

Alison MacKenzie is a Senior Lecturer at Queen's University, Belfast (and former secondary school teacher in Scotland). She is the Programme Director for the master's programme in Special Educational Needs and Inclusion, and former Director of the Postgraduate Certificate in Teacher Education at Queen's University. Her research interests and publications are primarily concerned with social injustice, which she examines through epistemic injustice, epistemologies of deceit and ignorance, feminism, and the Capabilities Approach; she also has a keen interest in Bourdieu's sociological analysis of inequality. Alison has been nominated, shortlisted for, and won a number of awards related to her teaching and supervision.

Ibrar Bhatt is a Senior Lecturer at the School of Social Sciences, Education and Social Work at Queen's University, Belfast. He has active research interests in writing and literacy as a social practice, digital literacies, and contemporary digital epistemologies. These interests emerged through some recent works, which include *Academics Writing: The Dynamics of Knowledge Creation* (2019) and *Assignments as Controversies: Digital Literacy & Writing in Classroom Practice* (2017), both published by Routledge/Taylor & Francis, as well as many published research articles. He is also a member of the Governing Council of the Society for Research into Higher Education, a convener of its Digital University Network, and Executive Editor for the journal *Teaching in Higher Education: Critical Perspectives*. His previous academic affiliations include Lancaster University and the University of Bradford.

Jennifer Rose's academic background is in Philosophy of Education. Her research is in the philosophy of knowledge and its use in epistemic relations in and between the social and material world. Her PhD thesis focused on the epistemology of testimony, epistemic injustice, and the decoloniality of knowledge in voice practices in higher education. Two recent publications of her work, 'To Believe or not to Believe: An Epistemic exploration of Fake News, Truth, and the Limits of Knowing' and 'The Mortal Coil of Covid-19, Fake News and Negative Epistemic Postdigital Inculcation', exemplify her unique theoretical approach to knowledge construction. Her professional background is entrepreneurial, focused on course development and delivery in a lifelong learning context.

About the Authors

Eamon Costello is Head of Open Education at Dublin City University. He has worked in a variety of roles in the University from mopping floors as a late-night janitor, to designing online learning in virtual environments, and as a lecturer heading up a department of highly committed staff. He is curious about how we think, learn, and work online, offline, and everywhere in between. He wonders about non-humanness and what this might mean for how we learn and unlearn each other. He has led a number of funded research projects and published on various topics around digital learning and open education. In line with the theme of this book, one item of this biography has been deep faked**.**

Prajakta Girme (Lily) is a researcher in Dublin City University currently working in the area of digital assessment in STEM education and with an interest in posthuman educational futures. She is currently working as a research assistant on the Assessment of Transversal Skills in STEM project (www.atsstem.eu), a large-scale initiative working in schools across Europe to help teachers and students figure out this strange thing we call STEM. She also moonlights as a posthuman graphical wizard and has a secret past relating to teeth. In line with the theme of this book one item of this biography may or may not have been deep faked.

Benjamin Green is a 2020 Asia Society-CEAIE Zhi-Xing China Fellow, and a third-year PhD candidate at Beijing Normal University, Faculty of Education. He has lectured at Beijing Foreign Studies University and China Foreign Affairs University, while also maintaining a position as section editor for the *Springer Encyclopedia of Educational Innovation.* As a critical scholar, his interest in complex adaptive social systems aims to foreground subaltern voices within Chinese Higher Education. However, his work has more recently been focused on US-China relations, global governance, digital nationalism, critical cosmopolitanism, and Chinese Internationalism as a contested project of alternative modernity.

Mike Hajimichael is Associate Professor and Head of The Department of Communications at the University of Nicosia, Cyprus. His PhD was in Cultural Studies at The Centre for Contemporary Cultural Studies (CCCS) in England. CCCS was an important experience as it defined many aspects of his academic, cultural, and political perspectives. In addition, Mike is a performance poet, recording artist, DJ, radio presenter, and freelance writer. These experiences have enhanced and informed his writing and research for the last two decades. He is particularly interested in media literacy, citizen's media, colonial writing/texts, applied ethnomusicology, and media representation and semiotics.

Petar Jandrić is Professor at the Zagreb University of Applied Sciences, Croatia, and Visiting Professor at the University of Wolverhampton, UK. His previous academic affiliations include Croatian Academic and Research Network, National e-Science Centre at the University of Edinburgh, Glasgow School of Art, and Cass School of Education at the University of East London. Petar's research interests are situated at the postdisciplinary intersections between technologies, pedagogies, and the society, and research methodologies of his choice are inter-, trans-, and antidisciplinarity. He is Editor-in-Chief of *Postdigital Science and Education* journal and book series. Personal website: http://petarjandric.com/.

Jialei Jiang completed her PhD in Composition and Applied Linguistics at the Indiana University of Pennsylvania. Her research interests include digital rhetoric, feminist new materialism, and multimodal composition. Her works have appeared in *Computers and Composition*, *Composition Forum*, *Kairos: Journal of Rhetoric, Technology, and Pedagogy*, *Postdigital Science and Education*, and edited collections. She is currently working on a collaborative research project that explores how instructors across writing studies design and deploy multimodal pedagogies for the purposes of social justice and advocacy.

Tess Maginess Principal Fellow, Higher Education Academy, is Professor of Lifelong Learning at Queen's University, Belfast. A literature specialist, she has developed a range of innovative adult learning pedagogies over the course of 25 years, often using critical and creative digital approaches. Tess has received many awards, including a national Teaching Fellowship. She has gained funding to develop a wide spectrum of partnerships, local, national, and international. Her research spans World Literature, adult education, especially non-traditional learners, mental health and disability, and the values and purposes of education. In her spare time, she gardens, cooks, sings, and writes poetry. She lives on the family farm with her husband, Ian, and dog, Kahl.

Peter McLaren is Distinguished Professor in Critical Studies at Chapman University, USA, and Co-Director of the Paulo Freire Democratic Project and International Ambassador for Global Ethics and Social Justice. He is also Emeritus Professor of Urban Education, UCLA, USA, and Emeritus Professor of Educational Leadership, Miami University of Ohio, USA. He is Honorary Director of the Center for Critical Studies in Education in Northeast Normal University, China. He is the author/editor of over 40 books, including *Postdigital Dialogues on Critical Pedagogy, Liberation Theology and Information Technology* (McLaren and Jandrić 2020).

Victoria O'Sullivan is a doctoral candidate in the School of Critical Studies, Faculty of Education and Social Work, University of Auckland. Prior to focusing on her PhD full time, she was a lecturer in secondary teacher education at Auckland University of Technology, where she taught philosophy of education. She is also an experienced Secondary teacher, having taught visual art for many years. Moved (in the sense of being affected and propelled into action; made mobile) by the slow, but also increasingly accelerated violence of the Anthropocene (as materialised by events like the 2019–2020 Australian bushfires, the Covid-19 pandemic and the Gulf Livestock 1 multi-species tragedy), her research explores ethical ways to think with/in the world at this moment in time.

Selman Özdan (PhD) is Assistant Professor Dr in the Department of Public International Law at the Ondokuz Mayıs University, School of Law in Turkey. He holds a PhD in Public International Law from Queen's University, Belfast, School of Law in Northern Ireland, UK and LL.M. (with Honours) from Case Western Reserve University, School of Law in Cleveland, USA. Previously, Selman worked at Erciyes University, where he was Head of Department for Public International Law. He is a member of the Society of Legal Scholars (SLS), Case Western Reserve University Law Alumni Association, and the National Association for Media Literacy Education. He has recently published in the *International Journal of Human Rights* and *Postdigital Science and Education.*

Shane J. Ralston is an ethicist, philosophy professor, and Dean of Richard Wright College, Woolf University, the world's first Blockchain-based university. His projects revolve around six broad areas: politics, ethics, education, environment, business, and sports. Shane's current research and writings focus mainly on issues of public corruption, higher education, and human resources ethics. He is the author of two books, *John Dewey's Great Debates—Reconstructed* (2011) and *Pragmatic Environmentalism: Towards a Rhetoric of Eco-Justice* (2013), and the editor of a collection, *Philosophical Pragmatism and International Relations: Essays for a Bold New World* (2013).

Jennifer Saul is Waterloo Chair in Social and Political Philosophy of Language at the University of Waterloo, in Canada. Previously she spent 24 years at the University of Sheffield. She is the author of *Lying, Misleading and What is Said* (OUP 2012), and the co-editor (with Michael Brownstein) of *Implicit Bias and Philosophy, Volumes 1 and 2* (OUP 2016). Currently she is working on racism, sexism, and deception and political speech, and the world is keeping her very busy. She plans a book on the method to use to evade responsibility for such speech.

Christine Sinclair is an Honorary Fellow in the Centre for Research in Digital Education of the Moray House School of Education and Sport at the University of Edinburgh from where she recently retired. For the final three years of her career, she was programme director for the MSc in Digital Education. She graduated from this programme herself in 2010, when working as a lecturer in academic practice at the University of Strathclyde in Glasgow. She enjoyed researching student experience through being a student and continues to be interested in student engagement with academic writing. She has written two books for students: *Understanding University: A Guide to Another Planet* (2006) and *Grammar: A Friendly Approach* (2010).

Albin Wagener holds a PhD and a Habilitation in discourse analysis and general linguistics. He currently works as an associate professor at the Université Rennes 2 (France) and also shares his research duties at the INALCO (France). His work mainly focuses on digital humanities and postdigital narratives, as well as culture and identity. Drawing on these topics, he has issued various publications in both French and English regarding applied online case studies in political discourse, discrimination, memes, communities, and social networks. These works in applied linguistics have been fuelling his theory of discourse and the way social representations are rooted in the neoliberal model of western democracies.

Jake Wright PhD, is a senior lecturer in philosophy at the University of Minnesota Rochester's Center for Learning Innovation (Rochester, Minnesota, USA). His research focuses on two areas: the ethical and pedagogical justifications for in-class practices, especially at the introductory level, and how we ought to respond to bullshit and other claims that reject the value of truth. He is particularly interested in how these areas overlap via the phenomenon of *naïve skepticism*, the predisposition to uncritically reject the idea of universal truth commonly held by introductory students.

Matthew A. Vetter is Associate Professor of English and affiliate faculty in the Composition and Applied Linguistics PhD program at Indiana University of Pennsylvania, where he teaches graduate courses in rhetorical theory, composition, critical pedagogy, and digital rhetoric and literacy. Vetter's work has appeared in journals such as *College English*, *Composition Studies*, *Computers and Composition*, *Pedagogy*, *Social Media & Society*, *Rhetoric Review*, and *Postdigital Science and Education*. In addition to these journal articles, Vetter has also contributed to publications sponsored by the Wiki Education Foundation.

Part I
Epistemology of Deceit

Chapter 1
Bad Faith, Bad Politics, and Bad Consequences: The Epistemic Harms of Online Deceit

Alison MacKenzie and Ibrar Bhatt

Introduction

In politics, in social media, indeed, whenever and wherever humans engage in communication, some form of deceit will commonly result. Lying, it seems, is an integral part of communication, and there are myriad opportunities for lying (MacKenzie and Bhatt 2020a). We expect politicians to lie, and we all know that online platforms are prodigiously efficient at spreading misinformation, disinformation, malinformation, lies, and similar epistemic vices. Key events in the UK and the USA, such as the 2016 UK referendum on EU membership and the 2020 US Presidential election, have inundated us with deceits that strike us as qualitatively and quantitatively different from other times. This is mainly because of the power and reach of online platforms, which, according to the Netflix documentary, *The Social Dilemma* (Orlowski 2020),[1] is altering human behaviour. Google and Facebook, for example, use algorithms that create individualised versions of reality, exploit behavioural addictions (through 'clickbait' and 'likes'), manipulate belief, and increase polarisation, and on which fake news spreads six times faster than other goods (Vosoughi et al. 2018).

[1] *The Social Dilemma* (Orlowski 2020) is a Netflix documentary-drama aired on 27 August 2020. It explores the dangers of social networking, using accounts from tech experts who worked for Google, Facebook, and Apple. It focuses on, among other issues, the vulnerability of teenagers to the platforms' methods of addicting them to social media, leading to high rates of depression and anxiety.

A. MacKenzie (✉) · I. Bhatt
School of Social Sciences, Education and Social Work, Queen's University Belfast, Belfast, UK
e-mail: A.Mackenzie@qub.ac.uk; I.Bhatt@qub.ac.uk

A. MacKenzie et al. (eds.), *The Epistemology of Deceit in a Postdigital Era*, Postdigital Science and Education,
https://doi.org/10.1007/978-3-030-72154-1_1

It is also deeply troubling that these giants have created a system that favours disinformation so that users may have no idea what is true or false (Orlowski 2020). They can control what we see, read, and believe – and we are not aware of it. We do know that lies proliferate as contagiously, it seems, as a SARS virus, and we expect to be lied to, particularly by those who govern us (Bradshaw and Howard 2017). When we critically consider the quality of the British political elite and learn how online platforms, on which we are so dependent, manipulate us, the dark realisation is that we seem to be in the grip of Machiavellian forces: scheming and self-interest, cunning and deceit, along with unprincipled lust for power, and power-for-power's sake.

In his best-known treatise on political power, *The Prince*, Machiavelli (2003), the Renaissance political philosopher, was critical of the view that a good leader was one who had moral character and exercised virtue and that by those qualities would earn respect and the right to be obeyed. 'Everyone' Machiavelli stated, 'admits how praiseworthy it is in a prince to keep faith, and to live with integrity and not with craft' (48) but goodness, he asserted, is not necessary to rule or to authority. As a political pragmatist, he understood that great princes put little faith in good conduct and circumvent the intellect of men by 'craft'. Anyone who pays attention to the sayings and doings of key political figures such as the current British Prime Minister, Boris Johnson, and the US President Donald Trump and his Republican acolytes will appreciate that they are not known for honesty or acting in good faith.[2]

Machiavelli also advised that the political rules of power are such that the prince must understand 'how to avail himself of the beast and the man … and that one without the other is not durable'. And if the prince must adopt the beast, he 'ought to choose the fox and the lion; because the lion cannot defend himself against snares and the fox cannot defend himself against wolves. Therefore, it is necessary to be a fox to discover the snares and a lion to terrify the wolves' (Machiavelli 2003: 48).

Machiavelli's political realism led him to propose that '[i]f men were entirely good this precept would not hold, but because they are bad, and will not keep faith with you, you too are not bound to observe it with them'. He cites, by way of example, how many treaties and engagements 'have been made void and of no effect through faithlessness', and the prince who knows how to employ the fox 'has succeeded best' (and the UK provides a good example of this, namely, the Brexit negotiations). Nevertheless, necessary though the half-man-half beast is to maintaining power, Machiavelli cautions that it is wise to 'disguise the fox and to be a great pretender and dissembler' on the grounds that men are 'so simple, and so subject to present necessities, that he who seeks to deceive will always find someone who will allow himself to be deceived' (Machiavelli 2003: 48).

The suspension of commonplace ethics in politics is recommended, and pre-emptive lying is justified because men are 'bad' and will not keep 'faith'. Nevertheless, deception means that the prince must appear to have all the ethical

[2] See Washington Post's ongoing database of the false or misleading claims made by President Trump during his time in office: https://www.washingtonpost.com/graphics/politics/trump-claims-database/. Accessed 5 January 2021.

qualities desired of a leader: to appear upright, religious, humane, and faithful 'but with a mind so framed' (49) that, when expedient, the leader can behave contrary to appearances. Machiavelli's analysis is compelling because he does not begin with an ideal person, an ideal theory of justice, or an ideal polity. There are no ideal states, just states in which injustice and inequality are the norm.

Social media has become one of the most significant arenas in which 'faithlessness' can be found. It is, on many accounts, one of the biggest enablers of deceit, conspiracy theories, disinformation, and malicious information, epistemic vices that are not 'incompatible with [enabling] authoritarianism' (Deibert 2019: 26). What does one do when bad faith, lying, and other vices are not aberrations, but have become the brazen norm? We contend that platforms which willingly and wilfully create systems that favour deceit over truth in order to pursue profit, erode trust, increase polarisation, threaten democratic processes, and destabilise democracy (Deibert 2019; Rid 2017). This is a grim analysis, but we need to be realistic if we are to confront the prodigality of deceit, and we will suggest some ways to epistemically resist and oppose these vexatious epistemic onslaughts.

We begin by discussing how social and mass media have been used to disseminate disinformation and its bad consequences: polarisation, distrust, and anger in the USA and the UK. The UK is often compared to the USA because of the populism and mendaciousness of Trump and Johnson. While these are the countries we know best, the analysis we present here could be readily applied to India, Brazil, Poland, Hungary, and numerous other countries. Our analyses throw up inevitable comparisons with totalitarianism and fascism, and we draw on Arendt's (1966) incomparable analysis of totalitarianism to explore just how harmful is deceit in all its nefarious varieties. We do not, however, suggest that there is a direct comparison between Trump and Hitler, or Trump and Stalin; what is of concern is that the power of social media is such that 'authoritarian practices are being propelled worldwide' (Deibert 2019: 31) and public discourse is being degraded because of the interconnected nature and viral speed of the Internet.

We explore how useful it is to counter the 'polariser's toolkit (Cassam 2020) with the humanist version, since retaliating in anger against anger or in calling the duped 'stupid' will get us nowhere. Contrary to Machiavelli, there are no proxies for truth, since truth and truthfulness are critical to a healthy polity.

Bad Politics and the Media: Beware Overlooking the Mass Media in Strategic Disinformation Campaigns

Months before the 2020 US Presidential campaign, President Trump began to claim that the 2020 election would be fraudulent and rigged against him, claims he continued to make after the election was called for Biden and despite the election being judged as one of the 'most secure in American history' by the Cyberspace and Infrastructure Security Agency (2020) on 3 November. The Security Agency Chief, Chris Krebs, was soon after fired from his post for contradicting Trump's claims.

During a White House press briefing on the 23 September 2020, Trump declined to say whether he would transfer power peacefully to Biden should he lose the election. Instead, he responded saying: 'We're going to have to see what happens, you know that. I've been complaining very strongly about the ballots, and the ballots are a disaster' and continued '[t]he ballots are out of control. You know it. And you know who knows it better than anybody else? The Democrats know it better than anybody else' (The Guardian 2020). His assertions about voter fraud were also shared by Republicans. According to Benkler et al. (2020: 2), citing a Pew poll from 16 September 2020, 61% of Republicans whose major source of news was Fox News or talk radio thought voter fraud by mail was a 'major issue'. By contrast, only 4% of Democrats who relied on the New York Times, the Washington Post, NPR, CNN, or MSNBC thought voter fraud was a problem. There were and are starkly different views about the safety of the election and whether mail-in votes and counting machines in counties and states that voted for Biden are legitimate. This is no surprise. As Benkler et al. (2020) demonstrate, Trump and his supporters engaged in a strategic disinformation campaign to undermine trust in the legitimacy and security of the election.

Benkler et al.'s (2020) research examines how political beliefs and attitudes are shaped at mass population scale. They engaged with three common conceptions about how public opinion is shaped by mass and social media. The first, and most common, is that social media is the driving force in shaping beliefs and attitudes by platforms such as Facebook which enable the dissemination of fake news, falsehoods, disinformation, and so on and through which propaganda, trolls, and bots proliferate. Actors who are neither political nor members of the media elite are empowered by these media to influence public perception. The second conception accepts that social media is the origin of falsehoods, which can be spread through mass media by influencers and which can transform public discourse through activism. Videos of police violence and Black Lives Matter protests are the most recent and powerful examples of mass media. The third conception is that social media has had less of an impact on political beliefs than is generally supposed and that political elites drive the agenda through mass media, while social media recirculates activist agendas (Benkler et al. 2020: 3).

The best example of this kind of mass media influence, according to the researchers, is mail-in ballots, voter fraud, and the legitimacy of the 2020 election. As Benkler et al. state: '[d]ecisions that mass media journalists and editors make about what they cover and how appear to be more important than what happens on Facebook'. Notably, given the analysis in the previous section, these decisions 'appear to be driven by the actions of political and media elites, principally President Trump' (4). Moreover, the 'largely-ignored' TV networks such as ABC, CBS, NBC, local TV, and CNN appear to be the primary source of news for the 'least politically pre-committed one-third of Americans' and, in the case of local TV, 'the least politically knowledgeable' (3).

The basis of Benkler et al.'s analysis rests on fifty-five thousand online media stories, five million tweets, and seventy-five thousand public posts on Facebook. This analysis is consistent with their earlier findings about the American political media ecosystem from 2015 to 2018, in which they found that 'Fox News and Donald Trump's own campaign were far more influential in spreading false beliefs than Russian trolls or Facebook clickbait artists' (Benkler et al. 2020: 4).

The fundamental insight that the researchers offer us is that polarised beliefs about mail-in voter fraud 'is an elite-driven, mass media leads model' (Benkler et al. 2020: 9). Trump, in particular, has driven the media agenda. His statements in tweets, press conferences, and television interviews have driven the debate over mail-in voting and were given credence by the communications teams of the White House and his re-election campaign, the Republican National Committee, and by leading Republican officials at federal and state levels. Benkler et al. (2020: 9) suggest that the coordinated messaging was part of a 'strategic disinformation campaign', motivated by fear that increasing voter participation during the Covid-19 pandemic would harm Republican chances of re-election – which it did. The disinformation was supported by a right-wing media ecosystem that 'marginalizes or suppresses dissenting views within the conservative sphere that try to push back against the mail-in voting fraud narrative'. The relationship between Trump and the media was one of mutual benefit. The President of CBS in an interview conducted after Donald Trump was elected said that his election win 'May Not Be Good for America, but It's Damn Good for CBS' (Bond 2016).

The 'cure' for elite-driven mass media disinformation campaigns? It's not fact-checking, since 'facts' have their alternatives and can be readily denounced as untruths or shameless propaganda. The situation is too polarised for fact-checking alone. Rather, Benkler et al. (2020: 10) suggest that what is necessary is 'aggressive editorial counteraction' by media editors and journalists of the Associated Press, television networks, and local TV news. They can make choices about how they cover the 'propaganda efforts of the President and his party, and how they educate their audiences'.

Mass Media and Social Media Consumption Driven by Dis/Mistrust

But is there something more to this disparity between mass media and social media? Newman et al. (2015) argue that this needs to be set in a context of wider news consumption and digital practice, the extent of which is significantly affected by age. As part of the annual study of the Reuters Institute for the Study of Journalism, Newman et al. (2015) found that when examining people's main sources of news split by age, for every group under 45, online news was deemed more important than television news, with Facebook holding the dominant position of the platform through which most young people access news and opinion. Since online news can be of all ideological stripes, including hyper-partisan, centrist, and mainstream, and given that a news consumer's exposure to online and alternative news is likely to be increased by greater levels of scepticism and mistrust of mainstream and traditional sources such as newspapers and television (see Elvestad et al. 2018), there is a need to better understand how and why people make news choices and how alternative news sources have risen to the ranks of the most trusted (Edelman's Global Trust Barometer 2017).

According to Edelman's Global Trust Barometer (2017), trust in mainstream broadcast media has declined precipitously in recent times. When faced with a choice between different sets of 'facts' offered by mainstream and 'alternative' online media, there is a need to ask: What ideals do audiences associate with their preferred go-to source? Why do seekers of news online turn to news purveyors such as Breitbart, InfoWars, and Blaze instead of more mainstream and legacy outlets like the BBC, Newsweek, or Aljazeera? Is it distrust, antipathy, or downright derision?

Two notable studies may offer some answers – and these accord with our analysis so far: Jonathon Ladd's *Why Americans hate the Media* (2012) and Mann and Ornstein's *It's Even Worse Than It Looks: How the American Constitutional System Collided With the New Politics of Extremism* (2012). According to Ladd (2012), lack of trust and confidence in mainstream media in the USA is closely related to democratic electoral processes and the kind of political messages consumed in the run up to elections. Since the 1970s, as political parties became more polarised and messages more intense, public acceptance of, and trust in, mainstream mass media has declined, and more partisan sources of news have emerged as salient in the development of citizens' views. He argues that much of this mistrust has been nurtured by elite media criticism of the media, particularly Republican Party elites, a process that intensified under the Trump administration.

Political analysts Mann and Ornstein came to a similar conclusion. They place the blame squarely on the contemporary Republican Party, characterising it as 'an insurgent outlier – ideologically extreme; … scornful of compromise; unpersuaded by conventional understanding of facts, evidence and science; and dismissive of the legitimacy of its political opposition' (Mann and Ornstein 2012: xiv). Importantly for our argument, the authors also caution against acerbic campaign approaches perpetuated by the mass media and the resultant steer towards the erosion of democratic accountability in the US politics.

Almost a decade later, there is now a much more complex relationship between mainstream journalism, alternative and online political news, and citizen knowledge. Media distrust and the rise of algorithmically mediated hyper-partisan alternatives has had significant civic and political ramifications. People who do not trust the media and who subsequently access hyper-partisan alternative sources are less likely to access accurate information and more likely to vote along partisan lines. It is, therefore, necessary to explore public responsiveness and people's credibility perceptions of online news consumers in order to ensure full exercise of democracy.

Most people access political messages via digital media, and digital infrastructures have become inextricably part of society's structures. This is the genesis of a 'postdigital' conception that there is no opposition between a 'virtual' or 'cyber' world and a corresponding 'face-to-face' world. Instead, the digital is now 'integrated and imbricated with our everyday actions and interactions' (Feenberg 2019: 8). Its structures and divisions, mediated by human behaviour but exacerbated by algorithms, are the very drivers which shape the conditions of knowledge production, circulation, and consumption. As we mentioned earlier, the documentary-drama, *The Social Dilemma* (Orlowski 2020), offers a powerful explanation of how these systems operate to manipulate our beliefs and behaviours.

Instead of a unified public sphere of 'the masses', people are now targeted with political messages as a multitude of very particular niche groups or micro-populations (Maly and Varis 2016). This has led to a decidedly algorithmic populism (Maly 2018) in which there is not a singular or exclusive 'mass media' instrument by which a linear flow of propaganda and political messages will flow. As a case in point, the Brexit referendum in the UK was won in favour of the UK leaving the European Union by the coming together of people from across the political spectrum, described by Blommaert (2020: 393) as the 'loose, temporal and unstable coalitions between ... micro-audiences'.

Another attempt at such digital micro-marketing of political messages was the campaign to deter Afro-Americans from voting for the Democratic party in the 2016 US election. The highly sophisticated campaign divided a data set of 200 million voters in to 8 different subcategories for niche targeting of political messages. One sub-group, labelled as 'Deterrence', consisted overwhelmingly of black and other groups of colour and were fed anti-Clinton adverts which focussed on out-of-context quotes to discredit her record on race relations (Channel 4 News Investigations Team 2020). The National Association for the Advancement of Colored People (NAACP) called the report an example of 'modern-day voter suppression' (Derysh 2020).

Mass media still has a place in political messaging, as Benkler et al. (2020) and others (Maly and Varis 2016) have argued. Today's public must, however, contend with a double-whammy of political messages from both mass media and social media sources. Mass media will also utilise social media platforms and their infrastructural logics to drive traffic to their pages and circulate information. According to Jarvis (2008), it is sometimes a case of 'blogs all the way down' in a model of information flow dubbed as a 'link economy'. In this model, news sources will borrow content from blogs and other online sources, sometimes with little or no verification, and add a layer of commentary as part of a 'new' story. The burden of proof can differ considerably compared to print and televised news, and as news providers contend with tighter deadlines and reduced staff, traditional standards for verification become much more difficult to sustain.

The case of a fake quotation attributed to the deceased French composer Maurice Jarre is one example. In this case, an Ireland-based student experimentally posted a fake quotation on the deceased composer's Wikipedia page shortly after his death. The quotation then appeared in the Guardian, BBC Music Magazine, and Australian newspapers. The hoax only came to light after the student contacted offending newspapers to tell them that the quotation was in fact a fabrication concocted by him as an experiment to 'show how journalists use the internet as a primary source and how people are connected especially through the internet' (Carbery 2009).

Polarisation for One's Own Bad Faith Ends: The Cynic's Toolkit and the Humanist's Response

Worryingly, these analyses show that we are living in highly polarised societies and that media of whatever kind are powerful instruments in driving and sustaining that polarisation, abetted by the kinds of deceits we have adumbrated. There is no doubt too, of course, that the deep cynicism of politicians such as the British Prime Minister, Boris Johnson[3] and the former United States President, Donald Trump, and all their enablers, nutrify polarisation. As Edsall observed in the New York Times (2018), '[h]ostility to the opposition party and its candidates has now reached a level where loathing motivates voters more than loyalty' (2019). Polarisation can be used as a political strategy to further political ends (re-election, English nationalism, protection from criminal prosecution, question the legitimacy of elections). Polarisation is also driven by propaganda that predates on religious, ethnic, political, economic, moral fears, and preferences for social/mass media. To counter polarisation, and the vices that accompany it, such as mistrust, deceit, epistemic blindness, and so on, we need to know the strategies and tactics that are employed to keep populations divided, angry, and mistrustful. Machiavelli's foxes and lions need to be rendered less cunning, mendacious, and treacherous.

Core features of the 'polarisation toolkit', according to Cassam (2020), consist of the following: mythmaking, stereotyping, propaganda, othering of an out-group, conspiracy theories, and polarising speech. Mythmaking, at which the Nazis excelled and with which our ardent Brexiteer politicians and spads (special advisers) have been busy, consists in creating mythic pasts which have been lost but which can be recreated in the future if we take the right action (e.g. leave the EU) and stand our ground (defy EU intransigence). Mythmakers also use myths to explain present divisions, discord, and lack of sovereignty (in the case of Brexit), the 'them' and 'us'. By 'taking back control', the mantra of the British Conservative Party under Johnson, the UK can, we are told, become a great nation again. It is aberrant nonsense, in our view, but recourse to rational debate, facts, and truthfulness seem to have no purchase among such supporters (see Parris 2020: fn 3). As Arendt pointed out, the ideal subjects of totalitarian rule 'are people for whom the distinction between fact and fiction (*i.e.*, the reality of experience) and the distinction between true and false (*i.e.*, the standards of thought) no longer exist' (1966: 474) (emphasis from the original).

[3] See Philip Stephens of the Financial Times (2019) who opines that Johnsons' lies are 'plunging Britain into a dark morass' at https://www.ft.com/content/645d8786-d9f2-11e9-8f9b-77216ebe1f17; and Mathew Parris of The Times (2020) who says of him that 'in his lonely soul he is darkly cynical' at https://www.thetimes.co.uk/article/were-heading-for-a-true-believers-brexit-xgkmhvl6x. Accessed 6 January 2020.

Mythmakers also create stereotypes, or generics, about disfavoured or out-group people, such as immigrants, Muslims, Blacks, or George Soros[4] (Cassam 2020). They are vilified as endangering treasured ways of life and of threatening our services, stealing our jobs, putting the Othered at serious risk of violence, discrimination, or loss or denial of citizenship. Another polarising trick is to assert, indignantly, that anyone who does not support the national effort to, for example, 'take back control' or to Make America Great Again (MAGA), is charged with not being 'patriotic'. Polarising speech is called into the services of mythmaking and stereotyping to provide loci around which to accuse that 'they' are not like 'us'. As political propaganda, mythmaking, stereotypes, and polarizing speech 'uses the language of virtuous ideals to unite people behind otherwise objectionable ends' (Stanley 2018: 24).

And no toolkit would be complete without conspiracy theories. Conspiracy theories 'function to denigrate and delegitimate their targets, by connecting them, mainly symbolically, to problematic acts' (Stanley 2018: 58). Among the best-known conspiracy theories are those concerned with Covid-19, vaccinations, and the Deep State in the USA, a hidden government within the legitimately elected government that is based on cronyism and corruption, all of which interfered with Trump's agenda and election success. But why are people so susceptible to what appears to most of us as insane nonsense? Is it, as Arendt suggested, the

> unexpected and unpredicted phenomena as the radical loss of self-interest, the cynical or bored indifference in the face of death or other personal catastrophes, the passionate inclination toward the most abstract notions as guides for life, and the general contempt for even the most obvious rules of common sense? (1966: 316)

Radical loss of self-interest and bored indifference might be seen in Britain's exit from the EU, despite all the warnings of how damaging it will be to country's economy; being stirred by the abstract notion of sovereignty when, in fact, striking favourable trade deals are all about managing interdependence, not safeguarding sovereignty; and refusal, by some, to accept the existence of Covid-19 and to refuse vaccination, in contravention of the obvious rules of scientific common sense: vaccines have been around for a long time and are considered by the medical and pharmaceutical industry to be safe.

The Allure of Deception

It is baffling why so many people are allured by the patently false and why, when confronted with what seems incontrovertible evidence time and time again, they dogmatically persist with the false belief. This persistence may be explained by

[4] The right wing in the United States is obsessed with George Soros, who is caricaturised by every anti-Semitic stereotype. Besner (2018) writes that that 'the red-meat crowds ... view him as a "sort of sinister [person who] plays in the shadows" ... Even to conservatives who reject the darkest fringes of the far right, Breitbart's description of Soros as a "globalist billionaire" dedicated to making America a liberal wasteland is uncontroversial common sense.'

confusion and fear and the consequent need for certainty from the chaos of opinions and endless streams of information. Another reason is fanaticism and insecurity. In her typically perspicuous analysis of the rise of totalitarianism in Nazi Germany and the Stalinist Soviet Union, Arendt (1966: 305) noted that Hitler believed that the bedlam of opinions could be 'avoided by adhering to *one* of these many opinions with "unbending consistency"' (emphasis from the original), despite the fact that one of the permanent features of the fascist and communist movements was their brazen and arbitrary lack of continuity. Totalitarian propaganda was also 'invariably frank as it was mendacious' (307) and routinely forged history. Even when the movements started to devour their own members through purges, mass deportations, and industrial scale murder, even when it turned on its own members, Nazism and Bolshevism retained mass support, not because of masterful propaganda and lying, stupidity, or ignorance, but because of the attraction of evil and mob mentality (307) and, more significantly, the 'selflessness of its adherents'.

Idealism could not explain this phenomenon since 'foolish or heroic' idealism 'springs from some individual decision and conviction and is subject to experience and argument' (307) and can outlive the movement. Fanaticism, however, cannot, but while the movement holds together, fanaticised members who adhere with total conformity 'cannot be reached by experience or argument' (308). Once the leader loses or dies, the movement dies with him, though that does not mean that Nazism or Stalinism disappears altogether; the lure of fascism survives in far-right groups and in populism (The Proud Boys, in the United States, for example). We see similar effects when people disappear 'down the rabbit hole' and into the mendacious embraces of conspiracy theorists, mythmakers, and peddlers of prejudicial stereotypes, to become trapped in alternative realities produced by echo-chambers and pernicious epistemic bubbles (Nguyen 2018).

It is tempting to believe that Arendt's analysis is relevant only to a particular time in the twentieth century European history. However, her analysis has a foreboding cogency to our current situation. There has been alarm that Trump's pathological lying, solipsistic fantasies, amorality, vulgarity, misogyny, and inability to concede defeat, enabled by what appear to be fanatical Republican devotees, were examples of fascistic tendencies (see Applebaum 2020; Kendizor 2020). Indeed, there have been calls to pay very close attention lest the USA lose her democracy. Had Trump won a second term, there was real concern that he would be unleashed, free to do whatever he liked, including changing the constitution so that he could go on being President in 2024, 2028, 2032: 'Trump Forever'.

As with Hitler, we were warned: ignore Trump at our peril. Hitler entered the political world legally, through democratic elections; Trump entered his likewise and on a conspiracy theory – the birther movement. Obama was declared to be a non-American and was therefore not the legitimate president: he was, the conspiratorialists claimed, a fraud; and 72% of registered Republicans believed this regardless of whether they were high or low knowledge republicans (Clinton and Roush 2016). One third, Applebaum wrote, not only believed this absurdity, but that one third went on to become Trump's infamous base.

> Over four years, they continued to applaud him, no matter what he did, not because they necessarily believed everything he said, but often because they didn't believe anything at all. If everything is a scam, who cares if the president is a serial liar? If all American politicians are corrupt, then so what if the president is too? If everyone has always broken the rules, then why can't he do that too? No wonder they didn't object when Trump's White House defied congressional subpoenas with impunity, or when he used the Department of Justice to pursue personal vendettas, or when he ignored ethics guidelines and rules about security clearances, or when he fired watchdogs and inspectors general. No wonder they cheered him on when he denigrated the CIA and the State Department as the 'deep state,' or laughed and smiled when he called journalists 'enemies of the people.' (Applebaum 2020)

Trump could do all this because many Americans had lost faith in democracy, and Trump exploited this distrust, primarily through Twitter and Fox News. Even now, at the time of writing, having lost the electoral college and the popular vote, despite the baseless court litigations that the election was stolen from him, Trump continues to sow distrust in and to demean not just respected figures and institutions but also the democratic process itself.[5] This is no accident. Biden, like Obama, will be regarded as an illegitimate president. The vilification of democratic processes and legitimate leaders continues, and that serves the interests of Trump and his enablers in the Republican Party.

How did the USA get to this, and will it ever recover? Arendt's own analysis of totalitarianism is that it emerges from, and requires, not classes but the masses (or 'the base' of MAGA).[6] Democratic governments rest on the silent approbation and tolerance of the indifferent and inarticulate sections of the country (Arendt 1966: 312), social atomisation and extreme individualisation, and apathy and hostility of the social strata who were exploited and excluded from active participation in politics. 'Chief characteristic of the mass man is not brutality or backwardness, but isolation and lack of normal social relations.' (317)

In the USA of today, and on Kendizor's (2020) analysis, many Americans believe they are not culturally or politically represented (as the masses in Germany and the Soviet Union were not). The masses lack economic clout; they feel betrayed. Kendzor also suggests that authoritarianism is networked and powerfully positioned to 'bombard users with propaganda, conspiracy theories and personal attacks' (Kendizor 2020: 154). Hostile states, as Putin's Russia is continually alleged to be, are prepared to use digital technology not only to attack their own citizens but also to transform democracies into their own authoritarian likeness (Brexit, India, U.S.A.).

---

[5] One can follow the twists and turns of Trump's actions and claims by looking up any news outlet. For example, The Independent at https://www.independent.co.uk/news/world/americas/us-election-2020/electoral-college-2020-trump-republicans-senate-ron-johnson-b1781745.html. Accessed 6 January 2020.

[6] 'The base' refers to Trumps' committed supporters. Rather than making America great again, the base seem to support efforts to destroy the Republican Party, institutions, electoral processes, and the health of the nation by refusing to wear mask or socially distance to prevent the spread of Covid-19.

The extent, reach, and phenomenal responsiveness of social media and the highly fragmented mass of people for whom messages are mediated by complex micro-marketing algorithms means that we are contending with a troll epidemic, mass online harassment, and the spread of toxic online culture in ways that cannot be readily monitored or policed. These vices are accompanied by a most brazen aspect of our social media lives – colossally impudent lies and insane conspiratorial theories. Spread by bots, propaganda ministries, validated by retweets and trending topics, and repeated through aggregated content, lies corrode trust. The elite, as well as the 'base', the 'mob', or whomever counts as the disaffected, must bear responsibility for the harms of lying. To return again to Arendt, this time to her analysis of the elite's delight in the destruction of respectability and the undermining of history which was regarded anyway as a façade to fool the people:

> the terrible, demoralizing fascination in the possibility that gigantic lies and monstrous falsehoods can eventually be established as unquestioned facts, that man may be free to change his own past at will, and that the difference between truth and falsehood may cease to be objective and become a mere matter of power and cleverness, of pressure and infinite repetitions. Not Stalin and Hitler's skill in the art of lying but the fact that they were able to organise the masses into collective unit to back up their lies with impressive magnificence, exerted the fascination [of the elites] … an atmosphere in which all traditional values had propositions had evaporated … made it easier to accept patently absurd propositions than the old truths which become pious banalities, precisely because nobody could be expected to take the absurdities seriously … those who traditionally hated the bourgeoise … saw only the lack of hypocrisy and respectability, not the content itself. (Arendt 1966: 333–34)

The modern variants of the alliance between the elite and the mobs are those who want to 'drain the swamp' in US politics and 'free' the UK from the EU. The elite are able to appeal to and command support from a significant portion of the population. Delusional and destructive though these mass appeals appear to be, they hold a fascination, and the leaders of these movements are indisputably popular. The appeal of lies and conspiracy theories can partly be explained by the fact that they offer simple answers to complex problems, shield us from confusion and complexity, and assure us that what happens in the world is not mere chance. They can offer, indeed impose as some authoritarians have sought to do, an alternative reality, though one that is far removed from that in which the majority lives. Lies and conspiracy theories also, of course, sow fear, anger, and mistrust (Deibert 2019).

Alternative realities may pose a further threat: delusional cognitive omnipotence to create a reality according to one's will and whim, and to which supporters must subscribe, prevents its adherents from learning from others and, indeed, from escaping from its shackles (Kendizor 2020). Trump appears to exercise a hold on the Republican party, even despite his absurd attempts to overturn the election, because they fear his vindictive rage should he return in 2024. Trump will not forget those who did not support him, and so, in an unprecedented move in US history, 126 House Republicans formally asked the Supreme Court to overturn the election results in four swing states (Michigan, Minnesota, Pennsylvania and Georgia). The Supreme Court unanimously rejected the lawsuit in a brief, one-page order, as having no standing under Article III of the Constitution. The promise of cognitive omniscience likewise poses a similar threat: it disables us from learning from others and from sharing our epistemic resources. The powerful (those who control the means of dissemination) seek to 'undermine the powerless in their very humanity – to undermine reason and deny them he capacity to give knowledge' (Fricker 2007: 44).

Countering Bad Consequences of Deception: Reducing Harm

Political theories or moral philosophies which presume justice as the norm may keep everyday injustices hidden, contribute to practices of ignorance, and desensitise our critical faculties. It is wise, perhaps, to begin one's analysis of online (and offline) deceptions with the assumption that we will inevitably have to contend with all manner of deceits perpetrated by wolves and lions and, of course, the naïve and indignant.

Lying about one's enemies, successes, mistakes, agenda, and reality is a prevalent feature of human engagement (Bok 1999). Political parties or heads of states will go to great lengths to dehumanise, discredit, or delegitimise what is contrary to, or advances their interests. 'Crooked Hillary' or 'Sleepy Joe', 'Remoaners', 'Libtards', and 'Antifa' are now well-known derogatory epithets which can be chanted or repeated ad nauseam to underscore their supposed cunning or their threat to the polity. We have ample evidence that all moral scruple will be thrown to the wind if the circumstances demand it; and we understand more fully than we ever did, the power of propaganda to subvert and dupe reason. Lies can spread rapidly online not just because of the casual way in which reality is distorted and the justification for calumny given but also because of the emotional, titillating, or outrageous tone of the lie.

Lying could be justified if it prevents harm and if white supremacists are roaming the city streets looking for Antifa or Black Lives Matter to shoot or intimidate. However, we need to be careful, because casual lying is harmful and calls for clear evidence that lying to one's enemies is warranted, particularly if paranoia plays a role in the justification for lying to one's adversaries: how has the enemy become the 'enemy'? Paranoic individuals or states may see enemies where none exist but righteously insist that their lies are merited because of the adversaries' bad faith (and why we must caution against Machiavellian arts). However, lying may not just result in prejudicially stereotyping the adversary so that bias is inevitable, but also in retaliations and sanctions, until one approaches a state of war or cold war hostility, or withdrawal from political, economic, and health unions (the European Union or the World Health Organisation) and polarisation: lying can spectacularly backfire. As Bok (1999: 142) warns, when governments 'build up enormous, self-perpetuating machineries of deception in adversary contexts', lies while occasionally excusable 'are weighted with very special dangers; dangers of bias, self-harm, proliferation, and severe injuries to trust' (143). Indeed. Antisemitic and anti-Muslim tropes are such dangers.

We also hear much about online epistemic bubbles and echo chambers which, in their worst effects, perpetuate the spread of lies, conspiracy theories, and propaganda, enchanting and embolding – enslaving – the mind with the belief that these channels espouse the truth (Nguyen 2018). In effect, however, they come to resemble the brainwashed who develop a 'peculiar' kind of cynicism which is:

> an absolute refusal to believe in the truth of anything, no matter how well it may be established. In other words, the result of a consistent and total substitution of lies for factual truth is that the lie will now be accepted as truth, and truth be defamed as lie, but that the sense by which we take our bearings in the real world – the category of truth versus falsehood is among the mental means to this end – is being destroyed. (Arendt 1968: 252)

Pernicious propaganda feeds, develops, and spreads false claims: it aims to transform critical faculties such that our judgements, values, and actions are enlisted into the forces of 'systematic falsification' (Ellul 1965: 61) of the kind that supports misinformation, disinformation, malinformation, misdirection, omissions, forgeries, exaggeration, underemphasis, and de-emphasis of information and seedy solipsism at which the former President of the USA excels. This is realism, a normal part of our everyday discursive lives, in which it seems impossible to argue for ideal theory or ideal states of being.

How do we counter the baneful effects of the vices we outlined above? Cassam (2020) suggests that, just as propaganda can be used for bad ends with its false, deceitful, and manipulative messages, it can also be used positively to humanise what has been dehumanized or distorted. Humanising propaganda means ethically and kindly engaging with people's emotions to understand why people are fearful, angry, or mistrustful, and why they are so ready to be duped by the absurd or the seemingly true. As has been well established, by themselves facts and evidence are not enough to make people understand why they are mistaken, misguided, or misinformed. McRaney explains what happens:

> Once something is added to your collection of beliefs, you protect it from harm. You do this instinctively and unconsciously when confronted with attitude-inconsistent information…When someone tries to correct you, tries to dilute your misconceptions, it backfires and strengthens those misconceptions instead. Over time, the backfire effect makes you less skeptical of those things that allow you to continue seeing your beliefs and attitudes as true and proper. (2014: 145)

Few like to be mistaken. Facts and evidence that are, therefore, presented in an empathic, non-judgmental way supported by critical questioning are more likely to be effective in encouraging the other person to be open to alternative views. Using 'eloquent' rhetoric (Cassam 2020) that rests on compassion or sympathy can help form prosocial beliefs and attitudes (and see also Dennett 2013).

Nevertheless, idealists and cynics alike will recognise that the polarisation toolkit is, as Cassam (2020: 20) observes, 'far superior to the depolarization toolkit'. It is 'a depressing thought' that eloquent rhetoric infused by compassion or sympathy is not enough to topple the power of dupery, even while compassion can provide a 'bridge' from the self to others not closely associated to us, reducing the distinctions between disparate groups of people. Polarisation is effective because 'polarizers have all the best tools' (Cassam 2020: 20) – myths, stereotypes, the power to other, polarising speech, and propaganda. These tools can trigger fear, loathing, and anger and also, critically, a sense of identity (e.g. as found among MAGA supporters).

Conclusion

The suspension of commonplace ethics in politics and online environments and pre-emptive lying because men are 'bad' and will not keep 'faith', as Machiavelli advised, has bad consequences. Ethical conduct, such as truth-telling, is critical to democracy and positive human relations; it is also critical in online environments. The answer to the onslaught of dupery in social and mass media is not the curtailment of free speech which would not, in any case, work since suppression or oppression rarely eradicate belief and may simply confirm the correctness of the belief or stir resentment and determination to hold fast on to the belief, as we discussed above (see Özdan, this volume, for an excellent human rights analysis of this issue; for an alternative view, see Wright, also in this volume). There are legitimate concerns about perceived loss of identity, the state of our democratic processes, the economic impact of Covid-19, and in whom we can trust when our societies seem so divided. It is a truism to say that education is critical, particularly awareness-raising around our own everyday digital practices in our current complicated and overwhelming information landscape (see, e.g. Bhatt and MacKenzie 2019; MacKenzie and Bhatt 2020a, b).

In the current postdigital times, our context has altered so radically that to fall back on standard educational approaches would be futile. Neither can we rely on existing information intermediaries (e.g. mainstream media and social media), though online platforms could do more to develop ethical technology that tries to inhibit the patently false and harmful. For example, Twitter has recently responded to calls that they put disclaimers on tweets that are clearly and evidentially false, such as President Trump's claims about electoral fraud. We need to enable people to be exposed to differing perspectives and to engage substantively across existing social divides. But we also need to understand that disarming conspiracy theorists, propagandists, peddlers of myths, and lies mean getting to the source of what animates their beliefs, listening with empathy to those concerns, while asking critical questions, activities which can yield ethical epistemic goods on which we can effectively act.

Francis Bacon told us that truth-telling is the 'sovereign good of human nature' (in Bok 1999: 262) and a fundamental principle of justice. Shabby or elaborate deceits impair the distribution and sharing of these goods. Goodness, contrary to Machiavelli's claim, is surely necessary to rule and to authority. Whether Machiavelli exhorted tongue in cheek that the Prince lie, or sought to do so in all seriousness, divorcing politics from ethics has consequences: such a polity cannot flourish. Further, appearing to have the ethical qualities desired of a leader but with a mind primed, when expedient, to behave contrary to appearances sows distrust, as we have sought to show here.

Lying is a vice that must be treated with the greatest caution and should never be done simply because it suits us. Lies undermine the political system, public trust in government and institutions, and trust in each other and, in the process, polarise society (Bok 1999). For these reasons, no ethically minded person should ever employ Machiavellian statecraft, however expedient. However, we must again be realistic. We have to acknowledge that there are many who admire the leader who 'avail[s] himself of the beast and the man' in the combined guise of the fox and the lion. Many MAGA supporters are loyal to Trump because he has created the illusion that he can 'drain swamp' because he is 'super smart, a genius'.[7] We also know that there is a calibre of politician who will resort to the dark arts of statecraft to exploit as many means possible to gain advantage, and they have most powerful mechanism ever available to us: social and mass media. We need to know how to begin to resist these forces.

References

Applebaum, A. (2020). Trump Won't Accept Defeat. Ever. The Atlantic, 6 November. https://www.theatlantic.com/ideas/archive/2020/11/trumps-forever-campaign-is-just-getting-started/617021/. Accessed 1 December 2020.

Arendt, H. (1966). *The Origins of Totalitarianism*. San Diego, CA: Harcourt Inc.

Arendt, H. (1968/2006). *Between Past and Future. Eight Exercises in Political Thought*. USA: Penguin Group.

Benkler, Y., Tilton, C., Etling, B., Roberts, H., Clark, J., Faris, R., Kaiser, J., & Schmitt, C. (2020). *Mail-in Voter Fraud: Anatomy of a Disinformation Campaign*. Research Publication No. 2020–6. October 2, 2020. Cambridge, MA: Berkman Klein Center for Internet & Society. https://doi.org/10.2139/ssrn.3703701.

Besner, D. (2018). The George Soros Story – and its Fatal Flaw. The Guardian, 6 July. https://www.theguardian.com/news/2018/jul/06/the-george-soros-philosophy-and-its-fatal-flaw. Accessed 25 December 2020.

Bhatt, I., & MacKenzie, A. (2019). 'Just Google it': Digital Literacy and the Epistemology of Ignorance. *Teaching in Higher Education, 24*(3), 302–317. https://doi.org/10.1080/13562517.2018.1547276.

Blommaert, J. (2020). Political Discourse in Post-Digital Societies. *Trabalhos em Linguística Aplicada, 59*(1), 390–403. https://doi.org/10.1590/010318136847016202004 08.

Bok, S. (1999). *Lying. Moral Choice in Public and Private Life*. New York: Vintage Press.

Bond, P. (2016). Leslie Moonves on Donald Trump: 'It May Not Be Good for America, but It's Damn Good for CBS'. The Hollywood Reporter, 29 February. https://www.hollywoodreporter.com/news/leslie-moonves-donald-trump-may-871464. Accessed 13 December 2020.

Bradshaw, S., & Howard, P.N. (2017). Troops, Trolls and Troublemakers: A Global Inventory of Organized Social Media Manipulation. Computational Propaganda Research Project. Working Paper No 2017.12. Oxford: University of Oxford. https://comprop.oii.ox.ac.uk/wp-content/uploads/sites/89/2017/07/Troops-Trolls-and-Troublemakers.pdf. Accessed 6 January 2021.

[7] For a brief survey of why Trump's supporters have remained loyal to him, despite the drift towards authoritarianism, see Lempinen (2020).

Carbery, G. (2009). Student's Wikipedia Hoax Quote Used Worldwide in Newspaper Obituaries. The Irish Times, 6 May. https://www.irishtimes.com/news/student-s-wikipedia-hoax-quote-used-worldwide-in-newspaper-obituaries-1.759391. Accessed 13 December 2020.

Cassam, Q. (2020). The Polarisation Toolkit. In A. Tanesini & M. P. Lynch (Eds.), *Polarisation, Arrogance and Dogmatism: Philosophical Perspectives*. Abingdon, Oxon: Routledge.

Channel 4 News Investigations Team (2020). Revealed: Trump Campaign Strategy to Deter Millions of Black Americans from Voting in 2016. Channel 4 News, 28 September. https://www.channel4.com/news/revealed-trump-campaign-strategy-to-deter-millions-of-black-americans-from-voting-in-2016. Accessed 13 December 2020.

Clinton, J., & Roush, C. (2016). Poll: Persistent Partisan Divide Over 'Birther' Question. NBC News, 10 August. https://www.nbcnews.com/politics/2016-election/poll-persistent-partisan-divide-over-birther-question-n627446. Accessed 13 December 2020.

Cyberspace and Infrastructure Security Agency (2020). Joint Statement from Elections Infrastructure Government Coordinating Council & The Election Infrastructure Sector Coordinating Executive Committees. 12 November. https://www.cisa.gov/news/2020/11/12/joint-statement-elections-infrastructure-government-coordinating-council-election. Accessed 1 December 2020.

Deibert, R. J. (2019). The Road to Digital Unfreedom. Three Painful Truths about Social Media. *Journal of Democracy, 30*(1), 25–39. https://doi.org/10.1353/jod.2019.0002.

Dennett, D. (2013). *Intuition Pumps and Other Forms of Thinking*. London: Penguin Books.

Derysh, I. (2020). Data Leak: 2016 Trump Campaign Listed 3.5 Million Black People it Wanted to Stop from Voting. Salon, 29 September. https://www.salon.com/2020/09/29/data-leak-2016-trump-campaign-listed-35-million-black-people-it-wanted-to-stop-from-voting/. Accessed 13 December 2020.

Edelman. (2017). 2017 Edelman Trust Barometer: Global Report. https://www.slideshare.net/EdelmanInsights/2017-edelman-trust-barometer-global-results-71035413. Accessed 12 December 2020.

Edsal, T. B. (2019). What Motivates Voters More than Loyalty? Loathing. New York Times, 1 March. https://www.nytimes.com/2018/03/01/opinion/negative-partisanship-democrats-republicans.html. Accessed 6 January 2020.

Ellul, J. (1965). *Propaganda: The Formation of Men's Attitudes*. New York: Random House.

Elvestad, E., Philips, A., & Feuerstein, M. (2018). Can Trust in Traditional News Media Explain Cross-national Differences in News Exposure of Young People Online? A Comparative Study of Israel, Norway and the United Kingdom, *Digital Journalism, 6*(2), 216–235. https://doi.org/10.1080/21670811.2017.1332484.

Feenberg, A. (2019). Postdigital or Predigital? *Postdigital Science and Education, 1*(1), 8–9. https://doi.org/10.1007/s42438-018-0027-2.

Fricker, M. (2007). Epistemic Injustice. Power & The Ethics of Knowing. Oxford: Oxford Univeristy Press.

Jarvis, J. (2008). The Link Economy v. the Content Economy. Buzzmachine, 18 June. https://buzzmachine.com/2008/06/18/the-link-economy-v-the-content-economy/. Accessed 13 December 2020.

Kendzior, S. (2020). *Hiding in Plain Sight: The Invention of Donald Trump and the Erosion of America*. New York: Flatiron Books.

Ladd, J. M. (2012). *Why Americans Hate the Media and How It Matters* Princeton, NJ: Princeton University Press.

Lempinen, E. (2020). Despite drift toward authoritarianism, Trump voters stay loyal. Why? Berkeley News, 7 December. https://news.berkeley.edu/2020/12/07/despite-drift-toward-authoritarianism-trump-voters-stay-loyal-why/. Accessed 6 January 2021.

Machiavelli, N. (2003). *The Prince*. London: Penguin Classics.

Mackenzie, A., & Bhatt, I. (2020a). Opposing the Power of Lies, Bullshit and Fake News: The Value of Truth. *Postdigital Science and Education*, 2(1), 217–232. https://doi.org/10.1007/s42438-019-00087-2.

Mackenzie, A., & Bhatt, I. (2020b). Lies, Bullshit and Fake News: Some Epistemological Concerns. *Postdigital Science and Education,* 2(1), 9–13. https://doi.org/10.1007/s42438-018-0025-4.

Maly, I. (2018). Populism as a Mediatized Communicative Relation: The Birth of Algorithmic Populism. Tilburg Papers in Culture Studies, paper 213. https://www.tilburguniversity.edu/research/institutes-and-research-groups/babylon/tpcs. Accessed 13 December 2020.

Maly, I., & Varis, P. (2016). The 21st Century Hipster: On Micro-populations in Times of Superdiversity. *European Journal of Cultural Studies 19*(6), 637–653. https://doi.org/10.1177/1367549415597920.

Mann, E. T., & Ornstein, N. J. (2012). *It's Even Worse Than It Looks: How the American Constitutional System Collided with the New Politics Of Extremism.* New York: Basic Books.

McRaney, D. (2014). *You are Now Less Dumb: How to Conquer Mob Mentality, How to Buy Happiness, and All the Other Ways to Outsmart Yourself.* New York: Gotham Books.

Newman, N., Levy, D. A. L., & Nielsen, R. K. (2015). Reuters Institute Digital News Report 2016: Tracking the Future of News. Oxford: Reuters Institute for the Study of Journalism. https://reutersinstitute.politics.ox.ac.uk/sites/default/files/research/files/Digital%2520News%2520Report%25202016.pdf. Accessed 13 December 2020.

Nguyen, T. C. (2018). Echo Chambers and Epistemic Bubbles. *Episteme, 17*(2), 141–161. https://doi.org/10.1017/epi.2018.32.

Orlowski, J. (2020). *The Social Dilemma* [Documentary Film]. Los Gatos, CA: Netflix.

Parris, M. (2020). We're heading for a true believers' Brexit. *The Times*, 12 December. Accessed 6 April, 2021.

Rid, T. (2017). Why Twitter Is the Best Social Media Platform for Disinformation. Motherboard, 1 November. https://www.vice.com/en/article/bj7vam/why-twitter-is-the-best-social-media-platform-for-disinformation. Accessed 5 January 2020.

Stanley, J. (2018). *How Fascism Works: The Politics of Us and Them.* New York: Random House.

The Guardian. (2020). Trump Refuses to Commit to a Peaceful Transfer of Power: 'There Will Be a Continuation' [Video]. https://www.theguardian.com/us-news/video/2020/sep/24/trump-refuses-to-commit-to-a-peaceful-transfer-of-power-there-will-be-a-continuation-video. Accessed 1 December 2020.

Vosoughi, S., Roy, D., & Aral, S. (2018). The Spread of True and False News Online. *Science, 359*(6380), 1146–1151. https://doi.org/10.1126/science.aap9559.

Chapter 2
An Epistemology of False Beliefs: The Role of Truth, Trust, and Technology in Postdigital Deception

Jennifer Rose

Introduction

In *Truth and Lying in a Nonmoral Sense*, Nietzsche wrote:

> This art of dissimulation reaches its peak in humankind, where deception, flattery, lying and cheating, speaking behind the backs of others, keeping up appearances, living in borrowed finery, wearing masks, the drapery of convention, play-acting for the benefit of others and oneself-in short, the constant fluttering of human beings around the one flame of vanity is so much the rule and the law that there is virtually nothing which defies understanding so much as the fact that an honest and pure drive towards truth should ever have emerged in them. (Nietzsche 1873/1999: 142)

As Nietzsche observes, humans deceive in many cunning ways and for multiple reasons. Dupery manifests in various guises, and we should know that seeing is not believing. Over two centuries later, Nietzsche's words still resonate, no less than with the 45th US Presidents' incitement of violence leading up to the 6 January 2021 riots. While one may interpret Nietzsche's reflections as overly pessimistic about the human condition, he does raise a point worth noting: if deception has reached its pinnacle among humans, and is so pervasive, why has truth come to dominate traditional epistemological analytic discourse and secure its status as the primary epistemic good?[1] This debate I do not address; however, I do question truth as a primary epistemic aim.

[1] *Defining* what *constitutes* truth is under debate (see Kirkham 2001); however, traditional analytic epistemologists have focused on how to *achieve* 'truth' through discussing various forms of justification, which are connected to achieving 'truth'. For one example see Goldman (1986).

J. Rose (✉)
School of Social Sciences, Education and Social Work, Queen's University Belfast, Belfast, UK
e-mail: jrose02@qub.ac.uk

A. MacKenzie et al. (eds.), *The Epistemology of Deceit in a Postdigital Era*, Postdigital Science and Education,
https://doi.org/10.1007/978-3-030-72154-1_2

My claims are not an all-out assault on the truth. Possessing truthful information and knowledge is central to the workings of any society. Truthful and accurate information and knowledge allow us to navigate our seas, roads, and aircrafts or help reduce disease risks. The coronavirus pandemic is the most recent worldwide example of how the lack of truthful and accurate information can exacerbate humans suffering (Rose 2020b). In this sense, it seems reasonable that we might adopt truth as a primary epistemic aim, as many traditional analytic epistemologists have done because truth is a requirement of knowledge (Kvanvig 2003; David 2001). Truth is a necessity in life that *can* help our planet's survival, overturn oppression, or increase equality; it is embedded into our knowledge construction. Some may argue for the intrinsic *value* of truth, pursuing truth for the sake of truth rather than for pragmatic reasons; however, trivial pursuit, whereby players win by knowing the most little-known facts, is not *valuable* during a pandemic other than, perhaps, to pass the time in isolation. Debates over *the value of truth* are ongoing,[2] complex, and not quickly resolved, and I do not attempt to resolve them in this chapter. However, in a human social environment where deceit is woven throughout our daily lives, social, technological, media, and epistemological ecosystems have become corrupted with false beliefs through pervasive deception; it is critical to revisit truth as a primary epistemic aim because achieving deception is directly related to ideals of truth.

In this chapter, I construct an *epistemology of false beliefs* to reveal one way in which audiences acquire technologically mediated false beliefs specifically focusing on the relationships between truth, trust, and technology in postdigital deception. I begin this argument by explicating the most fundamental way in which we acquire knowledge or information in social relations. I argue that we are dependent upon one another for constructing and disseminating information and knowledge. This dependence places us in a relationship where we must trust others to tell the truth if we are to acquire a true belief over a false one. I add an additional layer of analysis through a discussion on deception. Here I argue that the social relations in which we are embedded are absent from discussions on deception in epistemology; therefore, in discussions of deception, we must consider the deceiver as well as the audience to understand how false beliefs are engendered.

Next, I discuss the role of audiences' epistemic and psychological certainty of truth. I argue that a *holistic account of epistemic certainty* is something we simply do not possess because not all knowledge is epistemically certain and that commitments to truth about uncertain knowledge are through commitments to truth based on psychological certainty. I then add in the role of trust in social relations. I illustrate that trust can be established by deceivers exploiting an audiences' psychological certainty of truth. Lastly, in the final layer of analysis, I discuss the role that technology has in deception and how a postdigital lens can assist us in understanding an epistemology of false beliefs in postdigital deception. I conclude that truth ought to remain an epistemic aim. However, education can additionally focus on

---

[2] For an example on debates on the *value* of truth see James (2001) on the pragmatic value of truth and Bonjour (1985) for an account that claims that truth is the primary epistemic value.

engendering the value of understanding and a healthy scepticism to help people consider explanatory relationships in their social contexts, rather than solely focusing on truth.

Interdependence and the Search for Truth

Deriving from the Enlightenment tradition is the idea that we are autonomous individuals who can individually and independently generate and acquire knowledge, abstracted from social relations (Fricker 2006; Goldman 1999). For instance, Fricker (2006: 225) explains that '[t]he wholly autonomous knower will not accept any proposition, unless she herself possesses the evidence establishing it'. One of the founding philosophers of the Enlightenment era, Descartes (1637/1960: 51), contributed to the understanding that we were individual autonomous knowers when he wrote that we should 'never accept anything for true which I did not clearly know to be such' and to 'comprise nothing more in my judgment than what was presented to my mind so clearly and distinctly as to exclude all ground of doubt'.

Descartes focuses on the individual, agency, and self-reliance for ascertaining truth by focusing on one's own mind. He is sceptical of the certainty of knowledge deriving from the external world. However, he realises he cannot doubt all knowledge as he observes, 'I think, hence I am' (Descartes 1637/1960: 63), because in think*ing*, he *knows* that he exists. Descartes is certain of his knowledge deriving from his thoughts, experiences, and rationalizing, and it is the only with this evidence that he can *know with certainty* about how to obtain or establish *knowledge*. He writes that 'such evidence, that no ground for doubt...could be alleged by the sceptics capable of shaking' (63). Therefore, he suggests with certainty that one must rely upon oneself and accept this as the first principle of rationality.

Descartes was influential in the development of epistemological principles upon which to establish knowledge in traditional analytical epistemology. Additionally, his meditations were influential in the development of the modern individual knower (Coady 1994). However, Descartes' meditations do not capture the social nature of knowledge and the fundamental way in which we construct, disseminate, and acquire it. Goldman (1999: 4) observes that Descartes meditations are 'highly individualistic, focusing on mental operations of cognitive agents in isolation or abstraction from other persons'. However, knowledge is a social endeavour, so it requires consideration of its 'social routes to belief acquisition' (Goldman 1999: 4). Fricker (2006: 225) identifies Descartes' meditations as 'extreme purism' which circumscribes what we can come to know. Fricker (2006: 225) writes: 'it is not clear that we do or could possess any knowledge at all which is not in some way, perhaps obliquely, dependent upon testimony'.[3]

[3] While Fricker's analysis focuses upon learning from testimony, testimony can come in verbal or written forms.

Fundamentally, we owe much to others because most of what they learn derives from others in some kind of form (Fricker 2006). Our social relations readily evidence this understanding. We learn from our education, educators, families, doctors, neighbours, materials written by others, and many other human sources in life. However, the autonomous individual as the epistemic agent who pursues knowledge, knowing, and truth individually dominates Westernized thinking and traditional analytic epistemology (Coady 1994). Upon consideration of what we do know, we would be constrained in what we know if we did not learn from others. For example, from an epistemological point of view, Fricker (2006) explains that the autonomous knower is an extreme case of a knower and whose learning of the world will likely be severely restricted. Our world is social; others' words, in its varied forms, are how we acquire knowledge in and about the social world.

Consider how one comes to know one's birthdate. We rely upon others' testimony to tell us that we were born on a particular day at a particular time and in a particular year. We carry this belief with us for a lifetime. Suppose we look at our birth certificate or the birth registry to verify our birthdate if we do not believe our family. The accuracy and truthfulness of our birthdate still ultimately rely upon the individuals who completed the forms. We can trace our birthdate back through written testimony; however, it is traced back to an individual's first-hand experience, whose testimony we *unquestionably* accept, although there are no guarantees it is true or accurate. We have no avenue for verifying our birthdate through first-hand experience. We are necessarily reliant upon testimony. We learn from one another through written texts, dialogue, interlocutions, and what we read and see in online environments.

Rather than accepting arguments that knowledge construction and dissemination are fundamentally social processes, on the one hand, one may believe that Descartes' method is appropriate for combating online deception because we cannot trust what we read, see, or hear online, so we therefore ought to question it. However, Descartes' methods for determining what is true, while they may *seem* helpful for combatting online deception, can encourage individuals to only rely upon themselves which can lead to sceptical extremism, or 'full-fledged scepticism' (Gelfert 2014: 9). If we adopted Descartes' meditations, we would not believe anything we saw online or through digital media because we simply could not verify what we see through first-hand experience. However, we do indeed believe some information that we see online.

On the other hand, Descartes' search for truth excludes the fact that the language he uses in his philosophy is infused with meaning that he has learned from others. This meaning influences how he interprets the world. The epistemic clarity and certainty about what he can know can be questioned whether or not the epistemic sources he uses when rationalising are genuinely his representation of the world and are certain. What he rationalizes and comes to believe with certainty is fundamentally based on the meaning within the language that he uses and learned throughout his life. Although Descartes' ideas became influential over the development of the modern self as the independent, agential knower, they do not address the most fundamental way in which we acquire information or knowledge from others and their verbal, written, or shared representations of meaning, in social relations.

An obvious problem is that if deception is pervasive and we are reliant upon each other to learn and acquire information and knowledge, how have we learned anything at all? Indeed, we have managed to communicate information and knowledge that is true enough (I will discuss the nature of truth, knowledge, and certainty later on) so that we can come to *know*. However, because others' words can be deceitful, careless, inapt, or unreliable, questions about trust are raised. For this reason, Burnyeat and Barnes (1980) argue that testimony is not a sound method for acquiring knowledge. The authors explain that to accept knowledge through testimony is a credulity. Knowers may accept testimony too quickly in everyday life or knowers may illustrate a propensity towards gullibility, an inapt epistemic practice. Resultantly, knowers should be sceptical of testimony and not use others' testimony in everyday actions as a source for epistemic beliefs but to search for knowledge ourselves (Burnyeat and Barnes 1980).

The arguments that Burnyeat and Barnes and Descartes put forth are tempting to adopt because we do need some kind of scepticism because others may attempt to deceive us. However, wholescale adoption of a sceptical stance is untenable because we cannot escape learning information or knowledge from others in all of its forms; we are necessarily dependent upon others for coming to know things. Because we do learn from others, we inherently, and necessarily, *trust* others' and their words; otherwise, what we would learn and know would be very little. Students will not verify the truth, certainty, or validity of everything they learn from educators, and we do not and cannot possibly verify the truth, certainty, or validity of everything we read or hear. Learning from others is the fundamental way we acquire knowledge and information because knowledge and information is fundamentally socially constructed and disseminated. It is to be expected that it has problems, as people may be careless about speaking, and as I will discuss, deception further exacerbates these problems by exploiting truth, certainty, and trust. First, let us explore deception.

Dupers and Dupees: The Missing Link in Deception

A truism is that humans deceive. As Nietzsche (1873/ 1999) observed, there are many motivations for why people deceive. Deception by lying, for example, may be told to benefit oneself, but it may also be told to benefit others, such as an altruistic lie (Stokke 2018). Lies may be perpetrated about public or private life, to ensure social graces; to impress, define, or protect oneself; to cope with stressful situations; or to avoid embarrassment or punishment (Solomon 2009). Alternatively, and fundamentally, lies are told to change a belief or to obstruct the flow of knowledge or information (Marsili 2019). Why people deceive us just is as multifarious as how they deceive, making understanding deception highly complex.

Lying, for example, is *often* taken to be part and parcel of deception; insofar they are considered mutually constituted; if there is a lie, there is deception, and if there is deception, there is a lie. However, there are differences between lying and deception. *Deception* implies that the hearer has been deceived (Carson 2010). A case of deception is only deception if someone is caused to have false beliefs. Merely uttering a lie, or aiming to deceive, does not mean that the hearer believes the lie. The hearer can reject the lie and not be deceived.

A common understanding of lying comprises a speaker making an utterance, assertion, or statement that is false and intending to deceive, resulting in the audience acquiring a false belief. Ironically, this common understanding of lying 'deceives' us because it only accounts for one kind of lying and deception. Carson (2010: 3) argues that to be considered a lie, a liar must make 'a deliberate false statement that the speaker warrants to be true'. The liar may not necessarily *intend* to deceive a hearer, but a lie occurs when the speaker breaches an implied guarantee that his words are true when they are not. For Carson, the liar invites his hearer to trust him and then betrays the trust by speaking a statement that he does not believe to be true, though he has no intent to deceive. For example,

> I witness a crime and clearly see that a particular individual committed the crime. Later, the same person is accused of the crime and, as a witness in court, I am asked whether or not I saw the defendant commit the crime. I make the false statement that I did not see the defendant commit the crime, for fear of being harmed or killed by him. However, I do not intend that my false statements deceive anyone. (Carson 2010: 20)

Similarly, Sorenson (2007) points out that lying does not require intent to deceive. 'Bald-faced lies', Sorenson (2007: 645) explains, occur when a speaker lies without intention to deceive because they think that the hearers know they are lying, such as a person telling their partner that burnt rice tastes good when they both know that it does not. It is still a lie because the person does not believe the utterance made, but there is no intention to deceive, or to change another's belief or obstruct the flow knowledge. While the reasons for telling a bald-face lie, or it may be called a 'fib' (the gravity of which is not as serious as the calculated intention to deceive), may improve human relations, Sorenson still fundamentally considers it a lie.

Additionally, a true statement can be spoken to deceive if it misleads one to believe or continue to believe a falsehood (Carson 2010). Bill Clinton, for example, stated 'I did not have sexual relations with that woman, Miss Lewinsky'.[4] Relying on a specific definition of what constitutes sexual relations, Clinton did not lie. However, he certainly aimed to deceive though he spoke a true statement. Saul (2012: 65) defines lying as one that the speaker must not be the victim of linguistic error such as malapropism, using a 'metaphor, hyperbole, or irony'. People lie if they state a proposition that they believe to be false, are in a warranting context, and intend that their audience believe it to be true, and the audience believes they are in a warranting context.

Deception can also occur through 'half-truths'. These are true statements that selectively emphasize facts that support a particular interpretation of an issue to selectively ignore or minimize other pertinent facts or statements that may be

[4] See Yagoda (2018).

contrary to one's intended interpretation (Fallis 2019). For example, half-truths are a grey area 'of deceptive utterances that are difficult to classify' (Marsili 2019: 170). The 'grey area' is an area for which deceivers strive because it includes statements that are not entirely believed to be false but are also not believed to be true (Marsili 2019). Similarly, there are quarter truths and 'spin' (Solomon 2009). Additionally, Stokke (2018) points out that people are skilled at navigating the spaces between lying and deception. Stokke argues that people 'exploit the difference between outright saying what we do not believe and conveying disbelieved information in other ways' (3). These other ways include feigning emotions or attitudes by using non-declarative language such as 'questions, imperatives, or exclamations' (3). Sometimes there is no aim to deceive; people just speak insincerely.

Chisholm and Feehan (1977: 143–145) present eight basic ways deception can occur when the speaker intends to deceive. A speaker intentionally acts to:

(a) Cause a hearer to believe a false belief
(b) Cause a hearer to continue to believe a false belief
(c) Cause a hearer to lose a true belief
(d) Prevent a hearer from acquiring a true belief

Alternatively, a hearer may intentionally omit information and fail to engender a true belief by:

(e) Allowing the hearer to believe a false belief
(f) Allowing the hearer to continuing to believe a false belief
(g) Allowing the hearer to cease having a true belief
(h) Allowing a hearer to continue to believe a false belief

As seen with Chisholm and Feenan's conceptualization of deception, deception can occur by omission or concealment of information that leads to one's audience not acquiring a true belief. Deceivers can cause someone to falsely believe by withholding information if that is information that would affect them acquiring true belief. Deception by omission or concealment is not a lie because it requires someone to make a statement, but it entails the withholding or concealing of information that the hearer might need to know. This kind of deception through misleading can occur with or without a word as well as overt behaviour when deceivers suggest 'in their actions what they might never put into words' (Solomon 2009: 16). Additionally, silence can be a form of deception if a person knows that their silence will be understood as an agreement, that person intends that their silence be understood that way, and they remain silent on purpose (Fallis 2019). The complexity of deception increases because it is intertwined and intimately connected to self-deception.

Self-deception is inducing a false belief in oneself; it is intentional and motivated and simulates wilful ignorance (Beier 2019). What people deceive themselves about is broad and can include themselves or others, politics, economics, or anything that a person wilfully misconceives. The complications with self-deception are exacerbated because it is intertwined with deception. Martin (2009) explains that the lies that people tell others can be intricately entangled with the lies they tell themselves. Believing one's lies and the lies told to others may be done for strategic reasons.

Deceivers have motivated deceptions and self-deception that enables them to convincingly persuade their audiences of their deceptions because they speak with real sincerity (Martin 2009). Self-deception is not merely a linguistic activity like the nature of lying was initially thought to be; it involves more than an assertion of a false proposition. It includes a range of psychological attitudes, such as 'self-love, self-pity, self-respect, and self-loathing', and one can deceive oneself about others or the self (Solomon 2009: 23). In any account of deception, the self is central and critical because people are not deceitful in the traditional sense if they believe the falsehoods they tell.

Definitions of lying *presume* that one is certain about the truth oneself, as it is usually contradictory to believe something that is knowingly false. However, deception can also occur through various certainty levels, such as psychological certainty, the 'highest degree of confidence that a subject can have in the truth of a proposition' (Marsili 2019: 171). However, psychological certainty is always 'relative to *someone's standpoint*: it does not matter if the subject has no ground (or bad grounds) for holding that belief, because certainty requires only that *the subject* be supremely convinced of its truth' (Marsili 2019: 171). The deceiver need not believe that the uttered statement is false; her belief may simply be on a continuum of uncertainty/certainty about the belief. Beliefs can be understood with degrees of certainty; we can believe things in which we are not wholly certain (Marsili 2019), such as a person believing that a political party will win.

Typically, this illustrates a discrepancy between speakers' psychological state, such as intent or belief, and the psychological state expressed by the linguistic action, such as asserting, requiring, or promising (Marsili 2019). If people believe what they are assert is partially true but are not confident of it, they are not lying, though their statements can be misleading because they do not represent their psychological state. These 'graded beliefs' become lies when deceivers express 'certainty when [they] are uncertain', 'expressing uncertainty when [they] are certain', and 'expressing certainty or uncertainty to a higher degree than being adequate with respect with [their] knowledge base' (Marsili 2019: 177). So when deceivers pretend to have a higher or lower degree of belief and knowledge than expressed, they lie.

Traditional understandings of lying also *presume* that people knowingly and intentionally, often maliciously, deceive (Solomon 2009). This further supposes that people are autonomous, transparent, and rational because it is assumed that they *rationally* deceive (Solomon 2009). Deceivers may be blatant about self-interested lies, but self-deception is not individually self-contained, insofar, as we merely deceive ourselves. Self-deception is connected to social and personal relationships. Solomon (2009: 25) explains: 'to fool ourselves, we must either fool or exclude others; and to successfully fool others, we best fool ourselves'. Self-deception is a 'surreptitious, social construction of the self' (Solomon 2009: 27). We can deceive ourselves about who we 'are'. However, self-deception is also about one's particular role in social relationships, such as one posturing to be thought of or treated in particular ways by other people (Solomon 2009). Self-deception increases deception's complexity because the deceivers need not necessarily believe that what they convey is false. Deceivers may be disillusioned about what is true, which raises questions about if it is a case of deception or if deceivers merely believe and spread false beliefs because they have deceived themselves. Deception and self-deception are complex phenomena, which are not easily or readily apparent to any observer, I will not aim to explicate the complexity of deception and deceivers' possible self-deceptive epistemic states, but only to expose that a broad understanding of deception is thorny, and deceivers' states are not easily categorized into simple states of intention and lying.

However complicated the notion of deception is, the problem with this epistemological literature about deception is that it is still fundamentally based upon an individualistic Cartesian understanding. It focuses on deceivers, beliefs, behaviours, language, epistemologies, psychological states, and intentions to deceive. However, it does not consider the hearers, the learners, or the audience's role in accepting or rejecting the lie or believing the deceptive statement. If deceivers aim to deceive, achieving deception is about the audience as much as it is about the deceiver. As deceivers lie, mislead, or manipulate, it only is a case of deception if the audience believes their corrupt attempts to deceive. My claim is that deceivers can use 'truth' or what is *believed to be true* by the audience with *psychological certainty* to achieve deception. Therefore, I include the *audience's* psychological states of certainty with respect to the development of false beliefs because deception requires that audience *believe the false statement*. There is no case of deception if the hearers do not believe what information the deceivers present. Also, focusing on the deceiver as well as the deceived is necessary to understand the accumulation of false beliefs because we are reliant upon one another to create, share, and *learn* new information or knowledge. Deception is a blockage in the accumulation of true or accurate information. For these reasons, an audience's psychological certainty is of importance because deceivers can exploit it to engender false beliefs.

Certainty and Truth

There are two types of certainty that I distinguish here to illustrate that psychological certainty is the primary kind of certainty that people operate on when justifying their beliefs: psychological certainty and epistemic certainty. Psychological or subjective certainty is 'an attitude that persons can have towards a proposition' (Klein 1998: 1358). As Marsili (2019) observed, psychological certainty does not require that individuals have good doxastic reasons for their belief; it only requires that the individual has psychological certainty in what one believes is true. Psychological certainty is one's commitment to truth in a particular proposition. However, epistemic certainty 'is a measure of the epistemic warrant for a proposition' (Klein 1998: 1358). Alternatively, as Stanley (2008: 35) observes, a case of epistemic certainty is when a person knows that a given statement is true based on evidence that 'gives one the highest degree of justification for one's belief'. One has *absolute epistemic certainty* if one has infallible doxastic reasons for believing a stated proposition as truth, because if it is fallible, it is not certain. This is an absolute case of certainty; certainly if we removed gravity and oxygen from the earth, we know with *certainty* that we would be nothing more than floating dead bodies, without grounding and breathing paraphernalia.

These are particular aspects of life we might be certain about; however, because we do not have this same epistemic certainty with all aspects of life, such as what will the weather be tomorrow, we can *predict* what the weather will be like tomorrow, but we do not *know* it with certainty. *In consideration of a holistic view and account of knowledge, we do not have epistemic certainty.* Some things about how our world functions are more certain than others, but epistemic certainty is not something that pervades all knowledge because certainty is not a requirement for knowledge (Stanley 2008). Holistically, if we do not have *certainty in all* knowledge, then we must necessarily be operating on psychological certainty, unless we speak about only those things that are epistemically certain. Wittgenstein (1969: 52e) makes a similar point; he writes, 'it's not that on some points men know the truth with perfect certainty. No: perfect certainty is only a matter of their attitude'. Wittgenstein also distinguishes between epistemic certainty and subjective certainty, highlighting that epistemic certainty is not absolute because it is not perfect; therefore, any absolute certainty is a psychological function of certainty.

While we can be certain about particular aspects of life, *holistically* we do not possess epistemic certainty. However, we *do* make certainty claims, such as one believes with certainty that the election was stolen from Trump or that the democratic party is corrupt. If we do not have epistemic certainty about all aspects of life, then many claims of certainty we make are those of psychological certainty, our attitude of certainty of truth towards the claims we make. As I will discuss next, a deceiver can exploit psychological certainty in one's trusted relationship, positioning an audience in a state of vulnerability to blindly believe the statements of a deceiver.

The Exploitation of Trust Through Psychological Certainty of Truth

Because we are dependent upon the word of others, in any of its forms, we necessarily do trust some of what we hear or read; otherwise, we simply would not learn new information or knowledge. Trust is central to our social relations and operations of any society. We trust that other drivers on the road are competent and will not cause an accident. We trust that our doctors are truthful and competent. We trust the person we ask for directions to tell us truthfully and accurately how to get to our destination. Alternatively, we trust in a particular political party over another. My concern is not with explicating the central nature of trust. Processes of trust are complex, and the reasons and source of trust are many. However, my central concern here is with the relationship between truth, trust, and deception. We live by a fundamental maxim that we place trust in people when we know they tell or are telling the truth. Nooteboom (2006: 249) identifies this as 'intentional trust', trust in the honest or truthful individual, group, or organization. A broad definition of intentional trust is when the trustor trusts the trustee and accepts the risk associated with vulnerability to opportunistic actions (Nooteboom 2006). Intentional trust is primarily concerned with individuals' intentions in the trusted relationship; individuals can generally be benevolent, honest, or truthful in their intentions in the relationship or opportunistic, which entails 'lying, stealing, and cheating to expropriate advantage' (Nooteboom 2006: 249). With respect to learning from others, benevolent intentions are related to truth-telling and trust, conducive to learning from others in any form, and necessary in the epistemic relationship between givers of information and an audience.

Opportunistic intentions are where I place the relation between trust, truth, and deception. I take opportunistic intentions to be an abuse of relationships in deception. As Lackey (2008) explains, the hearer who places blind trust in a speaker because she has a relationship with her, and therefore cannot provide reasons for her belief, is an inapt knower. While Lackey takes a strict view on always justifying one's belief when learning from others, there is reason to heed her observations because trust involves risk. The audience is at risk of betrayal, opportunistic advantage, and exploitation by givers of statements. Audiences are at risk when the messenger does not enact the trustworthiness expected when one places trust in someone, thereby making blind trust a relevant concern to deception and the development of false beliefs. In online environments where the audiences need to determine who and what sources, and information to trust, rather than trust prima facie because deception is pervasive, my claim is that audiences with psychological certainty of truth are in a position of vulnerability to deceivers' opportunistic exploitation of the trust.

O'Neill (2020) argues that trust can be exploited when people abuse the trust they have been afforded. Stated another way, trust is corrupted when people abuse trustful relations with others and breach an implicit warrant of truthfulness. As already discussed, trust is central to acquiring any kind of knowledge or information simply because we cannot know everything, much of what we do know is limited, and what we can come to know in online environments is limited (Rose 2020a). Because the audience must necessarily decide who or what to trust, they are vulnerably situated in the relation to the giver of statements or potential deceiver because the deceiver can exploit that trust. My claim is that the deceiver exploits trust through his audiences' psychological certainty of truth and limited knowing because they do not have epistemic certainty. The deceiver builds trust by telling what appears to be truthful or believed to be truthful by the deceived. For instance, Trump has touted that he does not believe that systemic racism is problematic. 'Trump says he doesn't believe racism is a systemic problem within US police forces. He has positioned himself as a firm advocate of law enforcement but has opposed chokeholds and offered grants for improved practices.' (BBC 2020) Moreover, we see here in the testimonial of one of his supporters that the supporter also does not believe in systemic racism. 'I am not racist or sexist. I believe in personal responsibility and equal opportunity for all, not equal outcomes. Outcomes are left up to individuals. Man, 40s.' (Dunn et al. 2017)

The supporter's belief and psychological certainty in personal responsibility, equal opportunity, and unequal outcomes reveal the inherent belief in the nonexistence of systemic racism. Otherwise, he would not believe that outcomes are solely an individual problem. In relation to Trump's stances and stated policies, he garnered his supporters' trust by mirroring their ideologies and psychological certainty. In honest relations, a politician does as the people wish and communicates his pledge; people vote for the candidate that promises to address their needs. However, in dishonest relations, a pledge can be conveyed to establish trust, and once trust is established, it can be exploited. We justify our beliefs in others in two general ways: through prima facie trust and using our beliefs and knowledge as criteria for evaluating another's claim.[5] Because deception is rampant, we are less inclined to trust a speaker prima facie because we aim not to be deceived. However, we necessarily justify our belief in a speaker when they tell us things we already believe with certainty, simpliciter, and trust is established. Because we must trust someone or some institution to acquire our information or knowledge, once we trust, we are vulnerably positioned to be exploited and acquire false beliefs from the trusted. While it may seem absurd that anyone would trust in Trump's word, O'Neill explains that trust can be misplaced:

> Trust may be misplaced in liars and fraudsters, in those who are incompetent or misleading, and in those who are untrustworthy in countless other ways. Equally, mistrust and suspicions may be misplaced in those who are trustworthy in the matters under consideration. (O'Neill 2020: 17)

The central concern here, if trust is misplaced, and once trust it is established, the trusted can exploit the trust and deceive the trustee, who, consequently, is vulnerable to developing false beliefs based on a foundation of trust.

We now know that we are interdependent with one another for learning new information or knowledge. Therefore, conceptualizations of deception must necessarily consider the deceiver as well as the deceived to fully understand deception. Additionally, we have seen that we do not have a holistic account epistemic certainty, and many claims we make with certainty are done so upon psychological certainty. Psychological certainty about truth is directly related to how we justify our belief in our interlocutor and can be used by a deceiver to establish trust, which can later be exploited. An additional layer of analysis in the epistemology of false belief in a postdigital era requires consideration of technology's role in deception.

Postdigital Deception: Virtual Reality or Reality as Virtual?

Postdigital is a term, though messy and not concretely defined, that captures human relationships between humans and technology (Jandrić et al. 2018). Postdigital complexity is evident when we consider the complexity of people, life, the societies in which we reside, and the multitude of technological and digital devices that we

[5] See Gelfert (2014) for a discussion on reductionism and anti-reductionism in testimony.

use. In this view, technology is not a benign construction of materials into a cultural artefact; technology can be defined by how we use it (Dusek 2006). Technology, as Dusek (2006: 33) observes, can be understood as a tool (e.g. a phone) or as rules (e.g. software), and it can be understood as a system that 'needs to be set in the context of people who use it, maintain it, and repair it' (Dusek 2006: 33). Understood as a system, technology encompasses the postdigital condition and the complicated relationships we have. Our relationship to technology is further complicated when considering the nature of deception, us, and technology. Dusek (2006) explains that what we see through technology is not a direct route to visualizing what we see but is represented by technology (Dusek 2006). When someone sends us an electronic photo, we only see a representation mediated by technology; we do not see the actual objects or people in the photograph.

In honest relations, we trust that what we see in an online photograph is a true or accurate representation of reality. However, in deception, technology can be used not only to fabricate or manipulate images, words, and sounds but also to emulate the reality of one's audience and geographical context. For instance, Rose (2020a) revealed that online news consumers are limited in their knowing when attempting to determine the truth of what they see online because fake news posted online represents plausible truths that exist offline. In this instance, when individuals use their epistemic orientations to assess truth, they will arrive at false beliefs because they individually cannot 'know' what is true or false by simply viewing what they see online because it mirrors reality. This is because technology enables the digitized creation of audiences' realities, such as Trump using technology to build trust with his supporters by telling what they wish to hear and what corresponds to their beliefs and certainty of truth. Furthermore, technology enables the provision of new digitized realities for audiences, such as online epistemic bubbles.

Understanding technology, specifically in the role of deception, exposes it as a mediator between the deceivers and the deceived. This point is vital because, through technological mediation, deceivers can manipulate reality and establish trust. For instance, deceivers can easily and craftily omit, conceal information, and present half-truths or spins that prevent an audience from developing a true belief. Deceivers can embed lies, deceitful, or misleading information directly into images, text, sound, or videos. These latter tactics are readily seen in fake news memes, stories, and deep fake video productions. Technology enables an abundance of new ways to deceive because deception is not merely about a person misleading, deceiving, or lying verbally, or through body language face-to-face, technology affords deceivers with the instruments, such as software, to digitally create and recreate lies through misrepresentations of reality, which is well documented through the genre of fake news. Technology also enables asynchronous deception. For instance, deceivers may post a fake news story online, and while it can potentially reach millions of online users instantaneously, once it is online users can be exposed to it at a later date and time, which could entail days, weeks, or even months. The deceit stays embedded into the technology and lingers there for users to knowingly or unknowingly consume asynchronously from the original deceptive act. Deception is ongoing though the deceptive act is long over. These new forms of deceit are directly related to the development and advances in technology. This raises questions about what new ways of deceiving are emerging as technology rapidly changes.

A Way Forward: Revisiting Epistemic Values

The Enlightenment philosopher Voltaire (1778) wrote: 'those who make you believe absurdities can make you commit atrocities'. Though written over two centuries ago, Voltaire's insights seem to resonate with the events of American politics over the last 4 years as the 45th American President is credited with inciting fascism, violence, white supremacy, imperialism, and many other violent and unjust actions within some of the American people, leading up to the insurrection on 6 January 2021. When people trust and believe in a leader, they can be led to violent action by believing in falsehoods. An epistemology of false beliefs arises from trust being established on psychological certainty of truth and people's vulnerability to deceivers and being deceived. Once trust is established, people are vulnerable to believing any falsehood that the trusted makes, including dismissing or discrediting opposing views for which there is significant more evidence. These processes are further exacerbated and complicated in consideration of technology because technology mediates between deceivers and the deceived and can emulate truth and reality, or it can create new realities as people engage in online communities, such as social media groups.

Deceit is a broader problem of humanity, and it is remiss to address it only in online environments. We are situated in historical, social, gendered, and racialized contexts with politics, economics, laws, and unspoken structures by which we abide, such as capitalism that can motivate deceivers to deceive (Rose 2020b). Though I have discussed an epistemology of false belief, deceivers and the deceived will utilize their broader social contexts in digitally mediated communications. We simply cannot step outside of our societal and cultural context, particularly when establishing trust, because it is psychological certainty about the truth that establishes trust in givers of statements and potential deceivers and is directly related to our cultural context. Often what we believe as 'truth' is related to our context, such as the Trump supporter who does not believe systemic racism is a problem because he lives in a political environment that values individualism, individualist achievement, and disregards the fact that racial inequalities are socially constructed notions that are embedded into the fabric of our societies. Holistic epistemic certainty is something that we do not possess, so we ought to always foster truth-telling; however, truth as the sole epistemic aim is insufficient. As discussed, it can be used to establish trust, which can be exploited.

As Nietzsche (1873/1999) observed, deceit is pervasive, so much so, that it defies understanding how truth as a primary epistemic aim emerged from traditional analytical epistemology. Nietzsche's observations point towards deceit as being deeply embedded in human psychology and from this one might postulate that people fundamentally need to focus on truth to overcome their deceitful 'nature'. While this is an argument well beyond the scope of this chapter, one way to help soften the effects of postdigital deception is to add the value of understanding to epistemic aims.

Kvanvig (2003: 193) explains that understanding helps us grasp explanatory connections between pieces of information or the propositional compartmentalization of knowledge because 'it focuses on the question of whether the person has seen the right kinds of relationships among the various items of information grasped'. Understanding requires that individuals grasp the relationships between information and propositions, but also that it has a psychological component because the person must be able to *comprehend* the relations, and the relations must be within their awareness (Kvanvig 2003). This takes people beyond notions of knowing the truth as the epistemic aim because it helps them organize and systematize their thinking about the world's explanatory relationships. Helping people understand how to 'make sense' of their contexts and their relationships between each other, technology, knowledge, beliefs, and social structures can help combat deception because they are enabled to more aptly understand the relationships they have with the world, rather than merely being certain of truth claims and beliefs. Additionally, people ought to acquire a *healthy scepticism* about their truth *claims* and *beliefs* about truth.

Descartes' (1637/ 1960) methods for determining what is true, while they may *seem* to be helpful to combat postdigital deception, can encourage extreme scepticism and position people to develop false beliefs because they are limited in what they can know in technologically mediated environments (Rose 2020b). We do rely upon others to acquire accurate information and knowledge and cannot solely rely upon ourselves, because we are necessarily dependent upon one another, in some form, to acquire accurate information and knowledge: we cannot help but learn from the contexts in which we are born. A healthy scepticism requires us to consider our psychological certainty of truth about our beliefs. As discussed, we simply do not have a holistic account of epistemic certainty, so any claims of certainty about truth are primarily psychologically based. Until there is radical change in the social structures that contribute to deception, education can help people understand the limits to what they know, the certainty of what they know, and what they can reasonably know, not only in online environments but also through any technologically mediated communication.

This epistemology of false belief is critical to *understand* because it explicates a fundamental way in which deceivers aim to deceive us. If we can begin making the necessary connections in our world through a postdigital understanding, we will be further equipped to combat postdigital deception.

References

BBC. (2020). US Election 2020: What are Trump's and Biden's policies?. BBC, 18 October. https://www.bbc.com/news/election-us-2020-54507550. Accessed 20 January 2021.

Beier, K. (2019). Lying and self-deception. In J. Meibauer (Ed.), *The Oxford Handbook of Lying* (pp. 203–213). Oxford, UK: Oxford University Press.

Bonjour, L. (1985). *The Structure of Empirical Knowledge*. Cambridge, MA: Harvard University Press.

Burnyeat, M. F., & Barnes, J. (1980). Socrates and the jury: Paradoxes in Plato's distinction between knowledge and true belief. *Proceedings of Aristotelian Society. Supplementary Issue, 54*(1), 173–206. https://doi.org/10.1093/aristoteliansupp/54.1.173.

Carson, T. L. (2010). *Lying and deception theory and practice*. Oxford, UK: Oxford University Press.

Coady, C. A. J. (1994). *Testimony: A Philosophical Study*. Oxford, UK: Clarendon Press.

Chisholm, R. M., & Feehan, T. D. (1977). The intent to deceive. *The Journal of Philosophy, 74*(3), 143–159.

David, M. (2001). Truth as the epistemic goal. In M. Steup (Ed.), *Knowledge, Truth, and Duty: Essays on Epistemic Justification, Responsibility, and Virtue* (pp. 151–169). Oxford, UK: Oxford University Press.

Descartes, R. (1637/1960). Discourse on method meditations. In R. Descartes, B. Spinoza, & G. W. von Leibniz, *The rationalists* (pp. 39–107). Trans. J. Veitch. New York: DoubleDay.

Dunn, A., Kiley, J., Scheller, A., Baronavski, C., & Doherty, S. (2017). Voters say those on the other side 'don't get' them. Here's what they what they want them to know. Pewresearch, 17 December. https://www.pewresearch.org/politics/2020/12/17/voters-say-those-on-the-other-side-dont-get-them-heres-what-they-want-them-to-know/. Accessed 9 January 2021.

Dusek, V. (2006). *Philosophy of Technology; An introduction*. Malden, MA and Oxford, UK: Blackwell Publishing.

Fallis, D. (2019). Lying and omissions. In J. Meibauer (Ed.), *The Oxford Handbook of Lying* (pp. 193–192). Oxford, UK: Oxford University Press.

Fricker, E. (2006). Testimony and epistemic autonomy. In J. Lackey & E. Sosa (Eds.), *Epistemology of Testimony* (pp. 225–312). New York: Oxford University Press.

Gelfert, A. (2014). *A Critical Introduction to Testimony*. New York: Bloomsbury Publishing.

Goldman, A. I. (1986). *Epistemology and Cognition*. Cambridge, MA: Harvard University Press.

Goldman, A. I. (1999). *Knowledge in a Social World*. Oxford, UK: Clarendon Press.

James, W. (2001). *Pragmatism and Other Writings*. New York: Penguin Group.

Jandrić, P., Knox, J., Besley, T., Ryberg, T., Suoranta, J., & Hayes, S. (2018). Postdigital science and education. *Educational Philosophy and Theory, 50*(10), 893–899. https://doi.org/10.1080/00131857.2018.1454000.

Kirkham, R. L. (2001). *Theories of Truth*. Cambridge, MA: Massachusetts Institute of Technology.

Klein, P. D. (1998). Certainty. In E. Craig (Ed), *Routledge Encyclopedia of Philosophy* (pp. 1358–1361). London and New York: Routledge.

Kvanvig, J. L. (2003). *The Value of Knowledge and the Pursuit of Understanding*. Cambridge, UK: Cambridge University Press.

Lackey, J. (2008). *Learning from Words Testimony as a Source of Knowledge*. Oxford, UK: Oxford University Press.

Marsili, N. (2019). Lying and certainty. In J. Meibauer (Ed), *The Oxford Handbook of Lying* (pp. 170–182). Oxford, UK: Oxford University Press.

Martin, C. (2009). Introduction: the intersections of deception and self-deception. In C. Martin (Ed), *The Philosophy of Deception* (pp. 3–11). New York: Oxford University Press.

Nietzsche, F. (1873/1999). On truth and lying in a non-moral sense. In R. Geuss & R. Speirs (Eds), *The Birth of Tragedy and Other Writings* (pp. 139–153). Trans. R. Speirs. Cambridge, UK: Cambridge University Press.

Nooteboom, B. (2006). Forms, sources and processes of trust. In R. Bachmann & A. Zaheer (Eds.), *The Handbook of Trust Research* (pp. 247–263). Cheltenham, UK: Edward Elgar Publishing.

O'Neill, O. (2020). Questioning trust. In J. Simon (Ed), *The Routledge Handbook of Trust and Philosophy* (pp. 17–20). New York: Routledge.

Rose, J. (2020a). To believe or not to believe: an epistemic exploration of fake news truth and the limits of knowing. *Postdigital Science and Education, 2*(1), 202–216. https://doi.org/10.1007/s42438-019-00068-5.

Rose, J. (2020b). The mortal coil of covid-19, fake news, and negative epistemic postdigital inculcation. *Postdigital Science and Education, 2*(3), 812–829. https://doi.org/10.1007/s42438-020-00192-7.

Saul, J. (2012). *Lying, Misleading, & What is Said an Exploration in Philosophy of Language and in Ethics*. Oxford, UK: Oxford University Press.

Solomon, R. C. (2009). Self, deception, and self-deception in philosophy. In C. Martin (Ed.), *The Philosophy of Deception* (pp. 15–36). New York: Oxford University Press.

Sorensen, R. (2007). Bald-faced lies! Lying without the intent to deceive. *Pacific Philosophical Quarterly, 88*(2), 251–264. https://doi.org/10.1111/j.1468-0114.2007.00290.x.

Stanley, J. (2008). Knowledge and certainty. *Philosophical Issues, 18*, 35–57. https://doi.org/10.1111/j.1533-6077.2008.00136.x.

Stokke, A. (2018). *Lying and Insincerity*. Oxford, UK: Oxford University Press.

Voltaire. (1778). Voltaire (d. 1778): On injustice. https://ballandalus.wordpress.com/2013/05/26/voltaire-d-1778-on-injustice/. Accessed 24 January 2021.

Wittgenstein, L. (1969). *On Certainty.* New York: Basil Blackwell.

Yagoda, M. (2018). Bill Clinton: The infamous moment US president denied affair with White House intern Monica Lewinsky. Independent, 19 December. https://www.independent.co.uk/news/world/americas/bill-clinton-monica-lewinsky-speech-affair-relationship-sexual-relations-impeachment-a8689511.html. Accessed 28 January 2021.

Chapter 3
Towards a Response to Epistemic Nihilism

Jake Wright

Introduction

On 3 November 2020, voters elected former Vice President Joe Biden as the 46th President of the United States, defeating incumbent Donald Trump. Because the election took place amidst the Covid-19 pandemic, over 100 million voters – an unprecedented number – voted early. This tsunami of early voting had a number of effects, including delayed vote-counting in the decisive states of Michigan, Pennsylvania, Arizona, and Georgia. This delay meant that news organizations were unable to project a winner until the morning of 7 November (Edelman 2020a) and that the final states of Georgia and North Carolina were not projected until 13 November, a full 10 days after Election Day (Edelman 2020b). Such a delay was similarly unprecedented,[1] since election winners are typically known on election night. Further, because of partisan messaging regarding the safety of early voting and the manner in which votes were cast,[2] several states that contributed to Biden's

[1] The closest modern parallel to the 2020 vote count is the 2000 presidential election, which was not resolved for over a month because of a miniscule margin in the ultimately decisive state of Florida. Following a series of recounts and legal challenges, George W. Bush was declared the winner by a margin of 529 votes after the United States Supreme Court ordered an end to the recount in mid-December.

[2] Republicans, led by Donald Trump, largely tried to paint early voting as insecure and a source of widespread voter fraud, while Democrats encouraged early voting as a safe way to vote amidst a pandemic (Silver 2020). Thus, while early voting typically does not show a partisan lean in the United States, the early vote in 2020 skewed heavily towards Democrats. Further, in many states,

J. Wright (✉)
Center for Learning Innovation, University of Minnesota Rochester, Rochester, MN, USA
e-mail: jwwright@r.umn.edu

A. MacKenzie et al. (eds.), *The Epistemology of Deceit in a Postdigital Era*, Postdigital Science and Education,
https://doi.org/10.1007/978-3-030-72154-1_3

victory initially showed a significant lead for Trump that would later be chipped away at and ultimately surpassed by votes for Biden (Bronner et al. 2020).

As a result of the delayed vote count and the marked shift towards Biden as early votes were tabulated, several right wing social media accounts pushed widespread narratives of voter fraud, leading to significant doubts about the fairness of the election and the validity of Biden's victory, especially among Republicans (Badger 2020; Mehta 2020). For example, in the three weeks following Election Day, Twitter flagged tweets from Donald Trump's account (@realDonaldTrump) over 200 times as containing false information about the election (Spangler 2020). These baseless accusations potentially undermine not only the perceived legitimacy of a Biden administration but also faith in future elections.

Liberal democracy depends on good faith engagement. For example, democratic institutions must be responsive to stakeholders' needs via a 'process of reasoned discussion and deliberation on equal footing' (Christiano 2018). As Mill notes, 'the rights and interests of every or any person are only secure from being disregarded when the person interested is himself able, and habitually disposed to stand up for them' (1861: 54). In short, the ideal of democracy involves participation by individuals who are forthright about their interests via good faith engagement on a level playing field. The further we slip from this ideal, the worse democracy operates – potentially to the point of a complete breakdown of democratic systems themselves. Efforts like those above, baselessly painting the legitimate winner of a presidential election as fraudulent, are, simply put, not good faith engagement, and it is not hard to see how such efforts and the degree to which they have been advanced constitute a threat to democratic processes and institutions.

Recent scholarship has focused on rhetorical efforts to undermine the democratic process belying a commitment to good faith engagement, such as bullshitting and trolling. While efforts have been made to address such phenomena, they have largely focused on the individual phenomena themselves – for example, how we can disabuse belief in bullshit (Wright 2020a) or counter trollish behavior (Ebner 2019) – rather than considering these phenomena under a broader, more unified umbrella.

I have noted elsewhere that parallels existing between these phenomena are 'instructive and worthy of further study' (Wright 2020b) both because of their shared similarities as phenomena and because of the shared threats they collectively pose to democratic institutions. This chapter represents a first step in that further study, outlining what I term *epistemic nihilism* – briefly, a worldview that rejects the intrinsic value of truth – and outlining how we ought to respond to extreme cases of such nihilism. Essentially, cases of epistemic nihilism depend on rejecting truth as

in-person votes are tabulated first, with early votes counted later. Such states, like Pennsylvania and Georgia, showed an initial 'red mirage' due to Trump's significant lead in votes cast on election day itself. By contrast, states like Ohio and Texas, which counted early votes first, created a 'blue mirage' because the vote counting was reversed relative to states like Pennsylvania and Georgia.

a necessary condition for achieving one's aims, often depending on one's interlocutor being unaware of this rejection. Thus, when deployed in the context of the democratic process, such actions constitute a form of cheating where one does not engage in good faith, creating an advantage precisely because one expects one's interlocutor to be engaging in the good faith that the epistemic nihilist has rejected.

The question thus becomes how we ought to respond to cases of epistemic nihilism. While a number of remedies exist to address one-off instances of nihilism – for example, the ability on many social media platforms to flag nihilistic posts for removal or as disputed – the question of how to respond becomes more challenging when considering serial offenders whose nihilism becomes something of a way of life. Put differently, we must consider what to do with, for example, serial liars, inveterate bullshitters, and unrepentant trolls who do not merely engage in nihilistic behavior but are properly considered epistemic nihilists. I argue that, in such extreme cases, we are justified in denying the nihilist a platform from which to speak.

Such a response is, in some sense, extreme, seeming to violate norms of discourse at a minimum and potentially violating rights to free speech at a maximum. I argue that such an extreme response is warranted when it is only through our ability to enforce such penalties that the nihilist's advantage can be countered, drawing a parallel with the legal designation of vexatious litigants, who are barred from petitioning the courts – despite the right to do so – specifically because the harm is created by the vexatious litigant's abuse of that right. Put slightly differently, an epistemic nihilist like Trump might have the right to free expression under normal circumstances, but the abuse of that right to cause significant, repeated harm to democratic institutions may justify actions like denying a platform from which he can make his claims.

Epistemic Nihilism

I take *epistemic nihilism* to be the rejection of truth as an intrinsic or instrumental good. Often, discussions employing the term focus on at least the view that knowledge via universal epistemic principles is unobtainable[3], sometimes accompanied by further claims – for example, Nietzsche's claim that knowledge would not be useful if it were obtainable (Nehamas 2010) or Rorty's claim that epistemology as an enterprise is fatally flawed and should be dismantled (2009). When I use the term epistemic nihilism, however, I do not mean to suggest cases where a speaker believes that truth is unobtainable or cannot be adjudicated using universal principles, and I take epistemology generally to be a fruitful endeavor. Further, though I will not

[3] See, for example, Goldman (2010).

argue for it here, I accept a correspondence view of truth that accepts claims as true insofar as they align with an actual state of affairs in the world.

Perhaps the closest use of the term to my own is Arendt's view of nihilism as 'a way of thinking that can look rational but is really an attack on the purpose of rationality' (Gertz 2019: 104). As I discuss cases of epistemic nihilism, a common thread that emerges is the obscurance of truth because the truth is not valuable to the speaker who is attempting to influence their interlocutor's rational deliberations. This section examines such nihilism by considering the similarities between three exemplars of nihilistic speech – lying, bullshitting, and trolling – as well as the advantages of viewing activities like these as tokens of a larger type. I also discuss how epistemic nihilism can transcend individual instances and become an identity or way of life, which has implications for how we ought to respond when combatting extreme cases of such nihilism.

It takes no great imagination to see how lying constitutes epistemic nihilism. The goal of a lie is to convince one's interlocutor to believe a falsehood spoken by the liar because their belief in that falsehood would advantage the speaker in some way. For example, one may lie and deny an extramarital affair, but such a lie would only be successful if the interlocutor (e.g., the speaker's spouse) believed the lie and presumably would be uttered only if the speaker viewed it as to their advantage. Even white lies – for example, the claim that dinner was delicious when it was not or that one's dress is attractive when it is not – advantage the speaker at some level, for example, by allowing the speaker to seem supportive or to grease the wheels of social cohesion. Thus, the lie requires the recognition that the value of truth is outstripped by the value obtained by others' belief in one's falsehood.

Bullshit similarly rejects the value of truth, though for somewhat different reasons. Bullshit is essentially a claim that the speaker wishes their interlocutor to believe, though the speaker themselves has no regard for the claim's truth value (Frankfurt 1986). For example, Donald Trump regularly claims that unflattering coverage such as reports regarding crowd size (Concha 2018; Dale 2019; Levine 2019; O'Neil 2019), his handling of the Covid-19 pandemic (Trump 2020c), and his reelection campaign (Trump 2020b) is 'fake news'.

As I have argued previously (Wright 2020a), Trump's claims are bullshit precisely because of his aim in expressing them. Some cries of fake news are accurate, while others are not; Trump desires his audience to believe him not because they are true or false, but because they are unflattering. Unlike the lie, where truth matters, the truth value of the bullshitter's claim is simply irrelevant.

As a third example, trolling differs from lying and bullshitting in that success depends not on the interlocutor believing the troll but rather because the interlocutor is unsure what to believe because it is unclear what the troll believes. Essentially, trolling is a behavior in which outlandish claims are made or actions are undertaken for the purpose of garnering a reaction (Buckels et al. 2014; Edstrom 2016). Often, though not universally, such activities are otherwise aimless (Shachaf and Hara 2010), resulting merely from a desire to disrupt (Hardaker 2010). As noted later in this chapter, the generally aimless nature of most trolling provides vital cover for more nefarious instances of trolling that seek to disrupt in order to achieve a particular aim, like mainstreaming extremist views, retreating to familiar trollish responses that their actions are unserious and ought to be taken as such.

The generally provocative aim of trolling provides crucial cover for cases where trolling is employed as a recruiting or persuasive tool. For example, trolling often involves a 'humorous ambiguity [that] offers access points for undecided and not-yet politicized users to develop affinities with and support for far-right causes' (Bogerts and Fielitz 2019: 151). Such ambiguity allows the troll 'ironic distance' (May and Feldman 2019: 26) when the troll is confronted with claims that their speech or actions are out-of-bounds. Indeed, trolls typically respond that they are, in Internet parlance, 'doing it for the lulz',[4] suggesting that their actions or speech ought not be taken seriously because they seek to provoke. This idea of doing it for the lulz suggests that there is something wrong with the interlocutor themselves *because* they took trolling at face value, rather than embracing the 'nothing matters' ethos of trolling (Wright 2020b).

A Unified Theory of Epistemic Nihilism

There are important differences between lying, bullshitting, and trolling, such as whether their success depends on the interlocutor believing a false claim or whether the interlocutor must believe the speaker is representing genuinely held views. Further, significant literature exists discussing how to address each activity individually, ranging from innumerable discussions of dishonesty in various subfields of applied ethics to discussions of the psychological motivations behind bullshit acceptance[5] – as well as how to counter such openness[6] – to strategies for countering trollish behavior.[7]

It is not my goal to suggest that nothing can be learned by such focused attention. Instead, I suggest that grouping nihilistic activities under a common umbrella also carries with it certain advantages. First, approaching the problem through a common lens allows us to note similarities between actions that abandon truth as useful or intrinsically good. Second, insofar as commonalities exist, we are better

[4] 'Lulz' is a transformation of the common chat/text acronym LOL (laugh out loud), frequently deployed when the goal is to generate laughter based on offensive or provocative behavior. For example, UrbanDictionary.com lists several user-provided definitions with examples, including 'Why did I post a giant image of 50 Hitlers? I did it for the lulz,' or claiming that Truman authorized the atomic bombings of Hiroshima and Nagasaki, killing 'thousands of innocent women and children… for the lulz' (Urban Dictionary n.d.).

[5] See, for example, Nyhan and Reifler (2010); Pennycook and Rand (2018); Prior et al. (2015); Schaffner and Luks (2018); Wood and Porter (2019).

[6] See, for example, Andre (1983), Delaney (2004), Erion (2005), Momeyer (1995), Paden (1987, 1994), Satris (1986), and Wright (2019) for discussions of how to combat bullshit in a classroom environment.

[7] See, for example, Bogerts and Fielitz (2019), Ebner (2019), Edstrom (2016), May and Feldman (2019), and Tuters (2019).

positioned to develop general strategies and apply extant strategies focused on one token of this type. Third, grouping actions under a common banner allows us to sidestep questions of taxonomy when such questions are not useful. We need not parse whether a difficult case is a lie, bullshit, trolling, or something else if little rides on such a distinction; we may simply note an instance of epistemic nihilism and respond accordingly.

Many of the similarities between activities like lying, bullshitting, and trolling have been noted above. Briefly, each activity depends on rejecting the value or utility of truth in order to achieve some further aim by, for example, inducing one's interlocutor to believe a particular claim or to obscure the speaker's true beliefs or intent. Recognizing such similarities allows us to examine other behaviors with a critical eye towards whether they, too, constitute cases of epistemic nihilism. For example, one may examine the naïve skepticism often expressed by introductory-level students as a kind of (well-intentioned) nihilism that results from students' desires to avoid offense or appear tolerant (Wright 2019). Similarly, one might recognize that there are cases, like those discussed below, where one can engage in nihilism despite total transparency about one's genuine beliefs because the beliefs themselves are obviously nihilistic.

By collecting such disparate activities under a common framework, we can not only consider common responses – like my proposed response in this chapter – that may apply across all forms of epistemic nihilism but also consider how particular targeted responses may be appropriated to respond to other forms of nihilism. For example, I have discussed how strategies for addressing naïve skepticism can be reapplied to combat people's openness to political bullshit (Wright 2020a). Certainly, there will not be perfect overlap in such cases, and differences between kinds of nihilism ought to be taken into account, but this is not, I take it, a reason to reject such considerations any more than being sensitive to the relevant details of a particular instance of bullshit is a reason to reject general anti-bullshit strategies. One may look for broad trends and general strategies while attending to the details of a particular case.

Indeed, there may be instances where working in broad strokes is preferable to a fine-grained analysis. Such cases illustrate the third advantage of a broad theory of epistemic nihilism – the ability to sidestep irrelevant detail. To see what I mean, consider the following cases:

During racial justice protests in Buffalo, New York, an elderly peace activist named Martin Gugino was pushed to the ground by Buffalo police officers, hitting his head on the concrete sidewalk and sustaining a brain injury. Gugino's case attracted widespread media attention because video of the incident demonstrated that the officers' actions were unprovoked and directly contradicted an initial statement from the police department that Gugino 'was injured when he tripped & fell' (Herbert 2020). Donald Trump responded to this incident by suggesting via tweet that Gugino was a member of antifa[8] who had faked injury (Trump 2020a). Trump's

[8] Antifa is an umbrella term for a loose collection of left-wing protestors formed in the wake of white supremacy protests in Charlottesville, Virginia in 2017 (Anti-Defamation League n.d.). The term itself is a portmanteau of 'anti-fascist'.

tweet immediately drew widespread condemnation as 'baseless' (Spencer and Farley 2020), 'without evidence' (Phelps and Cathey 2020), a 'conspiracy theory' (Kessler 2020; Phelps and Cathey 2020; Reuters Staff 2020), and 'outrageous' (Kessler 2020). Because a Republican Senate conference lunch was scheduled for the afternoon Trump tweeted his comments, Republican senators became obvious media targets for journalists in search of comment. One such senator was Ron Johnson, who initially claimed to have not seen the tweet in question. But when asked by a reporter if he would like to have the tweet read to him so that he might comment, Johnson responded, 'I would rather not hear it' (Raju et al. 2020).

One might wonder how to classify such a comment, where the clear implication is a desire to avoid knowing the truth. The plain meaning of 'I would rather not know' is *a desire to not know* rather than a desire to wait for context or a request for time to formulate a response. By saying he would rather not hear Trump's comment, Johnson is not lying; he genuinely did not want to know what Trump said. Neither was his comment bullshit, since the truth of Johnson's claim seems central to our analysis. Finally, it is not trolling, since there is no evidence Johnson made his remarks to get a rise out of reporters. In addition, there is no doubt about his genuine view. Yet his actions seem almost brazenly nihilistic; he simply declares he does not want to know the truth because the truth would be, in some sense, bad for him.

One might, out of a sense of charity, argue that Johnson may have demurred out of a wish to avoid commenting without knowledge of the full context. Even if we apply such strenuous credulity, however, Johnson's comment is a particularly overt instance of a pattern among Republican politicians who refuse to contradict obviously false, malicious statements by Trump to the point where 'Republicans asked about Trump's comments on *x*' has become something of a journalistic genre. Thus, it is instructive to consider a second example where, in response to Trump's baseless claims that he won the 2020 election and is the victim of widespread fraud, each Republican member of Congress was asked, one month after the election, who won the 2020 Presidential election. Out of 249 Republican members, 27 acknowledged former Vice President Joe Biden as the winner, two claimed that Trump had indeed won, and 220 refused to answer (Kane and Clement 2020). Like the Gugino case, Trump's false claims to be the victim of fraud are dangerous, but unlike the Gugino case, unfamiliarity with the issue is simply impossible, rather than seemingly implausible, since the question was posed a month after the election itself, after a clear winner had emerged. Yet again, it is not clear that those who refused to answer lied, bullshitted, or engaged in trolling.

Classifying such cases as instances of epistemic nihilism affords those of us who stand opposed to such behavior the opportunity to name it without having to more precisely diagnose or taxonomize. Insofar as labeling such remarks as instances of nihilism is sufficient in considering a response, further analysis is unnecessary. It is nihilism and ought to be treated as such.

Epistemic Nihilism as a Worldview

Thus far, discussion of epistemic nihilism has focused on individual cases in order to provide a sense of what sorts of actions constitute epistemic nihilism. However, it is important to note there is a difference between one-off instances and serial commission. For many of the actions that constitute epistemic nihilism, one common thread seems to be that repeated instances of such actions can impact one's identity through how one is perceived by others or how one perceives oneself. For example, we may judge one who lies regularly as *a liar*. 'Internet troll' is not merely pejorative; it can also be part of one's self identity, used to enforce community boundaries among fellow trolls (Bartlett 2014) or as justification for one's socially undesirable actions (Reed 2019).

If we take seriously the idea that repeated instances of particular forms of epistemic nihilism can result in identities like 'liar', 'bullshitter', or 'troll' either being assigned or self-declared, it seems one can similarly be an epistemic nihilist, full stop. It may be sufficient to note that an individual simply is an epistemic nihilist. Such labeling may be useful, both in terms of pushing back on more nuanced denials of being a liar, etc., but also because such labels have important implications for how we ought to respond in particularly egregious cases, as I discuss below. We may be justified in enforcing stricter penalties against a liar than one who lies occasionally, and we may be similarly justified enforcing strict penalties against epistemic nihilists. Before discussing how we ought to respond, however, it is worth discussing in some detail the threat posed by nihilistic behavior.

The Threat of Epistemic Nihilism

Liberal democracy is premised on active, good faith participation from forthright members of the community, which provides a more-or-less level playing field. Epistemic nihilism rejects this premise by abusing the assumption that interlocutors are engaging in good faith. When successful, such actions advantage nihilistic behavior. In addition to providing a rhetorical advantage that is the direct result of bad faith engagement, nihilism has the further deleterious effect of encouraging conspiracists and other fringe actors willing to engage in actions well outside the scope of normal democratic participation. These advantages are further exacerbated by a balkanized media landscape that favors consumers' own partisan or tribal preferences, creating environments where nihilism is not adequately confronted.

The Nihilist's Rhetorical Advantage

It seems obvious that epistemic nihilism is advantaged over a commitment to truth and accuracy, since nihilistic speech needs only be rhetorically advantageous, while truthful or accurate speech much also attends to those criteria. For example, the ironic distance provided by nihilistic acts like trolling allow an ambiguity that advantages the speaker by allowing a response to claims that one's speech is racist, misogynistic, and so forth along the lines that the speaker is only kidding or being provocative for provocation's sake, masking the speaker's seriousness with unseriousness (Bogerts and Fielitz 2019). Essentially, nihilistic speech need not reveal itself as such unless pressed, so potential fellow travelers who view such speech favorably gain access to the views expressed because opponents cannot clearly establish that the views are sincerely held by the speaker (May and Feldman 2019).

Nihilistic speech similarly advantages the speaker when the context of discussion drifts from sincerely held beliefs towards meta-discussion of the speaker's seriousness. There may be widespread agreement that sincerely believing a particular claim would be problematic. However, the ironic distance provided by seemingly unserious provocation leads not to a discussion of the view itself, but whether the view is sincerely held or whether it is acceptable to insincerely express the view in question. When such debate occurs, the ironic or unserious use of language expressing genuinely held beliefs communicates meaning to those who understand the rules of a particular form of nihilistic communication as a form of dog whistle (Tuters 2019). The farcical nature of claims that Joe Biden's electoral victory was fraudulent has led to a robust meta-discussion of the degree to which these claims are genuinely held (Rucker et al. 2020), distracting from the fact that they are damaging precisely because they are false. Meanwhile, the message to those 'in the know' is quite clear; despite a clear victory free of fraud or interference, Joe Biden is not to be viewed as a legitimate president.

Finally, nihilistic speech allows for deflection or avoidance of undesirable lines of inquiry. Donald Trump, for example, has avoided questions about his rhetoric's effect on white nationalists by arguing such questions are themselves 'racist' (Farhi 2018). Similarly, he refused to answer a question about the removal of a high-ranking public health official who contradicted Trump's unsubstantiated claims about an ineffective Covid-19 treatment on the grounds that the reporter who asked the question was from a 'fake news' organization (Cortright 2020). Ron Johnson refused to hear what Trump had to say about the Gugino case. Like Trump's claims that his electoral defeat was the result of fraud, these cases drew media scrutiny away from the substance of the claims towards a general refusal to answer (Lewandowsky et al. forthcoming).

Refusing to engage on specious grounds to avoid uncomfortable or unflattering lines of inquiry obscures what one believes, as well as why they believe it. At best, we as interlocutors are able to evaluate actions and motivations at a meta level, judging them for their willingness to obfuscate and engage in nihilistic behavior, rather than evaluate actions in their own right. We may, perhaps, infer certain things from how someone responds to certain questions, but inference is no substitute for a genuine answer.

The Dangers of Nihilistic Speech

In addition to providing a rhetorical advantage, nihilistic speech can encourage actions that are anathema to reasoned deliberation that is the ideal of democracy. While the nihilist themselves might not be concerned with the truth, their interlocutors often are, thus creating the possibility of such individuals accepting genuinely dangerous claims.

For example, public health efforts aimed at reducing the spread of Covid-19 have been implemented to varying degrees of success globally. One of the largest factors impacting success is the degree to which they are countered by what the World Health Organization has called an 'infodemic' of misinformation (Evanega et al. 2020; United Nations Department of Global Communications 2020). In the United States, preliminary analysis has found that the largest driver of misinformation has been Donald Trump himself (Evanega et al. 2020). 37.9% of all misinformation captured by the study were directly associated with Trump, and a 'substantial proportion – possibly even the majority – of the [discussion surrounding] "miracle cures"' (7) may have been driven by Trump as well, since he frequently touted supposed cures like hydroxychloroquine and injecting bleach. Such misinformation is not a theoretical exercise; it impacts individuals' view of the pandemic itself and the trustworthiness of genuine sources of medical knowledge. Partisan differences regarding the seriousness of the pandemic and the efficacy of preventative measures exist (Allcott et al. 2020) and can reasonably be explained, at least in part, by the fact that a major American political party is led by an epistemic nihilist.

The threat posed by nihilistic speech goes beyond public health, however, promoting actions that directly threaten the pillars of liberal democratic institutions. Adherents to QAnon – the conspiracy theory that Donald Trump is overseeing a federal investigation into Satan-worshiping, blood-drinking, cannibalistic Democratic Party leaders (including and especially 2016 nominee Hillary Clinton) and Hollywood celebrities who are collectively responsible for a global child sex trafficking ring (Neiwert 2018) – anxiously await the 'Storm', supposed coordinated raids intended to crack down on the cabal (Coaston 2019). QAnon's growth has occurred on the far right with 'surprising rapidity' (Neiwert 2018), and a number of 2020 electoral candidates endorsed the theory either tacitly or explicitly. This includes Marjorie Taylor Greene, whose election to represent Georgia's 14th district elevated an explicit adherent to the House of Representatives (Allam 2020). Following a congratulatory tweet to Greene after her victory in the Georgia primary, Donald Trump was asked whether he endorsed QAnon. Refusing to denounce the theory, he replied that he 'didn't know anything about them, other than they supposedly like me' and that 'if I can help them save the world from problems, I'm willing to do it' (Rogers and Roose 2020).

It is not hard to imagine how such failure to denounce a conspiracy by its supposed leader can be viewed as at least tacit approval by conspiracists. Again, such seeming endorsement is no theoretical exercise; adherents have been described by the FBI as individuals willing to 'commit criminal and sometimes violent activity'

(FBI Phoenix Field Office 2019: 1) and have, in fact, done so. QAnon conspiracists, along with adherents to QAnon's progenitor, Pizzagate, have attempted armed liberations of nonexistent trafficking victims, blocked traffic with an armored truck to force the release of nonexistent, supposedly confirmatory documents, and assassinated a member of the New York mafia because the crime boss was a purported member of the so-called 'deep state' conspiring against Trump (Amarasingam and Argentino 2020). In the latter case, the mafia assassin's lawyer reported that he viewed himself as 'Trump's chosen vigilante' (Amarasingam and Argentino 2020: 40).

Such violence, generally speaking, is a breakdown of the sort of discourse democracy depends on; it is the application of power in lieu of reasoned discussion and deliberation. Thus, any violence is, at some level, problematic for democracy. But when such violence is cloaked in extrajudicial actions where conspiracist actors believe they have the tacit approval of the president, such violence becomes a threat to democracy itself. It does not matter whether the speaker actually believes in the underlying conspiracy theory. The refusal to say that a conspiracy theory is just that, instead remarking that one is 'willing to [help]', gives conspiracists permission to operate and act in a way that undermines democracy via terrorism and other actions anathema to democracy.

The Media's Effect on Epistemic Nihilism

Though the examples used throughout this chapter are recent, epistemic nihilism and its dangers are not new. Conspiracists have acted against the state long before the advent of 24-hour news, Tokyo Rose did not require the Internet to spread propaganda, and Socrates decried the rhetorical advantage of sophistry[9] over two millennia ago. What has changed, though, is a media landscape which exacerbates the advantages of and dangers posed by epistemic nihilism. This change is the result of what Rose and Bartoli (2020) call the 'balkanization' of media, where previously hegemonic media structures like local and national newspapers or television networks are supplanted by an explosion of new journalistic and quasi-journalistic sources, reflecting both consumers' own partisan preferences and the shift towards so-called viral content.

Such balkanization can invite nihilism not only by catering to cognitive biases like motivated reasoning or intellectual laziness but also because new media outlets often favor the enforcement of tribal boundaries over a commitment to truthfulness. For example, the conservative Gateway Pundit claims that they 'report the truth – and leave the Russia-Collusion fairy tale to the Conspiracy media' [sic] (Hoft n.d.).

---

[9] See, especially, the dialogues *Sophist*, *Gorgias*, and *Protagoras*. John M. Cooper describes the Socratic view thusly: 'Though aware that he does not know anything, [the sophist] produces in words totally inadequate "copies" of the truth on important subjects, one he makes appear to others to be the truth, even though, being false, they are hardly even like it.' (Cooper 1997: 326)

The conservative Daily Caller's Twitter bio brands itself as '[t]he journalists who love America' (@DailyCaller n.d.). Fox News successfully defended itself and its highest-rated host, Tucker Carlson, in a defamation lawsuit by arguing that the substance – not the expressed opinions, but the *substance* – of Carlson's commentary 'cannot reasonably be interpreted as facts' (Vyskockil 2020: 5) because 'given Mr. Carlson's reputation, any reasonable viewer "arrive[s] with an appropriate amount of skepticism" about the statements he makes' (12).

In an environment where the epistemic nihilist seeks the cover of ambiguity to mask their beliefs or seeks to mainstream their beliefs by introducing them through seemingly respectable outlets in palatable forms, media balkanization is a godsend. As noted previously, ambiguity offers a powerful opportunity to introduce extremist ideologies, and mainstreaming can be easily bootstrapped in a media ecosystem of innumerable outlets. This is especially true when options include hyperpartisan outlets, as well as outlets committed to fastidiously presenting both sides of an argument, regardless of how supported the evidence for both sides is.

In the latter case, media's provision of the so-called false balance not only provides avenues for unsupported contrarian opinions but also obscures the degree to which genuine expert consensus exists on phenomena like climate change (Koehler 2016; Merkley 2020; Park 2018). For example, a significant driver of the Covid-19 infodemic seems to have been that the overwhelming majority of Trump's baseless claims were not presented in a context where fact checking took place (Evanega et al. 2020), obscuring the degree to which expert consensus was aligned against Trump's unfounded claims, creating an environment where Trump's claims seemed more reasonable than they objectively were.

Countering Epistemic Nihilism

Given the threats posed by epistemic nihilism, one might naturally ask how we ought to respond. Here, I argue that we must be willing, in extreme cases, to deny epistemic nihilists a platform from which to speak, similar to how vexatious litigants are denied the ability to seek relief from the courts. In both cases, denial seems to at least violate fundamental norms and may involve curtailing an individual's rights. Like the vexatious litigant, I argue that the epistemic nihilist may be denied a platform even though doing so may curtail free speech rights precisely because the way in which those rights are invoked are abusive and harmful.

Nihilistic speech succeeds because it is able to subvert the norms of democratic discourse that assume a level of good faith and honest representation of sincerely held views, for example, convincing interlocutors that insincere views are held sincerely, or masking sincerely held views behind a veil of ambiguity. Efforts to counter such speech face a trilemma, either (a) stooping to the level of the nihilist by employing nihilistic tactics, (b) using established norms to counter the nihilist, or (c) breaking established norms of discourse without resorting to nihilistic speech.

Embracing nihilism to overcome the nihilist is, I take it, a nonstarter. It may have the proximate effect of overcoming a particular instance of nihilistic speech, but the ultimate effect is a universal descent into nihilism. Surely the cure cannot be more of what ails us.

Ideally, nihilistic speech would be countered by employing strategies falling within established norms. For example, social medial platforms have begun applying tools meant to counter nihilistic behavior – like fact-checking, flagging, and post removal – more widely and evenly than in the past, going so far as to flag and remove posts made by political leaders, such as Facebook's and Twitter's removal of posts from Donald Trump claiming seasonal flu was more dangerous than Covid-19 (O'Sullivan 2020) or Twitter's flagging false and misleading claims about voter fraud and other issues with the tag, 'This claim about election fraud is disputed' (Romm 2020). Such actions are the result of the claims at issue being both false and dangerous.

It would be best if the nihilist could be countered by such tactics, but it also seems reasonable to assume that staying within established norms of discourse will not always be successful *precisely because* of the advantages afforded nihilistic speech. Thus, there may be cases where one has no choice but to break established norms in an attempt to counter epistemic nihilism. The question is how best to do so, especially in edge cases where the nihilist's behavior is particularly egregious.

In extreme cases, the epistemic nihilist is essentially weaponizing the right to speak by abusing the assumption that interlocutors are operating in good faith. If this is so, we must be willing to deny the nihilist a platform. Nihilistic politicians, for example, ought not have their remarks broadcast, nor should they be the subject of interviews. Social media platforms must be willing to ban nihilists outright if other strategies prove unsuccessful. Obviously, such a strategy raises a number of concerns, from effectiveness to the rights of the nihilist to speak. There may be a public interest in knowing how a political figure explains policies, even if they do so nihilistically. Platform denial may be abused via partisan appeals to 'obvious' or 'widely accepted' truths that are genuinely disputed. Though space prevents a robust defense of each of these important concerns, I do note the following.

First, I acknowledge that attempts to ban lesser-known nihilists can result in a sort of whack-a-mole where the offending individual simply registers another account. Banning John Smith may not be as effective as banning Donald Trump, in part because of Trump's notoriety. However, I note that any roadblock that potentially slows or discourages nihilistic speech may be valuable. Also, John Smith cases seem unlikely to be the main focus of extreme measures like platform denial, since the potential harm of such anonymous actors seems far less likely to reach the point where extreme measures are warranted.

Second, I grant that the public right to know is vital to a healthy democracy and political leaders should generally be encouraged to explain their actions. However, the good faith assumed by such encouragement is precisely what the nihilist seeks to exploit to their advantage. Denying nihilists a platform not only neutralizes this advantage but also potentially incentivizes good behavior; a platform may welcome back a sufficiently reformed or repentant nihilist. Nihilists who depend at some level on being well-known – like politicians or media commentators – will not have the option of simply registering a new account and may be forced to choose between their nihilism and their access to a ready-made audience.

Third, the decision to deny a platform to an epistemic nihilist is clearly value-laden. We deny nihilists a platform because their nihilism is dangerous (i.e., bad). Such value judgments risk smuggling in more problematic judgments, like denying a speaker a platform because their political views do not align with my own. Though such concerns are serious, a basic response can be offered by invoking Heather Douglas' (2009) distinction between the direct and indirect application of values in the decision-making process. While me may use our values to directly determine what sorts of actions are permissible – for example, the permissibility of denying a platform based on our values regarding liberal democracy – we may *not* use our values to directly determine what counts as an instance of permissible or impermissible action. Instead, we may use our values to indirectly inform how evidence in difficult cases ought to be evaluated. For example, it may be the case that one political party is more likely to engage in nihilistic behavior than another, and we may look more skeptically on the claims of that party as a result. But we may not simply say, 'They are Tories and are therefore denied a platform because I disagree with Tories'. On Douglas's view, we may rule out advocacy via epistemic nihilism in the same way we rule out human subject trials that do not obtain informed consent; our values as a society directly tell us that such efforts are impermissible. (Indeed, it is precisely the fact that such values ought to be forthrightly and openly deliberated upon that gives this discussion import.) However, we cannot judge that a particular claim is an instance of nihilism or that a particular speaker is a nihilist simply because of their political views.

Finally, denying a platform does not constitute a violation of free speech rights. In the first place, my proposal does not call for imprisoning nihilists, nor am I arguing that the positions held by nihilists are automatically out-of-bounds. Instead, I argue we ought not provide platforms to egregious nihilists because of their tactics. If they wish to argue honestly for odious views, this discussion has nothing to say on the matter. Further, the denial of a platform is not speech prevention; it is at best an effort to curtail the reach of nihilistic speech to be heard. However, the right to speak does not entail a right to be heard, an obligation to listen, or any obligation to amplify a speaker's message. In essence, it is a declaration that we collectively will not help nihilistic speech find an audience. If the speaker can find an audience or a fringe platform willing to countenance nihilism, that is their business. However, even if denying a platform involved curtailing the right to speak, there are analogous circumstances demonstrating why such action is justifiable.

Within the US legal system, as in many liberal democracies, individuals have a fundamental right to petition the courts to seek redress. Yet, there exist individuals who invoke this right to the point of abuse, using the system to harass [opponents], to postpone a result he considers unfair, or simply to satisfy some urge to engage in litigation' (Manwell 1966: 1770). Such litigants are harmful not only because of the harm they cause their legal opponents but also because of the harm they cause the legal system itself by overtaxing it and preventing or delaying justice for petitioners whose motives are genuine. Thus, regular abusers may be legally declared *vexatious litigants* and prevented from filing further legal claims without involving outside counsel[10] or the express permission of the courts.[11]

Two features of this designation are worth discussing here. First, a finding that one is a vexatious litigant goes beyond other measures intended to prevent frivolous lawsuits, like anti-SLAPP[12] laws. It is an extreme response reserved for extreme offenders. Second, the bar that must be cleared for such a declaration is quite high, involving 'situations where litigants have filed dozens of motions either during the pendency of an action or relating to the same judgment' (Rushing 2007). In essence, one must engage in a great deal of genuinely harmful, specious litigation before being denied access to the courts.

The vexatious litigant designation and associated penalty is analogous to the sanction I suggest when denying epistemic nihilists a platform. My suggestion is not that we should liberally deny a platform at the first instance of nihilism or that no other steps be taken, but rather that extreme measures are justifiable in extreme circumstances. If there are individuals who cannot be trusted to engage in good faith, their refusal to do so poses significant harm, and less strenuous efforts have not proved corrective, we should be willing to deny them a platform.

Conclusion

Epistemic nihilism is all too common in contemporary discourse, in part because of the advantage it affords. While there are particularly obvious offenders whose speech regularly serves as a paradigm for nihilistic speech, like Donald Trump, it seems unlikely that one electoral defeat or one individual receding into the background of public life will address the wider problem of epistemic nihilism as a phenomenon. As research into the phenomena that constitute epistemic nihilism clearly demonstrates, Trump is not *sui generis.* There were epistemic nihilists before Trump, and there will be epistemic nihilists after Trump. If anything, Trump's success during his campaign and administration highlights the need for heightened

[10] Vexatious litigants frequently represent themselves, and a requirement to obtain outside counsel discourages abuse because such counsel is equally subject to sanction if they themselves abuse the courts. As practicing lawyers whose livelihood depends on access to the legal system, they presumably do not wish such sanction.

[11] See, for example, California's vexatious litigant statutes (Title 3A: Vexatious Litigants 1963.)

[12] Anti-SLAPP (strategic lawsuits against public participation) statutes are intended to prevent litigants from filing lawsuits specifically designed to discourage public access to the courts by, for example, making participation so expensive as to be prohibitive. For example, a corporation may engage in SLAPP if they file a lawsuit against a critic they expect to lose, but the costs of defending oneself from the lawsuit would bankrupt the critic. Such suits incentivize not speaking out, even when making legally protected claims, by making the price of participation too high (Randazza 2012).

vigilance so that the mistakes that led to the success of his nihilism will not be repeated.

While there are many steps one might take to discourage such nihilism, I have argued that, in extreme cases, we ought to simply deny the nihilist a platform from which to speak. Such sanction would apply only to egregious offenders whose nihilism is not only dangerous, but has not been corrected by more taciturn measures. While some platforms have taken steps to ban anonymous nihilists, such efforts do not seem to have extended regularly to more widely known offenders. Furthermore, when such deplatforming does occur, it is not only the exception to the rule, but it is also predicated on other behavior like abuse or sockpuppeting. Conspiracist Alex Jones, for example, has repeatedly suggested that the 2012 mass shooting at Sandy Hook Elementary was staged, but was banned from Twitter for abusive behavior towards other users (Schneider 2018). Similarly, the Krassenstein brothers, known mostly for hyperbolic criticism of Trump, were banned for maintaining multiple accounts under the guise that they were operated by different individuals, as well as purchasing interactions in order to publicize their antagonism of Trump (Concha 2019).

Clearly, the discussion here leaves many further questions to be answered, like what precisely constitutes an 'extreme' case or the precise circumstances in which we ought to deny nihilists a platform. However, these, I think, represent fruitful avenues of future deliberation. Regardless of the specifics generated by such discussion, if we are to take the fight against epistemic nihilism seriously, we must be willing to not only take effective measures against nihilists and nihilistic speech but also apply those measures evenly, no matter who is engaging in such speech.

References

Allam, H. (2020). From Fringe To Congress: QAnon Backers Are On The Ballot In November. NPR.org, 13 August. https://www.npr.org/2020/08/13/901985118/from-fringe-to-congress-qanon-backers-are-on-the-ballot-in-november. Accessed 30 December 2020.

Allcott, H., Boxell, L., Conway, J., Gentzkow, M., Thaler, M., & Yang. D. (2020). Polarization and Public Health: Partisan Differences in Social Distancing during the Coronavirus Pandemic. *Journal of Public Economics, 19*, 104254. https://doi.org/10.1016/j.jpubeco.2020.104254.

Amarasingam, A., & Argentino, M. A. (2020). The QAnon Conspiracy Theory: A Security Threat in the Making? *Combating Terrorism Center at West Point, 13*(7): 37–44.

Andre, J. (1983). Dealing with Naive Relativism in the Philosophy Classroom. *Metaphilosophy, 14*(2), 179–182. https://doi.org/10.1111/j.1467-9973.1983.tb00129.x.

Anti-Defamation League (n.d.) Who Are Antifa? 29 October. https://www.adl.org/antifa. Accessed 30 December 2020.

Badger, E. (2020). Most Republicans Say They Doubt the Election. How Many Really Mean It? The New York Times, 30 November. https://www.nytimes.com/2020/11/30/upshot/republican-voters-election-doubts.htm. Accessed 30 December 2020.

Bartlett, J. (2014). OG Internet Trolls Are Upset Their Hobby's Been Ruined. Vice, 3 October. https://www.vice.com/en/article/bn538w/trolls-jamie-bartlett-289. Accessed 30 December 2020.

Bogerts, L., & Fielitz, M. (2019). "Do You Want Meme War?": Understanding the visual memes of the German far right. In M. Fielitz & N. Thurston (Eds.), *Post-digital cultures of the far right: Online actions and offline consequences in Europe and the US* (pp. 137–154). Bielefeld: transcript Verlag.

Bronner, L., Wiederkehr A., & Rakich, N. (2020). What Blue And Red 'Shifts' Looked Like In Every State. FiveThirtyEight, 12 November. https://fivethirtyeight.com/features/where-we-saw-red-and-blue-mirages-on-election-night/. Accessed 30 December 2020.

Buckels, E., Trapnell, P., & Paulhus, D. (2014). Trolls Just Want to Have Fun. *Personality And Individual Differences, 67,* 97–102. https://doi.org/10.1016/j.paid.2014.01.016.

California Code of Civil Procedure. (1963). 391 https://leginfo.legislature.ca.gov/faces/codes_displayText.xhtml?lawCode=CCP&division=&title=3A.&part=2.&chapter=&article=. Accessed 30 December 2020.

Christiano, T. (2018). Democracy. In N. Zalta (Ed.), *The Stanford Encyclopedia of Philosophy*. Stanford, CA: Stanford University. https://plato.stanford.edu/archives/fall2018/entries/democracy/. Accessed 30 December 2020.

Coaston, J. (2019). The Mueller Investigation Is over. QAnon, the Conspiracy Theory That Grew around It, Is Not. Vox, 29 March. https://www.vox.com/policy-and-politics/2019/3/29/18286890/qanon-mueller-report-barr-trump-conspiracy-theories. Accessed 30 December 2020.

Concha, J. (2018). NYT Corrects Crowd Size Estimate at Nashville Rally after Trump Criticism. The Hill, 30 May. https://thehill.com/homenews/media/389925-nyt-corrects-crowd-size-estimate-at-rally-after-trump-criticism. Accessed 30 December 2020.

Concha, J. (2019). Anti-Trump Krassenstein Brothers Receive Permanent Twitter Ban. The Hill, 24 May. https://thehill.com/homenews/media/445376-anti-trump-krassenstein-brothers-receive-permanent-twitter-ban. Accessed 30 December 2020.

Cooper, J. (1997). *Plato: Complete Works*. Indianapolis, IN: Hackett.

Cortright, B. (2020). Trump Refuses to Answer Question About Vaccine Expert's Reassignment. Independent Journal Review, 23 April. https://ijr.org/trump-refuses-answer-question-experts-reassignment/. Accessed 30 December 2020.

Dale, D [@ddale8]. (2019). Oh Man. I Was Just Watching Dozens of People Walk out of the Room as They Sensed Trump Was a Minute or Two from Concluding...Then Trump Said That He's Been Watching the Doors and Not One Person Has Left. https://twitter.com/ddale8/status/1101924636281974785. Accessed 30 December 2020.

Delaney, J. (2004). Tolerance and Tact: A Critical Thinking Strategy for Dealing with Relativism. *Inquiry: Critical Thinking Across Disciplines, 22*(4): 27–31. https://doi.org/10.5840/inquiryctnews200322438.

Douglas, H. (2009). *Science, Policy, and the Value-Free Ideal*. Pittsburgh, PA: University of Pittsburgh Press.

Ebner, J. (2019). Counter-creativity: Innovative ways to counter far-right communication tactics. In M. Fielitz & N. Thurston (Eds.), *Post-digital cultures of the far right: Online actions and offline consequences in Europe and the US* (pp. 169–182). Bielefeld: transcript Verlag.

Edelman, A. (2020a). Biden Defeats Trump to Win White House, NBC News Projects. NBC News, 7 November. https://www.nbcnews.com/politics/2020-election/biden-defeats-trump-win-white-house-nbc-news-projects-n1246912. Accessed 30 December 2020.

Edelman, A. (2020b). With Final States Called, Biden's Projected Electoral College Victory Matches Trump's in 2016. NBC News, 13 November. https://www.nbcnews.com/politics/2020-election/final-states-called-biden-s-projected-electoral-college-victory-matches-n1247766. Accessed 30 December 2020.

Edstrom, M. (2016). The Trolls Disappear in the Light: Swedish Experiences of Mediated Sexualised Hate Speech in the Aftermath of Behring Breivik. *International Journal for Crime, Justice and Social Democracy, 5*(2), 96. https://doi.org/10.5204/ijcjsd.v5i2.314.

Erion, G. (2005). Engaging Student Relativism. *Discourse, 5*(1), 120–133.

Evanega, S., Lynas, M., Adams, J., & Smolenyak, K. Coronavirus Misinformation: Quantifying Sources and Themes in the COVID-19 'Infodemic'. https://www.uncommonthought.

com/mtblog/wp-content/uploads/2020/12/Evanega-et-al-Coronavirus-misinformation-submitted_07_23_20-1.pdf. Accessed 30 December 2020.

Farhi, P. (2018). 'What a Stupid Question': Trump Demeans Three Black Female Reporters in Three Days. Washington Post, 9 November. https://www.washingtonpost.com/lifestyle/style/what-a-stupid-question-trump-demeans-three-black-female-reporters-in-two-days/2018/11/09/272113d0-e441-11e8-b759-3d88a5ce9e19_story.html. Accessed 30 December 2020.

FBI Phoenix Field Office. (2019). Anti-Government, Identity Based, and Fringe Political Conspiracy Theories Very Likely Motivate Some Domestic Extremists to Commit Criminal, Sometimes Violent Activity. https://www.justsecurity.org/wp-content/uploads/2019/08/420379775-fbi-conspiracy-theories-domestic-extremism.pdf. Accessed 30 December 2020.

Frankfurt, H. (1986). *On Bullshit.* Princeton, NJ: Princeton University Press.

Gertz, N. (2019). *Nihilism.* Cambridge, MA: MIT Press.

Goldman, A. (2010). Alvin I. Goldman. In J. Dancy, E. Sosa, & M. Steup (Eds.), *A Companion to Epistemology* (pp. 144–152). West Sussex: Wiley.

Hardaker, C. (2010). Trolling in Asynchronous Computer-Mediated Communication: From User Discussions to Academic Definitions. *Journal of Politeness Research, 6*(2), 215–242.

Herbert, G. (2020). Buffalo Police Shove Elderly Man to Ground, Injuring Him; Claim He Tripped (Graphic Video). Syracuse.com, 5 June. https://www.syracuse.com/state/2020/06/buffalo-police-shove-elderly-man-to-ground-injuring-him-claim-he-tripped-graphic-video.html. Accessed 30 December 2020.

Kane, P., & Clement, S. (2020). Just 27 Congressional Republicans Acknowledge Biden's Win, Washington Post Survey Finds. Washington Post, 4 December. https://www.washingtonpost.com/politics/survey-who-won-election-republicans-congress/2020/12/04/1a1011f6-3650-11eb-8d38-6aea1adb3839_story.html. Accessed 30 December 2020.

Kessler, G. (2020). Analysis | Trump Tweets Outrageous Conspiracy Theory about Injured Buffalo Man. Washington Post, 9 June. https://www.washingtonpost.com/politics/2020/06/09/trump-tweets-outrageous-conspiracy-theory-about-injured-buffalo-man. Accessed 30 December 2020.

Koehler, D. (2016). Can Journalistic 'False Balance' Distort Public Perception of Consensus in Expert Opinion? *Journal of Experimental Psychology: Applied, 22*(1), 24-38. https://doi.org/10.1037/xap0000073.

Levine, J. (2019). Donald Trump Calls Out Washington Post Reporter, Defends Inauguration Crowd Size. The Wrap, 8 May. https://www.thewrap.com/trump-calls-washington-post-reporter-defends-crowd-sizes. Accessed 30 December 2020.

Lewandowsky, S., Jetter, M., & Ecker, U. (forthcoming). Using the President's Tweets to Understand Political Diversion in the Age of Social Media. *Nature Communication.* https://psyarxiv.com/ar8d9/. Accessed 30 December 2020.

Manwell, E. (1966). The Vexatious Litigant. *California Law Review, 54*(4), 1769–1804.

May, R., & Feldman, M. (2019). Understanding the Alt-Right: Ideologues, 'Lulz' and hiding in plain sight. In M. Fielitz & N. Thurston (Eds.), *Post-digital cultures of the far right: Online actions and offline consequences in Europe and the US* (pp. 25–36). Bielefeld: transcript Verlag.

Mehta, D. (2020). More Republicans Distrust This Year's Election Results Than Democrats After 2016. FiveThirtyEight, 20 November. https://fivethirtyeight.com/features/more-republicans-distrust-this-years-election-results-than-democrats-after-2016. Accessed 30 December 2020.

Merkley, E. (2020). Are Experts (News)Worthy? Balance, Conflict, and Mass Media Coverage of Expert Consensus. *Political communication, 37*(4), 530–549. https://doi.org/10.1080/10584609.2020.1713269.

Mill, J.S. (1861). Considerations on Representative Government. Parker, son, and Bourn. https://www.gutenberg.org/files/5669/5669-h/5669-h.htm. Accessed 30 December 2020.

Momeyer, R. (1995). Teaching Ethics to Student Relativists. *Teaching Philosophy, 18*(4), 305–311. https://doi.org/10.5840/teachphil199518450.

Nehamas, A. (2010). Friedrich Nietzsche. In J. Dancy, E. Sosa, & M. Steup (Eds.), *A Companion to Epistemology* (pp. 551–552). West Sussex: Wiley.

Neiwert, D. (2018). Conspiracy Meta-Theory 'The Storm' Pushes the 'Alternative' Envelope yet Again. Southern Poverty Law Center. https://www.splcenter.org/hatewatch/2018/01/17/conspiracy-meta-theory-storm-pushes-alternative-envelope-yet-again. Accessed 30 December 2020.

Nyhan, B., & Reifler, J. (2010). When Corrections Fail: The Persistence of Political Misperceptions. *Political Behavior, 32*(2): 303–330. https://doi.org/10.1007/s11109-010-9112-2.

O'Neil, T. (2019). Trump Insists 'Not One Person' Has Left – as People Are Walking out of His CPAC Speech. PJ Media, 8 May. https://pjmedia.com/video/trump-says-not-one-persons-left-as-people-leave-his-cpac-speech. Accessed 30 December 2020.

O'Sullivan, D. (2020). Facebook Removes Trump Post Falsely Saying Flu Is More Lethal than Covid. CNN, 6 October. https://www.cnn.com/2020/10/06/tech/facebook-trump-covid-flu-false/index.html. Accessed 30 December 2020.

Paden, R. (1987). The Student Relativist as Philosopher. *Teaching Philosophy, 10*(2), 97–101. https://doi.org/10.5840/teachphil198710228.

Paden, R. (1994). The Natural History of Student Relativism. *The Journal of Thought, 29*(2), 47–58.

Park, D. (2018). United States News Media and Climate Change in the Era of US President Trump. *Integrated Environmental Assessment and Management, 14*(2), 202–204. https://doi.org/10.1002/ieam.2011.

Pennycook, G., & Rand, D. (2018). Lazy, Not Biased: Susceptibility to Partisan Fake News Is Better Explained by Lack of Reasoning than by Motivated Reasoning. *Cognition, 188*, 39–50. https://doi.org/10.1016/j.cognition.2018.06.011.

Phelps, J., & Cathey, L. (2020). Trump Tweets Conspiracy Theory about Buffalo Protester Police Officers Knocked to Ground. ABC News, 9 June. https://abcnews.go.com/Politics/trump-tweets-conspiracy-theory-buffalo-protester-police-officers/story?id=71150154. Accessed 30 December 2020.

Prior, M., Sood, G., & Kabir Khanna, K. (2015). You Cannot Be Serious: The Impact of Accuracy Incentives on Partisan Bias in Reports of Economic Perceptions. *Quarterly Journal of Political Science, 10*, 489–518.

Raju, M., Foran, C., & Fox, L. (2020). Senate GOP Dodges over Trump's Baseless Buffalo Tweet: 'I Would Rather Not Hear It.' CNN, 9 June. https://www.cnn.com/2020/06/09/politics/trump-buffalo-protester-set-up-tweet/index.html. Accessed 30 December 2020.

Randazza, M. (2012). The Need for a Unified and Cohesive National Anti-SLAPP Law First Amendment Essays. *Oregon Law Review, 91*(2), 627–534.

Reed, L. (2019). 'Personally Invasive': Inside the World of 'Plainpotatoess,' Self-Described Troll. Washington Post, 12 February. https://www.washingtonpost.com/local/public-safety/personally-invasive-inside-the-world-of-plainpotatoess-self-described-troll/2019/02/12/62690100-2ef1-11e9-86ab-5d02109aeb01_story.html. Accessed 30 December 2020.

Reuters Staff. (2020). White House Defends Trump's Conspiracy Theory Tweet on Buffalo Protester. Reuters, 10 June. https://www.reuters.com/article/us-minneapolis-police-protests-buffalo-idUSKBN23H2AU. Accessed 30 December 2020.

Rogers, K., & Roose, K. (2020). Trump Says QAnon Followers Are People Who 'Love Our Country.' The New York Times, 19 August. https://www.nytimes.com/2020/08/19/us/politics/trump-qanon-conspiracy-theories.html. Accessed 30 December 2020.

Romm, T. (2020). Twitter Labels Trump's Latest Claim about Election Fraud as 'Disputed' but Doesn't Limit Dissemination. Washington Post, 7 November. https://www.washingtonpost.com/technology/2020/11/07/trump-election-outcome-tweet-label. Accessed 30 December 2020

Rorty, R. (2009). The Idea of a 'Theory of Knowledge'. In R. Rorty, *Philosophy and the Mirror of Nature, Thirtieth-Anniversary Edition* (pp. 131–164). Princeton, NJ: Princeton University Press.

Rose, L., & Bartoli, T. (2020). Agnotology and the Epistemology of Ignorance: A Framework for the Propagation of Ignorance as a Consequence of Technology in a Balkanized Media

Ecosystem. *Postdigital Science and Education, 2*(1), 184–201. https://doi.org/10.1007/s42438-019-00084-5.

Rucker, P., Dawsey, J., & Parker, A. (2020). Trump Insists He'll Win, but Aides Say He Has No Real Plan to Overturn Results and Talks of 2024 Run. Washington Post, 11 November. https://www.washingtonpost.com/politics/trump-election-results-strategy/2020/11/11/a32e2cba-244a-11eb-952e-0c475972cfc0_story.html. Accessed 30 December 2020.

Rushing, C. (2007). (California Court of Appeals) Morton v. Wagner.

Satris, S. (1986). Student Relativism. *Teaching Philosophy, 9*(3), 193–205. https://doi.org/10.5840/teachphil19869336.

Schaffner, B., & Luks, S. (2018). Misinformation or Expressive Responding? What an Inauguration Crowd Can Tell Us about the Source of Political Misinformation in Surveys. *Public Opinion Quarterly, 82*(1), 135–147. https://doi.org/10.1093/poq/nfx042.

Schneider, A. (2018). Twitter Bans Alex Jones And InfoWars; Cites Abusive Behavior. NPR, 6 September. https://www.npr.org/2018/09/06/645352618/twitter-bans-alex-jones-and-infowars-cites-abusive-behavior. Accessed 30 December 2020.

Shachaf, P., & Hara, N. (2010). Beyond Vandalism: Wikipedia Trolls. *Journal of Information Science, 36*(3), 357–370. https://doi.org/10.1177/0165551510365390.

Silver, M. (2020). Some In GOP Fear Trump's Push Against Mail-In Voting Could Harm The Party's Chances. NPR.org, 31 August. https://www.npr.org/2020/08/31/907091223/some-in-gop-fear-trumps-push-against-mail-in-voting-could-harm-the-party-s-chanc. Accessed 30 December 2020.

Spangler, T. (2020). Twitter Has Flagged 200 of Trump's Posts as 'Disputed' or Misleading Since Election Day. Does It Make a Difference? Variety, 27 November. https://variety.com/2020/digital/news/twitter-trump-200-disputed-misleading-claims-election-1234841137. Accessed 30 December 2020.

Spencer, S., & Farley, R. (2020). Trump Tweets Baseless Claims About Injured Buffalo Protester. https://www.factcheck.org/2020/06/trump-tweets-baseless-claims-about-injured-buffalo-protester. Accessed 30 December 2020.

Trump, D. [@realdonaldtrump]. (2020a). Buffalo Protester Shoved by Police Could Be an ANTIFA Provocateur. 75 Year Old Martin Gugino Was Pushed Away after Appearing to Scan Police Communications in Order to Black out the Equipment. @OANN I Watched, He Fell Harder than Was Pushed. Was Aiming Scanner. Could Be a Set Up? https://twitter.com/realDonaldTrump/status/1270333484528214018. Accessed 30 December 2020.

Trump, D. (2020b). I Keep Reading Fake News Stories That My Campaign Is Running Low on Money. Not True, & If It Were so, I Would Put up Money Myself. The Fact Is That We Have Much More Money than We Had 4 Years Ago, Where We Spent Much Less Money than Crooked Hillary, and Still Easily Won, 306–223! https://twitter.com/realDonaldTrump/status/1315871589129498625. Accessed 30 December 2020.

Trump, D. (2020c). Totally Negative China Virus Reports. Hit It Early and Hard. Fake News Is Devastated. They Are Very Bad (and Sick!) People! https://twitter.com/realDonaldTrump/status/1316146752685174784. Accessed 30 December 2020.

Tuters, M. (2019). LARPing & liberal tears: Irony, belief and idiocy in the deep vernacular web. In M. Fielitz & N. Thurston (Eds.), *Post-digital cultures of the far right: Online actions and offline consequences in Europe and the US* (pp. 37–48). Bielefeld: transcript Verlag.

United Nations Department of Global Communications. (2020). UN Tackles 'Infodemic' of Misinformation and Cybercrime in COVID-19 Crisis. United Nations, 29 October. https://www.un.org/en/un-coronavirus-communications-team/un-tackling-%E2%80%98infodemic%E2%80%99-misinformation-and-cybercrime-covid-19. Accessed 30 December 2020.

Urban Dictionary (n.d.) Lulz. 20 July. https://www.urbandictionary.com/define.php?term=lulz. Accessed 30 December 2020.

Vyskockil, M. K. (2020). (Southern District of New York) McDougal v. Fox News Network, LLC.

Wood, T., & Porter. E. (2019). The Elusive Backfire Effect: Mass Attitudes' Steadfast Factual Adherence. *Political Behavior, 41*(1), 135–163. https://doi.org/10.1007/s11109-018-9443-y.

Wright, J. (2019). The Truth, but Not yet: Avoiding Naïve Skepticism via Explicit Communication of Metadisciplinary Aims. *Teaching in Higher Education, 24*(3), 361–377. https://doi.org/10.1080/13562517.2018.1544552.

Wright, J. (2020a). 'Many People Are Saying…': Applying the Lessons of Naïve Skepticism to the Fight against Fake News and Other 'Total Bullshit.' *Postdigital Science and Education, 2*(1), 113–131. https://doi.org/10.1007/s42438-019-00051-0.

Wright, J. (2020b). Review of Maik Fielitz and Nick Thurston (Eds.). (2019). Post-Digital Cultures of the Far Right: Online Actions and Offline Consequences in Europe and the US. *Postdigital Science and Education*. https://doi.org/10.1007/s42438-020-00201-9.

Part II
Dupery, Politics, and Democracy

Chapter 4
Duperation: Deliberate Lying in Postdigital, Postmodern Political Rhetoric

Tess Maginess

Introduction

In this first section, I will concentrate on definitions. I will begin by offering some definitions of 'dupery' and of postdigital and then will try to consider the connection between them. The word 'dupe' is, apparently, derived from fifteenth century French and is said to be cognate with 'de huppe' (of the hoopoe), an extravagantly crested and reputedly stupid bird. If you wanted to dupe people, you might try to gull them into thinking you were stupid; this might be because you deliberately present yourself as a caricature, perhaps with an extravagant gold crest – on your head (Online Etymology Dictionary n.d.).

Applebaum (2020) has argued that the dupers are not from the world of the othered; they are from the world of the elite. They can write a fair hand and with a fountain pen, predigital chaps, assuring the right-wing middle class, subliminally, that they are, really, underneath all the blond bombshell eccentricity, the right sort. As MacKenzie et al. (2020) point out, information disorders are not always intentionally spread. My focus here is the deliberate dissemination of misinformation and malinformation. Montaigne (in Docherty 2019: 95) distinguishes between unintentional lying and true liars, if I may risk a paradox: 'those who say the opposite of what they know, to go against one's conscience'. As Kalsnes adumbrates:

> Fake news was named the term of the year in 2016 by the Oxford Dictionary and in 2017 by the Collins Dictionary. In 2017, the usage of the term had increased by 365% since 2016 (Collins Dictionary 2017). The American presidential election in 2016 put the phenomenon on the international agenda. Websites with fabricated content gained massive attention, such as the story that falsely claimed that the Pope endorsed the republican candidate

T. Maginess (✉)
School of Sociology, Education and Social Work, Queen's University Belfast, Belfast, UK
e-mail: t.maginess@qub.ac.uk

A. MacKenzie et al. (eds.), *The Epistemology of Deceit in a Postdigital Era*, Postdigital Science and Education,
https://doi.org/10.1007/978-3-030-72154-1_4

> Donald Trump (Ritchie 2016). Shortly after, President Donald Trump politicized the term and used it to discredit established media outlets. But even though the term seems fairly new, the phenomena it covers are old. (Kalsnes 2018)

In my view, dupery is not the child of the postdigital era; nor is the postdigital era the child of dupery, but there is a collocation between the two. Indeed, MacKenzie et al. (2020) provocatively question whether the very design of social media is to be implicated in the problems that we face. I hope to address this later in the section on medium and message.

Turning to the second term in the title, what is meant by the term 'postdigital era'? There have been a number of definitions and meanings growing around the phrase. For some, the term seems to usher a new era where the human, the authentic, replaces the unctuous flatteries of the advertising algorithm, sycophantically reassuring the 'users' that their advertising keyword choices are fantastic. Interestingly, the most optimistic 'spins' on the postdigital era have come from the advertising sector. These are the sites which have engineered their way to the top. Their euphemistic human touch may proceed from exactly the same brazenly cynical motivation. The difference from older forms of advertising is that the 'customer' gets immediate attention and ratification from the advertiser (Daugherty 2019) and even more 'personalisation' (Badara 2019).

Within the academic world, 'postdigital' has received considerable attention also, often linked to calls for greater digital literacy and critical thinking and theory. Knox (2015) argues that the critical theory associated with the Frankfurt School is important in the consideration of digital culture and education. This kind of critical theory emphasises the analysis and critiques of dominant ideologies and understandings. Knox contends that such a perspective shifts the focus from the orthodox fixation with the individual to a richer engagement with the way education itself is shaped through the digital. Yet, it might be the case that within academia, critical thinking is a term so often used as to have become, ironically, hegemonic. We exhort our students to think critically, but we do not always spell out exactly what this means. By critical thinking we mean a willingness to question and interrogate what we read and what we see, to investigate, to dig deeper, to weigh arguments rather than simply reproducing them, to challenge our own prejudices and received ideas, and to think, based on evidence from a range of perspectives, not to be supine. Perhaps, deeply embedded in this concept of critical thinking in Europe is a postwar minatory conscience – not to question is to accept, to obey orders, to collude, and to collaborate with a monstrous scale of evil. Montaigne, cited by Docherty (2019: 97), offers a more sanguine but challenging definition: 'Thinking … marks itself out as something that enables the possibility of radical fundamental and political change.'

It is important to bear in mind that we must always question our own ideas, our own assumptions and hegemonies, before we attack, effectively, beliefs we find repugnant. Thinking – critical thinking – is now more than ever critical because the academy itself, as Knox implies, is in danger of viewing education as an individual private gain, at the expense of broader, more humanist vision. This is in line with scholars such as Barnett (2015) and Collini (2012) who have argued that universities, especially in the more prosperous global 'north' (or affluent West), are increasingly focused on private good rather than public good.

Florian Cramer (2014) offers a wide-ranging and complex commentary on the meanings of postdigital. Significantly, for our focus here, Cramer argues that the postdigital can be disenchanted and sceptical – can look awry in the best sense. He cites The Guardian's revelations about the mass surveillance undertaken by the NSA's Prism programme [American's National Security Agency's National Electronic Surveillance Program] as an example of the postdigital shift from simply gathering daily news, to investigative and critical journalism.

A more laconic definition is critiqued by Tinworth (2012), citing Fraser Speirs; the postdigital era signals a phase where everybody simply accepts digitality as vernacular and hegemonic and nobody passes any remarks about it. Tinworth credits Russell Davies for coming up with the term in 2009, but argues that he made a quasi-apology the following year:

> Post Digital was supposed, if anything, to be a shout against complacency, to make people realise that we're not at the end of a digital revolution, we're at the start of one. The end game was not making a website to go with your TV commercial and it's not now about making a newspaper out of your website. Post Digital was supposed to be the next exciting phase, not a return to the old order. It's the bit where the Digital people start to engage in the world beyond the screen, not where the old guard reasserts itself. (Tinworth 2012)

In contrast to the sceptical and critical exposé of PRISM, Davies seems to balefully view the reassertion of the status quo as a kind of lost opportunity to be more human. There is a chilling implication here too; if you can persuade people that the 'new normal' is unquestioning acceptance of the digital, then the potential for wholescale Dupery is immense. Yet, as Jandrić (2018: 101), citing Whitty and Johnson (2008: 56), acknowledges, 'the Internet has simply provided a new place for individuals to lie'. Whether regarded as an equation or a metaphor, perhaps the third term – the term which connects dupery and the postdigital era, is 'post-truth'.

Post-truth Politics

Jandrić (2018: 101) cites the definition of post-truth offered by the Oxford Dictionaries: 'Circumstances in which objective facts are less influential in shaping public opinion than appeals to emotion and personal belief.' A little later, Jandrić (2018: 106) elaborates an opposition between the rational and irrational in relation to Donald Trump's presidential campaign. He concludes, 'the emotional, the irrational and the instinctive cannot be counterbalanced with truth and reason'. Jandrić (2018: 109) sees post-truth as 'a poisonous public pedagogy oriented towards raising future generations of people with distorted worldviews, opinions and ethical judgements'. However, this is a rather imprecise formulation because how are we to know what distortion really means here.

Koro-Ljungberg et al. (2019: 583) also draw attention to the Oxford Dictionaries' definition, adding that 'post-truth' was the international word of the year in 2016. They cite Mair (2017: 584) who suggests that in the post-truth world, the dishonesty of 'politicans has changed from "covering up" to presenting "alternative facts"'. They further contend that 'post-truth' involves receiving information from inner circles – confirming what has already been found advantageous, inevitably diminishing any possibility of critical thinking. Germane to this discussion, Koro-Ljungberg et al. (2019: 584) cite Butler-Adam (2017) who emphasised the role of academia and the universities in becoming more active in fighting post-truth and untrustworthy data. Some recommendations will be advanced at the end of this chapter.

The potential for dupery is a hardy perennial in all political systems. It might even be argued that lying is a vital part of the game – discreetly withheld 'home truths' and 'nuanced' diplomacy between contending parties, involving not just the withholding of potentially catastrophic truths, but of fudges, obfuscations, dances of angels upon pinheads, and, consequentially, some species of conflict resolution and the avoidance of war. Docherty (2019: 117) cites Hannah Arendt's urbane acceptance of lies in politics: 'No one has ever doubted that truth and politics are on rather bad terms with each other… lies have always been regarded as necessary and justifiable tools not only of the politicians' or demagogue's but also of the statesman's trade.' Turning to contemporary politics, Docherty (2019: 118) offers this caveat: 'We might say that the important thing is not that Donald Trump or Boris Johnson are constitutional and inveterate liars; rather, the important and troubling thing is that they disable the very demand for truth itself.'

Docherty (2019: 116–117) quotes Lyndsey Stonebridge who suggests that the real danger with a political culture that openly trades in lies is that we lose our shared sense of truth; community vanishes and made-up version emerges – the myth of Nationalism. Stonebridge does not define what community is and so there is a danger that we are simply sliding from one myth to another. This 'pervasive chicanery' as MacKenzie et al. (2020: 2) have dubbed it, is dangerous because it is not confined to politicians, but is becoming accepted as normal.

From Postmodern to Post-truth

It may be argued that, up until fairly recently, intellectuals were living in what has been identified as the postmodern era, a term coined by Lyotard (1979/1984). As Nandy et al. (2018) suggest, '[p]ostmodernists believe that society, culture and language are arbitrary and they accepted the limitations of people's disparate views, fragmentation and indeterminacy'. Aylesworth (2015) notes that in postmodernism, 'the model of knowledge as the progressive development of consensus is outmoded'. In this era, and in this rather privileged space, it is considered gauche to speak of absolutes. We accept, as hegemonic, that truth is fragmentary, unstable, contentious, and riven. However, this new hegemony is not, in fact, in the real world, 'true' (if I may risk a paradox). Many people have not 'done' postmodernism or, for the matter of that, modernism. These are First World, elite, intellectual concerns. Yet, most people are, in fact, postmodern in many ways. People understand that an absolute truth is a *rara avis*. They know history and culture politics are complicated and even downright contradictory. Furthermore, some people have been duped and ripped off, at least once, and so perhaps conclude that lies and dupery are a fact of life and that a sceptical stance is probably about the most realistic option combining coherence and correspondence, if we are privileged enough to have any choices. There remain areas where the desire for the absolute, especially in matters of love and religion, remains strong among some people. There is much talk also about those Enlightenment ideals of being authentic, about being true to ourselves, and of being, above all, rational (Duignan 2019).

Medium and Message: Politics as a Digital Commodity

Digital capitalism is now well established. The simple, reductive, repeated 'messages' of the advertiser can be easily repurposed to create a market for certain kinds of political products – once very hard to sell, but coming right back into fashion. Some imagine propaganda to be a purely political business, but it seems to me that it is also purely business. In the bad old days, politicians bought newspapers, controlled cinema, and popular culture (Föllmer 2020) and peddled their 'line' at a number of levels, from the apparently 'objective' editorial (that myth of truth) to the product placement of certain goods and services likely to support the political position or, if you will, 'cause'.

Digital forms such as Facebook and, even better, Twitter are the media of choice for populist politicians. It must be acknowledged also that they have also been the choice for politicians like Barrack Obama, who would not, I think, be described as Populist. As Marshall McLuhan (1964) has said, the medium is the message. It is not possible to present a nuanced, quietly built argument on Twitter. The 'message' needs to be simple and recursive – like an advertising slogan. 'Make America Great', 'Take Back Control', and 'Get Brexit Done'. The only difference is that political sloganeering deploys a higher ratio of verbs than is the case with advertising which is content to assert, 'Coke is it', 'Because I'm worth it', and 'Beans Means Heinz'.

The Degradation of Language

Docherty (2019: 3) inveighs against the degradation of language in the political rhetoric of our time. As he sees it, this is 'conditioned by boastful egocentricity, insult, diatribe and violence'. As a consequence, such rhetoric 'reduces the range of thought as it infantilises its vocabulary … degraded language … engenders the decay of daily and living politics.' Like Docherty, my own field is language and literature and so I am trained to be tuned to words. The decay and degradation Docherty speaks of has an almost Hamletian tone, conveying how language itself can betoken that there is something rotten in the State. There are many aspects to this linguistic degradation (Maginess 2019), but in this chapter I can only highlight a few of them. There is, as Docherty (2019) implies, one kind of degradation, which is the increasingly pervasive lexis of insult and name-calling. I will address this in more detail when I consider revenge and insult politics.

There is another kind of degradation which weaponizes language for the purposes of dupery, reassigning the meanings of keywords. The Polish Jewish philosopher Victor Klemperer (Adams 2017) argued that the Nazis commandeered language before they commandeered the country. The word 'radical' is a prime example. Both American Alt-Right and Islamic Fundamentalists have reassigned the meaning of this word. I was brought up in Northern Ireland in the late 1960s and early 1970s and, being from the Catholic minority, viewed the word 'radical' as a very positive word, denoting a commitment to Civil Rights and a challenge to discrimination. Now, for the Alt-Right, this is a very bad word. Yet for Islamist Fundamentalists, it is a good word – denoting approbation for active Conservative values. The unwitting identification of two sets of Conservative movements who consider themselves antithetical contains its own ironies.

Another phrase bristling with irony is 'fake news'. This is how the Alt-Right dismisses news it does not like, with a certain sinister agility, reversing the status of investigative journalistic truth into lies by a lie. And then there is 'libtard'. Here we get two insults for the price of one. 'Liberal' used to be a good word too (though not, in my world view as a young person, as good as radical). Now 'liberal' is collocated with the elite – so liberal values are, thus, repudiated and then fused with 'tard', a contracted form of 'retard', and American slang for a person with learning difficulties. We have the cruel and crass implication that liberals are not smart, but actually have learning deficiencies, and that people with learning difficulties must also be, by inference, condemned for liberal views. Another obvious aspect of how political language has become oversimplified is the reduction to very simple vocabulary and diction; polysyllables or complex words are absent. This is, of course, more suitable for Twitter where there is a very sheer character limit and is paralleled by a grammar which tends to emphasise verbs (calls to action) rather than modal adjectives or the complex embedded clauses to be expected from a conceptual outlook.

Paradoxically, the very call to action, the passionate exhortation to the people to become agents, to engage, to 'Make America Great', and 'to Get Brexit Done', masks an increasingly totalitarian outlook and way of working. The very last thing that the dupers want is for people to be active. They just want them to be sufficiently active to go out and buy the product, accept the message because it is simple, and deliver via a medium that does not allow for elaboration, caveat, and critical or creative thinking. In that sense, the messaging of the dupers on Twitter is like fast food – finger lickin' good – visceral, simple, and instantly gratifying. Then there is the content of the message, the short sharp sub-messages, Build the Wall, China has invented Covid-19 and exported it. Mexicans are violent rapists. The Police are right to shoot. Everybody should bear arms. In sex and violence, the thrill is not gone. But, trumping sex and violence is the thrill of raw, brazen power; people who lie for me, I will set free.

Some people may not take the euphemistic claims of advertisements seriously, yet some think that simply by repeating the slogans of transformation, often, it may be noted, backward looking, they will come true. 'Take *back* control', 'make America great *again*'. The trick is to get more people thinking like that, buying into that brand. Using algorithms for pernicious purposes, we find our data is 'harvested' (who knew?) from all sorts of apparently unrelated stuff we have done online: what we have bought, what our Facebook reveals, our Twitter, and our Snapchat. I take it to be that since these platforms are all financed (big time) by apparently incidental background advertising, it is in the interest of business to make even more money by allowing other companies to 'harvest' what to us is casual, of the moment, into mathematically powerful, rich data.

This offers a wide proscenium to entertain not the Scottish Ballet (which would be great) but all manner of clever hackers, hawkers, and stakers in hate (the natural children of resentment). However, the far more important attraction is power, specifically power as product, sellable, and reproducible. What the data harvesters have is a commodity which is vital to the supply and demand nexus of the Populists. And, as we have learned, data is Big business, control of 'data' advertising techniques replicable within a totalitarian politics.

The rise of the Alt-Right, globally, has followed the modus operandi of many such movements in history. That rise is not, in any sense a new spectre, somehow created by social media. The sanctioned 'Realist' posters of Stalinist Russia are but one example of how to deliver mass media simple and compelling 'messages' (Beale 2019). Now, of course, I am aware that what we know about all this is often via Western, Anti-Communist 'messaging', yet it would be hard to argue that these idealising posters did not hide an often grim and panoptical reality. I acknowledge that this is a topic so vast and complex that it would be impossible to do anything but glance at it here.

I have used the word 'beliefs' rather than reasoned arguments, and this is because I want to convey the emotional and even visceral intensity of the current brand of politics in many places. Let me be very clear before going any further, I do not believe 'emotional' to be either positive or negative as a psychic space, even though, historically, the word 'emotional' has been negatively applied to women, for example, and equated with irrational or sub-rational, or instinctive. This hackneyed and despicable construction, a lie among many other such oppressing lies, has given people the excuse to dominate and enslave in a great many places and in a great many circumstances. With an appropriating irony, truly deserving the adjective 'mordant', certain current politicians are now stealing the clothes of those who they have historically subjugated. In a sort of recurring impulse of colonisation and domination, the language deployed on social media plays and trades, above all, on the *emotional* and *instinctive* levels of response in the hearer and watcher. As MacKenzie (2020) and Docherty (2019) argue, feelings now seem more attractive than reasons and, indeed, as MacKenzie et al. (2020: 2) astutely note, 'render reasons unnecessary'. So, could it possibly be that politicians favouring (slavering, you should pardon the punning) a post democratic, autocratic (call it Presidential style) form of rule, akin to Power Management (you're fired, now where is the pussy, so I can celebrate?), will follow the basic Pig in a Poke Dupery manual? The familiar dialectical opposite, the rational, white, male dominating, expansively conquering and mastering 'hero', is, of course, also very much on show, pecking for the cameras.

The Lie of the Real

It is perhaps this brazen posturing which also sponsors another kind of paradox and that is the Populist, Alt-Right pretending to be 'real', to be of the people, to be distinct from the very elite out of which they came, as attested by Applebaum (2020), cited at the start of the chapter. Significantly, Applebaum's target is not just Trump or the British Tories but the Far Right across Europe. 'We are all in this together', the British Conservatives chanted about austerity, when it was blatantly obvious that the pain was not being borne by the elite.

The effect of this faux identification is to manipulate or even disarm the body politic, creating a carnival of confusion in which the citizens are meant to be bedazzled about who or what the real deal is. And since there is a terror of being other, the easiest option is just to follow the leader. Trump boasted that he is there to act for the people, to clear the swamp, and to rebuild the neglected, rusted margins of the kingdom. Anthony Scaramucci, White House Director of Communications, 21 July–31 July 2017, claimed on a BBC programme (2020) that the Presidential tweets emanated from a strategic desire to 'put people on their heels' (i.e. put them into a state of surprise or bemusement). This obvious bullying is theatricalised in Trump's taunts about the leader of North Korea as the 'little Rocket Man'. The transgressive visceral tone is, of course, ironically petty, but part of a riskier playground preening match. It looks as if Trump has won and the little Rocket Man is now part of the ranks of his new best friends.

Famously, or infamously, Margaret Thatcher questioned the concept of society (Thatcher 1987). Perhaps she meant that she conquered class and societal prejudices to come into her particular kingdom and so, no matter how humble, one could succeed. In fact, her father was an important local public figure, part of the Establishment. Not that there was any element of dupery, surely. Or perhaps it is a matter of *L'Etat, c'est moi.* What was good enough for Louis XIV seems to be good enough for a few contemporary leaders who would attempt to dupe us into thinking they are, really, when you get beyond the jokey cartoon, modern day sun kings, astrut in the colonnades, behind their golden cock comb.

From Flattery to Abuse: Cultivating Internal Resentment

The dupers play cynically upon what Foa and Wilmot (2019) have termed a 'resentment epidemic'. Analysing the deepening divide between urban and rural and viewing the protection of the metropolitan centres at the expense of the ex-industrial 'regions' of America, Europe, and the UK, they argue that Populists play on this. And there seems to be in recent times, a kind of compensatory promise to 'do' infrastructure, to tackle the potholes, to build houses. But who will really profit? The marginalised ex-steelworkers and forgotten small towns in America, England, France, or Real Estate? As Birdwell (2018: 255) points out, 'as dupery, myth cannot ensure any salutary social change; since no prediction is rationally justified, no goal assured'.

Applebaum (2020) maintains that this elite (of which she was a part) is powered by resentment; this seems to be becoming rather a theme among commentators. Her argument is that certain figures, already elite, consider themselves to be a mite overlooked. A recent tell-tale biography of the Trump family written by Donald Trump's niece, Mary, also headlines on this theme of resentment and revenge (Trump 2020). So, for some dupers, it may indeed be personal, but of course the duper, waking at dawn, knows that being the lightning rod for resentment is great TV and reckons the gladiatorial to be almost the biggest thrill of all, after his own sneering laughter at the dressed doll he has so lovingly crafted of the Okie from Muskogee. Our old Princes of Thieves, Hyperbole and Euphemism join with red wattled Brother in Arms: Revenge (this is personal, guys – another form of privatisation) and hey presto, the ground is beaked for recycled despotism, totalitarianism: 'post-democracy'.

From Abuse to Revenge

There is much euphemism in the tweeting rhetoric; in the manner of advertising claims, you will look great, the wrinkles will fall off you like scales from a fish, and for your arthritis there is a miracle cure. Snake oil, they used to call it. However, what is perhaps even more powerful is incitement to revenge. Now some have suggested (Applebaum 2020; Trump 2020) that in the case of some of these Populists, the motive is personal – a settling of old scores. That may be true, but far more dangerous, it seems to me, is the licensing, indeed the exhortation towards revenge. The ex-steelworkers and the ex-miners and the ex-brass banders and the ex-beauty Queens get to hear a leader who ventriloquises their anger and vexation and beats up that anger, fuels it, courts, and sparks it. Thus, we have that essential ingredient for conflict – an enemy. The enemy is the plush skinned elite, shimmering in you-will-not-understand theory.

From Revenge to Panoptical Surveillance: The Enemy Within

So, the stage is set for dictatorship and its greatest tool, surveillance. This is one of the oldest tricks in the dupery playbook. Data harvesting is a form of surveillance which can be used in very sinister ways. Interpretation of data on individuals can lead to them being labelled negatively, as, for example, radical Left. And it is not a big step to labelling them as the enemy within. We may recall that the Nazis also adopted a narrative of national persecution, whipping up resentment at the Versailles Treaty, before they demanded greater room and with chilling precision, proceeded to persecute all who were 'other' who were awry, Jews, people living with disabilities, Roma; you name them, we will dispossess them, outcast them, and arrange for their efficient disposal. Lest we forget.

Docherty (2019) suggests that the political Left (as he defines them, the intellectual elite) has in the past decades since the rise of neoliberal capitalism, taken refuge in language and theory at the expense of material facts. He draws upon philosophical discourse to suggest that the Left has chosen internal coherence over correspondence with reality. The danger of this is that it leaves the experts, and their slightly more comprehensible relations, the media, open to the charge of elitism. The intellectuals can then be vilified and ignored and made the whipping boy of Populists and Demagogues.

Resisting Dupery

What do the people who follow the golden crested do about dupery? They collude because they have become convinced where they will survive better, either as those who already hold money and power or as those who have been fooled by Big Talk that they, too, can get to be rich and, if not, then at least they have freedom – to get to say whatever they damned well like about anybody. They can rip the gloves off and blame the foreigners, which is precisely the narrow reservation the dupers have herded them into. They churn up the mud as they try to get out. Mud sticks, but not to the sun kings. They flick with their heavy claws, imaginary dandruff off the shoulders of Europeans. But then there are the other others who are not convinced. There are those who have the temerity not to play the game, to look askance, awry, at this model of humanity. Some of those who look awry are viewed by the 'normons' as different – they are not truly British or American, they are alien. They are beyond the pale.

The French philosopher, Lacan, talked quite a lot about dupery. And he came up with a pun, which is, to be sure, rather lost in translation: The non-duped err. Now, it seems what he meant by this was that if you want to not be duped, you must err (cited in Flieger 1996:106). That seems odd, until it is explained that a semantic shift has taken place – a reassignment of language. Now, for Lacan, to 'err' is good. Lacan seems to imply that erring is part of being human – embracing our fallibility, our capacity to be wrong, to go wrong. But Lacan means something more specific – for him, to err is to look awry. And as far as I understand, it means that looking at our normality, events or people or phenomena as if we were an alien, a foreigner, is vital. Now, another way of putting this, and perhaps a lot more simply, is that we need to look coolly, quietly, and critically, if we cultivate questioning as a habit of mind, a bit like Socrates. If we look awry, we refuse to accept the official version of events, the myth that the only purpose for us being in the world is private gain, preferably, amorally, and in a spirit of *braggadocio* which might remind us of a an extravagantly crested bird who is, not a fool but a duper, robbing us blind. Behind sight there is insight. And with this looking awry there is maybe some bitterness and anger and even paranoia. However, there may be such a thing as good paranoia as well as the bad paranoia, as Žižek has argued (cited in Flieger 1996: 102). That bad paranoia we have seen before too, the other side of resentment, is the imagination of persecution. We may note how lexically recursive the word 'witchhunt' has become on Trump's Twitter. If the Highest in the Land leads the charge toward the complete casualisation of fakery, of dupery as a national(ist) imperative, it will not be long before it is too late to say 'no surrender'.

MacKenzie et al. (2020: 6) refer to the report of the UK House of Commons Committee for Digital Culture, Media, and Sport Committee recommendation that digital literacy should be the 'fourth pillar' of education, along with reading, writing, and maths. More specifically, MacKenzie et al. (2020: 6) recommend that we begin to fashion techniques for developing emotional scepticism to override our tendency to be less critical of content that promotes an emotional response. Or, perhaps to qualify this slightly, I would add emotional responses propelled by fear, revenge, hatred, contempt for the oppressed, and marginalised.

We might begin by listening to the voices of the oppressed and marginalised, and we might proceed by teaching our children and our students ourselves that unless we create solidarity the nightmare of history will ineluctably advance and in that dark night there will be no escape. There is an important role for universities to enact critical thinking and critical pedagogy, but also for greater consideration of how the academy can become what has been termed 'the engaged university' (Watson et al. 2013). This means greater knowledge sharing and exchange between global north and south, as Munck et al. (2012) and Brennan et al. (2004) have advocated. And it means greater generosity and understanding of the role of universities within society and in the creation of society in terms of encouraging active democracy and participation, of challenging supine adherence to neoliberal values and silence in the face of the rise of intolerant, racist, and hateful politics.

References

Adams, T. (2017). How to Resist the New Right. The Observer, 9 March, 33.

Applebaum, A. (2020). How My old Friends Paved the Way for Trump and Brexit. Interview with Nick Cohen. The Observer, 12 July. https://www.theguardian.com/books/2020/jul/12/anne-applebaum-how-my-old-friends-paved-the-way-for-trump-and-brexit. Accessed 10 December 2020.

Aylesworth, G. (2015). Postmodernism. In E. N. Zalta (Ed.), *The Stanford Encyclopedia of Philosophy*. https://plato.stanford.edu/entries/postmodernism/. Accessed 21 August 2020.

Badara, O. (2019). The Unhidden Mysteries of the Post-digital Era. Towards Data Science, 14 May. https://towardsdatascience.com/the-unhidden-mysteries-of-the-post-digital-era-6a6b26c4551. Accessed 21 August 2020.

Barnett, R. (2015). *Understanding the University: Institutions, Ideas, Possibilities*. London: Routledge.

Beale, A. D. (2019). History of Art in the Soviet Union: Propaganda, Rebellion and Freedom in Socialist Realism. History Now, 21 May. http://www.historyisnowmagazine.com/blog/2019/5/19/history-of-art-in-the-soviet-union-propaganda-rebellion-and-freedom-in-socialist-realism. Accessed 21 August 2020.

Birdwell, R. (2018). *The radical novel and the classless society: Utopian and proletarian novels in U.S. fiction from Bellamy to Ellison*. Lanham, MA: Lexington Books.

Brennan, J., King, R., & Lebeau, Y. (2004). The Role of Universities in the Transformation of Societies: An International Research Project. London: Association of Commonwealth Universities, Centre for Higher Education Research and Information. http://oro.open.ac.uk/6555/. Accessed 21 August 2020.

Collini, S. (2012). *What Are Universities For?* London: Penguin.

Cramer, F. (2014). What is 'Post-digital?' *A Peer-Reviewed Journal About, 3*(1), 11–24.

Daughterty, P. (2019). The post-digital era is coming: Are you ready? Accenture, 12 February. https://www.accenture.com/us-en/blogs/technology-innovation/daugherty-digital-transformation. Accessed 18 August 2020.

Docherty, T. (2019). *Political English: Language and the decay of politics*. London: Bloomsbury.

Duignan, B. (2019). Jeremy Bentham. Britannica. https://www.britannica.com/biography/Jeremy-Bentham. Accessed 21 August 2020.

Flieger, J. A. (1996). The Listening Eue: Post-Modernism, Paranoia and the Hypervisible. *Diacritics, 26*(1), 90–107.

Foa, S., & Wilmot, J. (2019). The West has a Resentment Epidemic. Foreign Policy, 18 September. https://foreignpolicy.com/2019/09/18/the-west-has-a-resentment-epidemic-populism/. Accessed 21 August 2020.

Föllmer, M. (2020). *Culture in the Third Reich*. London: Oxford University Press.

Jandrić, P. (2018). Post-truth and critical pedagogy of trust. In M. A. Peters, S. Rider, M. Hyvönen & Tina Besley (Eds.), *Post-Truth, Fake News: Viral Modernity & Higher Education* (pp. 101-111). Singapore: Springer. https://doi.org/10.1007/978-981-10-8013-5_8.

Kalsnes, B. (2018). Fake News. In J. Nossbaum (Ed.), *Oxford Research Encyclopedias, Communication*. London: Oxford University Press. https://doi.org/10.1093/acrefore/9780190228613.013.809.

Knox, J. (2015). Critical Education and Digital Cultures. In M. Peters (Ed.), *Encyclopedia of Educational Philosophy and Theory*. Singapore: Springer. https://doi.org/10.1007/978-981-287-532-7_124-1.

Koro-Ljungberg, M., Carlson, D. L., & Montana, A. (2019). Productive Forces of Post-truth(s)? *Qualitative Inquiry, 25*(6), 583–590. https://doi.org/10.1177%2F1077800418806595.

Lyotard, J. F. (1979/1984). *The Postmodern Condition: A Report on Knowledge*. Trans. G. Bennington & B. Massumi. Minneapolis, MN: University of Minnesota Press.

MacKenzie, A., Rose, J., & Bhatt, I. (2020). Dupery by Design: The Epistemology of Deceit in a Postdigital Era. *Postdigital Science and Education*. https://doi.org/10.1007/s42438-020-00114-7.

Maginess, T. (2019.) Cyberlect in the Classroom: Dialogical Approaches to Languages. *Educational Role of Language Journal*, *1*(1), 35–46. https://doi.org/10.36534/erlj.2019.01.04.

McLuhan, M. (1964). *Understanding Media: The Extensions of Man*. New York: Mentor.

Munck, R., McQuillan, H., & Ozarowska, J. (2012). Civic Engagement in a Cold Climate: A Global Perspective. In L. McIlrath, & A. Lyons (Eds.), *Higher Education and Civic Engagement: Comparative Perspectives* (pp. 15–29). New York: Palgrave Macmillan. https://doi.org/10.1057/9781137074829_2.

Nandy, U. K., Nandy, S., & Nandy, A. (2018). A Perceptive Journey through Postmodernism. *Journal of Civil Engineering and Environmental Sciences, 4*(1), 20–23. https://doi.org/10.17352/2455-488X.000022.

Online Etymology Dictionary (n.d.) Dupe. https://www.etymonline.com/search?q=dupe. Accessed 18 August 2020.

Scaramucci, A. (2020). Trump and Tweets. BBC2, 19 July. UK: British Broadcasting Company.

Thatcher, M. (1987). No Such Thing as Society. Interview for BBC Radio 4, 23 September. https://www.margaretthatcher.org/document/106689. Accessed 18 August 2020.

Tinworth, A. (2012). What is post-digital? https://nextconf.eu/2012/01/what-is-post-digital/#gref. Accessed 18 August 2020.

Trump, M. (2020). *Too Much and Never Enough: How my Family Created the world's most Dangerous Man.* New York: Simon & Schuster.

Watson, D., Hollister, T., Stroud, S. E., & Babcock, E. (2013). *The Engaged University: International Perspectives on Civic Engagement.* London: Routledge.

Chapter 5
The Right to Freedom of Expression Versus Legal Actions Against Fake News: A Case Study of Singapore

Selman Özdan

Introduction

Content, including fake news or disinformation, has become one of the prominent challenges around the world, since it spreads rapidly through digital platforms and may cause serious harms, affecting millions of people, influencing, and impacting on health, financial markets, elections, and so on. To deal with fake news, policy-makers have taken precautions against, or have placed sanctions on, digital platforms. Anti-fake news laws adopted by states such as Singapore focus on short-term solutions such as penalising the producer of fake news. The aim of enacting such laws are, *inter alia*, to prevent the communication of false statements of facts, to suppress any support (financing, promotion) of online locations which repeatedly report fake news, and to detect and control against misuse of online accounts and bots. Regarding the penalties against the circulation of fake news, the law in Singapore imposes criminal penalties of up to 10 years imprisonment or a fine not exceeding 100,000 SGD. While it is surely important to control the dissemination of harmful fake news, there is a danger that laws restricting fake news may suffocate free speech, and the adoption of heavy legal sanctions to restrict the circulation of fake news should be reviewed in the light of international human rights laws.

Two key questions will be explored in this chapter: first whether legal remedies, sanctions, or restrictions against the circulation and publication of fake news are compatible with international human rights law and its criteria and second whether remedies or sanctions are proportional. Although there is no international legal obligation for online platforms to abide by international human rights law, those platforms have, arguably, a responsibility to respect them.

S. Özdan (✉)
School of Law, Ondokuz Mayıs University, Samsun, Turkey
e-mail: selman.ozdan@omu.edu.tr

A. MacKenzie et al. (eds.), *The Epistemology of Deceit in a Postdigital Era*, Postdigital Science and Education,
https://doi.org/10.1007/978-3-030-72154-1_5

Fake news will be analysed from the perspectives of legal and international human rights laws. While the circulation of fake news may infringe several fundamental international human rights (to health, to free and fair elections, to non-discrimination), legal sanctions against the flow of fake news may violate international human rights such as the right to freedom of expression and opinion. Finally, this chapter will offer recommendations on how to fight against fake news in compliance with the standards of international human rights law, such as adopting, for example, transparent policies and improving digital/media literacy.

International Human Rights Law Challenges to Fake News

International human rights law imposes a number of obligations on States in order to guarantee certain fundamental human rights to people residing in their own territory and, to some extent, non-residents.[1] International human rights law provides a helpful, inclusive, and normative framework with regard to human rights which applies to online or digital platforms, as well as the offline sphere. Digital platforms do not have an international obligation to comply with international human rights law principles; however, they have a clear responsibility to respect them. In this sense, international human rights law plays a critical role because it has as much impact on peoples' lives as national governments and the number of people to whom it penetrates appeals to an even wider sphere. In this respect, international human rights law provides an important framework for directing the activities of commercial enterprises such as digital platforms.

Human rights law is a legitimate concern in the international arena. The Universal Declaration of Human Rights (UDHR) was the first protocol to commence legitimate about the protections of the international community. Although the UDHR is a soft law, namely, a non-binding legal text, it has played a crucial role in the emergence of hard law documents, or legally binding texts for State parties in terms of their provisions. Further, the UDHR considers human rights as a protection mechanism for all individuals against abusive power by an authority. The International Covenant on Civil and Political Rights (ICCPR) and International Covenant on Economic, Social, and Cultural Rights (ICESCR), which are legally binding international documents for State parties, ensued from the UDHR. Regional conventions, such the European Convention on Human Rights (ECHR) and the Inter-American Convention on Human Rights (IACHR), also include similar principles in terms of protection of human rights.

In some cases, the jurisprudence of regional courts such as the European Court of Human Rights (ECtHR) provides a useful guide on the content, meaning, and

[1] The State authority for persons outside of the country is a controversial issue. Considering the sovereign equality principle and non-intervention principle, that restricts the ability of foreign nations to interfere with the internal affairs of another nation, any intervention of a State outside its own territory may infringe such principles of public international law.

interpretation of rights in a regional sense. Article 46(1) of the ECHR, for example, states that 'the High Contracting Parties undertake to abide by the final judgment of the Court in any case to which they are parties'. International courts serve as an important authority in drafting regulations regarding digital platforms. Taking into account all of these, principles of international human rights conventions and jurisprudences of international courts help us in evaluating the damage of fake news or disinformation to people in a legal sense. They also help us understand how legal measures taken against fake news or disinformation by national authorities negatively affect the enjoyment of international human rights.

While the State authority has extensive impact on peoples' lives, the influence of digital platforms has become more influential on people than State authorities. The Facebook Investor Relation's report in the second quarter of 2020 can corroborate that claim. According to the report, Facebook's daily active users numbered 1.79 billion on average for June 2020, an increase of 12% year-over-year. Facebook monthly active users numbered 2.70 billion as of June 30, 2020, an increase of 12% year-over-year (Facebook Investor Relations 2020). These statistical data may not prove the high impact of digital platforms on people; however, it can show that misleading content or fake news produced on digital platforms can seriously influence people's choices and opinions.

The development of communication technologies has made progress in favour of human rights by ensuring pluralism of expression in the digital sphere, by commencing new freedom of association, and by giving wider access to information than ever before. This development in communication technologies may, however, weaken democracy and democratic processes by causing some distortions in the field of freedom of expression and opinion, the right of privacy, the right to health, and electoral processes. Another critical issue is the lack of coherency between legal regulations and rapidly changing communication technologies (Jones 2019: 4). The national government of Singapore, the case study for this chapter, has taken legal measures against the dissemination of fake news and disinformation on digital platforms for infringing some basic human rights principles.

Violations of fundamental human rights, the polarisation of societies, the widespread use of hate speech, the weakening of democratic structures and processes, and the increase in incitement to violence are some of the problems that the digital age has created through disseminating fake news and disinformation. These cases need urgent action by either national governments or international structures.

The Right to Freedom of Expression and Opinion

A number of the UN's Human Rights Council Resolutions affirm that the human rights that people enjoy in the offline sphere should also be guaranteed and protected on the online sphere, particularly the right to freedom of expression, irrespective of frontiers, and on any platform of one's choice, in conformity with article 19 of the UDHR and of the ICCPR (UN Human Rights Council 2018: para. 1).[2]

The implementation of restrictions on the right to freedom of expression and opinion by governments without being circumstantiated by convincing and strong evidence that show that those restrictions are necessary and will serve their purpose may raise serious concerns about the protection of fundamental human rights. There are a number of regulations in public international law to prevent the abuse or arbitrary use of law in limiting freedom of expression and opinion. At this point, the UDHR, ICCPR, and ECHR are leading declarations and conventions. Such regulations stand against national legal regulations which can be adopted to suppress an independent and critical discourse. They prohibit manipulative activities on the right to freedom of expression and opinion. Article 18 of UDHR states that: 'Everyone has the right to freedom of thought, conscience and religion; this right includes freedom to change his religion or belief, and freedom, either alone or in community with others and in public or private, to manifest his religion or belief in teaching, practice, worship and observance.' Further, article 19(1) of ICCPR underscores the right to hold opinions without interference, and article 19(2) of ICCPR and article 19 of UDHR similarly state that: 'Everyone has the right to freedom of opinion and expression; this right includes freedom to hold opinions without interference and to seek, receive and impart information and ideas through any media and regardless of frontiers.' Article 19(3) of the ICCPR highlights that some restrictions may be imposed on the rights in question depending on certain conditions. It accordingly states that:

> The exercise of the rights provided for in paragraph 2 of this article carries with it special duties and responsibilities. It may therefore be subject to certain restrictions, but these shall only be such as are provided by law and are necessary: (a) For respect of the rights or reputations of others; (b) For the protection of national security or of public order (*ordre public*), or of public health or morals.

Article 20 of the ICCPR includes the following statements in respect of imposing restrictions on the right to freedom of expression: 'Any propaganda for war shall be prohibited by law. Any advocacy of national, racial or religious hatred that constitutes incitement to discrimination, hostility or violence shall be prohibited by law.' As can be seen, the UDHR and ICCPR guarantee a broad right to freedom of expression. The UN Human Rights Committee also underscore that any coercive attempt to the holding or not holding of any opinion is prohibited. The Committee accordingly states that freedom to express a person's opinion indispensably covers freedom not to express her/his opinion (UN Human Rights Committee 2011: para. 10).

Freedom of expression, then, is an integral part of democracy. The European Commission expresses that any jarring, disturbing, or offensive speech that does not

[2] See the resolution adopted by the Human Rights Council on 5 July 2018 for the Council's recommendations for States to adopt a human rights-based approach (UN Human Rights Council 2018: para. 5).

include hate speech or incitement to violence and that does not infringe the rights of others falls within the scope of the right to freedom of expression. Further, the Commission emphasises that reporting errors, parody, satire, and/or clearly defined partisan news or comments is not deemed as disinformation (European Commission 2019). The European Commission's approach should be kept in mind when national regulations against fake news is being discussed later in the chapter.

With respect to freedom of expression, article 10(1) of the ECHR states that:

> Everyone has the right to freedom of expression. This right shall include freedom to hold opinions and to receive and impart information and ideas without interference by public authority and regardless of frontiers. This Article shall not prevent States from requiring the licensing of broadcasting, television or cinema enterprises.

As a consequence, protection of freedom of expression cannot be limited only to the expression or dissemination of true information or facts.

The protection in question also covers opinions and thoughts. Ideas, facts, and value judgments cannot be equated and cannot be identically evaluated. In this regard, the jurisprudences of the ECtHR make precise distinction between value judgments and factual claims. While the existence of facts can be proven, the truth of value judgments and ideas is harder to prove or establish. The truth of value judgments is not susceptible to proof. In respect of value judgments, such a requirement is unobtainable and could infringe upon the right to freedom of opinion itself, which is a fundamental part of the right guaranteed under article 10 of the ECHR (Lingens vs Austria 1986: para. 46). Hence, it is difficult to claim that the verification obligation for which journalists are responsible applies to their value judgments. The ECtHR also states in its judgment that:

> The classification of a statement as a fact or as a value judgment is a matter which in the first place falls within the margin of appreciation of the national authorities, in particular the domestic courts [...]. However, where a statement amounts to a value judgment, the proportionality of an interference may depend on whether there existed a sufficient factual basis for the impugned statement: if there was not, that value judgment may prove excessive. (GRA Stiftung gegen Rassismus und Antisemitismus vs Switzerland 2018: para. 68).

In the 1976 Handyside vs UK, the ECtHR clearly stated the right to freedom of expression and the exceptions to which this right is subjected. According to the Court's assessment, freedom of expression is an essential cornerstone for democratic societies, and it constitutes one of the basic conditions for the progress of such societies and for the full development of each individual. In the Handyside vs UK case, the Court further held that freedom of expression applies not only to information and ideas that are favourable, harmless, or inoffensive but also to information and ideas that offend, shock, or disturb the State or any segment of society.[3] These are necessary to pluralism, tolerance, and open-mindedness without which there is no way to speak of a democratic society. It means, *inter alia*, any formality, condition, restriction, or punishment imposed in this area must be proportionate to the legitimate aim pursued (Handyside vs The United Kingdom 1976: para. 49).

[3] Without prejudice to paragraph 2 of Article 10 of the ECHR.

However, the ECtHR decided in a case law that article 10 of the ECHR does not guarantee unlimited freedom of expression. In this sense, the Court stated that 'the safeguard afforded by Article 10 to journalists in relation to reporting on issues of general interest is subject to the proviso that they are acting in good faith in order to provide accurate and reliable information in accordance with the ethics of journalism' (McVicar vs The United Kingdom 2002: para. 73).

Here, it is important to designate the position of digital platforms. In determining whether digital platforms are bound by the principles and obligations derived from the ECtHR jurisdictions, it is crucial to ask whether these principles, obligations, or privileges apply only to traditional media. Although the ECtHR jurisdiction concerns the traditional press, the ECtHR states that the same principles apply to audio and visual media. The Court in one of its case laws held that:

> The Court has also repeatedly emphasised the essential role played by the press in a democratic society. Although the press must not overstep certain bounds, regarding in particular protection of the reputation and rights of others, its duty is nevertheless to impart – in a manner consistent with its obligations and responsibilities – information and ideas on all matters of public interest. Not only does the press have the task of imparting such information and ideas, the public also has a right to receive them. Were it otherwise, the press would be unable to play its vital role of public watchdog … Although formulated primarily with regard to the print media, these principles doubtless apply also to the audio-visual media. (Haldimann and Others vs Switzerland 2015: para. 45)

Any natural or legal person who has the right to freedom of expression has certain duties and obligations while exercising this right. The media, regardless whether it is printed, audio or visual, should not cross the boundaries regarding the rights and reputations of others. In accordance with the ethics of the journalism, it is essential to act in conformity with the principle of good faith in order to convey information to the public accurately and reliably. However, it should not be interpreted as the persons in question are obliged to tell the truth. Because even if journalists act on the basis of the principle of good faith, they may by chance report incorrect or incomplete information (McGonagle 2017: 208). As Carl Bernstein (1992: 24) underscored, 'reporting is not stenography. It is the best obtainable versions of the truth.'

The Concept of Fake News

The term 'fake news' has become a byword in our period of post-truth which was named international word of the year 2016 by the Oxford Dictionaries (2016) and defined as 'relating to or denoting circumstances in which objective facts are less influential in shaping public opinion than appeals to emotion and personal belief'. If the concept of fake news is not properly and correctly identified, disproportionate and arbitrary practices or interventions may occur against content or the producer of that content. For the sake of protecting basic principles of international human rights law, it is highly important to designate whether a content is deemed to be fake or not. Fake news is such information which is intentionally produced and disseminated with the aim of deceiving the public towards believing in false statements and doubting verifiable truths (McGonagle 2017: 203). When that information is presented as news regardless of whether by a satirical news website or a regular one, it may also be seen as disinformation. Further, fake news is often used as a comprehensive concept for any information or content that is deceptive, fallacious, or including biasedly and unfairly reported true news (Rose 2020: 815).

In the information ecosystem, fake news may appear in different ways and by different methods. As Katsirea (2018: 164) states, fake news 'is but one permutation of many different types of potentially misleading content in our information ecosystem'. For example, Wardle (2017) enumerated seven types of problematic information which were circulated during the 2016 US presidential election: (i) Satire or parody: there is no intention to give rise to damage; however, such content has the potential to deceive; (ii) Misleading content: misleading transfer or dissemination of information to frame a person or an issue; (iii) Imposter content: presenting real sources in imitation; (iv) Fabricated content: the content is one hundred percent false, and it is generally designed to deceive or damage; (v) False connection: titles, captions, and images do not support the content; (vi) False context: sharing original content with unfounded or incorrect contextual information; (vii) Manipulated content: manipulation of genuine information or images to deceive people.

Fake news can be deceitful or fabricated, conduce to hostile discourse or propaganda, and infect news content such that it encourages violence. Ball (2017: 224) states that the 'top performing stories list shows how fake news ranges from the harmless to the deeply dangerous: from dubious and colourful true crime tales to stories playing on racial tensions amid Black Lives Matter protests; from fake promises of political concerts to claims of secret political murders – many naming celebrities in their headlines for an extra viral boost'. Fake news can be '100-percent-false stories predominantly published by sites that exclusively traffic in hoaxes to generate clicks' (Cunningham 2017). In this respect, it is important for what purposes and intent fake news and disinformation are served. Therefore, it is essential to distinguish between three types of content: the first, false or fake content which is intentionally posted or circulated by the media; the second, content that contains mistakes despite meticulous research; and the third, content that is not obviously fake or false but which is, however clearly biased, tendentious or exaggerated (Katsirea 2018: 162). It follows that determination of the intention or the implied meaning of the content is required before that content can be considered to be fake news or disinformation.

Accordingly, the Independent Monitor for the Press, in its March 2017 report, defined fake news as 'the knowing and consistent publication of predominantly false information in the guise of news' (IMPRESS 2017: para. 158). In this sense, we have four elements by which to accept content as fake news: deliberative, consistent publication, mainly falsehoods and providing content in the guise of news. Having said that, legal regulations against content, including fake news and disinformation should be heedfully drafted and adopted by governments. Failing that, arbitrary or malicious implementation of the law may occur, and international human rights principles, including the right to freedom of expression and opinion, will quite likely be infringed. This chapter both analyses the law against fake news and provides some alternative implementations in order to deal with dissemination of fake news by complying with international human rights law.

Legal Acts Against Fake News and Freedom of Expression and Opinion

Since the emergence of digital platforms, the scope and limits of freedom of expression and opinion have been a matter of debate. The rights to freedom of expression and opinion require having an idea and freely expressing it without being subject to any interference. The UN Human Rights Committee in its General Comments stated that the

> free communication of information and ideas about public and political issues between citizens, candidates and elected representatives is essential. This implies a free press and other media able to comment on public issues without censorship or restraint and to inform public opinion. The public also has a corresponding right to receive media output. (UN Human Rights Committee 2011: para. 13)

The Committee also stressed that the free communication of opinions and information regarding public and political matters between people is essential. This assuredly requires and implies a free press and other media platforms able to comment on public issues and to inform public opinion without being exposed to any censorship or constraint (UN Human Rights Committee 2011: para. 20).

It may be claimed that manipulating opinions of users on digital platforms via social media for political or other purposes infringes the right to freedom of expression and opinion. Fake news or disinformation produced by manipulative methods will reduce peoples' belief in democracy and eventually prevent them from recognising the difference between real and fake news.

Some States have passed resolutions in order to fight against fake news and disinformation disseminating through digital platforms. Some interventions by governments to prevent the spread of fake news are deemed incompatible with a number of international human rights principles, such as restricting freedom of expression and blocking or censoring Internet access (Bradshaw and Howard 2018: 6). In this sense, the Human Rights Council called upon States 'to ensure effective remedies for human rights violations, including those relating to the Internet, in accordance with their international obligations' (UN Human Rights Council 2018: para. 6).

There are a number of States fighting against the dangers and disadvantages of fake news and disinformation. Some have adopted specific legal measures which may be strongly criticised for infringing upon fundamental human rights principles. To explore this issue further, I will take Singapore and its Protection from Online Falsehoods and Manipulation Act (POFMA) as a case study.

Singapore: A Case Study

Singapore has not experienced an election manipulated or destabilised by fake news or disinformation (Kaye 2019: 131). However, the Government of Singapore, by making reference to the election disputes in Europe and North America, argued that 'Singapore should not wait for an incident to occur' (Kaye 2019: 131; Neo 2020: 724). In April 2019, the Government drafted POFMA requiring correction or, in more serious cases, the removal of fake accounts, deactivation of fake bot accounts, or counterfeit online accounts. The POFMA came into effect on 2 October 2019.

By this means, the Government criminalised the spreading fake or false news for the purpose of manipulation and posting or disseminating fake content on digital platforms. The POFMA forbids the communication of false statements of facts. According to the POFMA, a false statement of fact is described as a deceptive, false, fallacious, or misleading statement that a rational person hearing, seeing, or otherwise perceiving it would consider to be a representation of fact (Protection from Online Falsehoods and Manipulation Act 2019). In particular, according to section 7 of the POFMA, a person must not perpetrate any acts whether in or outside of Singapore territory, in order to communicate a statement which that person is aware or has reason to consider that the statement is a fabrication or untruth, and the communication of that falsehood in Singapore is likely to:

> i) be prejudicial to the security of Singapore or any part of Singapore; ii) be prejudicial to public health, public safety, public tranquillity or public finances; iii) be prejudicial to the friendly relations of Singapore with other countries; iv) influence the outcome of an election to the office of President, a general election of Members of Parliament, a by-election of a Member of Parliament, or a referendum; v) incite feelings of enmity, hatred or ill-will between different groups of persons; or vi) diminish public confidence in the government. [Protection from Online Falsehoods and Manipulation Act 2019: sec. 7(1)].

Persons who maliciously distribute such fake news or falsehoods, in contravention of POFMA regulation, may be subject to fines or imprisonment or both. Individuals in violation of section 7 of the POFMA will be liable to a fine not exceeding 50,000 Singapore Dollars or a term of imprisonment not exceeding 5 years. For non-individuals, such as digital platforms, a fine not exceeding 500,000 Singapore Dollars will be imposed. On the other hand, where an inauthentic online account or bot account is used to disseminate or communicate such falsehoods or fake news, alleged offenders who are individuals will be liable to a fine not exceeding 100,000 Singapore Dollars or a term of imprisonment not exceeding 10 years. In respect of non-individuals, a fine not exceeding 1 million Singapore Dollars will be imposed [Protection from Online Falsehoods and Manipulation Act 2019: sec. 7(3)].

The POFMA gives ministers of the Singapore Government broad and arbitrary authority and power to issue correction notifications, to order the removal of content, and/or block access to online content if they are considered to be disseminating fake news or falsehoods that are against the public interest or to erode public confidence in the government (Han 2019). However, any independent audit body or committee for preventing arbitrary or malicious implementations is not prescribed by law in Singapore. The concept of public interest is a broad one. Threats to national security and elections and the public perception of the government may be related to the concept of the public interest. A broad interpretation of that concept may be easily abused or exploited. In other words, any digital platform content that could be interpreted or deemed as embarrassing or harmful to the government may be simply flagged as fake news.

The law minister of Singapore, K. Shanmugam, pointed out that the right to free speech should not be badly influenced by this Bill, POFMA, and that it is simply aimed at dealing with falsehoods, bot accounts, trolls, and fake accounts (Ministry of Law Singapore 2019). However, the POFMA has been criticised since it cannot, at the same time, fulfil the requirements of international human rights law. A number of political parties, civil society, and academics strongly warned that the POFMA was not impeachable and would give government ministers the authority and power to decide what is false and true in Singapore (Article 19 2019). The Freedom House, non-profit non-governmental organisation, stated that the law provides government ministers with great power 'to identify false online content and order its removal or correction; the measure's criminal penalties include fines up to a year in prison for failure to comply with removal or correction orders' (Freedom House 2020).

Such authority and power should be vested in an independent judiciary. Freedom House in its 2020 report questioned the independent judiciary system of Singapore and deduced that the highest judges of Singapore are appointed by the president upon the advice of the prime minister. The report claimed that the government's consistent success in cases that had a direct impact on the government's agenda raised serious doubts about judicial independence. It argued that this situation was particularly evident in defamation cases and litigations against the government opponents and people who raise dissenting opinions (Freedom House 2020: para. F1). Giving final decisions in conjunction with an independent judiciary mechanism may alleviate the legitimate concern in question to some extent.

POFMA cannot adequately provide clear protection of freedom of expression and freedom to receive and impart information. The International Commission of Jurists also criticised it since the POFMA fails to 'include exceptions or defences, including the defences of public interest, honest mistake, parody and/or artistic merit. There is no recourse available for a direction or order made under the bill to be quashed on judicial review grounds of illegality, irrationality and procedural impropriety' (Sivaprakasam 2019: 121). Further, the POFMA, as mentioned above, permits extraterritorial application of penalties on individuals or non-individuals whether in or outside of Singapore's territory, and it does not, therefore, comply with international obligations to protect and respect the right to free expression and information regardless of frontiers (Sivaprakasam 2019: 121).

Kirsten Han, a freelance journalist and human rights activist, has strongly criticised the POFMA. Han claimed that the legal regulation on fake news and disinformation would be very likely subject to malfeasance and abuse. She accordingly argued instead that regulation in Singapore (and alike countries such Malaysia) needs media, news, and information literacy systems and requires developing transparency policies in public institutions in order to mount social passive resistance against fake news and disinformation (Han 2018).

Further, the POFMA may hinder the economic development of Singapore, tarnish the country's image, and eventually damage national interests. Phil Robertson, deputy Asia director of Human Rights Watch, stated that 'Singapore's long intolerance of free expression virtually ensures the online falsehoods law will be used to silence dissenters'. He rightly apprised of the potential danger that would be faced by the Singaporean Government and remarked that the 'law's mere existence has already led critics of the government to self-censor online. Singapore's trading partners should tell the government that every new restraint on free expression makes the country a less hospitable place to invest and do business' (Human Rights Watch 2020).

The first reported case of applying POFMA occurred in November 2019. Brad Bowyer, a political member of the opposition party, was ordered by the POFMA Office to send out a correction notice under a post that Bowyer issued on Facebook less than 2 weeks before, in which he allegedly raised doubts about the independence of two companies (Temasek Holdings Pte. Ltd. and GIC Pte. Ltd) that are linked to the government. Further, he reportedly questioned these companies' investment strategies (Sivaprakasam 2019: 122; Ministry of Finance Singapore 2019). The correction directive was notified to Bowyer by the Minister of Finance of Singapore for the following reason: 'The post contains clearly false statements of fact, and undermines public trust in the Government. … It is necessary to state this for the record: GIC and Temasek operate on a commercial basis, and the Government is not involved in their individual investment decisions' (CNA 2019). Bowyer thereupon issued a correction notice on his Facebook account. He also pointed out that 'I am not against being asked to make clarifications or corrections especially if it is in the public interest … in general, I caution all those who comment on our domestic politics and social issues to do so with due care and attention especially if you speak from any place of influence' (CNA 2019). As can be seen, implementing POFMA raises serious questions. Applying POFMA rules against an opposition party member of a substantial opposition party in Singapore raises a concern that the law would be used to target someone who explicitly or implicitly expresses condemnatory or censorious views, or simply disapproving opposition.

Therefore, considering international human rights principles, there are a number of ill effects of adopting and applying legal regulations such the POFMA law. Pursuant to international human rights law, imposing restrictions on the right to freedom of expression and opinion on the grounds of disseminating fake news cannot be met on any legitimate ground. This situation may lead to the decrease in public trust of the legal system, particularly during electoral periods. Further, since it interferes with the freedom to receive and impart information outside of the country that law infringes the principle of sovereign equality and accordingly non-intervention principles in domestic affairs of other States which are deemed to be the principle of public international law. Further, it violates an international obligation that requires the protection of the right to freedom of expression and opinion regardless frontiers. The other point is that the mere relationship between the disseminated content on digital platforms and its damages should be clearly identified. Otherwise, imposing penalties for alleged fake news or disinformation cannot be fulfilled and enforced by legal perspective. Criminal sanctions should comply with the principle of proportionality. Another criticism is that the enforcement authority of the law is vested in the executive body of the government. However, such authority should be vested in independent judicial bodies. An impartial and fair supervisory board is necessary to protect individuals against disproportionate and unjust restrictions on the right to freedom of expression and opinion. Such boards are, further, required to prevent abuse of the law by the authorities. The POFMA law allows appeal to the High Court; however, since the feasibility of judicial review is unlikely, this aspect of the law has is weak (Article 19 2019).

The POFMA's perception of disseminating and creating fake news and disinformation is quite problematic since posting and disseminating such content are deemed to be crimes. This situation may easily impede the right to freedom of expression and opinion, as I have argued above. Taking account of non-governmental organisations as expressed in the British human rights organisation (Article 19) and the International Commission of Jurists, regulations pursuant to the principles of international human rights should be promoted. Legal regulations against fake news that offer censorship and/or criminalises discourse and opinions should be replaced with other policies which work compatibly with international human rights law, and States should not be encouraged to follow such regulations.

Alternative Methods and Recommendations

The Singapore case has clearly brought out that regulations or legal enforcements regarding digital platforms and textual or other content types on these platforms should not be drafted and adopted without taking account of international human rights law. Struggling with fake news and disinformation should be based on the respect for human rights principles, including the right to freedom of expression and opinion. Obeying international human rights law is the justificatory ground of this struggle.

Imposing criminal sanctions against fake news and disinformation-related contents or censoring such contents on digital platforms may cause problems for the protection of international human rights law principles. Before forbidding or criminalising expressions and opinions, it is necessary to accurately define the danger and risks posed by fake news and disinformation. When the boundaries of such contents' definition and the identification of their risks are hazy, arbitrary prohibitions and penalties will probably result. Further, governments should adopt responses which are proportionate to these risks and dangers (Katsirea 2018: 187). In other words, adopted mechanisms and regulations against fake news and disinformation should work in accordance with international human rights principles.

Therefore, rather than censoring content or penalising digital platforms, alternatives are needed to deal with fake news and disinformation, such as impeding financial incentives which support the dissemination of such content, strengthening reliable and trustworthy news and information sources, promoting transparency policies regarding digital platforms, and settling and improving media-news-information literacy.

In support of these alternatives, the UN 2017 Joint Declaration on Freedom of Expression and 'Fake News', Disinformation, and Propaganda pointed out three important issues in struggling with fake news and disinformation. Firstly, in accordance with international human rights law, national governments are not allowed to enforce censorship on expression and opinion merely by virtue of its falsehood. Governments that want to eliminate or limit fake news and disinformation would have to comply with well-established legal principles such as the principle of the right to freedom of expression and opinion. Regulations should not serve as a tool that censors expression or opinion, and they should be narrowly tailored to manage and answer a specific issue. The Joint Declaration, secondly, underscored that governments have an obligation to avoid producing or disseminating fake news, propaganda, and disinformation. Hereby, the governments' leaders and other authorities at government level should speak truthfully. For this reason, they should encourage a free and independent press and media, not enforce and promote censorship. Finally, the Declaration drew attention to transparency policies. It argues that digital platforms should follow transparent policies regarding the rules they implement and the regulations they adopt. The Declaration further emphasised that technical solutions regarding fake news and disinformation (such a fact-checking service) which can strengthen the ability of users to distinguish the truth from fiction should be encouraged (The UN Special Rapporteur on Freedom of Opinion and Expression et al. 2017).

A number of recommendations for national governments to cope with fake news and disinformation were submitted to the 2017 report of the Council of Europe. (i) National governments should commission research to delineate information disorder. For accurate research, the following questions should be considered: What are the most common types of information disorder? Which digital platforms are the main vehicles for dissemination of disinformation? What research has been done in order to examine people's reactions and responses to such contents in specific countries? (ii) National governments should request transparency around digital platforms' adverts (specifically Facebook) so that ad purchasers and relevant platforms can be held accountable. (iii) Advanced cybersecurity training should be provided by governments. The training should teach how to prevent attempts at hacking and phishing attacks. (iv) Digital platforms should be encouraged to work with independent and impartial public media organisations to produce quality news and helpful analysis available to their users. (v) While the digital platforms are attempting to prevent fake news sites from financially advantaging, other networks are getting involved to fill the gap. So, governments should draft regulations to prevent any advertising activities from coming out on such sites (Wardle and Derakhshan 2017: 82). These listed recommendations are a road map for governments to guide them on how they can minimise the negative effects of fake news and disinformation without censoring content on digital platforms and implementing penal sanctions.

Transparent, independent, and impartial policies are strongly encouraged. Also, the fact remains that the compliance with international human rights law should not be avoided.

Censorship Is Not a Way Out

Censorship arises when the government, special interest lobbies, or private individuals impose their own political, ideological, or moral values on others through proscribing or suppressing any type of content which they find dissenting. Censorship accordingly means the restriction of what people may state, hear, record, write, see and read (Day 2001: 10). Any measure taken against fake news and disinformation on digital platforms could probably create some infringements on the right to freedom of expression. International human rights law guarantees the right to seek, receive, and impart information and thoughts for everyone. However, international human rights law allows the necessary and proportionate restrictions by legal means to protect the right of others or to maintain national security and public order. Nevertheless, it does not tolerate an exception that allows limiting statements and opinions simply because they are false. As David Kaye (2019: 121) rightly underscored that '[w]e were worried that a rush to prohibit fake news, rather than finding a combination of technical, educational, and legal solutions, would almost certainly undermine the protections for free expression over the long term'. Fighting against fake news and disinformation by implementing punitive enforcement may probably discourage people from putting forward their own opinion, particularly if it strongly criticises the government. In this sense, Kaye (2019: 121) added that '[w]e wanted to caution governments and companies against taking precipitous steps that could undermine debate and dissent'.

Media and Information Literacy

The promotion and implementation of media and information literacy is one of the longest-term solutions to deal with fake news and disinformation. It is a useful and helpful tool for everyone, regardless of age range, to understand how to evaluate different information resources and how to think critically and analytically about information and news received from digital platforms. As Bulger and Davison (2018) highlight, media literacy 'has become a center of gravity for countering "fake news"' (2). It aspires to create a citizenship based on international human rights principles such the right to freedom of expression and further aims at enabling a responsible participation in the digital platforms. Media and information literacy require life-long learning, and it cannot be limited to specific age group (European Commission 2018: 25). Users should be informed and encouraged to check the accuracy of related content before disseminating or liking it on digital platforms.

Journalists, bloggers, or others should be trained how to distinguish reliable sources and fake news.

The Human Rights Council calls upon States 'while fully respecting their human rights obligations and commitments regarding freedom of opinion and expression, to encourage media training, educational campaigns and other efforts aimed at identifying and raising awareness about information online that may be deliberately misleading or false' (UN Human Rights Council 2018: para. 16). Media and information literacy are highly effective method to deal with disinformation and fake news on digital platforms. Thus, it should be embedded in education and should be an integral part of the curriculum. Such curriculum would be enriched thereby including following elements:

> i) traditional news literacy skills; ii) forensic social media verification skills; iii) information about the power of algorithms to shape what is presented to us; iv) the possibilities but also the ethical implications offered by artificial intelligence; v) techniques for developing emotional scepticism to override our brain's tendency to be less critical of content that provokes an emotional response; and vi) statistical numeracy.' (Wardle and Derakhshan 2017: 70)

There are a number of recommendations that governments or specific authority bodies (such a Ministry of Education) should take into consideration for conducting the qualified and efficient media and information literacy programme. First, since the domain of digital platforms is no longer limited by country borders, the curriculum of the media and information literacy programme should be drafted in accordance with international standards. The preparation and evaluation of such curriculum should, therefore, include a global discourse. For example, the media and information literacy should be added to the competencies evaluated in the OECD PISA rankings by national governments (European Commission 2018: 26). Second, the media and information literacy programme cannot be limited to the specific age group. Teachers, journalists, and other media professionals should be included to such programme. Third, an education programme of the media and information literacy should be formed by focusing on the critical assessment of information sources, the effect of emotions on critical thinking, the functioning and effects of algorithms, and artificial intelligence (Wardle and Derakhshan 2017: 84–85). Media and information literacy cannot prevent people exposure from fake news; it may, however, minimise damages by clarifying the difference between fact and fake, misleading, and reliable information.

Transparency

Transparency is an essential element of due process procedures recognised in international human right principles. It is also important for the right to freedom of expression. It 'does not raise the free expression issues that bedevil mandated requirements for removal of problematic material' (MacCarthy 2020: 8). The main purpose of adopting transparency policies on digital platforms is to make information, news, and other content understandable and above-board in order that users can distinguish fake news and disinformation from reliable content and facts. According to the 2018 report of the European Commission, transparency helps people find factual claims and arguments and thereby 'understand the process behind their online dissemination and popularity, the motivations and funding sources of those who make information publicly available' (European Commission 2018: 22).

Transparency may also increase the influence of media literacy activities by providing users with relevant information *inter alia* 'on patterns of circulation, necessary to critically assess the material facts quoted in news articles by journalists or in posts and blogs by citizens' (European Commission 2018: 22). Recommendation CM/Rec(2018)1 on media pluralism and transparency of media ownership highlights that States should ensure transparency on digital platforms, particularly their organisation and financial systems, and to encourage media-information literacy for the purpose of providing users with reliable information and critical awareness (Committee of Ministers of the Council of Europe 2018: para. 1.7). The Recommendation further proposes that States should promote

> the development of open, independent, transparent and participatory initiatives by social media, media actors, civil society, academia and other relevant stake holders that seek to improve effective exposure of users to the broadest possible diversity of media content online. (Committee of Ministers of the Council of Europe 2018: para. 2.5)

Furthermore, the Recommendation sets forth the feature of required regime of transparency and implicitly elucidates its significance for democratic societies as follows:

> States should promote a regime of transparency of media ownership that ensures the public availability and accessibility of accurate, up-to-date data concerning direct and beneficial ownership of the media, as well as other interests that influence the strategic decision making of the media in question or its editorial line. (Committee of Ministers of the Council of Europe 2018: para. 4.1)

Conclusion

The circulation and dissemination of fake news and disinformation have become easier in our information and news ecosystems. This situation can significantly damage a number of international human rights law; however, legal regulations adopted by governments against fake news and disinformation may also create significant human rights violations such as the right to freedom of expression and opinion. The POFMA law adopted by Singaporean government is a case in point, and it cannot fulfil its obligations to international human rights law.

To deal with fake news and disinformation, policy makers should adopt reasonable methods in conformity with the principles of international human rights law, as I have argued here. A policy of censorship is not the solution in the struggle against fake news and disinformation; rather, we need concerted and thoroughgoing digital and media literacy prorgammes, transparency policies, and independent, impartial, and fair supervisory boards.

References

Article 19. (2019). Singapore: New law on "online falsehoods" a grave threat to freedom of expression. https://www.article19.org/resources/singapore-new-law-on-online-falsehoods-a-grave-threat-to-freedom-of-expression/. Accessed 17 July 2020.

Ball, J. (2017). *Post-Truth: How Bullshit Conquered the World*. London: Biteback Publishing.

Bernstein, C. (1992). The Idiot Culture: Reflections of Post-Watergate Journalism. The New Republic, 8 June. http://carlbernstein.com/magazines_the_idiot_culture.pdf. Accessed 17 July 2020.

Bradshaw, S., & Howard, P. N. (2018). *Challenging Truth and Trust: A Global Inventory of Organized Social Media Manipulation*. Oxford: Oxford Internet Institute & University of Oxford.

Bulger, M., & Davison, P. (2018). The Promises, Challenges, and Futures of Media Literacy. *Journal of Media Literacy Education, 10*(1), 1-21. https://doi.org/10.23860/JMLE-2018-10-1-1.

CNA. (2019). POFMA Office directs Brad Bowyer to correct Facebook post in first use of 'fake news' law. https://www.channelnewsasia.com/news/singapore/brad-bowyer-facebook-post-falsehood-pofma-fake-news-12122952. Accessed 9 October 2020.

Committee of Ministers of the Council of Europe. (2018). Appendix to Recommendation CM/Rec(2018)1: Guidelines on media pluralism and transparency of media ownership.

Cunningham, G. (2017). Avoid the misnomer 'fake news'. Village, 20 February. https://villagemagazine.ie/avoid-the-misnomer-fake-news/. Accessed 11 August 2020.

Day, N. (2001). *Censorship or Freedom of Expression?* Minneapolis, MN: Lerner Publications Company.

European Commission. (2018). A Multi-Dimensional Approach to Disinformation: Report of the Independent High Level Group on Fake News and Online Disinformation. https://ec.europa.eu/digital-single-market/en/news/final-report-high-level-expert-group-fake-news-and-online-disinformation. Accessed 11 July 2020.

European Commission. (2019). Tackling Online Disinformation in the European Union. https://ec.europa.eu/digital-single-market/en/news/tackling-online-disinformation-brochure. Accessed 12 July 2020.

Facebook Investor Relations. (2020). Facebook reports second quarter 2020 results. https://investor.fb.com/investor-news/press-release-details/2020/Facebook-Reports-Second-Quarter-2020-Results/default.aspx. Accessed 22 September 2020.

Freedom House. (2020). Freedom in the World 2020: Singapore. https://freedomhouse.org/country/singapore/freedom-world/2020. Accessed 20 August 2020.

GRA Stiftung gegen Rassismus und Antisemitismus vs Switzerland App. no. 18597/13, (ECtHR 9 April 2018).

Haldimann and Others vs Switzerland App. no. 21830/09, (ECtHR 27 February 2015).

Handyside vs The United Kingdom App. no. 5493/72, (ECtHR 7 December 1976).

Human Rights Watch. (2020). Singapore: Free expression restrictions tighten: New 'online falsehoods' law further curbs rights. https://www.hrw.org/news/2020/01/14/singapore-free-expression-restrictions-tighten. Accessed 17 July 2020.

Han, K. (2018). A letter of complaint to the Select Committee on Deliberate Online Falsehoods. Medium, 29 March. https://medium.com/@kixes/a-letter-of-complaint-to-the-select-committee-on-deliberate-online-falsehoods-e84d5b484a55. Accessed 20 August 2020.

Han, K. (2019). Big Brother's regional ripple effect. *Index on Censorship, 48*(2), 67–69. https://doi.org/10.1177/0306422019858296.

IMPRESS. (2017). Written evidence submitted by IMPRESS: The Independent Monitor for the Press [FNW0112]. http://data.parliament.uk/writtenevidence/committeeevidence.svc/evidencedocument/culture-media-and-sport-committee/fake-news/written/48730.pdf. Accessed 11 July 2020.

Jones, K. (2019). *Online Disinformation and Political Discourse: Applying a human rights Framework*. London: Chatham House The Royal Institute of International Affairs.

Katsirea, I. (2018). "Fake news": Reconsidering the value of untruthful expression in the face of regulatory uncertainty. *Journal of Media Law, 10*(2), 159–188. https://doi.org/10.1080/17577632.2019.1573569.

Kaye, D. (2019). *Speech Police: The Global Struggle to Govern the Internet*. New York: Columbia Global Reports.

Lingens vs Austria App. no. 9815/82, (ECtHR 8 July 1986).

MacCarthy, M. (2020). Transparency Requirements for Digital Social Media Platforms: Recommendations for Policy Makers and Industry. Transatlantic Working Group. https://doi.org/10.2139/ssrn.3615726. Accessed 21 October 2020.

McGonagle, T. (2017). "Fake News": False Fears or Real Concerns? *Netherlands Quarterly of Human Rights, 35*(4), 203–209. https://doi.org/10.1177/0924051917738685.

McVicar vs The United Kingdom App. no. 46311/99, (ECtHR 7 August 2002).

Ministry of Finance Singapore (2019). Press Releases: Use of POFMA on an online posting by Mr Brad Bowyer, 25 November. https://www.mof.gov.sg/newsroom/press-releases/use-of-pofma-on-an-online-posting-by-mr-brad-bowyer. Accessed 17 July 2020.

Ministry of Law Singapore (2019). Second reading Speech by Minister for Law, K Shanmugam on The Protection from Online Falsehoods and Manipulation Bill, 7 May. https://www.mlaw.gov.sg/news/parliamentary-speeches/second-reading-speech-by-minister-for-law-k-shanmugam-on-the-protection-from-online-falsehoods-and-manipulation-bill. Accessed 8 October 2020.

Neo, R. (2020). The securitisation of fake news in Singapore. *International Politics, 57*, 724–740. https://doi.org/10.1057/s41311-019-00198-4.

Oxford Dictionaries (2016). Word of the Year 2016. https://languages.oup.com/word-of-the-year/2016/. Accessed 17 November 2020.

Protection from Online Falsehoods and Manipulation Act (2019), Bill No. 10/2019. https://www.parliament.gov.sg/docs/default-source/default-document-library/protection-from-online-falsehoods-and-manipulation-bill10-2019.pdf. Accessed 17 July 2020.

Rose, J. (2020). The Mortal Coil of Covid-19, Fake News, and Negative Epistemic Postdigital Inculcation. *Postdigital Science and Education, 2*(3), 812–829. https://doi.org/10.1007/s42438-020-00192-7.

Sivaprakasam, D. (2019). Dictating the Internet: Curtailing Free Expression, Opinion and Information Online in Southeast Asia. Geneva: International Commission of Jurists.

The UN Special Rapporteur on Freedom of Opinion and Expression; the OSCE Representative on Freedom of the Media; the OAS Special Rapporteur on Freedom of Expression and the ACHPR Special Rapporteur on Freedom of Expression and Access to Information. (2017). Joint Declaration on Freedom of Expression and "Fake News", Disinformation and Propaganda [FOM.GAL/3/17]. http://www.osce.org/fom/302796. Accessed 17 July 2020.

UN Human Rights Committee. (2011). General comment No. 34: Article 19: Freedoms of opinion and expression [CCPR/C/GC/34].

UN Human Rights Council. (2018). Resolution adopted by the Human Rights Council on 5 July 2018: The promotion, protection and enjoyment of human rights on the Internet [A/HRC/RES/38/7].

Wardle, C. (2017). Fake news. It's complicated. Medium, 17 February. https://medium.com/1st-draft/fake-news-its-complicated-d0f773766c79. Accessed 15 August 2020.

Wardle, C., & Derakhshan, H. (2017). Information Disorder: Toward an interdisciplinary framework for research and policymaking. [DGI(2017)09]. Strasbourg: Council of Europe.

Chapter 6
US Digital Nationalism: A Habermasian Critical Discourse Analysis of Trump's 'Fake News' Approach to the First Amendment

Benjamin Green

Us Protests as Foundational to American Democracy

Civil protest, as enshrined in both the US Constitution and the dogmatic mythos of the US' revolutionary origin story, represents the bedrock of the US democratic system. Graham (2019) adds that the Boston Tea Party represents a foundational act of patriotic civil disobedience, embodying a core narrative of freedom based on dissent-through-protest as a central tenant of US democracy. As a means of seeking redress for grievances or overall structural change, the First Amendment of the US Constitution guarantees citizens the right to peaceably assemble and petition the government (Egemenoglu 2020). Specifically, the First Amendment guarantees a negative freedom of expression from both federal and state (as outlined by the 14th Amendment) restrictions (Bechtold 2020). However, these freedoms are not absolute. The US Supreme Court has long allowed for restrictions that fall within constitutional limits (Winston 2014). Moreover, the First Amendment does not provide rights for protests in which 'there is a clear and present danger of riot, disorder or interference with traffic on public streets, or other immediate threat to public safety or order' allowing for statutes to be enacted which 'prohibit people from assembling and using force or violence to accomplish unlawful purposes' (Winston 2014). Notwithstanding, the American Civil Liberties Union (ACLU: 2020) has outlined that the First Amendment 'prohibits such advanced notice requirements from being used to prevent rallies or demonstrations that are rapid responses to unforeseeable and recent events'.

Black Lives Matter (BLM) protests, sparked by the murder of George Floyd by Minnesota police officers on 25 May 2020, the Trump administration has sought to restrict the First Amendment freedoms of BLM protesters – through both claims to

B. Green (✉)
Faculty of Education, Beijing Normal University, Beijing, China

A. MacKenzie et al. (eds.), *The Epistemology of Deceit in a Postdigital Era*, Postdigital Science and Education,
https://doi.org/10.1007/978-3-030-72154-1_6

'clear and present danger of riot' and/or 'threat to public safety and order'. Specifically, Trump has continued to paint BLM protesters as 'rioters' and 'angry mobs' who are 'trying to unleash a wave of violent crime in our cities' (The White House 2020a, b), a narrative which allows Trump to base the suppression of free speech on a constitutionally provisioned authority to restore law and order (Petersen 2020). Despite a recent study outlining the overwhelmingly peaceful nature (93%) of (Summer 2020) BLM protests (Kishi and Jones 2020: 3), partisan media outlets continue to drive a divisive 'fake news' narrative which casts protesters as anarchists, while framing Trump's attempts at First Amendment suppression as a positive facet of his 'law and order' presidency.

Egelhofer and Lecheler (2019) describe the crisis of 'fake news' as a two-dimensional form of media communication which creates and propagates pseudo journalistic disinformation while politicizing and instrumentalizing the term 'fake news' to delegitimize other sources of media information. Moreover, easily published pseudo journalism has allowed parallel media ecosystems to coalesce around Trumpian ideological positions which disregard reason or argument (Legg 2018). Benkler et al. (2017) highlight the existence of a hyper-partisan, insulated right-wing knowledge community in the US – a 'fake news' media ecosystem that reinforces shared ideologies, shields its members from outside journalistic challenges, and presents 'wholly fabricated falsities' which instil in its viewers a 'fundamentally misleading view of the world'. Kellner (2018: 92) adds that within this rightist fake news media bubble of deceit, Trump's pathologically deceitful practices are based in a 'politics of lying' which perfectly suit Frohm's diagnosis of an authoritarian personality. Echoing Kellner, Fuchs (2018: 197) has outlined 'Trumpology' as a mediated political spectacle of authoritarian-capitalism based in direct rule of the billionaire class, nationalism, scapegoating, the friend/enemy scheme, and law and order politics.

Given this state-sponsored authoritarian media discourse, Schneider's (2018) work on digital nationalism in China serves as a foundational reference for understanding the US' Trump-dominated authoritarian 'fake news' media ecosystem. Specifically, US digital nationalism is defined herein as state-sponsored nationalism shared through a complex ecology of information, an authoritarian technic governed by political institutions which promote partisan misinformation through political actors, commercial enterprises, NGOs, and Internet users, as a politically expedient means to indoctrinate the masses. Within the context of the continued BLM anti-racism protests as an exercise of First Amendment freedoms seeking to redress the government, and a state-sponsored media-driven attempt to undermine the public's understanding of these freedoms, the objectives of this study aim to highlight that rightist media outlets represent a bulwark of digital nationalism which facilitates Trump's authoritarian 'fake news' approach to the First Amendment.

Trump's 'Fake News' Approach to the First Amendment

Constitutional scholars argue that an environment of hyper partisanship, combined with President Trump's continued attacks against protesters and journalistic critics, is steadily eroding the good governance norms and constitutional understanding of a First Amendment which has provided the American people with a previously unparalleled freedom of expression (Price 2018; Grambo 2019). Specifically, Price (2018: 821) highlights that the problem of 'fake news' (deliberate propagation of demonstrably untrue statements that shape public opinion) could weaken First Amendment protections by allowing partisan officials to 'cherry-pick evidence' of offensive expression or incitement of violence as a rationale for the 'selective and discriminatory' enforcement-cum-repression of free speech. Such easily verifiable instances of free speech oppression/protection abound within the Trump Presidency (see Executive Order on Campus Free Speech, Executive Order on Preventing Online Censorship, Trump's labelling of BLM as 'terrorists', deployment of federal troops to quell protests in Oregon) (Camera 2019; Svrluga 2019; Allyn 2020; The White House 2020a; Choi 2020; Dewan 2020; Baker et al. 2020).

Trump's fake news approach to the First Amendment has allowed him to simultaneously shape institutional norms to provide protection for actors who reside on his side of the political spectrum, while impinging upon the freedoms of those institutions, groups, and individuals who present a challenge to his increasingly autocratic central authority. This 'fake news' approach to the First Amendment was especially clear during Trump's 'constitutionally murky' deployment of unidentified federal officers to suppress BLM protesters, under the guise of 'protecting government property' in Portland, Oregon, in July 2020 (Vladeck 2020). Thus, the problem of 'fake news' highlights an unsettling flaw of contemporary US democracy, one which continues to allow the president to cherry-pick rationales and procedural norms towards the selective suppression/protection of First Amendment freedoms.

Specifically, this chapter argues that Trump's bulwark of US digital nationalism deliberately propagates a deceitful image of 'criminality' (Grambo 2019) upon individuals and groups of BLM protesters as a means of promoting Trump's brand of 'fake news', First Amendment suppression/protection – undermining normative and legal boundaries of the First Amendment while legitimizing a tenuous law and order claim to political sovereignty. This underscores MacKenzie and Bhatt's (2019) argument that the destructive nature of fake news lies in its intentionally deceitful obfuscation of facts and its manipulative coercion of public gaslighting as a means to secure expedient political gains. Therefore, it is imperative that we understand how the hyper-partisan rightist media supports the legitimacy of the Trump regime's increasing authoritarianism through the propagation of state-sponsored disinformation – weakening First Amendment protections while eliciting an antithetically authoritarian brand of obsequious 'political correctness' within a large proportion of the US voting populace.

Theoretical Framework

Habermas' *discourse theory of law and democracy* argues that the increasing pluralism of modern western constitutional democracies creates a tension between 'facts and norms' that place 'aged constitutional frameworks under tremendous stress' (Rehg and Habermas 1996). Specifically, Habermas outlines 'validity' as the ideal legitimacy and rational legitimacy of the law as opposed to 'facticity' as the inherent certainty of the law's institutionalized coercive power (Baxter 2011). Moreover, Habermas (1996) notes the inherent conflict between the validity based Kantian 'liberal' understanding of law and legitimate government – framed by human rights and societally bound civil liberties and the factitious Rousseauean 'civic republican' view towards the legitimacy of laws and government as based in popular sovereignty.

Kant and Rousseau argue, therefore, for markedly different conceptions of political legitimacy. Kant frames the normative prescribed boundaries of society as an *autonomy of the will,* wherein the legitimacy of laws and institutions is derived from the rational will of the polity – often reflected through 'maxims to action' as a form of contrarian law that is not procedurally defined (Kaufman 1997). Rousseau critiques modern republics as suffering from a lack of 'civic republican virtues' which cause 'excessive attachment to institutions', rather than sovereign authority as the power from which these institutions gain legitimacy (Ward 2016). Therefore, within the USA we are witnessing Habermas's critique of modern democracy, with the Left seeking to uphold the autonomous will of the people by protecting long-standing yet normatively inscribed liberal Kantian democratic institutions and the Right's use of procedurally defined legal frameworks to support Trump's Rousseauean civic republican desire to reshape the boundaries of sovereign legitimacy.

Within a hyper-partisan bifurcated media discourse, a Habermasian understanding of Kantian liberal autonomy and Rousseauean republican sovereignty provides an important view of modern democracy from which to assess the current US crisis of institutional (il)legitimacy. Habermas argues that legal institutions within modern democratic systems exhibit 'adaptive programming' which allows powerful interests to effect 'macro-level legal change without the direct participation of the citizenry (Rehg and Habermas 1996). Habermas (1996) further describes 'public spheres' as structures or *social spaces* of communicative action which function as democratic sluices, feeding back into socially constructed, and therefore legitimate legal frameworks at the administrative level. Thus, the 'institutional core' of Habermasian political public spheres consists of 'communicative networks amplified by mass media', representing a necessary space for generating, acquiring, and maintaining administrative legitimacy (Baxter 2011).

However, the political public sphere 'in standard operation' is influenced by political economies (markets and governmental bodies) of money and power which operate as 'steering media', de-anchoring, and therefore delegitimizing the production and administration of law from the communicative power of its citizens (Baxter

2011). Thus, through the use of filtered, synthesized streams of communication – which highlight specific public opinions while promoting the moral leadership, competency, and authority of a given administration – 'success-oriented' steering media circumvent civic consensus as a legitimizing foundation of democratic institutional frameworks of authority (Habermas 1996; Baxter 2011).

US Digital Nationalism: Reconceptualizing the Hyper-Partisan Right

While there was once a belief that innovations to systems of information and communication technology (ICT) would catalyse a shift towards more open, democratic societies (Jandrić 2017), authoritarian governments are utilizing technology to tighten their grips on power through the spreading of propaganda and illiberal practices which undermine human rights (Barma et al. 2020). Benkler (2006) engages with a Habermasian critique of public spheres within the postdigital age by introducing the notion of online networked public spheres, arguing that any improvement to political public sphere must be weighed against the many failures of the networked information economy. Benkler et al. (2018) describe one such critical failure in their description of the US' far-right 'propaganda feedback loop', wherein political elites, media outlets, and the public inhabit a self-reinforcing media ecosystem which packages and delivers biased/identity confirming partisan narratives while labelling oppositional narratives as biased and untrustworthy 'fake news'. Moreover, Gambo (2019) highlights that Trump's campaign to erode faith in mainstream media, through the continued propagation of 'fake news' in all broad-range journalistic forms, is characteristic of authoritarians' desire to undermine all institutions and forms of media which contradict them.

Given this context, Schneider's (2018) concept of digital nationalism – as a sustained, mediated, and filtered nationalistic ecology of knowledge that precludes the materialization of Habermasian critical public forums of opposition and dissent – provides an accurate description of a right-wing hyper partisan media ecosystem dominated by Fox News and Breitbart within the USA (Benkler et al. 2018). This understanding of the US' current hyper-partisan *public sphere* belies the discursive nature of modern democratic institutions, underscoring a critical need to investigate how legal and democratic legitimacy is either conferred or questioned within public forums mediated by powerful economic and ideological interests.

Previous scholars have provided insights into this question. Highlighting the joint negotiation between political elites and respective rightist media outlets, the authors note that politicians who thrive in this ecosystem will have done so through a symbiotic relationship with supportive media outlets who gain broader public viewership in return for favourable coverage of identity-confirming politicians within the network (Benkler et al. 2018). Kaiser et al. (2019) expand upon networked media relationships by highlighting common 'identity forming linkages' between political elites, audiences who view mainstream media like Fox News, and consumers of fringe partisan sites like Breitbart. Ogan et al. (2018) outline this phenomenon throughout their study of the 2016 election cycle, wherein Trump's negative accounting of immigration led to a corresponding ideological shift in negative media coverage. Thus, conservative (GOP: Republican) political elites, right-wing media outlets, and their consumers constitute a rightist US media ecology which functions symbiotically to promote and reify a closed 'fake news' discourse based on expedient political gains, increased viewership (clicks, likes, retweets, shares and likes), and self-affirmed ideologies and values. It is important to note that our understanding of leftist media within this conceptual approach aligns with the position of Benkler et al. (2018) who state that, while hyper-partisanship exists within leftist media environments, 'there is no distinct left-wing ecosystem that parallels the right in its internal coherence or insularity'.

In light of this understanding, this chapter builds upon Mumford's (1964) notion of 'authoritarian technics', highlighting US digital nationalism as a technology of manufactured and sterilized intelligence based in an authoritarian ideology of uniform conformity. This notion supports the understanding that the Trump regime, in its continued galvanization of a political base mired in enmity and fear of the left, drives a 'politically correct' (Li 2017) 'Trumpology' of civic republican support for authoritarianism which allows for expedient political benefit at the cost of an overall weakening the First Amendment. Thus, hyper-partisan rightist 'fake news' media outlets represent a bulwark of US digital nationalism, which manufactures coercive content aimed at securing a political base of power founded in citizens who are manipulated into conforming to Trump's 'fake news' approach to the First Amendment. This chapter will show that a distinct rightist US media ecosystem is undercutting the democratic potential of online public spheres – propagandizing a 'fake news' form of political sovereignty which supports illegitimate authoritarian legal changes by alienating citizens from the productive role of critical civic discourse. The following method has been adopted to outline specific instances wherein the rightist media ecology (State, media), as an authoritarian technic of US digital nationalism, has evinced a clear effort to undermine the First Amendment.

Critical Incidents of Authoritarian Technic Within US Digital Nationalism

First, this analysis utilizes Critical Incident Technique (CIT) (Butterfield et al. 2005; Flanagan 1954; Bott and Tourish 2016) to outline 'critical incidents' wherein the Trump-led hyper-partisan Right has utilized a 'fake news' approach to undermine First Amendment Freedoms. Second, an Internet-based corpus review (Mautner 2005; Jensen 2011; Boellstorff et al. 2012; Marshall 2011; van Dijk 2014) of state media as authoritative text (via tweets, interviews, speeches, official press releases, executive actions) and leftist and rightist domestic media sources (news reports, editorials, commentaries) are used to construct a discursive *glonacal* media heuristic (State, Left, Right) (Marginson and Rhoades 2002) surrounding the issue of protest – as an embattled First Amendment freedom in the USA.

Specifically, based on their overall viewership and 'hyperpartisan' rightist or leftist 'skewing' media bias, Otero's Media Bias Chart (Ad Fontes Media 2019; Otero 2019) allows for the outlining of rightist and leftist media outlets within a subsequent *glonacal* analysis. Specifically, Otero's Media Bias Chart is utilized herein to outline a hyper-partisan rightist/leftist media discourse (see Table 6.1). This heuristic will also serve to foreground a damaging hyper-partisanship between competing Kantian liberal (leftist) and Roussean civic republican (rightist) claims to political legitimacy. Furthermore, an authoritative 'state media' heuristic of official tweets, press releases, executive orders, and speeches made by the president and his staffers will fill-out my *glonacal* (Left, State, Right) discursive media heuristic as a framework for assessing BLM protests as a critical incident relating to the current/future outlook of First Amendment freedoms. Finally, a critical discourse analysis (CDA) (Fairclough 1995; O'Keeffe 2006; Hassan 2018) of this *glonacal* media heuristic provides support for the understanding that the US' bulwark of digital nationalism propagates and promotes an intentionally deceitful discourse surrounding Trump's selective 'fake news' approach to the First Amendment. Thusly, this analysis outlines a discrete rightist US media discourse, which, in its support of Trump's attacks on First Amendment freedoms, represents the *authoritarian technic* (Mumford 1964) of US *digital nationalism* (Schneider 2018).

Critical Incident: BLM Protests

Trump's dehumanizing attacks against BLM protesters have been witnessed throughout his entire tenure as a politician. This is true of his 2016 attacks on former NFL Quarterback and BLM-supporter Colin Kaepernick (who took a knee during the national anthem in protest of continued police brutality towards African Americans). Trump proclaimed that team owners should 'get that son of a bitch off the field' and that Kaepernick should 'find another country' (Bixby 2016; Graham 2017; Jacobs 2017). Trump's dehumanizing rhetoric has been continuously lauded by his base, further emboldening his dehumanizing stance against BLM-affiliated First Amendment protesters throughout his presidency (Cancian 2020).

Table 6.1 Hyper-partisan US media outlets (Ad Fontes Media 2019)

Hyper-partisan leftist media	Hyper-partisan rightist media
CNN (40.8 million)	Fox news (133.15 million)
MSNBC TV (30.8 million)	Breitbart (23 million)
The Atlantic (16 million)	The daily caller (11.6 million)
Vanity fair (11.24 million)	The blaze (5.98 million)
Slate (10.53 million)	Infowars (4.8 million)

Black Lives Matter (BLM) is an ideological and political movement which emerged after the acquittal of Travon Martin's Killer, George Zimmerman, with the keyword #Blacklivesmatter framing conversation and debates surrounding legal murders, mass imprisonment, and a 'system of US values' wherein black bodies are deemed inherently criminal and therefore targeted for demise (Maraj et al. 2018; Szetela 2019). Founded by Alicia Garza, Partrice Cullars, and Opal Tometi in 2013 as an online campaign to raise awareness for the injustice of Trevon Martin's brutal murder (and the incredulity of George Zimmerman's subsequent acquittal), the movement quickly transitioned to real-world civic protests (both peaceful protest and riots) by activists fed-up with the seemingly endless killings of black citizens by members of various US police forces (Anderson 2019). Given the recent rise in BLM-affiliated protests across the nation and the government's attempts to crack-down on these protests, the subsequent media discourse surrounding BLM highlights a constitutional crisis between First Amendment freedoms and the government's authority to quell violence in the name of public health, safety, and welfare (Ferreri 2020). Thus, within the continued framework of the Habermasian (validity/facticity) crisis of democracy, the media discourse surrounding continuing BLM protests as either an unlawful movement for systemic change or unlawful civic unrest represents a critical incident for this study.

Glonacal Critical Discourse Analysis: State, Rightist, and Leftist

The State

On 25 May 2020, a startling video emerged on social media outlets across the globe. For 8 minutes and 46 seconds, this video laid bare the brutal murder (in graphic gut-wrenching detail) of George Floyd, a black US citizen, at the hands of a white US Minnesota police officer named Derek Chauvin (Hill et al. 2020). Following the public outcry, which spilled over into BLM protests and riots around the globe, on 1 June 2020, the president released this statement:

> I am your President of law and order, and an ally of all peaceful protesters … But in recent days, our nation has been gripped by professional anarchists, violent mobs, arsonists, looters, criminals, rioters, Antifa, and others … These are not acts of peaceful protest. These are acts of domestic terror. The destruction of innocent life and the spilling of innocent blood is an offense to humanity and a crime against God … That is why I am taking immediate presidential action to stop the violence and restore security and safety in America. I am mobilizing all available federal resources — civilian and military — to stop the rioting and looting, to end the destruction and arson, and to protect the rights of law-abiding Americans, including your Second Amendment rights … If a city or a state refuses to take the actions that are necessary to defend the life and property of their residents, then I will deploy the United States military and quickly solve the problem for them. (The White House 2020b)

Trump initially addresses the nation in whole before transitioning back towards his base through a show of concern for Rightist ideological talking points (God, Antifa, Second Amendment). Within his remarks, we witness his selective notions of equal justice, law and order, and how they fall within an ethnonationalist framework of civic republicanism. Specifically, Trump's ethnonationalist appeal to law and order highlights a critique of US civic republican constitutionalism as 'too culturally specific, too orthodox and too exclusionary' (Williams 1994).

This ethnonationalist framework of civic republican law and order requires that the protest of injustice exist within a 'constitutionally bound' moral and legal framework of coercive sovereign political authority/legitimacy which does not seek to overthrow the sovereign (Pettit 2012).

This understanding of civic republicanism helps explain why Trump can easily condemn BLM protests as 'terrorists' while defending armed (primarily white) militias who stormed the Lansing, Michigan, capitol building as 'very good people' (Panetta 2020). Nevertheless, as protests continued, Trump's rhetoric towards BLM anti-racist protests began to take an even more pugilistic stance. On 3 July 2020, in the midst of a devastating pandemic, during one of the most divisive points in US history, President Trump had this to say about the ongoing BLM protests:

> Our nation is witnessing a merciless campaign to wipe out our history, defame our heroes, erase our values, and indoctrinate our children. Angry mobs are trying to tear down statues of our Founders, deface our most sacred memorials, and unleash a wave of violent crime in our cities. This attack on our liberty, our magnificent liberty, must be stopped, and it will be stopped very quickly. We will expose this dangerous movement, protect our nation's children, end this radical assault, and preserve our beloved American way of life. The violent mayhem we have seen in the streets of cities that are run by liberal Democrats, in every case, is the predictable result of years of extreme indoctrination and bias in education, journalism, and other cultural institutions. (The White House 2020b)

Trump's 4 July speech (based in a political discourse of ethnographic fear) highlights what Orellana and Michelsen (2019) label as a benchmark of contemporary rightist US discourse, a return to American exceptionalism (manifest destiny) based on claims of God-given cultural superiority, representing the right's desire to 'unshackle the innate potential of birth-culture' through the abandonment and disestablishment of liberal normative frameworks (Peters et al. 2020). This desire to usurp liberal norms in favour of ethnonationalist civic republicanism highlights the dangers inherent to Price's (2018) notion of partisan suppression/enforcement/protection of First Amendment rights – opening the door to the authoritarian usurpation of State's Rights as well.

While he has not yet invoked the Insurrection Law, he has already utilized his 'fake news' approach to the First Amendment to hold a partisan 'peaceful protest for law and order' on 10 October 2020 at The White House – despite a D.C.-wide ban on mass gatherings due to Covid-19 (Murdock 2020). Finally, as part of his central 'law and order' campaign promise, Trump has continuously stated that he will do everything in his power to 'protect the suburbs', i.e., his base of support and legitimacy, falsely tweeting on 26 August that: 'TODAY, I will be sending federal law enforcement and the National Guard' to Kenosha, Wisconsin 'to restore LAW and ORDER' (Thomas and Phelps 2020). The president followed up these false claims on 1 September, stating that: 'My administration coordinated with the state and local authorities to very, very swiftly deploy the National Guard surge federal law enforcement to Kenosha and stop the violence' (Horton 2020).

The issue with these claims is not just that they are false but that they attempt to reframe the current boundaries of sovereign power held within the executive office. To be clear, Trump does not have the constitutional authority to 'send in the national guard', that is a decision which has to be made by the state in question, in this case, Wisconsin (Thomas and Phelps 2020). However, while it is important to note that Trumps' claims were false, the 1807 Insurrection Law does allow the federal government to direct federal troops into states as a means of protecting 'citizens rights' (Horton 2020).

While this act has not been invoked since 1992, Trump's continued pursuit of sovereign authority within a coercive procedural understanding of law and order (facticity) (rather than validity) is a critical blow to long-standing liberal US democratic norms which hold that political legitimacy is derived from the overriding will of the people. As a case in point, on 26 June 2020 Trump issued an executive order titled 'Executive Order on Protecting American Monuments, Memorials and Statues and Combating Recent Criminal Violence' (The White House 2020c). Under the guise of 'protecting monuments and federal buildings', this executive order provided procedural legitimacy for the creation and subsequent deployment of masked, unidentifiable 'paramilitary' troops by the Department of Homeland Security – called Protecting American Communities Task Force (PACT), to quell protesters in 'out of control liberal Democrat' run cities (Fox 2020).

These constitutionally precarious, yet politically expedient actions allowed Trump to bolster his claim of being a 'law and order president'. The realization of this authoritarian coercive notion of legitimacy, which views Trump's sovereign power within an autocratic civic republican framework, would also allow Trump to 'legitimately' supersede constitutionally mandated state and individual rights on the path towards the selective and politically beneficial administration of law and order. Providing a final glimpse into Trump's official position on the anti-racist campaign of BLM as a movement, Trump had this to say at campaign rally in Atlanta, Georgia, on 25 September 2020:

> As you know… many of those who are spreading violence in our cities are supporters of an organization called the Black Lives Matter or BLM. It's really hurting the black community. It's hurting the black community… The stated goal of BLM organization people is to achieve the destruction of the nuclear family, abolish the police, abolish prisons, abolish border security, abolish capitalism, and abolish school choice. That's what their stated goals are. (Trump 2020)

Historically, fears surrounding the censorial power of the government led to significant refinements of the First Amendment regarding interference, prosecution, or defamation on the part of the government towards its critics (Grambo 2019). Displaying Price's (2018: 821) 'highly selective and discriminatory enforcement of the First Amendment,' Trump has portrayed himself as 'a defender of free speech and foe of political correctness' (Graham 2018), while enacting a sustained and targeted defamation of BLM members seeking government redress. Lastly, leaving little doubt as to exactly who's rights matter most and why, Trump had this to say at a recent campaign rally on 13 October 2020:

> I'm about law and order. I'm about having you safe. I'm about having (sic) your suburban communities. I don't want to build low-income housing next to your house … Suburban women, they should like me more than anybody here tonight because I ended the regulation that destroyed your neighborhood. I ended the regulation that brought crime to the suburbs, and you're going to live the American dream … So can I ask you to do me a favor? Suburban women, will you please like me? I saved your damn neighborhood, OK? (Axelrod 2020)

Thusly, the state discourse surrounding the BLM protest movement entails a politically self-serving partisan, ethnonationalist civic republican, selective understanding of law, and order which frames BLM-affiliated protesters as terrorists, while drawing legitimacy via the protection of the rights, freedoms, and dreams of his singularly virtuous conservative white suburban base of support.

Hyper-partisan Right

The aforementioned 'State' definition of BLM as a terrorist organization hell-bent on destroying the fabric of American society allows for a more directed analysis of the hyper-partisan right as an echo-chamber for Trump's law and order rhetoric. On 20 July 2020, Breitbart posts an article titled 'Black Lives Matter Protesters Loot Businesses, Set Fires in Seattle' which uses the looting of an Amazon store in Seattle, Washington, as rationale for labelling BLM protesters as 'Antifa Militants' through a highlighted quote by police which stated: 'These are criminal acts, not peaceful protests' (Starr 2020). On 10 August 2020, a BLM-affiliated protest in Chicago in support of arrested protesters descended into looting and rioting. Fox News subsequently reports on this event by highlighting a quote (from an NBC affiliate in Chicago) which has BLM Chicago founder Aislinn Pulley stating:

> I don't care if someone decides to loot a Gucci or a Macy's or a Nike store, because that makes sure that person eats … That makes sure that person has clothes … That is (sic) reparations … Anything they wanted to take, they can take it because these businesses have insurance. (Aaro 2020)

The Fox News article further underscores the criminality of the BLM-affiliated protest turned riotous looting by highlighting an unnamed quote by Chicago PD which states:

> The shooting prompted hundreds of people to descend on downtown Chicago early Monday with vandals smashing the windows of dozens of businesses and making off with merchandise, cash machines and anything else they could carry. (Aaro 2020)

This quote was followed by a statement by Chicago Police Superintendent, David Brown: 'This was not an organized protest. Rather, this was an incident of pure criminality…This was an act of violence against our police officers and against our city.' (Aaro 2020)

The pointed nature of this article does not adequately frame Fox News' position on BLM; more importantly, however, the article does not allow for an adequate understanding of the events of that night. Specifically, in a peculiar Janus-faced journalistic positioning, a separate article (published the same day) by Fox News also reports the same events and the same statements made by BLM Chicago founder Aislinn Pulley within an entirely different context. The author of the article provides this quote by Pulley which states:

> I think the goal of the preoccupation around property damage and looting specifically, along the Mag Mile and in the heart of the city's commerce center, works to distract away from the actual cause of the outrage, the important thing is to intervene and remind people what the causal incident was and continues to be. (Craft 2020)

This strategic 'success-oriented' reporting by Fox News simultaneously frames Pulley as the unapologetic face of a radical left-wing Antifa-communist crime wave, yet also as thoughtful and mournfully self-aware of how looting hurts the community and undercuts BLM's core message. To some, this approach may seem to represent a novel form of journalistic integrity which serves the needs of all-comers – 'if you want veracity, we have you covered, if you want mendacity, we have that too'. Unfortunately, by mixing journalistic integrity with pseudo-journalistic ideological fodder, Fox News is contributing to the Trumpian campaign to undermine freedom of the press (Kharroub 2017).

Moreover, this pseudo-ethical journalistic posturing lends credence to Trump's continued insistence that the fourth estate (as a liberal institution) now represents nothing more than biased 'fake news' partisan politics. Lastly, these two excerpts should underscore the worrisome dissolution of journalistic integrity and pervasive radicalization of once-centrist conservative stalwarts like Fox News, an assertion that core right-wing outlets are failing to act as a 'truth-telling brake' on radical fringe sites like Breitbart (Benkler et al. 2018; Chambers 2020).

Thusly, media outlets within the US' hyper-partisan right-wing media ecology no longer constitute a check on mendacity but rather value it, promote consumerism over empirical evidence, and are driven by a logic of emotionally charged groupthink rather than journalistic ethics (Green 2020). As a final demonstration of this doleful notion of the crumbling fourth estate, this article presents a 6 September 2020 Breitbart article which cites the aforementioned ACLED and Princeton University's Bridging Divides Initiative (BDI) study. Specifically, this analysis underscores that despite the authors of the study clearly stating that their findings support the conclusion that 93% of BLM protests held in the summer of 2020 were overwhelmingly 'peaceful and nondestructive', the 6 September 2020 Breitbart article presents the following 'alternative' conclusion:

> Mainstream media seized on the data last week to argue that the 'Trump narrative' of violent demonstrations was false. The study itself speculated that public perceptions of riots were skewed by 'political orientation and biased media framing' and 'disproportionate coverage of violent demonstrations.' However, public perceptions may simply have reflected the wide geographic distribution of the violence…Thus in the public imagination, the pro-

> portion that matters most may not be the 7% of protests that were violent, but the 96% of major urban areas that experienced rioting. (Pollak 2020)

This analysis should highlight a clear symbiosis between the state and the rightist media as working in unison to create a misleading narrative of BLM as a violent criminal organization that threatens the safety and well-being of peaceful, law-abiding Americans. Moreover, while clinging to a semblance of journalistic integrity, what was once classifiable as 'the mainstream right' has allowed itself to be steered further afield into the purely success-oriented domain of pseudo-journalistic 'click-bait' alternative 'fake news'. In Habermasian terms, the potential for autonomous civic discourse (theoretically allowed for by an independent free press), in practice, has been coopted by authoritarian institutions of powerful self-interested elites (Staats 2004). Thus, the state and the rightist media together represent an authoritarian technic of US digital nationalism which utilizes 'fake news' disinformation to undermine democratic public opinion in favor of a pathological 'mass deception' which creates a citizenry incapable of self-conscious public debate.

Hyper-partisan Left

Trump's decision to send federal troops to Portland, Oregon, to quell BLM protests was met by leftist media articles which attempted to frame these actions as 'unconstitutional' and a threat to threat to First Amendment norms and values. A 17 July 2020 article by Vanity Fair, citing both the ACLU and Speaker Nancy Pelosi respectively, states the following:

> the ACLU said in a statement Friday. 'These actions are flat-out unconstitutional and will not go unanswered.' Democrats have chimed in. After Barr sicced federal law enforcement on protesters in Washington last month, **Nancy Pelosi** demanded they be identified. 'The practice of officers operating with full anonymity undermines accountability, ignites government distrust and suspicion, and is counter to the principle of procedural justice and legitimacy during this precarious moment in our nation's history,' she wrote. (Lutz 2020)

The article may be used to outline the following several characteristics of Leftist media:

Firstly, the presence of political elites as steering media that frame Leftist discourse, in this case Speaker Nancy Pelosi and the ACLU. Here, Speaker Nancy Pelosi and the ACLU attempt to address issues of Rousseauean legitimacy (procedural justice, constitutionality) and Kantean general will (principles, norms, and values) as a means to outline that Trump's actions fall outside the legitimate bounds of sovereignty.

Secondly, however rife with familiar 'fear-based' rhetoric (distrust, suspicion, unjust), this article, and many others by the left, fails to counter the Right's political manoeuvring on two fronts. Firstly, by incorrectly labelling Trump's actions as unconstitutional, Leftist discourse fails to accurately confront a First Amendment doctrine which 'leaves the door open' for government punishment when freedom of expression manifests in criminal conduct (Price 2018). Secondly, the Left (as a loosely affiliated political program) has continuously failed to grasp the underlying conflict of modern democracy as a battle between Rousseauean sovereign law (facticity) and Kantian notions of 'spontaneous self-legislation' (validity).

This understanding belies a more critical error within Leftist discourse, one which fails to understand that the current protections afforded by the First Amendment are primarily imperiled by the diminished intellectual climate which frames these constitutional disputes (Price 2018). Critically, rather than calling for legislative or judicial actions aimed at halting the erosion of the fourth estate as the font of critical civic discourse, as well as procedural protections to normative First Amendment freedoms, media articles on the left continue to argue the case against Trump's desire to erode erstwhile foundational liberal institutions via normative grounds. On 29 July 2020, Slate releases this article as an appeal to their readers:

> The right to assemble, protest, and gather is the neglected younger sister to the free speech clause. As the Supreme Court lavishes attention on commercial speech and money as speech and religious signage and union dues and cake baking as speech, the freedom to gather and protest is often forgotten. But this spring and summer, as protests broke out across the country initially in response to the police killing of George Floyd, a Black man, and increasingly in response to government crackdowns on protest itself, we are left with the grim prospect of protesters without much legal protection, despite the First Amendment. This much was plain to see in two congressional hearings on Tuesday, in which thousands of peaceful demonstrators were dismissed as anarchists and mobs, both by Republicans in Congress and by Attorney General William Barr. (Lithwick 2020)

In essence, the Slate article is arguing that Habermasian 'steering media' within the USA have successfully reoriented the First Amendment principle of free speech to protect elite political and economic interests rather than citizens wishing to redress a government grievance. True, but lamentably old news. What this article should highlight is that by ignoring the political climate of 'fake news' which has allowed Trump to retain a semblance of 'law and order' political legitimacy (to a base of misinformed followers and obsequious political elites), the Left is constantly put on the defensive, scrambling to guard against the next bulldozing of an erstwhile sacrosanct liberal norm or value.

However, this article makes a prescient point regarding the issue of 'guilt by association' – an issue at the core of current and future US First Amendment freedoms:

> In other words, in Barr's hands, the freedom of assembly is transformed to mass guilt by association. Neither he nor Monahan could explain when and how one protester hellbent on violence turns an entire peaceful protest into an angry mob… (Lithwick 2020)

The overwhelming selectivity by which mass guilt by association is imputed is clearly observable within the leftist narrative that the right is utilizing procedural law to institute politically partisan and selectively oppressive tactics to undercut the legitimacy of anyone and everyone (thugs, looters, rioters, criminals) seeking to protest injustices under the current administration. On 2 June 2020, The Atlantic had this to say on the matter:

> On May 28, Donald Trump demanded the First Amendment right of free speech for himself on privately owned social media, and then, four days later, declared war on the people, gathered on public property, as they sought, in the words of the amendment itself, 'to assemble, and to petition the Government for a redress of grievances.' ... The right of assembly is an important First Amendment right, one treasured by the founding generation and the First Congress, which wrote the amendment, and one re-won two centuries later at great pain by the labor, civil-rights, and anti-war movements ... That right has been under assault since the day Trump took office ... red-state legislatures have been indefatigable in debating and passing laws designed to penalize protesters for disfavored causes. (Epps 2020)

This research finds that Leftist media is driven by steering media (in the form of political elites) and is not above framing public discourse within familiar political 'hit piece' and fear-based tactics of the right. However, a unified pattern of intentional 'fake news' disinformation/misinformation that could potentially mirror the right's programmatic (technological, political, commercial, institutional) (see Benkler et al. 2018: 22) cohesiveness does not exist within leftist media outlets. This analysis of the hyper-partisan left should, however, provide an understanding that, while there exists a diversity of opinions on the left surrounding BLM protests and Trump's draconian efforts to quell them, it is primarily based in a flawed over-reliance on a Kantian liberal narrative (Habermasian validity claims) which aim to cast Trump's authority as illegitimate and therefore warranting of continued protest. However, this research identifies a Leftist media discourse, foregrounded within a Leftist political agenda, that continues to emphasize validity over facticity, failing to promote substantive frameworks (legislative, legal) which would protect either protesters or the right to protest from the Right's continued procedural manoeuvring. Thus, this analysis supports Price's (2018: 830) assertion that the USA will continue to experience 'a downward spiral with respect to First Amendment freedoms protected by norms and conventions rather than just judicial doctrine'.

Implications of US Digital Nationalism: A Potential End to the US Democratic Experiment

Firstly, this descent into 'fake news' pseudo-journalism portends a grave outlook for both democratic civic discussion and the ability of the press to hold US leaders accountable (West 2017). This understanding is highlighted by Ehrenfeld and Barton (2019) who find that the blurring lines between journalism and social media-style pseudo-journalism, the incentivization of 'fake news' over news, and engagement metrics which promote mass persuasion have engendered a society at odds with the principles of democratic deliberation and collective action. Finally, these attempts to steer public opinion away from liberal notions of free speech highlight Habermas' (1996: 5) conclusion that discourses within modern societies are mediated and rationalized by systemic imperatives which 'confer legitimacy on political will-formation, legislation and the administration of justice'. Specifically, the manipulation of public discourse towards a promotion of Trump's 'fake news' approach to the First Amendment represents an all-out effort by rightist media to further pull at the seams of contemporary US society. Using 'fake news' as an expedient political tool which exploits the inherent weakness of modern democracy, the hyper-partisan right, as the authoritarian technic of digital nationalism, has seized upon the US' inability to transcend plurality, its inability to produce 'context transcending validity claims' (Habermas 1996) surrounding First Amendment legal freedoms, and seeks now to reframe this doctrine within a Trumpian 'fake news' authoritarian framework.

Further, this research finds that the most pressing concern for the future protection of First Amendment rights and freedoms lies within the aforementioned 'mass guilt by association'. This is an issue which remains foundational to the future of US First Amendment freedoms. Case in point, in a striking reversal from the past, when the US constitution was viewed as a model for the rest of the world, the UN has seized upon current US constitutional failings, providing a framework for the right to protest which stands as exceedingly prescient. Specifically, in light of global BLM protests, which have transformed to protests against police brutality in general, such as the ongoing anti-brutality protests in Nigeria (Akinwotu 2020), the UN issued a groundbreaking 'authoritative interpretation' (Dickinson 2020) on the right of peaceful assembly. The UN's General Comment 31 on Article 21 (The Right to Peaceful Assembly) section 17 and 18 states the following:

> There is not always a clear dividing line between assemblies that are peaceful and those that are not, but there is a presumption in favour of considering assemblies to be peaceful. Moreover, isolated acts of violence by some participants should not be attributed to others, to the organizers or to the assembly as such.
>
> The question of whether or not an assembly is peaceful must be answered with reference to violence that originates from the participants. Violence against participants in a peaceful assembly by the authorities, or by agents provocateurs acting on their behalf, does not render the assembly non-peaceful. (United Nations 2020)

This recent decision by the UN strikes at the core of recent hyper-pluralist liberal-republican constitutional debates within the USA and further outlines Price's (2018: 73) assertion that the current social and political climate of 'partisan polarization and distrust' represents a critical challenge to the previously sacrosanct 'civic libertarian' understanding of the right to peacefully assemble. Thus, this research should highlight that within a contemporary framework of US digital nationalism, the hyper-partisan left must back their appeals to Kantian liberal norms and values with procedural and legal frameworks which ensure that the autonomy of will displayed within individual and group protest – as well as the ideals which support its use – are protected against the oppressive civic republican facticity which undergirds Trump's 'fake news' approach to the First Amendment.

Lastly, it must be noted that Trump's selective 'fake news' approach to the First Amendment has been used to protect himself against being flagged on social media, to defend conservative voices on university campuses, and to pardon right-winged armed militia groups who 'protested', i.e., committed arson and led an armed standoff against federal authorities (Landers 2018), and is now being used to defend an attempted coup of the office of the President of the United States of America. In his ongoing battle to overturn the democratic US election process, a recent report by the Washington Post provides a transcribed call between Trump and Georgia Secretary of State Brad Raffensperger which outlines Trump's continued use of 'fake news' to legitimize his selective use of 'law and order' as a coercive fulcrum of power:

> there's nothing wrong with saying that, you know, that you've recalculated … you should want to have an accurate election. And you're a Republican … We wanted Fulton County. And you wouldn't give it to us. the ballots are corrupt … And you are going to find that they are —totally illegal — it is more illegal for you than it is for them because, you know, what they did and you're not reporting it. That's a criminal, that's a criminal offense. That's a big risk to you … And that's a big risk … So look. All I want to do is this. I just want to find 11,780 votes, which is one more than we have because we won the state. (Gardner and Firozi 2021)

Within a Rousseauean civic republican notion of political legitimacy, the legitimacy of the sovereign, at its limit, is based upon the subordination of individual freedoms to a sovereign (individual, state, institution) endorsed by the overriding will (either majority or committee) of the people. Thus, any sovereign who seeks to either rule without or overturn this general will (in a Kantian sense, the social contract as general will) loses the civic republican legitimacy afforded to those states operating within constitutional constraints (Pettit 2012). In other words, having lost the general election, the electoral college, and more importantly the legitimizing will of the people, any further 'fake news' attempts by Trump to retain his 'law and order' sovereignty are illegitimate and should be met by a non-partisan reproach of authoritarian demagoguery.

Conclusion

Within the context of a hyper-plural liberal-republican US media landscape, this chapter has presented a Habermasian critique of the state as working in conjunction with hyper-partisan rightist media to foment an authoritarian technic of US digital nationalism. Specifically, this research has shown that elite politicians on the right enlist the support of media outlets, who have abandoned democratic precepts of 'truth-seeking journalistic integrity' in favour of 'success-oriented' fake news pseudo-journalism. Further, this joint quest for expedient political and economic gains has undermined Kantian liberal First Amendment norms and values, supporting a Trumpian desire to delegitimize the fourth estate as a means to substitute critical political discourse in favour of a civic polity mired in a state of pathological 'mass deception'.

Thus, I have argued that Trump's use of the authoritarian technic of US digital nationalism to propagandize his 'fake news' approach to the First Amendment has enveloped the hyper-partisan right in a shroud of obsequious – 'politically correct' rhetoric which seeks to legitimize his claim of sovereignty based in a wholly authoritarian civic republican notion of law and order. Finally, this research recommends that the Left adopt a unified discourse of reform which seeks to undergird longstanding First Amendment principles (validity) within procedurally defined (facticity) frameworks that will not so easily succumb to future instances of 'fake news' demagoguery. In other words, if immediate procedural steps are not taken (such as adapting the UN General Comment into current US legal frameworks), the Right will continue to utilize its bulwark of US digital nationalism to blaze a corrosive Rousseauean civic republican path towards the precipitous erosion of both the First Amendment and many other longstanding Kantian liberal norms and values within the US.

References

Aaro, D. (2020). Black Lives Matter holds rally in Chicago to support those arrested after looting, unrest. Fox News, 12 August. https://www.foxnews.com/us/black-lives-matter-holds-rally-chicago-support-arrested-looting-unrest. Accessed 16 October 2020.

ACLU (2020). Protesters' Rights. Know Your Rights. American Civil Liberties Union. https://www.aclu.org/know-your-rights/protesters-rights/. Accessed 17 September 2020.

Ad Fontes Media. (2019). Interactive Media Bias Chart. https://www.adfontesmedia.com/interactive-media-bias-chart-2/. Accessed 16 October 2020.

Akinwotu, E. (2020). Army warn they are on standby as police brutality protests intensify in Nigeria. The Guardian, 15 October. https://www.theguardian.com/global-development/2020/oct/15/army-standby-police-brutality-protests-nigeria. Accessed 16 October 2020.

Allyn, B. (2020). Twitter Flags President Trump's Tweet For The 1st Time. NPR, 26 May. https://www.npr.org/2020/05/26/862838470/twitter-flags-president-trumps-tweet-for-the-first-time. Accessed 15 September 2020.

Anderson, M. (2019). History of the hashtag #BlackLivesMatter: Social activism on Twitter. Pew Research Center: Internet, Science & Tech, 31 December. https://www.pewresearch.org/internet/2016/08/15/the-hashtag-blacklivesmatter-emerges-social-activism-on-twitter/. Accessed 15 September 2020.

Axelrod, T. (2020). Trump makes appeal to suburban women at rally: 'Will you please like me?'. The Hill, 14 October. https://thehill.com/homenews/campaign/520932-trump-makes-appeal-to-suburban-women-at-rally-will-you-please-like-me. Accessed 15 October 2020.

Baker, P., Kanno-youngs, Z., & Davey, M. (2020). Trump Threatens to Send Federal Law Enforcement Forces to More Cities. The New York Times, 20 July. https://www.nytimes.com/2020/07/20/us/politics/trump-chicago-portland-federal-agents.html. Accessed 15 October 2020.

Barma, N., Durbin, B., & Kendall-Taylor, A. (2020). Digital authoritarianism: Finding our way out of the darkness. War on the Rocks, 4 August. https://warontherocks.com/2020/02/digital-authoritarianism-finding-our-way-out-of-the-darkness/. Accessed 15 September 2020.

Baxter, H. (2011). *Habermas: the discourse theory of law and democracy*. Stanford, CA: Stanford Law Books.

Bechtold, E. (2020). The First Amendment: what it really means for free speech and why Donald Trump is trampling on it. The Conversation, 7 October. https://theconversation.com/the-first-amendment-what-it-really-means-for-free-speech-and-why-donald-trump-is-trampling-on-it-121274. Accessed 11 October 2020.

Benkler, Y. (2006). *The Wealth of Networks: how social production transforms markets and freedom*. New Haven, CT: Yale University Press.

Benkler, Y., Faris, R., Roberts, H., & Zuckerman, E. (2017). Study: Breitbart-led right-wing media ecosystem altered broader media agenda. Columbia Journalism Review, 3 March. https://www.cjr.org/analysis/breitbart-media-trump-harvard-study.php. Accessed 5 October 2020.

Benkler, Y., Faris, R., & Roberts, H. (2018). *Network Propaganda*. New York: Oxford University Press.

Bixby, S. (2016). Trump on Colin Kaepernick: 'He should find a country that works better for him'. The Guardian, 29 August. https://www.theguardian.com/sport/2016/aug/29/donald-trump-colin-kaepernick-national-anthem-protest. Accessed 15 September 2020.

Boellstorff, T., Nardi, B. A., Pearce, C., Taylor, T. L., & Marcus, G. (2012). *Ethnography and virtual worlds: a handbook of method.* Princeton, CA: Princeton University Press.

Bott, G., & Tourish, D. (2016). The critical incident technique reappraised. *Qualitative Research in Organizations and Management: An International Journal, 11*(4), 276–300. https://doi.org/10.1108/qrom-01-2016-1351.

Butterfield, L. D., Borgen, W. A., Amundson, N. E., & Maglio, A.-ST. (2005) Fifty years of the critical incident technique: 1954–2004 and beyond. *Qualitative Research, 5*(4), 475–497. https://doi.org/10.1177/1468794105056924.

Camera, L. (2019). Trump to sign executive order protecting campus free speech. U.S. News & World Report, 21 March. https://www.usnews.com/news/education-news/articles/2019-03-21/trump-to-sign-executive-order-protecting-campus-free-speech. Accessed 15 September 2020.

Cancian, D. (2020). Everything Donald Trump has said about NFL kneeling so far. Newsweek, 8 June. https://www.newsweek.com/everything-donald-trump-said-nfl-anthem-protests-1509333. Accessed 12 September 2020.

Chambers, S. (2020). Truth, Deliberative Democracy, and the Virtues of Accuracy: Is Fake News Destroying the Public Sphere? *Political Studies*. https://doi.org/10.1177/0032321719890811.

Choi, M. (2020). Trump tweets a letter calling protesters 'terrorists'. POLITICO, 5 June. https://www.politico.com/news/2020/06/04/trump-lawyer-protesters-terrorist-letter-302552. Accessed 15 September 2020.

Craft, A. (2020). Black Lives Matter Chicago co-founder says looting steps on message; condemns Mayor Lightfoot's inaction. Fox News, 12 August. https://www.foxnews.com/media/blm-chicago-looting-steps-on-message. Accessed 15 September 2020.

Dewan, A. (2020). Trump is calling protesters terrorists. That puts him in the company of the world's autocrats. CNN, 27 July. https://www.cnn.com/2020/07/25/politics/us-protests-trump-terrorists-intl/index.html. Accessed 15 September 2020.

Dickinson, D. (2020). How do you define lawful peaceful protest? The UN Human Rights Committee has a clear answer. UN News, 29 July. https://news.un.org/en/story/2020/07/1069211. Accessed 16 October 2020.

Egelhofer, J. L., & Lecheler, S. (2019). Fake news as a two-dimensional phenomenon: a framework and research agenda. *Annals of the International Communication Association, 43*(2), 97–116. https://doi.org/10.1080/23808985.2019.1602782.

Egemenoglu, E. (2020). First amendment. Legal Information Institute, March. https://www.law.cornell.edu/wex/first_amendment. Accessed 17 September 2020.

Ehrenfeld, D., & Barton, M. (2019). Online Public Spheres in the Era of Fake News: Implications for the Composition Classroom. *Computers and Composition, 54*, 102525. https://doi.org/10.1016/j.compcom.2019.102525.

Epps, G. (2020). Trump's Grotesque Violation of the First Amendment. The Atlantic, 2 June. https://www.theatlantic.com/ideas/archive/2020/06/trumps-grotesque-violation-first-amendment/612532/. Accessed 16 October 2020.

Fairclough, N. (1995). *Critical discourse analysis: the critical study of language.* London: Longman.

Ferreri, E. (2020). How first and second amendments apply in protests. Duke Today, 8 September. https://today.duke.edu/2020/09/how-first-and-second-amendments-apply-protests. Accessed 14 October 2020.

Flanagan, J. C. (1954). The critical incident technique. *Psychological Bulletin, 51*(4), 327–358. https://doi.org/10.1037/h0061470.

Fox, B. (2020). Heavily armed US agents on city streets: Can Trump do that? AP NEWS, 22 July. https://apnews.com/article/law-and-order-violence-politics-oregon-racial-injustice-b35e37208e261278ecc33154c37d5d85. Accessed 15 October 2020.

Fuchs, C. (2018). *Digital demagogue authoritarian capitalism in the age of Trump and Twitter*. London: Pluto Press.

Gardner, A., & Firozi, P. (2021). Here's the full transcript and audio of the call between Trump and Raffensperger. The Washington Post, 4 January. https://www.washingtonpost.com/politics/trump-raffensperger-call-transcript-georgia-vote/2021/01/03/2768e0cc-4ddd-11eb-83e3-322644d82356_story.html. Accessed 3 January 2021.

Graham, B. A. (2017). Donald Trump blasts NFL anthem protesters: 'Get that son of a bitch off the field'. The Guardian, 23 September. https://www.theguardian.com/sport/2017/sep/22/donald-trump-nfl-national-anthem-protests. Accessed 11 October 2020.

Graham, D. A. (2018). 'Maybe You shouldn't Be in the Country'. The Atlantic, 24 May. https://www.theatlantic.com/politics/archive/2018/05/trumps-double-standard-on-free-speech-and-the-nfl/561119/. Accessed 11 October 2020.

Graham, L. (2019). New anti-protest laws are incompatible with American democracy. The Conversation, 6 October. https://theconversation.com/new-anti-protest-laws-are-incompatible-with-american-democracy-74279. Accessed 17 September 2020.

Grambo, K. (2019). Fake News and Racial, Ethnic, and Religious Minorities: A Precarious Quest for Truth. *University of Pennsylvania Journal of Constitutional Law, 21*(5), 1299–1348.

Green, B. (2020). In Pursuit of an 'Ethos of Community': Postdigital Education in the Age of Covid-19. *Postdigital Science and Education, 2*(3), 681–689. https://doi.org/10.1007/s42438-020-00123-6.

Habermas, J. (1996). *Between Facts and Norms: Contributions to a Discourse Theory of Law and Democracy*. Cambridge, MA: The MIT Press.

Hassan, A. (2018). Language, media, and Ideology: Critical Discourse Analysis of Pakistani News Bulletin Headlines and Its Impact on Viewers. *SAGE Open, 8*(3), 215824401879261. https://doi.org/10.1177/2158244018792612.

Hill, E., Tiefenthäler, A., Triebert, C., Jordan, D., Willis, H., & Stein, R. (2020). How George Floyd was killed in police custody. The New York Times, 1 June. https://www.nytimes.com/2020/05/31/us/george-floyd-investigation.html. Accessed 14 October 2020.

Horton, J. (2020). Does Trump have the right to send in federal forces? BBC, 2 September. https://www.bbc.com/news/world-us-canada-52893540. Accessed 11 October 2020.

Jacobs, B. (2017). Kim Jong-un, the NFL and 'screaming at senators': Trump's Strange night in Alabama. The Guardian, 23 September. https://www.theguardian.com/usnews/2017/sep/23/kim-jong-un-the-nfl-and-screaming-at-senators-donald-trumps-strange-night-in-alabama. Accessed 15 September 2020.

Jandrić, P. (2017). *Learning in the Age of Digital Reason*. Rotterdam: Sense.

Jensen, K. B. (2011). New media, Old Methods – Internet Methodologies and the Online/Offline Divide. In M. Consalvo & C. Ess (Eds.), *The handbook of Internet studies* (pp. 43–58). West Sussex: Wiley-Blackwell.

Kaiser, J., Rauchfleisch, A., & Bourassa, N. (2019). Connecting the (Far-)Right Dots: A Topic modeling and Hyperlink Analysis of (Far-)Right media Coverage during the US Elections 2016. *Digital Journalism, 8*(3), 422–441. https://doi.org/10.1080/21670811.2019.1682629.

Kaufman, A. (1997). Reason, Self-Legislation and Legitimacy: Conceptions of Freedom in the Political Thought of Rousseau and Kant. *The Review of Politics, 59*(1), 25–52. https://doi.org/10.1017/s0034670500027145.

Kellner, D. (2018). Donald Trump and the Politics of Lying. In M. Peters, S. Rider, M. Hyvönen, & T. Besley (Eds.), *Post-truth, fake news: viral modernity & higher education* (pp. 89–100). Singapore: Springer. https://doi.org/10.1007/978-981-10-8013-5_7.

Kharroub, D. T. (2017). American democracy under threat: Fake news, alternative facts. Alaraby, 24 February. https://english.alaraby.co.uk/english/Comment/2017/2/24/American-democracy-under-threat-Fake-news-alternative-facts. Accessed 16 October 2020.

Kishi, R., & Jones, S. (2020). (rep.). *Demonstrations and political violence in America: New data for summer 2020*. Princeton: US Crisis Monitor.

Landers, E. (2018). Trump pardons ranchers whose case sparked Bundy takeover of Oregon refuge. CNN, 11 July. https://www.cnn.com/2018/07/10/politics/hammonds-trump-pardon/index.html. Accessed 11 October 2020.

Legg, C. (2018). 'The Solution to Poor Opinions Is More Opinions': Peircean Pragmatist Tactics for the Epistemic Long Game. In M. A. Peters, S. Rider, M. Hyvönen, & T. Besley (Eds.), *Post-Truth, fake news viral modernity & higher education* (pp. 43–58). Singapore: Springer. https://doi.org/10.1007/978-981-10-8013-5_4.

Li, J. (2017). Educational Policy Development in China for the 21st Century: Rationality and Challenges in a Globalizing Age. *Chinese Education & Society, 50*(3), 133–141. https://doi.org/10.1080/10611932.2017.1330992.

Lithwick, D. (2020). We've neglected the freedom of assembly for years before Portland. Slate Magazine, 29 July. https://slate.com/news-and-politics/2020/07/freedom-of-assembly-neglected-before-portland.html. Accessed 16 October 2020.

Lutz, E. (2020). The Trump administration is deploying "Secret Police" against protesters in Portland. Vanity Fair, 17 July. https://www.vanityfair.com/news/2020/07/trump-administration-deploying-secret-police-against-protesters-in-portland. Accessed 16 October 2020.

Mackenzie, A., & Bhatt, I. (2019). Opposing the Power of Lies, Bullshit and Fake News: the Value of Truth. *Postdigital Science and Education, 2*(1), 217–232. https://doi.org/10.1007/s42438-019-00087-2.

Maraj, L. M., Prasad, P., & Roundtree, S. V. (2018). #BlackLivesMatter: pasts, presents, and futures. *Prose Studies, 40*(1–2), 1–14. https://doi.org/10.1080/01440357.2019.1668638.

Marginson, S., & Rhoades, G. (2002). Beyond national states, markets, and systems of higher education: A glonacal agency heuristic. *Higher Education, 43*(3), 281–309. https://doi.org/10.1023/a:1014699605875.

Marshall, P. D. (2011). Newly Mediated media: Understanding the Changing Internet Landscape of the Media Industries. In M. Consalvo & C. Ess (Eds.), *The Handbook of Internet Studies* (pp. 406–423). West Sussex: Wiley-Blackwell.

Mautner, G. (2005). Time to get wired: Using web-based corpora in critical discourse analysis. *Discourse & Society, 16*(6), 809–828. https://doi.org/10.1177/0957926505056661.

Mumford, L. (1964). Authoritarian and Democratic Technics. *Technology and Culture, 5*(1), 1–9. https://doi.org/10.2307/3101118.

Murdock, J. (2020). Trump to go ahead with "law and order" protest amid D.C. mayor's ban on "mass gatherings". Newsweek, 10 October. https://www.newsweek.com/trump-law-order-protest-coronavirus-1538034. Accessed 16 October 2020.

O'Keeffe, A. (2006). *Investigating media Discourse*. New York: Routledge.

Ogan, C., Pennington, R., Venger, O., & Metz, D. (2018). Who drove the discourse? News coverage and policy framing of immigrants and refugees in the 2016 U.S. presidential election. *Communications, 43*(3), 357–378. https://doi.org/10.1515/commun-2018-0014.

Orellana, P. D., & Michelsen, N. (2019). Reactionary Internationalism: the philosophy of the New Right. *Review of International Studies, 45*(5), 748–767. https://doi.org/10.1017/s0260210519000159.

Otero, V. (2019). Ad Fontes media's first multi-analyst content analysis ratings project: White paper. Lafayette: Ad Fontes Media. https://www.adfontesmedia.com/white-paper-multi-analyst-ratings-project-august-2019/. Accessed 14 October 2020.

Panetta, G. (2020). Trump calls protesters who carried guns into the Michigan Capitol 'very good people' and says the governor should 'make a deal' with them. Business Insider, 1 May. https://www.businessinsider.com/trump-protestors-with-guns-in-michigan-capitol-are-very-good-people-2020-5. Accessed 14 October 2020.

Peters, M. A., Hollings, S., Green, B., & Ogunniran, M. O. (2020). The WHO, the global governance of health and pandemic politics. *Educational Philosophy and Theory.* https://doi.org/10.1080/00131857.2020.1806187.

Petersen, J. (2020). Trump's crackdown in Portland is an attack on free speech. The Washington Post, 22 July. https://www.washingtonpost.com/outlook/2020/07/22/trumps-crackdown-portland-is-an-attack-free-speech/. Accessed 17 September 2020.

Pettit, P. (2012). Legitimacy and Justice in Republican Perspective. *Current Legal Problems, 65*(1), 59–82. https://doi.org/10.1093/clp/cus016.

Pollak, J. B. (2020). Data: 48 of America's 50 largest cities hit by Black lives matter riots. Breitbart, 6 September. https://www.breitbart.com/politics/2020/09/06/data-48-of-americas-50-largest-cities-hit-by-black-lives-matter-riots/. Accessed 16 October 2020.

Price, Z. (2018). Our imperiled Absolutist First Amendment. *University of Pennsylvania Journal of Constitutional Law, 20*(4), 817–844.

Rehg, W., & Habermas, J. (1996). Translator's Introduction. In *Between facts and norms: Contributions to a discourse theory of law and democracy* (pp. ix-xxxvii). Cambridge, MA: The MIT Press.

Schneider, F. (2018). *China's digital nationalism.* New York: Oxford University Press.

Staats, J. L. (2004). Habermas and Democratic Theory: The Threat to Democracy of Unchecked Corporate Power. *Political Research Quarterly, 57*(4), 585. https://doi.org/10.2307/3219820.

Svrluga, S. (2019). Trump signs executive order on free speech on college campuses. The Washington Post, 22 March. https://www.washingtonpost.com/education/2019/03/21/trump-expected-sign-executive-order-free-speech/. Accessed 14 September 2020.

Szetela, A. (2019). Black Lives Matter at five: limits and possibilities. *Ethnic and Racial Studies, 43*(8), 1358–1383. https://doi.org/10.1080/01419870.2019.1638955.

The White House (2020a). Executive Order on Preventing Online Censorship. Washington, DC: The White House. https://www.whitehouse.gov/presidential-actions/executive-order-preventing-online-censorship/. Accessed 14 September 2020.

The White House. (2020b). Remarks by President Trump at South Dakota's 2020 mount rushmore Fireworks celebration. Washington, DC: The White House. 4 July. https://www.whitehouse.gov/briefings-statements/remarks-president-trump-south-dakotas-2020-mount-rushmore-fireworks-celebration-keystone-south-dakota/. Accessed 16 October 2020.

The White House (2020c). *E*xecutive Order on Protecting American Monuments, memorials, and statues and combating recent criminal violence. Washington, DC: The White House. 26 June. https://www.whitehouse.gov/presidential-actions/executive-order-protecting-american-monuments-memorials-statues-combating-recent-criminal-violence/. Accessed 16 October 2020.

Thomas, E., & Phelps, J. (2020). Trump says federal law enforcement, National Guard on way to site of violent protests in Wisconsin. ABC News, 27 August. https://abcnews.go.com/Politics/trump-federal-law-enforcement-national-guard-site-violent/story?id=72624520. Accessed 16 October 2020.

Trump, D. J. (2020). Black economic empowerment. Make America great again [Transcript], 25 September. Georgia: Atlanta. https://www.rev.com/blog/transcripts/donald-trump-black-economic-empowerment-speech-transcript-september-25. Accessed 15 October 2020.

United Nations (2020). UN treaty body database. https://tbinternet.ohchr.org/_layouts/15/treatybodyexternal/Download.aspx?symbolno=CCPR%2fC%2fGC%2f37&Lang=en. Accessed 17 September 2020.

van Dijk, T. A. (2014). Discourse, cognition, society. In J. Angermuller, D. Maingueneau, & R. Wodak (Eds.), *The Discourse Studies Reader: Main currents in theory and analysis* (pp. 388–399). Amsterdam: John Benjamins Publishing Company.

Vladeck, S. (2020). Are the Trump administration's actions in Portland legal? Are they constitutional? The Washington Post, 24 July. https://www.washingtonpost.com/politics/2020/07/25/are-trump-administrations-actions-portland-legal-are-they-constitutional/. Accessed 14 September 2020.

Ward, L. (2016). Civil Religion, Civic Republicanism, and Enlightenment in Rousseau. In G. C. Kellow & N. Leddy (Eds.), *Ancient Lessons for Global Politics* (pp. 246–268). Toronto: University of Toronto Press.

West, D. M. (2017). How to combat fake news and disinformation. Brookings, 18 December. https://www.brookings.edu/research/how-to-combat-fake-news-and-disinformation/. Accessed 15 October 2020.

Williams, D. C. (1994). European and U.S. Perspectives on Civic Republicanism. *Indiana Journal of Global Legal Studies, 2*(1), 71–77.

Winston, A. (2014). Right to peaceful assembly: United States. Law Library of Congress, 1 October. https://www.loc.gov/law/help/peaceful-assembly/us.php. Accessed 17 September 2020.

Chapter 7
A Project of Mourning: Attuning to the Impact of 'Anthropocentric-Noise Disorder' on Non-Human Kin

Victoria O'Sullivan

Introduction

> Reports state the sound of the dog hitting the car woke neighbours up as it sounded like a tyre explosion. They then found the dog lying dead on the ground with its blood staining the bricks. (NZ Herald 2020)

During the pandemic, transparent, synthetic surfaces (windows, camera lenses, and computer screens) provided the medium to marvel at animals 'reclaiming' exterior spaces, but also to jettison them from interior ones. Shortly after the World Health Organisation (WHO) declared a global health emergency in early February 2020, rumours that cats and dogs can spread the virus began to circulate, resulting in people throwing pets from apartment windows (NZ Herald 2020; Seven News 2020), dumping them on streets (Campbell 2020), and euthanising them at veterinary clinics (Berry 2020). The rumour likely emerged due to a media outlet 'tweaking' the words of a scientist who had appeared on a television network and then posting the modified version on the social-media platform 'Weibo' (NZ Herald 2020). Instead of saying that cats and dogs who had been in contact with Covid-19-positive patients should be quarantined, it was reported that they could spread the virus. It is difficult to dignify the death of the subject of the newspaper excerpt above (which another news-paper article identifies as a French Bulldog) with an exact date of death as the articles reporting the event do not provide this level of detail, only those of a more visceral nature concerning the event's

V. O'Sullivan (✉)
School of Critical Studies, Faculty of Education and Social Work, The University of Auckland, Auckland, New Zealand
e-mail: v.osullivan@auckland.ac.nz

A. MacKenzie et al. (eds.), *The Epistemology of Deceit in a Postdigital Era*, Postdigital Science and Education,
https://doi.org/10.1007/978-3-030-72154-1_7

aftermath—details we wouldn't be given if this were a human death—and that it took place at 4 am (NZ Herald 2020; Seven News 2020).[1]

The pandemic has heralded into existence instances of non-human animals becoming subjects of 'fake news'. Examples come in the form of erroneous conclusions they can spread the virus and viral micro-length videos that show them in the throes of continually 'reclaiming' space (this is not to say that individual animals are represented in a tautological mode of 'continually' reclaiming space; rather the sheer quantity of these stories creates a repetition of this narrative). These examples point to seemingly trivial, sometimes fleeting and insubstantial practices that in the first example, at least, are capable of producing dire consequences for non-human animals. This chapter thus attunes itself to mediated practices of information dissemination constitutive of 'information disorder', as they have emerged during the pandemic and pertain to non-human animals. How do these practices manifest and interact, and what ways of thinking and outcomes do they preclude and produce?

In attuning itself accordingly, this chapter considers the utility of an existing framework to describe information disorder when non-human animals are the

[1]However, it would be unfair to attribute these violent events exclusively to the singular event involving the 'tweaking' of information. A poster produced by the WHO, on how to 'protect yourself and others from getting sick', which, according to a 'reverse-image search' website, first appeared online on 20 January 2020 (not long before the French Bulldog was thrown from an apartment window) potentially sends mixed messages concerning the epidemiological role of companion animals in virus transmission, or at least leaves things wide open for interpretation. See https://www.who.int/images/default-source/health-topics/coronavirus/2handwash.tmb-549v.png?sfvrsn=cf9e093e_1c (accessed 20 January 2020). I have assumed that the poster is intended to provide Covid-19 health advice, although it is not possible to definitively associate it with the virus: unlike other WHO coronavirus-related posters, it does not include obvious phrases/words like '#coronavirus', but the URL to retrieve the image includes this word (additionally, I happened to stumble upon the poster in a public bathroom a month or so before New Zealand went into its first lockdown, i.e., the poster appeared contemporaneously with the virus). Whilst hygiene information contained in the poster is not 'incorrect' (it is indeed sensible to wash one's hands after handling animal waste to avoid getting sick, as advised in one bullet-point), if the poster intended to provide Covid-19 health advice, then the brevity of information in this bullet-point, and the lack of an obvious connection between the poster and the virus, might contribute to an ecology of information practices that generates ambiguity and leads people to conclude that animals might spread the virus. The events propelled by the event of information 'tweaking' prompted the WHO to produce another poster for its suite of 'myth-busting' posters that aim to dispel myths concerning how the virus can be contracted and treated. See https://www.who.int/images/default-source/health-topics/coronavirus/myth-busters/mythbuster-1.png (accessed 20 January 2020). Thus, a poster that aims to counter extreme violence towards non-human animals exists alongside ones aiming to counter beliefs that adding hot peppers to meals and taking hot baths are viable treatment methods. But other than this, the poster's minimal information on the topic of non-human animals and coronavirus, and quick shift to more generalised hygiene practices that humans should observe when engaging with animals seems to provide an underwhelming response to the violence engendered by beliefs that animals (in this instance, pets) might spread the virus. More thoughtful and complex information exists on the Centre for Disease Control and Prevention (CDC) website, which, amongst other topics, discusses how pets might be protected from the risks that humans infected with coronavirus may present to them. See https://www.cdc.gov/coronavirus/2019-ncov/daily-life-coping/pets.html (accessed 20 January 2020).

subject. Wardle and Derakhshan (2017: 5) argue that the term 'fake news', which has been co-opted by politicians to describe news coverage they find disagreeable and wish to clamp down on, is 'woefully inadequate to describe the complex phenomenon of fake news'. They propose an alternative framework for examining information disorder — one that the United Nations Educational, Scientific, and Cultural Organisation has recently used in their policy brief, 'Disinfodemic: Deciphering Covid-19 Disinformation' (UNESCO 2020). Wardle and Derakhshan's (2017) framework proposes three information types, no doubt familiar to readers, constitutive of information disorder. *Misinformation* and *disinformation* involve false information; however, the intent of the agent disseminating it differs: misinformation is shared without harm intended, contrary to the motivation behind the sharing of disinformation. *Malinformation*, 'genuine' information that is shared to cause damage 'often by moving information designed to stay private into the public sphere', is the third (2017: 5). Wardle and Derakhshan's (2017) conceptualisation seems much about information's 'presence', perhaps because it is easier to examine the 'truthfulness' of information that appears to us in the 'positive' and attach its appearance to agentic humans. I therefore argue that the model, which tends to be applied to scrutinise information ecologies where human interests only are at stake, is human-centric. As an analytical tool, its version of 'truth' seems to privilege a reality that appears to us in the positive (as that which is identifiable, fathomable and knowable), and information that demands our attention and response, not that which is altogether missing, absent, and excluded.

In the context of the pandemic, identifying instances of mis- and dis-information where non-human animals are the subject has been a 'hit and miss' affair that has led me to a smattering of disparate, sometimes seemingly trifling practices and episodes, which are nonetheless capable of producing dire consequences for non-human animals. Three instances I have identified include the previously mentioned episode involving the 'tweaking' of information. In this instance, posters produced by an organisation not typically associated with contributing to an information ecology that generates uncertainty and ambiguity possibly interacted with this fleeting moment of inaccuracy to produce unwarranted alarm. The second involves the viral, sometimes 'fake', videos and images of animals 'reclaiming' space during lockdown and the uplifting and amplification of this content by news agencies, resulting in frequently articulated conclusions of 'nature's' infinite and immediate capacity to heal (Searle and Turnbull 2020; Taylor and Fraser 2020a).[2] The third instance is a

[2] After having spent much time thinking about these visual artefacts, I have concluded that another harm may be the thought that is produced via a combination of their sheer quantity, micro-length, and representationalism. By 'representationalism', I mean that as a result of their abundance, the video-clips repeatedly show non-human animals in the act of performing, and only performing, the act which humans have assigned significance to. When watching, there is no need to wait for this footage, as it is all we are presented with: everything in the footage is significant, nothing is insignificant, and we do not have to attend (watch and wait) with patience. The experience of viewing these videos might be a very different experience to that produced by viewing three other screen-based visual artefacts that have emerged in the context of the pandemic, where the significant 'moment' is not immediately discernible. These artefacts are the data that is generated by small

more singular event involving the re-purposing of a video supposedly showing the removal of a 'Chrysanthemum' bat infestation from a rooftop in Wuhan (the species of bat scientists believe from which the virus originated). The video, which was uploaded to Facebook and went viral, may facilitate a reduced sense of human responsibility for the evolution of the virus by suggesting that it is a result of (and may be exacerbated by) 'out-of-control' nature (O'Sullivan 2020b). It was, in fact, filmed by a roofing company in Florida, almost a decade ago, and shows the removal of Mexican Fruit Bats—one of the other 1400 species of bat that are in existence (Kaur 2020).

But what of information's altogether omission: its absence? Concerning ourselves with information's absence might prompt us to think more carefully, and therefore caringly, about more-than-human perspectives and experiences. Hence, for example, it is not possible, or indeed relevant, to pinpoint precisely where and when political leaders fail to acknowledge how the virus instantiates the prevailing condition that is the exploitation of non-human animals because the failure to do so is a persistent, distributed, and generalised condition, one that is not so much about *mis-* or *dis*-information—a model that is premised on the truthfulness of information that is presented to us in the positive, as much as it is about its altogether omission. I argue that mediated responses to the disappearance of Gulf Livestock 1 (GL1), a tragedy I will discuss shortly, provide another example where information concerning the interests, experiences, and perspectives of the animal is omitted, and like practices of mis- and dis-information, that the practices that produce this omission are also constitutive of untruthfulness.

Hence, the consequences of Covid-19 on non-human animals manifest in the immediate present, in all their visceral materiality, but may also be diffuse and long range in nature. The lack of public reflection, stimulated by political leaders and/or the media, on the exploitative human-animal relationships involved in the virus's evolution may produce such longer-range consequences. Arguably, such invisibilsation renders links between everyday practices and a way of thinking that led to the virus unable to be drawn so that when lockdowns began to be lifted, the symbolic gesture signalling the 're-opening' of the economy came to be the rush to fast-food outlets and the eating of the flesh of another (Kirkness 2020). It is worth noting, too, that whilst the pandemic has given rise to mediated practices of information dissemination that not only obfuscate but also produce animal trauma, it has also

cameras that have been attached to animals by scientists either before or during lockdowns (see the 'Covid-19 bio-logging initiative', https://www.bio-logging.net, accessed 20 January 2020); the collection of 10-min length videos showing views through domestic windows, as recorded by people in lockdown (see https://www.window-swap.com, accessed 20 January 2020); and the long-take footage produced by an underwater camera that has been submerged in the depths of the ocean (see https://www.abc.net.au/news/2020-05-06/rv-falkor-on-research-expedition-with-no-scientists-on-board/12215962, accessed 20 January 2020). The viewing experience of these three artefacts might be characterised by affects additional to the delight that people appeared to experience when viewing the videos of animals 'reclaiming' space. Other affects may include boredom due to extended periods where nothing in particular happens—a result of the non-human nature of the recording resulting in the camera training itself on apparently insignificant, mundane detail.

created spaces for future 'mechanisms of obscurity' to materialise. Laws and policies, or 'ag-gag' bills (Bittman 2011), which threaten to 'deepen, instead of loosening, humans' grip on animals and the harmful ways we treat them', have been passed whilst the world has been distracted by anthropocentric concerns: the threat to human health that the virus poses (Oliver 2020). The passing of 'Bill 156', now known as the 'Security from Trespass and Protecting Food Safety Act 2020', by the Government of Ontario on 18 June 2020 will make it difficult for activists and journalists to reveal harms committed to animals and humans in the context of factory farming. The Bill was passed to supposedly 'protect Ontario's farms and farm animals from trespassers', including would-be whistle-blowers, and 'protect contamination' of the food supply' (Security from Trespass and Protecting Food Safety Act 2020). Therefore, the penning of a legal artefact will reinforce mediated omissions of animal perspectives, facilitating information practices that are productive of non-truthfulness, or truth's incompleteness, as it pertains to them.

Since the animal appears to be the disappeared other of politics and media, rather than exclusively use concepts like deceit, lies, and *mis-* and *dis-*information to describe practices of information dissemination where the animal is already absent and excluded (indeed, was likely never there in the first place), I am interested in patterns of omission that obscure the interests of animals and obfuscate their trauma—rendering it unintelligible. The concepts I am interested in are *omission*, *obscuration*, *obfuscation,* and *eschewal*—concepts that describe the outcomes of what I term a type of 'anthropocentric-noise disorder'. As a concept, anthropocentric-noise disorder draws attention to the fact that the privileging of human interests in our visual and auditory practices of information dissemination is also constitutive of an information disorder. The concept also quite obviously re-inscribes humans—subjects that are otherwise absent in terms like 'information disorder' (Wardle and Derakhshan 2017), 'disinfodemic', 'viral disinformation' (UNESCO 2020), and 'massive infodemic' (WHO 2020)—as being responsible for the cultivation of this disorder.

Following a line of thought offered by fake news discourse (and the word 'truth', a word that represents the antithesis of fake news, and is readily associated with transparency and thus visuality), humans' 'synthetic encounters' with non-human animals 'reclaiming' space during lockdowns (i.e., through windows, screens or camera lenses), and the disappearance of GL1 during Typhoon Maysak, a tragedy that took place during the pandemic, these words are sensorially, atmospherically, visually, and materially inflected. For instance, the word 'obfuscate' has a Latin derivation: 'ob' means 'in front of, before', and 'fuscare' means 'to make dark'. Fuscare comes from 'fuscus', meaning 'dark', which is related to the word 'dusk'—a liminal spacetime, which condenses transitions to do with light, temperature, sound, smell, and any other sense that may be intelligible to animals, but perhaps not to humans, into comparatively shorter, more accelerated chunks of time than that comprising day and night. Dawn and dusk happen to be time intervals when many species become active. We were reminded of this during the pandemic when we sensed the heightened presence of other animals, reporting an intensification of bird song, for instance. However, like the fish in the Venetian canals that people also reported noticing during lockdown, which were there all along, only invisible due to the level of visual and sonic 'noise' in the water (as created by boat engines making the water murky, and likely sonically inhospitable), the bird song may have been present all along, albeit—like the animal perspectives discussed in this chapter—channelled out and obscured by anthropocentric noise. To attend to the outcomes of anthropocentric-noise disorder (as something that makes its presence felt visually and sonically, materially, and discursively), I have therefore drawn on a list of words that come via non-human phenomena, such as light and water, and in the instance of 'obfuscation', via human encounters with non-human animals during the pandemic. In doing so, a sort of 'right of reply' to be taken up by animals emerges—one that manifests endogenous to the context of the production of a visual archive of animals allegedly reclaiming space.

I now wish to orient this introduction to the specific context that this chapter is focused on—the mediated eschewal of information pertaining to the disappearance of GL1. Beirne (2014: 49) argues that slaughterhouses have 'become all but invisible, tending to be built far from human populations, at sites that are both unseen and unknown'. However, this movement towards the invisible is also true of sites and spacetime zones of animal exploitation that are more liminal, less-anchored, than that represented by the 'bricks and mortar' of the slaughterhouse. The terrestrial transportation of farmed animals kept in holding pens until a suspension on live-export is lifted, to the port where a vessel waiting to be loaded with the animals is moored, is an apt expression of the space-time-site liminality of the live-export trade and its movement towards the invisible. In November 2020, this terrestrial, soon-to-be-oceanic transportation, took place 'under cover of darkness', when the 'Ocean Drover' (the world's largest 'livestock' vessel) was loaded with animals before departing from 'PrimePort Timaru' (Timaru Port) in Aotearoa New Zealand (Taunton 2020). This event, which was New Zealand's second live-export shipment after the GL1 tragedy, exists outside of the archive; outside of time: the ship's visit is not recorded on a schedule published on the port's website, where the arrival and departure times of other ships are included, nor is the visit of another livestock vessel, the 'Ocean Swagman', which arrived in the same port, 4 days later. The port allows 'customers' (whoever they are: they are not easy to identify) who do not want 'their movements to be on a shipping website' to be left off the schedule (see Mohanlall 2019). But in the context of live-export, omissions from shipping schedules instantiate just one way in which the animal is omitted (from the archive and our knowledge producing practices).[3] In the section that follows, I look further at how information practices relating to live-export, and to the GL1 tragedy, in particular, render the animal invisible and, that which concerns them, omitted.

[3] Strategies of 'synthetic activism', undertaken to produce and populate a different archive, coexisted with the act of writing this chapter. These strategies involved tracking livestock vessels' movements via an app that tracks ships via satellite and articulating propositions for possibly impossible artworks. I locate one such proposition literally in the margins, in the footnotes of this chapter (see f/n 11).

Gulf Livestock 1 and the Informatic Eschewal of Non-Human Animal Trauma

> In the future, most products, including plants and domestic animals, will probably be tagged with microchips which will supply, in real time, information as to their state (the wear and tear of materials, the maturing of plants, the health of animals, the obsolescence of foodstuffs and medicines), their localisation (Global Positioning System (GPS) or satellite surveillance devices) and movements (tagging of migrating birds, traceability of products, etc.). We sense, here, the danger that such a mechanism might be applied increasingly to human beings, a development which could, in parallel with the rise of security systems, open a new chapter: that of global surveillance systems. (UNESCO 2005: 48)

> We saw that money was no concern if it meant that experts could locate the missing Malaysian flight [MH370]; this is sold as a humanitarian concern, but one that is never extended to melting icebergs or collapsing ecosystems. (Turpin in Franke and Turpin 2015: 150)

At the intersection of science, technology, nature, and now zoonoses and pandemic, our capitalist condition refuses nature the 'right to opacity' that poet and philosopher Edouard Glissant argues that on behalf of everyone, we must clamour for (Glissant 1997: 194). Instead, we demand nature's complete visibility, knowability, and availability. Blas uses the term 'informatic opacity' to refer to aesthetic strategies that resist global surveillance, capture technologies and biometric profiling, and argues that Glissant's demand for opacity 'refuses a logic of total transparency and rationality, disrupting the transformation of subjects into categorisable objects of Western knowledge' (Blas 2018: 198). For Glissant, 'opacity is an unknowability—and, hence, a poetics.... [which] must be defended in order for any radically democratic project to succeed,'; it is also 'fundamentally aesthetic' (Blas 2016: 149–150).

I do not need to look far to identify some of the ways in which we attempt to deny nature the right to opacity; in fact, I only need to refer to textual sources endogenous to the research event that is the writing of this chapter. One of these sources happens to be UNESCO's policy brief: 'Disinfodemic: Deciphering Covid-19 Disinformation', which warns us that the 'disinfodemic', with its turn away from 'verifiable, reliable information, such as that produced in science and professional journalism', poses a threat to the formation of 'knowledge societies' (2020: 3). Knowledge societies is a concept referred to by UNESCO (2005), and some of the future (now current?) ways society might deny animals the right to opacity, in the context of a knowledge society, is pointed to in a paragraph of this 'survey' type publication (see quote above). Although UNESCO (2005: 48) cautions us on the risks posed by surveillance technology, asking 'are our societies going to be societies of technological surveillance? In the name of openness and the free circulation of information and knowledge, should knowledge societies always lead to confusion between knowledge for all and knowledge on all? Is there not a right *not* to know?', the potential incursion of such technology into animal bodies is not similarly troubled.[4]

Though UNESCO (2005) refers to a future that *could* be today, we can also look to a more actualised present for examples of how we endeavour to deny nature the right to opacity (the right to hide from our gaze and resist our desire to extract knowledge). In the context of the pandemic, two very different examples come to mind. In the first, ocean floor mapping continues unabated, even with coronavirus restrictions in place. In May 2020, the Schmidt Ocean Institute research vessel, 'Falkor', surveyed the depths of the Queensland Plateau in the remote Coral Sea Marine Park, with only crew and technicians on board (typically there might also be 10–15 scientists). On this month-long expedition, SuBastian, a camera-equipped remotely operated vehicle (ROV), recorded hours of seafloor footage. This footage, which included overlays of commentary from scientists at home across Australia, was live-streamed via YouTube (Shorey and Kim 2020). It is plausible to argue that the mapping of the ocean floor and other areas imperilled by human activity may provide a baseline from which to compare future deterioration. Additionally, Troon (2020) argues that the type of long-take footage produced by underwater cameras may provoke an ethic of attentiveness and care, fostering attunement to ecological degradation. I agree with both of these arguments, but perhaps we also need to consider the intersubject (human-nature) ethics involved during the actual recording of the footage, as well as the absurdity that is the contrast between what is possible to technologically perform in one context, but impossible to perform, or even consider performing, in another (such as in the search for GL1).

In the second example, an aquarium in Tokyo asked people to FaceTime their 'lonely' spotted garden eels who were supposedly missing humans so much during lockdown that they became 'shy', burying under the sand when staff walked by (Elliot 2020). The fact that a brief respite from the human-gaze may have prompted the eels to realise just how over-exposed they are to it—installed as they are in a small tank that provides humans 360° views of them, whilst listening to hotel-lobby style music—was not considered (O'Sullivan 2020a).

If we were to 'image' humans' relationship to animals according to a visual-register, on the one hand, we demand non-opacity, or absolute visibility, when we wish to extract from nature, or know nature absolutely. On the other hand, however, we are content with opacity at the point of finitude (death), when no more needs to be known, or can be extracted—and recent debates about cameras onboard fishing

[4] If the future outlined by UNESCO (2005) is representative of the 'knowledge society' (a concept summoned back into existence by UNESCO [2020]), the creation of which is threatened by the existence of the disinfodemic, might such a society be so desirable given that incursions into animal bodies to facilitate knowledge production represents the type of extractivist thinking that has brought us to this moment in the Anthropocene, and to the immediate pandemic situation we find ourselves occupying? Or, might UNESCO's commitment to iconic discursive-concepts like the 'knowledge society' need to be re-thought? This question is all the more pertinent given that UNESCO is an educational organisation that creates environmental education (EE) policy, such as education for sustainable development (ESD), the discourse of which often espouses an interest in more ethical human-environment relationships.

vessels drift into this terrain (Manch 2020). Perhaps the disappearance of Gulf Livestock 1(GL1), described as 'one of the greatest maritime disasters of recent years', also drifts into this terrain (Buitendijk 2020).[5] The ship left port on 14 August, during the country's second lockdown, when only local people could travel to the port to protest or 'bear witness' to the existence of otherwise invisible lives and the trauma such lives experience.[6] It was scheduled to arrive in the Port of Jingtang, Tangshan, China, on 3 September, but disappeared one-hundred nautical miles west of Amami Ōshima Island, southwest Japan, the day prior, almost three weeks after leaving New Zealand. Onboard were 43 crew (39 Filipinos, two New Zealanders, and two Australians) and 5867 cows, a figure that is often 'rounded-up' to 5800 (cf ODT 2020). Search and rescue attempts were called off after 8 days. Just 5 days after GL1 commenced its ill-fated journey, another livestock vessel, the 'Yangtze Harmony', left Port Taranaki (New Zealand) carrying 5400 cows, whilst the 'Dareen' left Napier Port (New Zealand) 11 days later, carrying 7300 cows.

Our acceptance, indeed cultivation, of opacity at the point of finitude comes into sharp relief when I try to imagine what inevitably ends up impossible: the conjuring of the chaos taking place, likely in the dark (the ship sent a distress signal at 1.40 am Japan Standard Time), as Typhoon Maysak bore down on GL1, somewhere in the Northwestern Pacific Ocean. There exists scant visual or other sensorial record of the event to help do this: an Internet image search yields few images, and just one of the animal toll exacted (an image of a dead cow floating in the water).[7] But surely more than one of the 5867 bodies would have drifted into the path of search and rescue teams and their cameras? What has prevented other images from finding their way online? The image of a cow, images of the orange canopy of a life-raft, and a short video that begins with the arresting footage of the night-time rescue of Eduardo

[5] The struck-out words are GL1's previous names before it became a livestock vessel. The names are written in this way to draw attention to conjecture surrounding the sea-worthiness of livestock vessels that were originally built as container ships, and often for short rather than deep-sea routes (Kevany 2020). It is also to draw attention to the apparent ease at which ships with previous functions are re-commissioned as live-export ships. Like the screen-shots included in this chapter (Fig. 7.1), which record moments in journeys made by livestock vessels, the struck-out text is an expression of an aesthetic the logic of which is to work backwards. This aesthetic enacts a response-ability to the past in that it resists animal trauma being overwritten and rendered invisible.

[6] Bearing witness may involve documenting conditions, providing water to de-hydrated animals, talking to and touching animals in a bid to offer comfort, and protesting with placards. In New Zealand, it is a nascent mode of protest / way to 'attend' to others (see https://www.rnz.co.nz/national/programmes/saturday/audio/2018777910/the-singing-vegan-animal-welfare-activist-sandra-kyle, accessed 20 January 2020). However, witnessing is more established elsewhere (see Scott-Reid [2020] and www.thesavemovement.org, accessed 20 January 2020).

[7] See https://www.nytimes.com/2020/09/04/world/asia/cattle-ship-capsized.html (accessed 20 January 2020). Although I have only been able to retrieve one image from the Internet of the animal toll exacted, photographs of cows on board the ship in 2019 can be seen here: https://www.flickr.com/photos/136647212@N08/albums/72157715834521802 (accessed 20 January 2020).

Sareno, the ship's chief officer, are about the sum of what I can locate online.[8] The video includes fragments of conversation between Sareno and the rescuers, all of whom wear masks to protect each other from the virus. From the viewer's point of view (and perhaps that of Sareno and rescuers), the conversation competes with the engine's racket, giving a feel for what it must be like for animals on board a ship, so far removed from earth and soil.

Contrary to Blas's concerns regarding the deployment of surveillance technology to marginalise human others, of the all-knowing nature of technology, and UNESCO's (2005) forecasting of how future technology may be used to track the health, localisation, and movements of animals, in this instance, technology fails to see, or perhaps even endeavour to see, the animal (to find the lost ship and document and archive lost animal lives). Curiously, 'alt-text' frequently does not see the animal either, or at least, not when they are spent; when there is nothing left to be extracted.[9] Or perhaps it *does* see animals but does so as inadequately as my attempt to imagine the chaos of the event: the description alt-text provides for the lone cow is 'a picture containing water, mammal, outdoor, blue'.

Prompted by the inadequacy of the existing visual archive documenting the loss of GL1, which would otherwise help imagine the event that took place, indeed to *mark it* as an event *that took place,* I purchase 'Marine Tracker', a $5.00 app that tracks ships via satellite. I buy the app as I want to find out what kind of visual information, if any, such an app can produce of a vessel that has vanished. However, since the live-export of 5867 cows only came to my attention *after* the ship carrying them vanished, on now learning that another vessel, the 'Yangtze Fortune', is about to leave Portland, Australia, to pick-up a shipment of cows from Napier Port (the first after a brief suspension, imposed by the New Zealand government after the loss of GL1, has been lifted), I realise I need to attend much more closely to the ethical problem that is live-export.[10] I therefore also purchase the app to track the Yangtze Fortune as it heads to New Zealand and once it is 'loaded' and on its way to the next

[8] See https://www.nytimes.com/2020/09/04/world/asia/cattle-ship-capsized.html (accessed 20 January 2020).

[9] Alt text is written copy that serves three purposes. It appears in place of an image on a website, in case the image does not load, allows search engines to crawl and rank websites when Internet users search for content, and helps screen-reading tools to describe images to readers with visual impairment (although perhaps not especially well).

[10] In fact, the ethical problem of live-export was only dimly present in my mind prior to the disappearance of GL1, hence also the exportation of live animals on the Yangtze Harmony, as well as the Dareen, just days after GL1 left New Zealand, also went under my radar. But whilst tracking the movement of the Yangtze Fortune, I became aware that another two ships were ploughing their way to New Zealand: the 'Ocean Drover' and 'Ocean Swagman'. That I only become aware of this whilst the ships were already in transit, and via an email from the organisation Save Animals from Exploitation (SAFE), requesting supporter action, is suggestive of a certain level of concealment of live-export practices in Aotearoa. As mentioned in the introduction, the visits by these two boats were not listed on PrimePort Timaru's website, something that Appelbe argues is representative of a more recent development in the country's practice of live-export (see Mohanlall 2019). On another note, the name 'Ocean Drover' says much about the industry's claim to farmed animal bodies; that the meat-industrial complex must forge ahead; must not be interrupted by something

port. This 'tracking' is a type of micro/virtual protest, or mode of bearing witness, which involves virtually following a livestock vessel, as protesters sometimes do when following a truck. However, it is also a way to mourn GL1's disappearance, via a type of equivalency. To resist the invisibility of practices concerning the animal-industrial complex (as instantiated by the inadequacy of the image-archive documenting the animal toll exacted by the disappearance of GL1), I record this tracking via screenshots (see Fig. 7.1).[11]

However, mourning via an app-assisted imaging/imagining of GL1's disappearance is rendered difficult because the slower speed of ships, as compared to planes, means that the app represents movement in a way that is less visually dynamic than that offered by equivalent 'flight radar' apps, thus thwarting my attempt to follow the vessels. On the app, each ship is represented by an arrow-type shape, whose progress through the water is only discernible when the user looks away from the screen and back again (if the fragmentary nature of everyday life does not make it challenging to remember to do so). In this sense, the app facilitates our 'turn away' from the event, instantiating the 'unprecedented looking away' that Haraway argues is the optic characteristic of our time:

> What is it to surrender the capacity to think? These times called the Anthropocene are times of multispecies, including human, urgency: of great mass death and extinction; of onrushing disasters, whose unpredictable specificities are foolishly taken as unknowability itself; of refusing to know and to cultivate the capacity of response-ability; of refusing to be present in and to onrushing catastrophe in time; of unprecedented looking away. (Haraway 2016: 35)

Despite the sophistication of maritime technology, which enables an ROV to map the ocean floor's depths during a pandemic, we have no trace of GL1 and are clueless about what happened to it. Whilst this is also true of the disappearance of Malaysian Airways flight MH370, on 8 March 2014, after it is believed to have

---

as alien to them as the ocean (drover is an Australian settler term for a person who moves animals over long distances, usually for 'market').

[11] 'HEAP', the title of a possibly impossible artwork herewith proposed, seeks to engage an aesthetic, ethic, and politic concerned with opacity, transparency, and light. A laser-cutting machine will be commissioned to write hashtags such as #bringthemhome, #findmymate, #alleyesonNZ, and #banliveexportNZ onto 5867 'ear-tags' (which will be re-cycled from cows that once had them pinned to their ears). The tags will then be assembled into a heap, and an industrial-strength torch will continually pass over it to project shadows of the jumbled-up phrases. Ideally, the ocean area where GL1 is thought to have sunk would 'host' the projection (the heap would therefore likely need to be smuggled onto a ship). This proposition will find its realisation when/if ship tracking apps have evolved to the extent that they can capture the kind of visual and temporally-specific information that the projection of these scattered phrases would represent. The artwork thus imagines entering into the data system of ship-tracking apps but generating an altogether different kind of information. The realisation of this artwork would also rely on torches being powerful enough and atmospheric conditions sufficiently conducive to allow at least some phrases, or even letters, to be visible on the water. Less ambitious — perhaps more realisable — would be the projection of the phrases (in the real or via pre-filmed footage) onto public and private surfaces. Such surfaces could include livestock vessels docked in New Zealand ports and buildings like 'Pastoral House' (the headquarters of New Zealand's Ministry for Primary Industries).

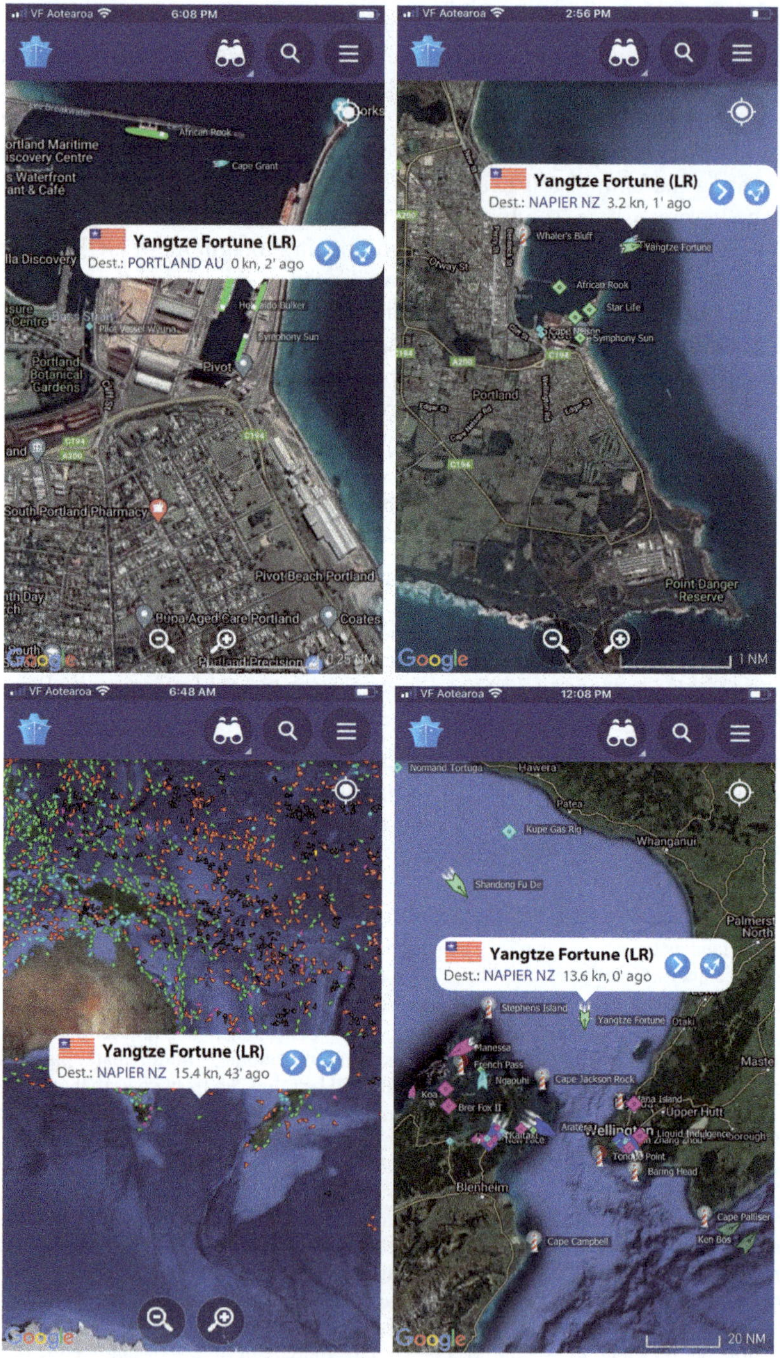

Fig. 7.1 The locations of the 'Yangtze Fortune', as it makes its way from Portland, Australia, to Napier Port, New Zealand, between 31 October 2020 and 6 November 2020, according to the app 'Marine Tracker'. Screenshots: Victoria O'Sullivan

crashed into the Southern Indian Ocean, efforts mobilised to locate each craft register as strikingly different. Bremner (2015) describes the search, one that Cetina (2009: 65) might characterise as unfolding as a 'synthetic situation' that 'invariably includes and may, in fact, be entirely constituted by, onscreen projections', accordingly: 'Looking for plane debris in the ocean began in outer space. It mobilised a vast array of satellites, floats, drifting buoys, data collection systems on ships, computer screens, imaging techniques, UN agencies and protocols, national agencies, and private companies' (Bremner 2015: 201).

According to Bremner, the search thus manifested as a 'distant and invisible operation made situationally present around the globe through an extended sensorium of remote-sensing and screen-based technologies' (2015: 199). However, the data produced by this scopic system 'did not merely presence the search', rather like the accumulative and exponential nature of social media 'dissemination structures' such as 'likes', 'shares', and 're-tweets' (Emmelheinz 2015: 136), it 'propelled … [the search] forward', giving it momentum (2015: 199). The argument is made tangible by Bremner's description of how amateur data analysts assisted the search:

> DigitalGlobe, the commercial US satellite operator, expanded its Tomnod crowdsourcing platform to engage the public in the search for the missing plane. Satellite imagery of the ocean's surface was uploaded to the Tomnod site; alerted on Facebook when new imagery was available, amateur data analysts were able to view it and tag potential signs of wreckage by dropping a pin onto a satellite map. A crowd-rank algorithm then identified overlaps in tagged locations before they were investigated by DigitalGlobe analysts. (Bremner 2015: 202)

According to Turpin, 'we have to wonder about the mental collateral damage', or 'psychotechnical vulnerability', that instances like the disappearance of MH370 produce (Turpin in Franke and Turpin 2015: 150). This vulnerability is a product of the fact that a plane, which is so 'carefully monitored and tracked', can go missing and is exacerbated by sophisticated technological systems' failure to locate it when it does. However, psychotechnical vulnerability is a pathology unlikely to emerge in the context of the search for GL1, which has unfolded seemingly outside of the scopic tracking-systems MH370 was/is enveloped within. Perhaps this is also true of the ship's actual disappearance (not just the search for it) depending on how closely livestock-vessels are monitored compared to commercial aircraft.

Whilst our lack of knowledge about what happened to MH370 and our inability to locate the aircraft is profoundly disturbing, it seems we are significantly less perturbed by the ship's disappearance and our cluelessness concerning what happened to it.[12] Like the single image of the animal toll exacted, the level of media attention to this tragedy has been underwhelming. According to Weekes (2020), disasters like the sinking of GL1 are a 'common but almost unreported occurrence worldwide'. Such ships, sometimes crewed by people paid as little as 90 cents per hour, 'disappear without the world paying much attention' (2020). Their

[12] Suffice to say that the loss of MH370 is profoundly disturbing for reasons greater than the fact that the search-mission 'undermines the aesthetic of a controlled system', and our confidence in systems we assume are failure-proof (Turpin in Franke and Turpin 2015: 15).

disappearance results in the deaths of 'inappropriate/d others' (Haraway 1992; Minh-ha 1986). Such deaths often go unnoticed; instead, they are 'de-individualised as a mass death which is understood as collateral damage in the service of "higher" purposes such as profit, progress, colonisation, civilisation, scientific breakthrough, ideological purity, neoliberal mass consumption etc.' (Radomska, Mehrabi, and Lykke 2020: 93). Perhaps we could add maintenance of the 'animal-industrial complex' to this list (Noske 1989; Twine 2012).

I sensed this lack of attention on social media, too: on Twitter, amid partisan debates concerning quarantining and mask-wearing, and the intersection of these debates with seemingly ever-increasing waves of Covid-19 mis- or dis-information, this multispecies tragedy, and its impact on humans, terrestrial, and marine animals, seemed to receive little attention and therefore generate little visibility (or vice versa). This lack of visibility is obviously problematic given that under regimes of 'communicative capitalism', it is how images and signs accumulate value and/or power (Emmelheinz 2015). Scrolling down to the first time that #GulfLivestock1 is used, after entering this hashtag into the search bar, does not take long (this hashtag is the one most obviously connected to the event, at least in the English-speaking world). A tweet including it was first posted on 19 September, more than 2 weeks after the ship disappeared. Other tweets that include the hashtag, mainly posted by friends and family of lost crew undertaking individualised search missions by scanning ocean satellite imagery, conjoin people to support efforts to crowdsource the costs of more official ones, but garner little attention, attracting few 'likes' and 'retweets'. These 'do-it-yourself' style missions are obviously very different to the social-media facilitated ones, undertaken in the search for MH370.

However, the phenomenon that is the eclipsing of the GL1 tragedy by waves of tweets relating to Covid-19 crept up on me, and I failed to take 'field notes' of a phenomenon that unfolded before I entirely registered its significance (such as recording what other #tags were popular/trending at the time). Social-media users' actions—their use of 'dissemination structures', or engagement with a Tweet simply by clicking on it—yield 'data' that has spawned an industry that sells it at a cost that is prohibitive to individual researchers and seems tailored to businesses that want to identify 'influencers' to help sell their products. Additionally, data more than 30 days old is apparently not retrievable (a bit like surveillance-camera data, or the ocean, which both 'overwrite' data/information unless it is 'reviewed' promptly).[13] I must remember to heed the advice given by Rutz et al., to scientists wanting to investigate how animals have responded to 'anthropause' (micro-pockets of Covid-19-induced human immobility) and take field-notes:

> We are confident that researchers will be keen to resume fieldwork, but recommend they take a few extra steps. First, we suggest they keep detailed records of official restrictions on (and where possible, observed changes in) human mobility in their study areas, as this information may be difficult to reconstruct after the fact. (Rutz et al. 2020: 158)

[13] However, one social-media data retrieval website that I consulted teased that data older than 30 days 'might' be retrievable, but it would only be possible to know on subscription to their service.

Writ large in fake news discourse are words that assume its antithesis, like 'truth'. But when did the media, or at least mainstream media, ever truthfully and comprehensively represent the concerns and perspectives of non-human animals? Hence, not specifically related to the mediated obfuscation of animal trauma during the pandemic, the Centre for Animal Ethics at the Universitat Pompeu Fabra recently published their 'Guidelines Towards an Ethical News Coverage of Non-Human Animals' (UPF-CAE 2020), aimed at journalists. A goal of the Guidelines is to:

> Unveil the speciesist power relations that legitimate the relationships of oppression imposed on other species due to the supposed superiority of the human species, which are structurally analogous to the oppressions we are already fighting against (sexism, racism, classism, homophobia, cultural discrimination, ableism, etc.). (UPF-CAE 2020: 4)

However, fake news discourse does gift the possibility to think optically and visually. Therefore, this chapter's aesthetic, ethic, and politic affirms animals' 'right to opacity' (as subjects), simultaneous to their right to 'informatic visibility'. This does not mean that they should be subject to the gaze of technologies of a biometric kind but that they should be subjects of media and political concern.

Conclusion

> Our minds are still racing back and forth, longing for a return to 'normality,' trying to stitch our future to our past and refusing to acknowledge the rupture. But the rupture exists. And in the midst of this terrible despair, it offers us a chance to rethink the doomsday machine we have built for ourselves. (Roy 2020)

Many, including Roy (2020) and Latour (2020), have asked how we might live differently come the end of the pandemic. Taylor and Fraser (2020b) have pondered this question hoping that we may develop a heightened sensitivity to our impact on other animals. If we imagine the animal-industrial complex as a component of the 'doomsday machine' (or even conflated the two), then one expression of this 'refusal' to acknowledge the rupture would be the rush to eat the flesh of another (a burger) after lockdowns began to be lifted. It is a phenomenon expressive of how the exploitation of animals and capitalism are linked if ever there was one. Perhaps the 'rupture' that the pandemic has brought into existence asks us to rethink the doomsday machine (or animal-industrial complex) and all other modes and sites of animal exploitation. But information practices constitutive of a type of 'anthropocentric noise disorder', which privileges humans' interests, renders the trauma of other animals invisible.

This chapter has explored some of the ways in which this disorder has manifested during the pandemic, as well as some ways to intervene. The practices that are constitutive of the disorder involve moments of misinformation that present themselves to us in the positive, but the condition that is the mediated omission, obscuration, obfuscation, and eschewal of the interests, perspectives, and experiences of non-human animals, as I have endeavoured to argue comes into play most notably in the instance of GL1, also contributes to untruthful information ecologies.

References

Beirne, P. (2014). Theriocide: Naming Animal Killing. *International Journal for Crime, Justice and Social Democracy, 3*(2), 49–66. https://doi.org/10.5204/ijcjsd.v3i2.174.

Berry, E. (2020). Pets: The voiceless victims of the Covid-19 crisis. Phys.org, 25 March. https://phys.org/news/2020-03-pets-voiceless-victims-covid-crisis.html. Accessed 1 November 2020.

Bittman, M. (2011). Who protects the animals? The New York Times, 26 April. https://opinionator.blogs.nytimes.com/2011/04/26/who-protects-the-animals/. Accessed 1 November 2020.

Blas, Z. (2016). Opacities: An Introduction. *Camera Obscura, 31*(2), 149–153. https://doi.org/10.1215/02705346-3592499.

Blas, Z. (2018). Informatic Opacity. In R. Braidotti & M. Hlavajova (Eds.), *Posthuman Glossary* (pp. 198–199). London: Bloomsbury Academic.

Bremner, L. (2015). Technologies of Uncertainty in the Search for MH370. In H. Davis & E. Turpin (Eds.), *Art in the Anthropocene: Encounters Among Aesthetics, Politics, Environments, and Epistemologies* (pp. 199–211). London: Open Humanities Press.

Buitendijk, M. (2020). Disappearance of livestock carrier Gulf Livestock 1 raises questions. SWZ Maritime, 10 September. https://www.swzmaritime.nl/news/2020/09/10/disappearance-of-livestock-carrier-gulf-livestock-1-raises-questions/. Accessed 30 December 2020.

Campbell, C. (2020). 'They are overwhelmed': China's animal shelters can't cope with the number of pets abandoned due to Covid-19. Time, 2 March. https://time.com/5793363/china-coronavirus-covid19-abandoned-pets-wuhan/. Accessed 30 December 2020.

Cetina, K. K. (2009). The Synthetic Situation: Interactionism for a Global World. *Symbolic Interaction, 32*(1), 61–87. https://doi.org/10.1525/si.2009.32.1.61.

Elliot, J. K. (2020). Lonely eels need video calls so they don't 'forget' humans during coronavirus. Global News, 1 May. https://globalnews.ca/news/6892746/coronavirus-eels-facetime-call/. Accessed 11 January 2021.

Emmelheinz, I. (2015). Images do not Show: The Desire to See in the Anthropocene. In H. Davis & E. Turpin (Eds.), *Art in the Anthropocene: Encounters Among Aesthetics, Politics, Environments, and Epistemologies* (pp. 131–142). London: Open Humanities Press.

Franke, A., & Turpin, E. (2015). The Fates of Negativity: Anselm Franke in Conversation with Etienne Turpin. In H. Davis & E. Turpin (Eds.), *Art in the Anthropocene: Encounters Among Aesthetics, Politics, Environments, and Epistemologies* (pp. 143–154). London: Open Humanities Press.

Glissant, E. (1997). *Poetics of Relation*. Ann Arbor: University of Michigan Press.

Haraway, D. (1992). The Promises of Monsters: A Regenerative Politics for Inappropriate/d Others. In L. Grossberg, C. Nelson, & P. A. Treichler (Eds.), *Cultural Studies* (pp. 295–337). New York, London: Routledge.

Haraway, D. (2016). *Staying with the Trouble: Making Kin in the Chthulucene*. Durham, NC: Duke University Press.

Kaur, A. (2020). Fact check: Old, unrelated video of bats streaming out from a roof linked to coronavirus outbreak. India Today, 13 February. https://www.indiatoday.in/fact-check/story/fact-check-old-unrelated-video-of-bats-streaming-out-from-a-roof-linked-to-coronavirus-outbreak-1646095-2020-02-13. Accessed 10 January 2021.

Kevany, S. (2020). Livestock ships twice as likely to be lost as cargo vessels. The Guardian, 28 October. Retrieved from https://www.theguardian.com/environment/2020/oct/28/exclusive-livestock-ships-twice-as-likely-to-be-lost-as-cargo-vessels. Accessed 5 December 2020.

Kirkness, L. (2020). Covid 19 coronavirus: Auckland Maccas' queues cause traffic jams. The New Zealand Herald, 29 April. https://www.nzherald.co.nz/lifestyle/news/article.cfm?c_id=6&objectid=12327917. Accessed 11 January 2021.

Latour, B. (2020). What protective measures can you think of so we don't go back to the pre-crisis production model? http://www.bruno-latour.fr/node/853.html. Accessed 19 November 2020.

Manch, T. (2020). Government delays mandatory cameras on fishing boats, again. Stuff, 5 June. https://www.stuff.co.nz/national/politics/121724465/government-delays-mandatory-cameras-on-fishing-boats-again. Accessed 11 January 2021.

Minh-ha, T. T. (1986). She, the Inappropriate/d Other: Introduction. *Discourse, 8*, 3–10.

Mohanlall, S. (2019). Livestock ship's "covert" entry to port "no secret." Stuff, 8 November. https://www.stuff.co.nz/business/farming/117273660/livestock-ships-covert-entry-to-port-no-secret. Accessed 11 January 2021.

Noske, B. (1989). *Human and Other Animals*. London: Pluto Press.

NZ Herald. (2020). Dogs and cats reportedly thrown from apartments in China over coronavirus fears. The New Zealand Herald, 1 February. https://www.nzherald.co.nz/world/news/article.cfm?c_id=2&objectid=12305201. Accessed 11 January 2021.

ODT. (2020). Cattle ship with two Kiwis on board reported missing off Japan coast. The Otago Daily Times, 3 September. https://www.odt.co.nz/star-news/star-national/cattle-ship-two-kiwis-board-reported-missing-japan-coast. Accessed 11 January 2021.

Oliver, C. (2020). Covid-19, 'more-than-human' research, and the reproduction of interspecies violence. Animals in Society, 2 July. https://animalsinsocietygroup.wordpress.com/2020/07/02/catherine-oliver-covid-19-more-than-human-research-and-the-reproduction-of-interspecies-violence/. Accessed 21 October 2020.

O'Sullivan, V. (2020a). Non-Human Animal Trauma During the Pandemic. *Postdigital Science and Education, 2*(3), 588–596. https://doi.org/10.1007/s42438-020-00143-2

O'Sullivan, V. (2020b). On the Educative Potential of Reservoir Bats: Practices of Response-ability for the Chthulucene. *Knowledge Cultures, 8*(2), 16–22. https://doi.org/10.22381/KC8220203

Radomska, M., Mehrabi, T., & Lykke, N. (2020). Queer Death Studies: Death, Dying and Mourning from a Queerfeminist Perspective. *Australian Feminist Studies, 35*(104), 81–100. https://doi.org/10.1080/08164649.2020.1811952.

Roy, A. (2020). The pandemic is a portal. Financial Times, 4 April. Retrieved from https://www.ft.com/content/10d8f5e8-74eb-11ea-95fe-fcd274e920ca. Accessed 5 December 2020.

Rutz, C., Loretto, M. C., Bates, A. E., Davidson, S. C., Duarte, C. M., Jetz, W., Johnson, M., Kato, A., Kays, R., Mueller, T., Primack, R. B., Ropert-Coudert, Y., Tucker, M. A., Wikelski, M., & Cagnacci, F. (2020). COVID-19 Lockdown Allows Researchers to Quantify the Effects of Human Activity on Wildlife. *Nature Ecology and Evolution, 4*(9), 1156–1159. https://doi.org/10.1038/s41559-020-1237-z.

Scott-Reid, J. (2020). Animal rights activist Regan Russell, 65, died trying to expose what Bill 156 will hide. Toronto Star, 23 June. https://www.thestar.com/opinion/contributors/2020/06/23/animal-activist-died-trying-to-expose-what-bill-156-will-hide.html. Accessed 21 October 2020.

Security from Trespass and Protecting Food Safety Act 2020. https://www.ontario.ca/laws/statute/20s09?_ga=2.122150219.1932982140.1610925544-358329435.1610925544. Accessed 17 January 2020.

Searle, A., & Turnbull, J. (2020). Resurgent Natures? More-than-Human Perspectives on Covid-19. *Dialogues in Human Geography, 10*(2), 291–295. https://doi.org/10.1177/2043820620933859.

Seven News. (2020). Coronavirus rumour that pets can carry virus results in animals thrown to their deaths. Seven News, 4 February. https://7news.com.au/news/animals/coronavirus-rumour-that-pets-can-carry-virus-results-in-animals-thrown-to-their-deaths-c-678046. Accessed 27 May 2020.

Shorey, K., & Kim, S. (2020). RV Falkor discovers unexplored depths of Coral Sea without a single scientist on board. ABC News, 6 May. https://www.abc.net.au/news/2020-05-06/rv-falkor-on-research-expedition-with-no-scientists-on-board/12215962. Accessed 14 October 2020.

Taunton, E. (2020). Thousands of cattle loaded on to live export ship in the dark. Stuff, 10 November. https://www.stuff.co.nz/business/farming/123337791/thousands-of-cattle-loaded-on-to-live-export-ship-in-the-dark. Accessed 11 January 2020.

Taylor, N., & Fraser, H. (2020a). Radically imagining human-animal relations after the Covid-19 pandemic. Animals in Society, 6 April. https://animalsinsocietygroup.wordpress.com/2020/04/06/radically-imagining-human-animal-relations-after-the-covid19-pandemic/. Accessed 11 January 2021.

Taylor, N., & Fraser, T. (2020b). Imagining human-animal relations after the pandemic. https://theotheranimals.com/podcasts. Accessed 11 January 2021.

Troon, S. R. (2020). How to care about coral: The cinematic realism of underwater camera systems. Eco_media II: Fire & Rain. https://criticalintimacies.wordpress.com/eco_media-2020/abstracts/. Accessed 11 January 2021.

Twine, R. (2012). Revealing the 'Animal-Industrial Complex': A Concept and Method for Critical Animal Studies? *Journal for Critical Animal Studies, 10*(1), 12–39.

UNESCO. (2005). *Towards Knowledge Societies*. Paris: UNESCO.

UNESCO. (2020). *Disinfodemic: Deciphering Covid-19 Disinformation*. Paris: UNESCO.

UPF-CAE. (2020). Universitat Pompeu Fabra Centre for Animal Ethics' Guidelines towards an ethical news coverage of non-human animals. https://www.upf.edu/web/cae-center-for-animal-ethics/for-journalists. Accessed 11 January 2021.

Wardle, C., & Derakhshan, H. (2017). Information Disorder: Toward an Interdisciplinary Framework for Research and Policy Making. Strasbourg: Council of Europe.

Weekes, J. (2020). Gulf Livestock tragedy highlights plight of poor seafarers, Kiwis stuck abroad. Stuff, 12 September. https://www.stuff.co.nz/national/300103367/gulf-livestock-tragedy-highlights-plight-of-poor-seafarers-kiwis-stuck-abroad. Accessed 11 January 2021.

WHO. (2020). Managing the Covid-19 infodemic: Promoting healthy behaviours and mitigating the harm from misinformation and disinformation. https://www.who.int/news-room/detail/23-09-2020-managing-the-covid-19-infodemic-promoting-healthy-behaviours-and-mitigating-the-harm-from-misinformation-and-disinformation. Accessed 13 October 2020.

Part III
Discourse and Digital Literacy

Chapter 8
Someone Is Wrong on the Internet: Is There an Obligation to Correct False and Oppressive Speech on Social Media?

Jennifer Saul

Introduction

The experience is not an uncommon one: over your morning coffee, you open up Facebook and find a friend of yours discussing someone else's false and offensive post and urging all right-minded people to go and comment on it. Alternatively, perhaps you read a false and offensive tweet from an acquaintance from high school, or even from someone close to you. You feel appalled and you feel a pressing obligation to say something, not to just let it sit.

Perhaps at this point you pause for a moment wondering what to do. And here the story gets a little more fanciful. If you are a philosopher (or interested in philosophy), you might turn to what philosophers have said about responding to false and hateful speech. You will find some arguments that may make you feel an urgent need to respond, reinforcing what your friends are saying, or what you are already feeling. For example, you will see arguments from Rae Langton on the importance of what she calls 'blocking' oppressive speech, which include powerful statements like this: 'Hearers and bystanders who do not block will sometimes, through that omission, make a speech act more evil, whether they mean to or no.' (Langton 2018: 161) You are likely to be deeply concerned by Ishani Maitra's (2012) argument that not objecting can confer authority on an utterer of hateful speech. Sandy Goldberg

I am very grateful for discussions of earlier drafts of the paper with audiences at the University of Sheffield and the University of Waterloo; for conversations with Patrick Connolly, Shannon Dea, Ray Drainville, Anna Klieber, Mathieu Marion, and Martina Rosola; and for research assistance from Anna Klieber. I'm grateful also for helpful feedback from the editors.

J. Saul (✉)
Department of Philosophy, University of Waterloo, Waterloo, ON, Canada
e-mail: Jennifer.saul@uwaterloo.ca

A. MacKenzie et al. (eds.), *The Epistemology of Deceit in a Postdigital Era*, Postdigital Science and Education,
https://doi.org/10.1007/978-3-030-72154-1_8

(2020a) will tell you that there is a default entitlement to take silence as acceptance, and you will worry about what it means if you do not speak up. You will also find Casey Rebecca Johnson (2018) arguing that there is an epistemic obligation to voice disagreement. All this may make you feel, all the more pressingly, that you need to throw yourself into those threads and speak your mind.

And yet, there is also another strand of thought. These authors acknowledge some serious problems that one may encounter in trying to speak up. And many others also discuss these problems, some giving them even more weight (Lepoutre 2019; McGowan 2012, 2018). Counterspeech may fail or even backfire. It may not be safe to speak up in a particular context, or for members of a particular group. Indeed, it may be that the structural injustices present in society make any claim of a duty to speak up a piece of ideal theory (Lackey 2018).

At this point, you might feel very uncertain what to do. You might think, perhaps with some reason, that philosophers may not have been the best people to consult on this matter. But one interesting fact is that these discussions have been built almost exclusively around a model of speech acts taking place in face-to-face conversations. In this paper my plan is to begin from the work of philosophers on counterspeech in general, but then turn to the particular issues posed by social media. I will discuss the special problems presented by social media, but also some interesting approaches to false and offensive speech that social media makes possible. In the end, I will offer some advice to the fictional you who is appalled by what you see on social media, but (as usual for philosophy papers) it will not be as detailed and concrete as you might like.

Why You Might Feel You Should Speak Up

Speech Act Strand

There is a substantial speech act tradition in social and political philosophy, which forcefully presses the point that speech acts can dramatically alter what is permissible, making racism and sexism more acceptable. The focus here is particularly on *unchallenged* speech acts, which can have the effects that they do precisely because they are not challenged. It is not hard to see how this focus could make one feel the pressing necessity of challenging. (Importantly, as we will see, these authors do acknowledge and grapple with difficulties for such challenges.)

Mary Kate McGowan (2012, 2018) is focused on the ease with which facts about what is permissible can be changed, especially with regard to racism and sexism. She argues that the ease with which permissibility facts change more generally leads to an overly smooth facilitation of racism and sexism. Any utterance, for McGowan, changes some permissibility facts simply by virtue of changing the state of the conversation. If I say, ‘hang on, my kitten is chewing the power cord’, it becomes permissible to assume that I have a kitten and impermissible to ask if I have any pets—as long as nobody follows up with, 'hey, you don't have kittens, what are you talking about?'. That much is unremarkable. But McGowan argues that the same sort of thing happens with racist utterances. If someone in a conversation makes a racist utterance and nobody objects, then racism (or at least racist utterances) becomes permissible in that conversation. For this reason, objecting becomes paramount. There are very high costs allowing a racist utterance to go unchallenged, because not challenging it allows the permissibility facts to change and make racism permissible for the conversational context and even beyond. McGowan extends this approach to oppressive speech and oppression more generally, building a compelling picture of how unchallenged speech acts can have serious oppressive effects. As we will see, however, McGowan does also raise concerns about the difficulty of such challenges.

Ishani Maitra (2012) directs our attention to the way that speakers may come to be vested with authority simply by other speakers not questioning linguistic moves that are made. So, for example, consider a case in which someone is racially abusive on a subway car, and nobody challenges them. The speaker, in her example, aims to rank his target as inferior, and this is licensed by the silence of the other passengers, who thereby give him the authority for this ranking (Maitra 2012: 115). It is crucial to Maitra's picture that this happens even if the other passengers are quite uncomfortable with what is taking place: 'Even if the hate speaker's fellow passengers have strong reservations about what he says to the woman he targets, as long as they fail to speak up, the speaker can end up with authority.' (Maitra 2012: 116)

Rae Langton's (2018) recent work has been on 'back door speech acts', which smuggle in assumptions in ways that may go unnoticed by participants. Presuppositions are a key example of an ordinary way that this happens—if I say, 'he is from Michigan but doesn't like Trump', my interlocutors may take on the assumption that a Michigander who dislikes Trump somehow defies expectations. And they may do this without even realizing that this is what they are doing. This can be easily stopped, though, by pulling out the assumption and criticizing it: 'Hey! Actually more than half of Michigan voters were opposed to Trump in 2016, and he only won the state due to third-party voting. And Biden won in 2020!'

More perniciously, racist and sexist background assumptions can be smuggled in this way. Here is an example from John McCain. Remarkably, this interchange has been repeatedly cited as an instance of John McCain's brave *anti*-racism.

> 'I gotta ask you a question,' Quinnell told McCain, who leaned in closer to hear her.
>
> 'I can't trust Obama,' she told McCain, and the world. 'I have read about him and he's not… he's not… he's an Arab. And…'
>
> This is when McCain politely took back the microphone and started shaking his head back and forth. He did so instinctively, without a hint of political motivation or strategic forethought.
>
> 'No?' Quinnell asked, her voice trailing off.
>
> 'No, ma'am,' McCain replied decisively.
>
> *'He's a decent family man, citizen, that I just happen to have disagreements with on fundamental issues,' McCain told the crowd.* (Davich 2018) (emphasis added)

McCain's utterance in italics presupposes that there is a contrast between being Arab and being a decent family man and citizen—it does not make sense without it. Yet this is hidden enough that most commentators (and quite likely McCain himself) failed to notice this. It is precisely this sort of thing that Langton is concerned with (although the example is mine). The right thing to do, she says, is to pull out these sorts of assumptions and criticize them. To do so is to engage in the speech act of *blocking*, an important counterspeech obligation. Indeed, she writes, '[h]earers and bystanders who do not block will sometimes, through that omission, make a speech act more evil, whether they mean to or no' (Langton 2018: 161). Although Langton very much acknowledges that blocking is not always possible, she builds an appealing picture of its power, describing it as offering 'a modest time machine' because it offers a way to undo what may have seemed successful pernicious speech acts.[1]

Silence as Assent Strand

There is another strand of argument that might make you feel even more uncomfortable about not speaking up. This is Sandy Goldberg's (2020a) argument that not speaking up will (generally) be interpreted as assent or at least acceptance.[2] The idea that we could be seen as accepting false and oppressive claims is one that motivates many people to feel a pressing urge to comment quickly or retweet angrily.

Goldberg (2020a) argues that if one is engaged in a cooperative conversation (in the sense of Grice 1991), then—if one does not speak up—one will generally be assumed to agree with what a speaker has said. This is because there is an assumption that if one rejects an assertion, one will say so. More precisely, he endorses the claim that he calls NO SILENT REJECTION (the capitals are his):

> In all speech exchanges which are Gricean conversations, all competent language users enjoy a default (albeit defeasible) entitlement to expect that an audience regarding whom it was manifest that he has remained silent in the face of a publicly made assertion has not rejected that assertion. (Goldberg 2020a: 176)[3]

If A says something false (or otherwise rejection-worthy) to B, then—if B is being cooperative and is aware of the falsehood—B should speak up. If B doesn't speak up, then there is a default entitlement to assume that B agrees. This is only a

[1] For a very close examination of undoing speech acts, see Caponetto (2020).

[2] Philip Pettit (2002) also argues for this conclusion, more briefly. His argument also turns on Gricean considerations (Grice 1991). According to Pettit, in conditions of genuine freedom of speech, silence can (generally) legitimately be presumed to communicate assent. This could be seen as motivating a very strong obligation to speak up on social media. Here I focus on Goldberg, due to his much more detailed discussion of possible defeating conditions for the presumption of acceptance. (For a response to Pettit 2002, see Langton 2007.)

[3] For an argument against Goldberg (2020a), see Klieber (2020).

default, not a guarantee: there may be reasons for not speaking up. But this default means that silence will, in general, be taken as assent. And this is what generates the obligation to set the record straight by speaking up. This duty holds, Goldberg argues, for both morally and factually problematic utterances. Indeed, one form of support that Goldberg offers for this is a collection of powerful statements about the obligation to speak up in the face of wrongdoing (not just wrong speaking). For example:

> When I was the rabbi of the Jewish community in Berlin under the Hitler regime, I learned many things. The most important thing that I learned under those tragic circumstances was that bigotry and hatred are not the most urgent problem. The most urgent, the most disgraceful, the most shameful and the most tragic problem is silence. (Joachim Prinz, quoted in Goldberg 2020a: 170)

Goldberg (2020a) acknowledges, as we will see, that this is merely a default—and that there will be many circumstances in which this obligation does not hold. But the mere fact (if it is one) that there is a default of interpreting silence as acceptance will contribute substantially to the felt need to *respond now* to problematic claims on social media.

Epistemic Obligation Strand

Rebecca Casey Johnson (2018) argues that there is a distinctly epistemic obligation to voice disagreements. She identifies several sources for this obligation, focusing in particular on self-regarding duties, obligations arising from cooperative endeavors or from efforts at enquiry, and obligations stemming from Millian concerns about the need to submit beliefs to proper scrutiny. Again, this obligation is merely a default. But it is the sort of default that could make you think you do need to put down your coffee and respond to that false and offensive tweet in the story that I mentioned at the start of this chapter.

Problems with Counterspeech

There is also a very substantial literature, on the other hand, itemizing serious problems with counterspeech.

Jennifer Lackey (2018) gives one of the most powerful statements of this in her objection to Goldberg (2020a). She argues that his NO SILENT REJECTION claim is motivated by ideal theory—by a picture of the world in which people are situated as equals—and that this claim only makes sense in such a world. However, in our actual world, power dynamics are omnipresent, and huge numbers of people are unable to object safely or to be taken seriously:

> No conversation is entirely free of differences in the distribution of epistemic goods, status, power, psychology, cultural expectations, practical constraints, or some combination thereof. Speaking up against others almost always involves a calculation—whether conscious or not—that is based on one's position and the costs and benefits of dissent on this topic at this time with this conversational participant. (Lackey 2018: 90)

To some extent, Goldberg's (2020a) view *does* acknowledge these varying power dynamics. He discusses circumstances in which NO SILENT REJECTION fails, and those circumstances include those in which objecting is very costly and those in which objecting is ineffective. But Goldberg treats these as particular circumstances which may or may not arise for individuals, noting that when they do, NO SILENT REJECTION will be undermined. Lackey argues that the corrosive effects of power dynamics are so widespread and systematic that there cannot be a *general* NO SILENT REJECTION, which she rightly notes would underpin a very general duty to reject. Instead, she suggests that there are different sorts of duties for members of different sorts of social groups (as well as the more contextual variations that Goldberg 2020a discusses). Importantly, she notes also that members of some social groups will have an *easier* time speaking up and being taken seriously—and that this gives them a heightened duty to object.

Mary Kate McGowan (2012, 2018), Robert Simpson (2013), and Maxime Lepoutre (2019) raise serious concerns about the idea that counterspeech can be effective or safe. These are rooted in the same concerns that Lackey has about the power dynamics of society. McGowan notes that speaking up—which can be dangerous—constitutes a serious extra burden for those targeted by hate speech, who are already suffering the harms of that speech (as well as of oppression more generally). She also notes that power dynamics may render counterspeech ineffectual: a woman who speaks up in a sexist environment, for example, is not all that likely to have her objections properly understood, taken seriously, and acted upon in an appropriate manner. She further notes that there is an important asymmetry: while it is relatively easy to carry out a speech act of oppression, it can be much harder to reverse it. Finally, building on work from Simpson (2013), she notes that counterspeech can backfire—a point that will be important later in this paper. Her concern, and Simpson's, is that objecting to something may serve to reinforce associations: repeatedly explaining that Black men are not disposed to violence may, for example, unwittingly reinforce the association between Black men and violence.[4] Lepoutre (2019) extends this point beyond hateful and oppressive speech, noting that the association reinforcement can happen with any attempt to

[4] McGowan (2018) suggests that these difficulties are serious, but sometimes possible to overcome. A skillful interlocutor can, in some circumstances, succeed in shifting the focus of a conversation. McGowan's example involves someone very politely and skillfully making sure that a colleague of color is considered for a leadership role (McGowan 2018: 192). As McGowan acknowledges, this will often not be possible. And as anyone who has tried to have a tactful conversation on the Internet knows, special challenges for this technique are presented by the dynamics of social media.

correct falsehoods, including reinforcing the association between vaccines and autism through one's speech denying this link.[5]

Importantly, the authors we have discussed are all sensitive to these concerns. Some of their arguments, as we have seen, can be taken to provide strong motivation for counterspeech. But they also show real concerns about how often this will be effective or safe, especially for members of marginalized groups. Rae Langton (2018) discusses the way that social location can impact one's efforts to object. Her concern is that oppressive power and social norms can render counterspeech less effective. The oppressive power of racism can mean that a Black person's utterance is not listened to or taken seriously. Norms that prescribe passivity and agreeableness for women may mean that when they object, they are dismissed as difficult and not worth paying attention to. Considering both of these, it may be far less effective when members of subordinated groups speak up. Both Langton and McGowan suggest that, due to these issues, members of dominant groups have a greater obligation to speak up. (Though, as they are aware, this does not solve all of the problems that they raise.)

Goldberg (2020a) and Johnson (2018) also acknowledge key factors which can affect an obligation to speak up. Goldberg notes that the default entitlement to think that a silent audience agrees does not hold unless one is in a cooperative conversation. So if the situation is either not cooperative or not a conversation, this entitlement is not present and there is not the same obligation to speak up. This will include, for example, situations in which a back and forth is not expected (a formal meeting with a hierarchy, perhaps), or situations in which one has opted out of cooperating (perhaps in protest). The entitlement is also removed if there is an outweighing explanation for the silence—for example, if the room is too noisy, or one has laryngitis. Or, importantly if there are difficult power dynamics—one might not be able to tell one's boss that they are saying something false. The cost of objecting might be too great—especially in cases like hate speech, where objecting could lead to violence. Johnson similarly notes that considerations of practicality, safety, and power dynamics can override the default obligation.

None of these authors specifically addresses the issues that arise with objections and counterspeech on social media. I'll turn to those now.

[5] Lepoutre (2019) invokes, in addition to other arguments, the much-discussed 'backfire effect' (Nyhan and Reifler 2010), a purported psychological phenomenon in which correcting a falsehood seems to lead to increased belief in the falsehood. It is not so clear, however, that this effect actually exists (see Swire-Thompson et al. 2020). If this effect is proven to exist, it only strengthens the arguments for difficulties of counterspeech.

Problems with Objecting on Social Media

So far, we have seen that there are arguments which seem to back up that pressing felt need to speak up in the face of false or oppressive speech. But we have also seen ways that it may be mitigated, especially if we are members of oppressed groups who may find objecting unsafe—or for whom it may also be less effective. But, this line of thought goes, unless there are such power dynamics present it really would be much better to speak up. However, these arguments come from authors focusing on our duties in face-to-face conversations. It is important, then, to think carefully about what happens when we turn our attention to speech on social media.

One reason for hesitating over the felt obligation to object on social media, which we will not dwell on much, is that false and offensive claims are *constantly* being made on social media. Trying to object to every claim would be a never-ending, exhausting, and fruitless task. But we'll set this aside—the demandingness of duties is a well-worn topic and not something specific to this one.[6] Instead, we will look at other features of online communication which set it importantly apart from face-to-face communication.

Even before the pandemic, social media speech had become enormously influential. But with a dearth of face-to-face human contact taking place, it takes on even more importance. The effects in the world are by now beyond doubt. Moreover, there are both a vast number of falsehoods circulating on social media and a torrent of opportunities to object to them, as well as considerable pressure to do so. Since conversational dynamics on social media are very different from those face to face, it is important to carefully consider their consequences for the duty to object. I will argue that these consequences are profound.

First, however, let's think a bit about some of the ways that social media conversations differ from face-to-face ones.[7] Here are some key ones that will be important to our discussion.

- Uncertain/changeable audience: In a face-to-face conversation, one usually knows to whom one is speaking. Even in the case of addressing a crowd, one knows that one is addressing a crowd. While the audience may sometimes change—one person leaves the table at the bar; another sits down—this is not a constant feature, and the speaker is reasonably likely to be aware of it. This is not at all the case on social media.
- Responses can drastically alter the makeup of a conversation. If someone with a large social media following—or just one very different from one's own—weighs in, the audience can be dramatically altered. This is unlikely to happen face to face.
- Audiences can be indefinitely vast—there is virtually no limit on the number of people who may become participants in, or audiences for, a social media

[6] Johnson (2018) has a nice discussion of this sort of limitation on the duty to object.

[7] Here I draw on work by Connolly (2020) and Goldberg (2020b).

conversation. Physical constraints alone mean that face-to-face conversation is not like this.

Amplification

As mentioned above, the philosophers who have pressed the importance of objecting have been very much focused on face-to-face interaction. In face-to-face conversations, a lot of awkward, unfortunate, or even terrible things can happen when one objects. One may be ignored; one may be made to feel that one was being rude; one may be attacked, verbally or physically. And all of these responses are more likely for those from marginalized groups. That is presumably a key reason why the authors we discussed all shy away from asserting a fully general duty to object. And yet, they argue, if one is safe from attack, then there may be good reason to endure the awkwardness or the frustration of being ignored—it is possible that one will be listened to. And, importantly, not objecting may either communicate agreement or confer authority on the speaker. If possible, it is important to object in order to avoid this.

One thing that will not happen in a face-to-face conversation: one will not, in general, bring it about that more people hear or pay attention to the problematic utterance. There are certain exceptions—e.g., if someone mutters something appalling, and many more people come to hear it when it is repeated by an objector. This exception, however, is an important one. The importance comes from the fact that it is not a bad analogy for what may happen on social media.

To understand this point requires a bit of information about how social media algorithms determine which posts are most likely to be presented to users. While this has changed over time (and there are also variations between platforms), a key feature has long been degree of engagement.[8] Engagement can take the form of simple reactions such as *likes*, but sharing, retweeting, or replying to a post is far more powerful. Such engagement is vital to—and much sought by—those hoping to build a following. Given these dynamics it is very easy to see that objecting to a post makes it *more* likely that it will be seen. And this is so whether one's reaction takes the form of a reply on Facebook or a retweet with commentary on Twitter (though the latter is the closest analogy to repeating something that has been muttered in order to criticize it). If one has politically engaged friends on social media, it is very common to see an angry post criticizing someone else on social media and directing all right-thinking people to go and register their objections. This instruction, when widely disseminated and followed, guarantees that the offensive original post will be seen far more widely than it otherwise would have been and is likely to bring notoriety to the original poster. In some instances, this

[8] This is just one key feature, but it is the most important one for the present argument. For more details, see, for example, Cooper (2020).

can be a devastating public shaming. But in others, this is how a career as a provocateur is built.

In 2010, Terry Jones, a small-town pastor without a huge following, declared his intention to burn the Koran. Initially, this was ignored by mainstream media. However, it was picked up on social media, largely by those who found his plan abhorrent. The outrage over his plan made it famous, so famous that eventually the mainstream media felt they had to cover it. Eventually, he backed away from the plan, but when that led to a reduction in media coverage, he decided to go ahead after all. The ensuing worldwide protests led to 12 deaths in Afghanistan. And none of this would have happened without social media sharing *by his opponents.* This sharing enormously amplified his message and led to horrendous real-world consequences.[9]

And this is a key problem with social media counterspeech: objecting to something on social media is very likely to *amplify* it. Since a central reason for thinking we should object is risk of harm from the utterance, we should be very worried about increasing that risk by increasing the number of people who are reached by the utterance. This concern applies equally strongly to the issue of correcting oppressive speech and to the issue of correcting falsehoods.

Generation of Sympathy

It is, and always has been, important to object in the right way, in order to avoid generating sympathy for those one is objecting to. Viciously insulting responses have always run the risk of alienating potential allies and of recruiting sympathizers to the cause one opposes. All this is true of ordinary conversations as well as social media ones. However, objecting on social media poses special risks that are worth taking note of.

When you speak up in a face-to-face conversation, you are aware of whether this is a part of a large pile-on or just an individual comment. If somebody else is raising the objection you want to raise, you generally hold back and let them do it. You do not add your voice repetitively. If you decide to add your voice to a crowd of people objecting, that is a decision you make—you do not accidentally find yourself doing it. On social media, however, things happen very quickly. You may object to something, thinking you are the only one speaking up, and then quickly find yourself part of a very large group. And this matters a great deal—small groups on social media quickly become large, and a large group may be perceived as a mob, and therefore generate sympathy for the person criticised.

Research bears this out. A study by Sawaoka and Monin (2018) compares reactions to criticisms of offensively racist or sexist posts, depending on the amount

[9] For a full discussion of this case and its implications for social media amplification, see boyd (2018).

of opposition they receive in comments. They found that a single commenter may be viewed favorably, but if there is a large group of commenters (even ten, quite a small group by social media standards), that same commenter will be viewed negatively. They take this to result from sympathy generated for a person who seems to be ganged up on by a large number of people, who come across as bullying. Since generation of sympathy is far from the desired goal of those who speak up against an offensive post, it does look like counterspeech may become counterproductive if it is too widely taken up. This concern is only enhanced by the fact that it is not always easy to know whether one is a part of a social media mob or not. As you sit there, over your coffee, you may see that nobody has responded to that problematic tweet. But by the time you retweet it with a pithy criticism, you may be one of hundreds.[10] This possibility of unknowingly inciting or joining a mob is a part of what motivates Norlock (2017: 188) to note that social media brings with it 'new responsibilities [which] include sorting out the extent to which we each have more power than we believe we do or than we think carefully about exerting, even as we exert it in online communication'.[11]

Abuse

When raising objections face to face, there is always a risk of verbal or physical abuse, especially if racist or sexist speech is at issue and if one is a member of a marginalized group. This is something that the philosophers we have discussed are well aware of and take into account. However, the risk of verbal abuse, including serious threats, is greatly magnified by social media. There are several relevant factors:

1. It is harder to assess the risk one faces, because one does not know who will end up seeing anything one writes.
2. It is very easy, and very fast, to mobilize armies of commenters to respond with vile threats and abuse.
3. This abuse can include such things as doxxing, which put one potentially in physical or financial jeopardy.

None of this is speculative. All of these behaviors are well-established. Attacks of this sort are especially common for members of marginalized groups, and especially when they speak up about racism or sexism. Soraya Chemaly writes:

> The phrase 'online harassment' is an anodyne catchphrase for a spectrum of behaviors, many of which break unenforced laws, degrade people's civil rights, reduce their ability to work, cause emotional and psychological harm, and actively inhibit their freedom of

[10] For further discussion of proportionality worries, specifically with respect to online shaming, see Billingham and Parr (2020). For further criticisms of online shaming, see Aitchison and Meckled-Garcia (2020).

[11] For more on these complexities, see also Aly and Simpson (2019).

> expression… The harassment often involves public shaming meant to humiliate and generates anxiety that comes with stranger threats and mob attacks. It also almost always alters, sometimes permanently, a person's ability to feel safe in 'real' space, to make a living, and to engage publicly and politically. (Chemaly 2019: 150)

Karen Adkins (2019: 83), similarly, discusses two prominent attempts at feminist online shaming, noting the disastrous consequences for the feminists who spoke up: 'Richards and St. Louis, as aspiring shamers, themselves became the objects of shame and rejection from their professional communities. They became the objects of sustained, public, and shaming scrutiny; they were condemned as professionals….' In the end, as Adkins notes, both were forced out of their professions.

Summing Up

Without looking at social media, the literature on counterspeech already included concerns about safety and power dynamics. We can see that these concerns are only intensified on social media. A post which might be meant as a response to one individual can end up travelling far and subjecting the poster to a quite stunning amount of vile abuse—and this is especially common for members of marginalized groups. The epistemic uncertainty introduced by this means that it can be far more difficult to know whether one is in a safe position to speak. The non-social-media literature also discussed the possibility that counterspeech might not be effective, either for practical reasons (e.g., the room is too noisy) or for political ones (bias makes one unlikely to be taken seriously). And it touched on the potential for backfire through reinforcing associations. But social media presents important new ways that this backfire can take place: through amplification via algorithms and through generation of sympathy if a lone voice unwittingly becomes part of a mob. Concerns about these sorts of backfires make social media counterspeech especially problematic. With that in mind, we now turn to alternatives. In other words, what other options do you have, as you survey the problematic posts you see online, and sip your coffee?

Not Objecting **on Social Media**

Alexander Brown (2019) has argued, quite compellingly, that remaining silent on social media does not have the same meaning or consequences that it has in face-to-face communication. There are three key points he makes here. First, it is rarely clear who has or has not seen a particular social media utterance. He makes a helpful comparison here to Maitra's subway car example. In that case, it is generally safe to assume that anyone conscious and in earshot hears the racist abuse,[12] which is why their silence has an authorizing effect.[13] On social media, however, any particular speaker's silence could be due to their not being aware of an offensive or false utterance. Remaining silent, then, does not have the same licensing effect. Returning to Goldberg's concerns, it is not at all clear that any one person's silence will be interpreted as acceptance, and a general lack of response seems also unlikely to be interpreted in this way.

Brown (2019) also notes the importance of different conventions in different speech communities. There may be some online communities in which the lack of critical comments is taken to signify acceptance, but this does not seem generally to be the case. Social media users do not in fact usually feel obligated to take the time to pass negative judgment on each post that they find or false. Finally, Brown (2019) draws attention to ways of registering disagreement or offense that do not involve replying to the original utterer. Social media presents many different ways that one can communicate, not all of which have clear correlates in face-to-face communication. When someone says something which is offensive or false, an objector may respond directly. But they may also start an entirely new thread discussing the problem that they witnessed. In order to avoid amplifying an offensive or false comment, it is important not to link to that comment in any way and not to discuss it in a way that will raise the profile of the person who made it. This is why social media conversations on controversial matters can sometimes take the form of rather roundabout descriptions of problematic utterances and what is wrong with them. This strategy can be very useful for avoiding both amplification and abuse. But it may be difficult to know what is being referred to, and the discussion may not be seen by those who most need to see it—those who might have been adversely affected by the original post.[14]

A decent case can be made, then, that any obligation to respond to false or offensive speech on social media is significantly less than it would be in a face-to-face situation, simply because a lack of direct response will not have the same meaning or effects. This case is only strengthened by considering the problems we saw earlier for responding on social media.

But we are still left with a serious problem to be solved. What should be done in response to false or offensive speech on social media? Given the lessened responsibility to directly respond, one might wonder whether silence could usefully act as a response. Alessandra Tanesini (2018) has recently argued that silence can

[12] This assumption, of course, may be false if the people within earshot are hearing impaired or if they are listening to headphones. But an assumption like this is nonetheless more plausible offline than online.

[13] Brown (2019) in fact argues that it should often not be seen as having this effect even offline, but I will not go into that here.

[14] This problem is very much heightened by the presence of online epistemic bubbles (which have the consequence that one's post may be seen only by those one already agrees with) and echo chambers (which have the consequence that one's objections will not be viewed as credible by those one is disagreeing with). See Nguyen (2020) for this distinction.

offer an eloquent means of objecting. However, for this to succeed, the silence has to be witnessed and understood as an objection. Key examples are resistant refusals to meet demands that one speaks and large silent protests. It is difficult to see how a failure to comment on a social media post could have the sorts of effects that one can obtain with these techniques. Eloquent silence, then, seems more likely in face-to-face situations.

So we still need to think through effective responses. The reflections so far have, I think, made it clear that there are very serious difficulties with any individual responding directly to offensive or false speech and hoping to correct it. So we turn now to institutional/group responses.

Institutional and Group Responses

Institutional Responses

To some extent, as we have already hinted, these issues are not new. In the 1960s, George Lincoln Rockwell, head of the American Nazi Party, carefully exploited the way that counterspeech could amplify and generate sympathy for his political movement. He did this by booking talks on liberal college campuses, where he knew he would be met with protests. This generated media coverage. The media coverage of the protestors who were (quite reasonably) angry also generated sympathy and financial donations for his cause. In response, Jewish groups developed a strategy that they called 'quarantine': they called on people, crucially including the media, to ignore the speeches. They asked campaigning groups not to protest, and they asked media not to cover the speeches.[15]

A key thing which is different now is the massive difficulty of succeeding in a quarantine strategy. Online responses are often not centrally organized in the way that a campaigning group might be, and even when they are, there may be many online campaigning groups—it would be very difficult to succeed in reaching all the relevant people and convincing them not to object. One *might* be able to get some mainstream media to agree not to cover something, but given media polarization, it seems clear that some large media operations, seeking to profit from controversy, would not be amenable to this idea. Even if they were, however, the Terry Jones case is quite a cautionary tale: mainstream media did ignore his announcement. But eventually the outcry on social media became strong enough that they felt they needed to cover it.

A quarantine as previously practiced, then, will not succeed. But social media also presents new methods that may be used. Certain recent moves by social media companies can be seen as attempts to reimagine quarantine for our times. Both

---

[15] See Beckett (2017); Donovan and boyd (2019).

Twitter and Facebook have made efforts to remove Q Anon conspiracy groups.[16] Social media companies are attempting to remove falsehoods about Covid-19.[17] They are also labelling certain false claims, about Covid-19 or the 2020 US Presidential election result, as false (not quarantining in this case, but providing a real-time correction rather than relying on users to do so).[18] Donovan and boyd (2019: 14) argue for a more nuanced proposal, *strategic amplification*, which they describe as 'a complex recognition that amplifying information is never neutral and those who amplify information must recognize the costs and consequences of publication'. One suggestion they offer is that amplification could be thought of as something that has to be *earned* from social media companies, suggesting that 'platforms can define successful recommendations and healthy feeds as those maximizing respect, dignity, and other productive social values. They can actively downweigh divisive, cruel, hateful, or antagonistic content.' (Donovan and boyd 2019: 13)

It remains to be seen how effective these efforts will be, but they seem clearly preferable to relying on individual users to take huge personal risks to raise objections and corrections that may only succeed in amplifying falsehoods and generating abuse.[19]

Group Responses

There are also some highly innovative group efforts to respond to false or offensive speech by reducing its prominence and/or raising the profile of countervailing views. In 2015, social justice advocates in Italy began a novel campaign to block the hatred being spread by far-right politician, Matteo Salvini. Salvini's social media feeds had become very effective vehicles for spreading anti-immigrant and racist sentiments, particularly targeting refugees and the Roma. In response, Progetto Kitten was born. This project involved activists flooding Salvini's social media feeds with photos of kittens—making it difficult to even find the posts stoking hatred.[20] An even more recent such effort involved taking over the twitter feed of the Proud Boys, a violent far-right group, with photos of 'proud boys', understood as meaning gay men expressing their pride (Bryant 2020). Similarly, the #iamhere group works to flood comment sections and social media feeds with supportive and accurate posts in order to combat online falsehood and misinformation (Eyre and Goillandeau 2019).

---

[16] See BBC News (2020), Timberg (2020).

[17] See Scott (2020), Reuters (2020).

[18] Individuals may, however, still have a role to play: these responses depend in some significant part on individuals reporting problematic posts.

[19] One problem with institutional responses so far has been biases and errors in how they are applied. See Chemaly (2019) for a discussion of these.

[20] My thanks to Martina Rosola for calling this to my attention. See Zaffarano (2015).

Responses like the above present one form of positive group-based counterspeech. But they are not the only one. Maxime Lepoutre (2019) discusses the importance of positive counterspeech, noting substantial evidence that it is more effective to combat a false story with a different, true story than with the mere negation of the false one. But Lepoutre also takes very seriously the difficulty of undoing the harms of false or oppressive speech. This is why he argues for a focus instead on *preemptive* counterspeech—educational efforts that can 'condition the conversational setting to make it inhospitable to ignorant speech' (Lepoutre 2019: 181). Although it may be too late to do anything helpful about your acquaintance's problematic social media post, Lepoutre would suggest, perhaps, it should serve as motivation to make preemptive efforts. This could consist of posting articles about how to spot untrustworthy sources, but at its most effective, it will surely involve large-scale educational efforts. Again, group-based (possibly institutional) counterspeech is likely to be more effective.

Adkins (2019) discusses one especially effective group-based response to sexist speech, especially notable because the original individual attempt at online shaming led to devastating consequences for the shamer while the group response was almost universally acclaimed. This was the case of Nobel Laureate, Tim Hunt, who made a stunningly sexist joke at a conference: 'let me tell you about my trouble with girls. 3 things happen when they are in the lab; you fall in love with them, they fall in love with you and when you criticize them, they cry' (Adkins 2019: 80). Connie St. Louis criticized this joke and ended up being forced out of science journalism. But women scientists started a hashtag, #distractinglysexy, featuring 'pictures of women vamping while holding test tubes, captions sarcastically praising themselves for managing to stave off sobs as they examine slides of tissue under microscopes or excavate archaeological sites' (Adkins 2019: 89). Adkins notes that this constructively redirected attention to the wide range of women scientists rather than to Hunt and also that participants gained safety and anonymity through the collective nature of the effort.

Conclusion

Many problems for counterspeech were already recognized in the philosophical literature which focused on face-to-face communication, such as oppressive power dynamics and dangers of speaking up (especially for members of marginalized groups). There were also concerns about impracticality and situations which make successful counterspeech less likely to succeed. All of these problems are greatly magnified by the workings of social media. Moreover, social media adds to this new ways of bringing about unwitting amplification and uncertainty regarding one's conversational context. Social media, however, also presents some new and potentially promising avenues for institutional and group approaches to false and oppressive speech. It is too early to tell which methods will be most effective for combatting falsehoods and hate-filled utterances on social media. But it does seem clear that direct individual responses are less likely to succeed than either group or institutional responses. The individual responsibility to issue corrections, then, is at the very least substantially lessened. So, to return to the scene from which we started: when you see those problematic utterances on your social media feed, you might be better off having another cup of coffee and thinking carefully and strategically about how to involve groups and institutions in fighting this problem, which is unlikely to be conquered through individual direct confrontations.

References

Adkins, K. (2019). When Shaming is Shameful: Double Standards in Online Shame Backlashes. *Hypatia, 34*(1), 76–97. https://doi.org/10.1111/hypa.12456.

Aitchison, G., & Meckled-Garcia, S. (2020). Against Online Public Shaming: Ethical Problems with Mass Social Media. *Social Theory and Practice*. https://doi.org/10.5840/soctheorpract20201117109.

Aly, W., & Simpson, R. (2019). Political Correctness Gone Viral. In C. Fox & J. Saunders (Eds.), *Media Ethics, Free Speech, and the Requirements of Democracy* (pp. 125–143). New York: Routledge. https://doi.org/10.4324/9780203702444.

BBC News (2020). Facebook Bans QAnon Conspiracy Theory Accounts Across All Platforms. BBC News, 6 October. https://www.bbc.com/news/world-us-canada-54443878. Accessed 11 December 2020.

Beckett, L. (2017). George Lincoln Rockwell, Father of American Nazis, Still in Vogue for Some. The Guardian, 27 August. https://www.theguardian.com/world/2017/aug/27/george-lincoln-rockwell-american-nazi-party-alt-right-charlottesville. Accessed 11 December 2020.

Billingham, P., & Parr, T. (2020). Online Public Shaming: Virtues and Vices. *Journal of Social Philosophy, 51*, 371–39. https://doi.org/10.1111/josp.12308.

boyd, d. (2018). Media Manipulation, Strategic Amplification, and Responsible Journalism. Data and Society: Points, 14 September. https://points.datasociety.net/media-manipulation-strategic-amplification-and-responsible-journalism-95f4d611f462. Accessed 11 December 2020.

Brown, A. (2019). The Meaning of Silence in Cyberspace. In S. Brison & K. Gelber (Eds.), *Free Speech in the Digital Age* (pp. 207–223). New York: Oxford University Press. https://doi.org/10.1093/oso/9780190883591.001.0001.

Bryant, M. (2020). LGBT Twitter Users Tease Far-Right Group By Taking Over Proud Boys Hash Tag. The Guardian, 5 October. https://www.theguardian.com/world/2020/oct/05/proud-boys-hashtag-lgbt-twitter-users. Accessed 11 December 2020.

Caponetto, L. (2020). Undoing Things With Words. *Synthese 19*, 2399–2414. https://doi.org/10.1007/s11229-018-1805-9.

Chemaly, S. (2019). Demographics, Design, and Free Speech. In S. Brison & K. Gelber. (Eds.), *Free Speech in the Digital Age* (pp. 150–169). New York: Oxford University Press. https://doi.org/10.1093/oso/9780190883591.003.0010.

Connolly, P. (2020). *Two Types of Conversation: Face-to-face and Digital*. PhD dissertation. Sheffield: University of Sheffield.

Cooper, P. (2020) How the Facebook Algorithm Works in 2020 and How to Make it Work for You. Hootsuite, 27 January. https://blog.hootsuite.com/facebook-algorithm/. Accessed 12 January 2021.

Davich, J. (2018). 'No, ma'am': McCain wasn't merely a politician, but a true patriot. Chicago Tribune, 30 August. https://www.chicagotribune.com/suburbs/post-tribune/opinion/ct-ptb-davich-john-mccain-no-maam-moment-st-0831-story.html. Accessed 15 January 2021.

Donovan, J., & boyd, d. (2019). Stop the Presses? Moving From Strategic Silence to Strategic Amplification in a Networked Media Ecosystem. *American Behavioral Scientist 65*(2), 333–350. https://doi.org/10.1177/0002764219878229.

Eyre, M., & Goillandeau, M. (2019). Here, Here: The Swedish Online Love Army Who Take on the Trolls. The Guardian, 15 January. https://www.theguardian.com/world/2019/jan/15/the-swedish-online-love-army-who-battle-below-the-line-comments. Accessed 15 January 2021.

Goldberg, S. (2020a). *Conversational Pressure.* New York: Oxford University Press.

Goldberg, S. (2020b.) The Promise and Pitfalls of Online Conversations [YouTube Video]. 7 February. London: Royal Institute of Philosophy London Lecture Series. https://youtu.be/DfxhOmRrDcE. Accessed 10 December 2020.

Grice, H. P. (1991). *Studies in the Way of Words.* Cambridge, MA: Harvard University Press.

Johnson, C. R. (2018). Just Say 'No': Obligations to Voice Disagreement, *Royal Institute of Philosophy Supplement 8,* 117–138. https://doi.org/10.1017/S1358246118000577.

Klieber, A. (2020). Conversational Silence Reconsidered (draft).

Lackey, J. (2018). Silence and Objecting. In C. R. Johnson, (Ed.), *Voicing Dissent. The Ethics and Epistemology of Making Disagreement Public* (pp. 82–96), New York: Routledge. https://doi.org/10.4324/9781315181189.

Langton, R. (2007). Disenfranchised Silence. In M. Smith, R. Goodin, & G. Geoffrey (Eds.), *Common Minds. Themes from the Philosophy of Philip Pettit* (pp. 199–214). Oxford: Oxford University Press.

Langton, R. (2018). Blocking as Counterspeech. In D. Harris, D. Fogal, & M. Moss (Eds.), *New Work on Speech Acts* (pp. 144–164), New York: Oxford University Press. https://doi.org/10.1093/oso/9780198738831.001.0001.

Lepoutre, M. (2019). Can 'More Speech' Counter Ignorant Speech?. *Journal of Ethics and Social Philosophy 16*(3), 155–191. https://doi.org/10.26556/jesp.v16i3.682.

Maitra, I. (2012). Subordinating Speech I. In I. Maitra & M.K. McGowan (Eds.), *Speech and Harm: Controversies Over Free Speech* (pp. 94–120), Oxford: Oxford University Press. https://doi.org/10.1093/acprof:oso/9780199236282.001.0001.

McGowan, M. K. (2012). On 'Whites Only' Signs and Racist Hate Speech: Verbal Acts of Racial Discrimination. In I. Maitra & M.K. McGowan (Eds.), *Speech and Harm: Controversies Over Free Speech,* (pp. 121–147). Oxford: Oxford University Press.

McGowan, M. K. (2018). Responding to Harmful Speech. In C. R. Johnson (Ed.), *Voicing Dissent* (pp. 182–200). New York: Routledge. https://doi.org/10.1093/acprof:oso/9780199236282.003.0006.

Nguyen, C. T. (2020). Echo Chambers and Epistemic Bubbles. *Episteme, 17*(2), 141–161. https://doi.org/10.5840/socphiltoday201762343.

Norlock, K. (2017). Online Shaming. *Social Philosophy Today,* 33, 187–197. https://doi.org/10.5840/socphiltoday201762343.

Nyhan, B., & Reifler, J. (2010). When Corrections Fail: The Persistence of Political Misperceptions. *Political Behavior, 32*, 303–330. https://doi.org/10.1007/s11109-010-9112-2.

Pettit, P. (2002). Enfranchising Silence. In P. Pettit, *Rules, Reasons, Norms* (pp. 367–378). Oxford: Clarendon Press. https://doi.org/10.1093/0199251878.001.0001.

Reuters (2020). Facebook Bans False Claims About Covid-19 Vaccines. NBC News, 3 December. https://www.nbcnews.com/tech/tech-news/facebook-bans-false-claims-covid-19-vaccines-rcna188. Accessed 11 December 2020.

Sawaoka, T., & Monin, B. (2018). The Paradox of Viral Outrage. *Psychological Science 29*(10), 1665–1678. https://doi.org/10.1177/0956797618780658.

Scott, M. (2020). Social Media Giants Are Fighting Coronavirus Fake News. It's Still Spreading Like Wildfire. Politico, 3 December. https://www.politico.com/news/2020/03/12/social-media-giants-are-fighting-coronavirus-fake-news-its-still-spreading-like-wildfire-127038. Accessed 11 December 2020.

Simpson, R. M. (2013). Unringing the bell: McGowan on oppressive speech and the asymmetric pliability of conversation. *Australasian Journal of Philosophy, 91*(3), 555–575. https://doi.org/10.1080/00048402.2012.704053.

Swire-Thompson, B., DeGutis, J., & D. Lazer. (2020). Searching for the Backfire Effect: Measurement and Design Considerations, Journal of Applied Research in Memory and Design Considerations. *Journal of Applied Research in Memory and Cognition, 9*(3), 286–299. https://doi.org/10.1016/j.jarmac.2020.06.006.

Tanesini, A. (2018). Eloquent Silences: Silence and Dissent. In C. R. Johnson (Ed.), *Voicing Dissent. The Ethics and Epistemology of Making Disagreement Public* (pp. 109–128). New York: Routledge. https://doi.org/10.4324/9781315181189.

Timberg, C. (2020). Twitter Banished the Worst QAnon Accounts. But More Than 93,000 Remain on the Site, Research Shows. Washington Post, 3 October. https://www.washingtonpost.com/technology/2020/10/03/twitter-banished-worst-qanon-accounts-more-than-93000-remain-site-research-shows/. Accessed 11 December 2020.

Zaffarano, F. (2015). La Pagina Facebook di Salvini e Invasa Dai Gattini. La Stampa, 7 May. https://www.lastampa.it/politica/2015/05/07/news/la-pagina-facebook-di-salvini-e-invasa-dai-gattini-1.35259558. Accessed 11 December 2020.

Chapter 9
Writing Against the 'Epistemology of Deceit' on Wikipedia: A Feminist New Materialist Perspective Towards Critical Media Literacy and Wikipedia-Based Education

Jialei Jiang and Matthew A. Vetter

Introduction

In their contribution to *Postdigital Science and Education*'s special issue of 'Lies, Bullshit, and Fake News Online', Jiang and Vetter (2019) argue that despite the programming of Wikipedia bots for combating problematic information, their efficacy is challenged by social, cultural, and technical issues related to misogyny, systemic bias, and conflict of interest (Bazely 2018; Gallert and Van der Velden 2015; Geiger and Ribes 2010; Glott et al. 2010). Problematic information, including types of misinformation and disinformation, points towards the urgency of building critical media literacy that has the potential to help students ward off the danger embedded in the 'epistemologies of ignorance' (Alcoff 2007; MacKenzie and Bhatt 2018) and 'deceit' (MacKenzie et al. 2020). In the postdigital era of problematic information, it is imperative that educators and students be on the alert for how the human and the nonhuman, the digital and the nondigital, interfere and exert agency in Wikipedia's complex and highly volatile processes of information validation.

In this chapter we continue these conversations by further exploring ways to counter the vices of problematic information on Wikipedia. We argue that a feminist new materialist perspective provides a promising theoretical lens for understanding critical literacy learning through Wikipedia-based writing projects. Employing feminist new materialist theories of intra-action (indicating a new materialist and posthumanist notion of shared agency) and lively assemblage (the multiplicity of diverse materials and actors that produce collective action) (Barad 2007; Bennett 2010; Lenz Taguchi 2010), we examine the ways that college students compose

J. Jiang (✉) · M. A. Vetter
Indiana University of Pennsylvania, Indiana, PA, USA
e-mail: mvetter@iup.edu

A. MacKenzie et al. (eds.), *The Epistemology of Deceit in a Postdigital Era*, Postdigital Science and Education,
https://doi.org/10.1007/978-3-030-72154-1_9

Wikipedia articles to address the encyclopedia's systemic biases, especially those related to misrepresentation and uneven coverage of women and minorities (Collier and Bear 2012; Glott et al. 2010; Gruwell 2015; Wadewitz 2013). More specifically, we attend to how students work together to identify marginalized topics on Wikipedia, evaluate the coverage of multiple perspectives in these Wikipedia articles, analyze information gaps and biases, and contribute knowledge to the global Wikipedia community.

The Wikipedia-based writing project, featuring the entanglement of human agents and digital technologies, challenges students to create sociomaterial assemblages (Bhatt 2017) that entice bodies into collective actions against the proliferation of problematic information within and beyond the encyclopedia. We ultimately contend that feminist new materialist perspectives add new vigor to the current theories and practices surrounding critical media literacy and conclude this chapter by envisioning the possibility of encouraging conscious use of the encyclopedia to more fully address the epistemic challenges of Wikipedia-based education.

Problematic Information and Critical Media Literacy in Wikipedia-Based Education

Problematic Information

The crisis of 'problematic information', what Jack (2017) defines as 'inaccurate, misleading, inappropriately attributed, or altogether fabricated' information, describes the failure of media ecologies (MacKenzie and Bhatt 2018) to address issues related to authenticity and rhetorical manipulation and the inability of formal education to teach critical media/information literacy. Terms like fake news, misinformation, and disinformation, while frequently used in public discourse, can be misleading. This chapter employs Caroline Jack's taxonomy, from 'Lexicon of Lies: Terms for Problematic Information' (2017), by utilizing her definition of misinformation and connecting it to epistemologies of deceit in Wikipedia.

According to Jack, misinformation includes 'information whose inaccuracy is unintentional', whereas disinformation is 'deliberately false or misleading' (Jack 2017: 2–3). In this chapter, we engage Jack's term misinformation to imply a type of problematic information that stems from broader social marginalizations and is translated in Wikipedia as specific knowledge gaps that repeat those marginalizations. For instance, Wikipedia's gender gap, or the disparity of content related to women, may be viewed as a general, cultural problem of patriarchy in addition to a lack of women Wikipedia editors. While these knowledge gaps are not actively planned or premeditated to spread 'deliberately false or misleading' information, their implications are significant and far-reaching just the same. Furthermore, these types of misinformation may be even more dangerous precisely because they are not intentionally promoted by identifiable actors—contributing to a larger epistemology of deceit in what has become the most widely used encyclopedia in human history.

The Wikipedia-based writing project, we contend, provides direct opportunities to write against the epistemology of deceit within the encyclopedia’s community. As students become more familiar with Wikipedia practices, they also realize the need to create sociomaterial assemblages that work towards increased and distributed reliability of the encyclopedia’s content, enticing bodies into collective actions and intra-actions both within and beyond the encyclopedia. In the following sections, we review and expand on conceptions of critical media literacy; introduce feminist new materialism as a method for studying critical media literacy practices; provide a review of two Wikipedia-based assignments (one at the undergraduate level and one at the graduate level); and apply theories of intra-action and lively assemblage to student edits and reflections. In considering the implications of critical media literacy, we ultimately make pedagogical realizations concerning (1) new understandings of agency, activism, and reliability within the specific context of Wikipedia and Wikipedia-based education and (2) opportunities for pedagogies of intersectional feminism while making note of the specific challenges related to Wikipedia-based assignments. Furthermore, these realizations demonstrate how Wikipedia-based writing assignments enable pedagogies that can work against the epistemology of deceit to battle problematic information.

Critical Media Literacy

Our use of critical media literacy engages Kellner and Share’s (2005) definition. For Kellner and Share, critical media literacy encompasses five core concepts:

1. Non-Transparency: All media messages are ‘constructed’.
2. Codes and Conventions: Media messages are constructed using a creative language with its own rules.
3. Audience Decoding: Different people experience the same media message differently.
4. Content and Message: Media have embedded values and points of view.
5. Motivation: Media are organized to gain profit and/or power. (374–376)

More specifically, the fourth concept emphasizes the ways that students are capable of addressing the values, assumptions, and ideologies underlying the representation of race, gender, and class in digital media spaces. While focusing on detailing the ideological nature of human communication, Kellner and Share nevertheless fail to attend to the robust roles played by nonhuman actors in shaping and reshaping the communicative acts in new media. Our extension of their work, particularly through the lens of feminist new materialist theories, has sought to highlight the complex processes through which subjectivity, ideology, and agency cut across nonhuman and human relations.

A range of scholarship exists on critical literacy (e.g., Duffelmeyer 2002; Jiang 2020; Kellner and Share 2005; LeCourt 1998; Selber 2004; Thomson-Bunn 2014) and feminist new materialism (e.g., Barad 2007; Bennett 2010), respectively, yet only recently is there work emerging on exploring the intersection between the two domains of research. In their recently published book *Affect, Embodiment, and Place in Critical Literacy*, Lenters and McDermott draw our attention to the possibility of rethinking feminist new materialisms in light of empathy and ethical encounters with literacy. Specifically, Barad's work on new materialism propels researchers towards 'intra-actions that matter in the world' (Lenters and McDermott 2019: 7). Reframing critical literacy through the lens of feminist new materialist thought, Lenters and McDermott pinpoint a form of critical literacy that opens up 'a generative worldmaking practice, one that goes beyond critique as an endpoint and looks towards ongoing commitment and action' (8). In what follows, we employ a feminist new materialist framework to approach Wikipedia-based writing as a site of critical literacy action.

Entangling with Differences: Feminist New Materialisms as a Method to Study Critical Media Literacy Practices

A robust theoretical framework, feminist new materialism, affords a new understanding of critical media literacy that looks towards 'ongoing commitment and action' (Lenters and McDermott 2019: 9). We draw on various conceptual contributions to feminist new materialism, particularly by Barad and Bennett. In this section, we first briefly introduce the assignments and course contexts for each Wikipedia-based writing project, and from which we draw our qualitative data regarding edits and student reflections. The first assignment was taught in a doctoral-level seminar in digital rhetoric and the second in a first-year, general education writing course. Taken together, these courses demonstrate the flexibility of Wikipedia-based pedagogy for engaging students' critical media literacy. Following the assignment descriptions, we provide a review of two conceptual frames that make up our feminist new materialist perspective, namely: (1) intra-action and (2) lively assemblage. These concepts are then employed to analyze and interpret qualitative data from student work on these assignments.

Assignment Descriptions

A final course project in English 846: Digital Rhetoric was a planned Wikipedia Edit-a-thon as a campus event. Edit-a-thons (a portmanteau of 'editing' and 'marathon') are typically one-day gatherings in which participants work together to improve a subject area in the encyclopedia by learning how to edit and contributing to Wikipedia. This specific event was further specialized in that we were working with the organization Art+Feminism to consciously engage representation of marginalized identities (women, LGBTQIA identities, related topics) through active editing and participation. While the actual event was cancelled due to Covid-19 and social-distancing measures, students were asked to do a small editing project of their own, in lieu of this event, focusing on articles and topics related to the course. For this project, students worked in small groups (2–3 students per group) to assess the quality of and improve a Wikipedia article related to the course topic of digital rhetoric. Overall, 12 student editors made a total of 170 edits and added approximately 3800 words to improve the following articles: 'Hashtag activism', 'Internet meme', 'Digital identity', 'Digital literacy', 'Digital rhetoric', and 'Visual rhetoric'.

In English 101: Composition I, students were assigned a similar project in which they would assess and develop 12 Wikipedia articles on marginalized topics. A major difference here was that topic selections were more open and not necessarily tied to the subject of the course itself. Overall, 46 student editors made a total of 363 edits and added approximately 103,000 words to improve specific Wikipedia articles. Articles edited included topics such as 'Violence Against LGBT People', 'Educational Inequality', 'Gender equality', 'Obesity in the United States', 'Assistive Technology Service Provider', and 'Exploitation of Women in Mass Media'. While Wikipedia is constantly being updated, a majority of the edits remained on the encyclopedia, which demonstrated the enduring power of this kind of pedagogical intervention.

In both courses, instructors led discussions on knowledge gaps in Wikipedia (especially the issue of Wikipedia's gender gap) in order to engage students' critical thinking. Students in the graduate course chose two essays from the recent book *Wikipedia @ 20: Stories from an Incomplete Revolution*: Alexander Lockett's (2020) 'Why Do I Have Authority to Edit the Page? The Politics of User Agency and Participation on Wikipedia' and Denny Vrandečić's (2020) 'Collaborating on the Sum of All Knowledge Across Languages'. With both an open-access and print version, Wikipedia @ 20 offers a number of accessible and current reflections on Wikipedia's failures and successes over the last 20 years (Reagle and Koener 2020).

Furthermore, both courses were supported by resources offered by Wiki Education, a nonprofit educational organization that works with higher education instructors to develop and integrate Wikipedia assignments.

Intra-action in Student Edits and Reflections

We turn to intra-action as a theoretical construct to better understand student-produced Wikipedia edits and their reflections on the edits. From a feminist new materialist perspective, agency is not fixed and predetermined. Karen Barad's 'intra-action' moves beyond viewing agency as solely produced in discourse and towards conceptualizing agency as emergent from and mediated by material reality, as well. This theoretical move has provided a new materialistic response to Foucault's notions of discursive and non-discursive practices that locate power and agency within social interactions. As Barad (2003) argues, for Foucault even the non-discursive practices have been reduced to social institutional practices; therefore, focusing on discourses alone is no longer a useful strategy for extending the new materialist view of agency beyond social dimensions.

Drawing inferences from the physicist Niel Bohr, Barad has developed the concept of *intra-action* as a rejection of observer-observed dichotomy in support of a 'flow of agency' permeated through both human and nonhuman forces (Barad 2003: 817). In Barad's words, 'the world is an ongoing intra-active engagement, and bodies are among the differential performances of the world's dynamic intra-activity, in an endless reconfiguring of boundaries and properties, including those of spacetime' (2008: 377). The focus here is on the entangled nature of the material and the discursive, as well as the lively relationship between humans and nonhumans (Barad 2003, 2007; Lenz Taguchi 2010). An intra-active account of literacy positions bodies within relationships with other bodies, opening the possibility of producing new literacies, meanings, and knowledge.

The application of *intra-action* as a methodology in literacy research can be glimpsed in Jackson and Mazzei's (2012) intra-active analysis of female faculty members' narratives that shifts the attention to 'entangled state of agencies' (125), viewing agency as emergent from both social and material relations. As a case in point, the intra-action between human and material spaces is vividly depicted in the narratives of Cassandra, a female African American college faculty member. In their qualitative research describing how intra-action takes place, Jackson and Mazzei delineate the ways through which the materiality of Cassandra's office co-constructs the power dynamics of 'belonging' and 'exclusionary' spaces, which in turn shape Cassandra's intersected identities as at once privileged and marginalized, at once a female professor and a person of color. Not unlike Jackson and Mazzei's assertions, Ehret, Hollett, and Jocius' (2016) intra-active study of adolescents' new media making documents the ways that the discursive-material practices of multimodal compositions might allow for a dissolution of boundaries between bodies, meanings, and materials. The researchers underscore that agency is dispersed across both human new media makers and nonhuman technologies and that the entangled agency holds robust implications for the co-production of knowledge and meaning.

Thinking of Wikipedia-based writing in a similar vein, in this chapter, we approach multimodal and digital composition through the lens of intra-action and entangled agencies. More specifically, we understand the production of knowledge on Wikipedia to be a distributed and enacted practice. Our analysis builds on Kennedy's (2016) theorization of Wikipedia authorship as a part of distributed curatorial practices: 'Given its [Wikipedia's] frequently collaborative nature, it also requires becoming comfortable with forms of authorial agency that are explicitly distributed and contextual.' (28) That is, since Wikipedia is a global platform that allows anyone to edit and collaborate, the collaborative nature of such work challenges us to reconsider the notion of single authorship in the traditional sense. We thus contend that writing against problematic information on the platform is a practice enacted through student editors' intra-active (and ethical) encounters with digital information literacy.

In both the undergraduate and graduate assignments, students' edits and reflections help students begin to understand agency in combatting problematic information as a distributed, social and material, intra-action (Barad 2003). English 846: Digital Rhetoric students working on the Wikipedia Hashtag activism for example, described the activist nature of hashtags #RealConvo and #FireDrillFridays as working in both material and discursive contexts through textual, human, and material agents. One student added the following to the article: 'Real Convo features guides for talking about mental illness and videos of celebrities such as Sasha Pieterse and Sydney Marguder sharing their mental health stories.' (Wikipedia 2020)

In another section of the Wikipedia article, another student worked to add representation of a different hashtag, #FireDrill Fridays. As in #RealConvo, this student also focused on the human/material entanglement of actors that bring about the hashtag's (intra-)activism, invoking celebrity actors and activists, political legislation, protest events, as well as specific and established outcomes of the hashtag: 'Inspired by Greta Thunberg and started by Greenpeace and Jane Fonda, #FireDrillFridays brings awareness to the climate change crisis...Calling for a Green New Deal in the United States government, the movement organized protests on the Capital every Friday beginning in October 2019...The campaign advocates no new fossil fuels and to phase out existing fossil fuel projects.' (Wikipedia 2020)

These students began to make realizations about intra-action as a distributed flow of agency by making the following edit to the Hashtag activism page: 'By initiating conversations and confronting problems, hashtags serve as a digitally-informed extension of the role language has always held in generating political action.' (Wikipedia 2020) Students working on the Hashtag activism article, in addition to making edits such as those represented above, also collaborated on a shared reflection. Their reflection further demonstrates their awareness of the capacity of hashtag activism to 'create change and/or community' through a sociomaterial and distributed process of intra-action. In describing their motivation to add the #RealConvo section, one group member observed how a paragraph on this hashtag represents 'a good addition to the Wikipedia page because it links users to a few mental health resources and emphasizes the importance of working to end stigmas associated with mental illness'. 'Given the current pandemic situation', they continue, 'it's essential to talk about mental health, and having a hashtag to use can, via social media, increase support and validation for individuals with mental illness'.

This reflection, in opposition to tropes regarding the insignificance of hashtag activism as 'armchair activism demonstrates students' understanding of how mental health awareness is created through an intra-action of multiple agents. They further describe the material impact of hashtags, and their representation and description in Wikipedia, by emphasizing the rhetorical connections made possible through their circulation:

> Drawing from Jones's (2018) piece about Pinterest as a site of both collaboration and individuality, we tried to show the emotional and practical benefits of using hashtags [by adding the following to the Wikipedia article]: 'Identifying shared experiences builds

rhetorical connections between people who would never otherwise meet, enabling users of hashtags such as #MeToo and #BlackLivesMatter to support and validate each other.'

'Intra-action' and enacted agency can also be glimpsed in undergraduate students' contribution to the article Gender Equality as well as the dynamic role played by their use of wikilinks, or internal hyperlinks to other Wikipedia pages. The student group working on the article 'Gender Equality' identified multiple intersectional actors that together generate forces and capacities to intra-act with other human and nonhuman affordances. For instance, in their reflection, the students turned to the support of gender equality by the United Nations, the violence against trans women, as well as issues related to women's health. The student who worked on expanding the section on the violence against trans women in the article contributed intersectional knowledge to Wikipedia's coverage of women:

> Trans women in the United States have encountered the subject of anti-trans stigma, which includes criminalization, dehumanization, and violence against those who identify as transgender. From a societal stand point, a trans person can be victim to the stigma due to lack of family support, issues with health care and social services, police brutality, discrimination in the work place, cultural marginalisation, poverty, sexual assault, assault, bullying, and mental trauma. The Human Rights Campaign tracked over 128 cases [*clarification needed*] that ended in fatality against transgender people in the US from 2013 to 2018, of which eighty percent included a trans woman of color. In the US, high rates of Intimate Partner violence impact trans women differently because they are facing discrimination from police and health providers, and alienation from family. In 2018, it was reported that 77 percent of transgender people who were linked to sex work and 72 percent of transgender people who were homeless, were victims of intimate partner violence (Wikipedia 2019).

While the article Gender Equality has largely overlooked the experiences of trans women, which leads towards problematic information, this student's contribution attests to the inter-active capacity of wikilinks (links to other Wikipedia articles) in addressing and challenging such negligence. In particular, the students' use of wikilinks speaks to intra-activity and relationality and demonstrates their complex understanding regarding the interconnected actors in contributing to the asymmetrical power relations and encounters in relation to trans women.

Lively Assemblage in Students' Edits and Reflections

The framing of lively assemblage in feminist new materialism further leads us to reconstrue Wikipedia as synonymous to a networked assemblage of social material relationships. As defined by Deleuze and Parnet (1987), an assemblage is 'a multiplicity which is made up of many heterogeneous terms and which establishes liaisons, relations between them across ages, sexes and reigns—different natures. Thus, the assemblage's only unity is that of co-functioning: it is a symbiosis, a sympathy (69). Bennett's (2010) agential assemblage takes Deleuze and Parnet's conception of assemblage a bit further to concentrate on a composite of vital things, both animate and inanimate. The act of tracing assemblages is particularly salient for studying digital composition practices for social action. Gries (2015) has deployed the method of iconoclastic tracing to analyze the online distribution of the 'Obama Hope' campaign. More recently, Gries (2019) further applies assemblage theory for analyzing the impact of student multimodal advocacy campaigns.

Beyond the acts of remixing and circulating, participants and researchers involved in multimodal writing projects also act as part of the assemblage. Continuing such conversations Gries (2019: 334) pinpoints that 'assemblage is limited when we solely think about it in terms of textuality' and that 'assemblage ought to be understood in terms of ontology—as a phenomenon that takes place on multiple scales, among intermingling human and nonhuman entities, to constitute collective life'. In short, practicing feminist new materialism would follow that we become attuned to the various, networked assemblage of human and nonhuman entities and bodies that contribute to social advocacy and collective action.

In our application of lively assemblage to the Wikipedia-based writing project, we read sociomaterial assemblages as dispersed textualities and agents that work to co-construct reliability within the encyclopedia. Furthermore, such assemblages entice users/bodies into collective actions against the proliferation of problematic information within and beyond the encyclopedia. From a feminist new materialism perspective, we understand human beings as more than capable of knowing; instead, human actions are inextricably intertwined with human-technology assemblages. So, when addressing college writers' use of Wikipedia, a feminist new materialism approach allows us to center on the ways in which human beings come together with digital technologies and material resources to generate capacities for combatting problematic information and, in doing so, challenge the epistemology of deceit on Wikipedia.

In order to reframe the notion of reliability in Wikipedia as assembled by multiple social actors, policies, and algorithmic processes, we employ the term ethical assemblage to describe the construction of reliability as a dynamic assembling of ethos (credibility) rather than a static or individual process. We invoke 'assemblage' in the tradition of Deleuze and Parnet, as well as scholars influenced by the material and ecological implications of their work in rhetoric and media studies (Barnett and Boyle 2016; Gries 2015; Nicotra 2016; Walker 2016). Furthermore, we view student edits and reflections, especially those centered on assembling multiple sources and agents, as uncovering the multiplicities of such ethical assemblages. While these processes are more pronounced in the graduate students' edits and reflections, discussed immediately below, we also view undergraduates' work as moving towards the production of ethical assemblages and an understanding of distributed reliability in Wikipedia.

In making edits to the article on Hashtag Activism', one student working to represent the #RealConvo hashtag, a campaign focusing on mental health awareness, created textual and material assemblages that synthesized organizations, people, identities, and other textual and material agents work towards an assembled ethos. The excerpt below displays wiki markup, such as wikilinks and reference numbers, to show the intertextual and material connections being made:

> **#RealConvo**
> #RealConvo represents the Real Convo project by the American Foundation for Suicide Prevention (ASFP). Begun in May 2019, Real Convo features guides for talking about mental illness and videos of celebrities such as Sasha Pieterse and Sydney Magruder sharing their mental health stories. AFSP created #RealConvo for people to share personal stories and combat mental illness stigma. Organizations such as National Alliance on Mental Illness and To Write Love on Her Arms have retweeted #RealConvo with links to mental health resources. (Wikipedia 2020)

Edits made to the #FireDrillFridays hashtag section of the same article, discussed above, also combine multiple wikilinks, references, and material/physical touchstones towards the assemblage of reliability and notability. Since the student's edit, that passage has been further developed to include a multiplicity of diverse sources:

> **#FireDrillFridays**
> Inspired by Greta Thunberg and started by Greenpeace and Jane Fonda, #FireDrillFridays brings awareness to the climate change crisis. Calling for a Green New Deal in the United States government, the movement organized protests on the Capitol every Friday beginning in October 2019. The campaign also advocates for complete stoppage of new fossil fuel projects and to phase out existing fossil fuel projects. #FireDrillFridays gained popularity with celebrity arrests. Due to the COVID-19 pandemic, Fonda moved #FireDrillFridays online to continue rallying for government action. (Wikipedia 2020)

Reflecting on these edits, this student discusses how they brought together multiple types of sources to build ethos in the article: 'I used news articles and the website created for the cause for additional resources for the reader.' As is apparent from the above excerpt, the integration of wikilinks and references to additional organizations, celebrities, and sources also provides a diverse and dispersed assemblage towards reliability and illustrates the notion of ethical assemblages often contained in a single section or paragraph of a Wikipedia article.

For undergraduate editors, they similarly position credibility and reliability within the complex assemblage of information in and across the Wikipedia platform, but from a novice standpoint. The student editors who worked on the article titled 'Violence against LGBT People' provide an illustration. These students, in their reflection essay, describe the challenges of finding relevant and productive sources that do not violate Wikipedia's Neutral point of view and No original research policies (McDowell and Vetter 2020), without inserting their own emotional responses to the topic:

> I think that the most difficult part was actually finding information for what I wanted to specifically write about. Most of the articles I came across on google scholar talked about a specific group in the LGBT community and I was searching for information on the LGBT people as a whole. Also, I think another difficult thing about the Wikipedia was being careful not to insert my own personal feelings or emotions into my writing especially because the LGBT community is such a sensitive topic touch on.

> When someone edits a Wikipedia page they have to cite where they got these information [*sic*] from. So at the bottom of every Wikipedia page there is a place of links that will take you to a website where the information came from. This can be really helpful because most of these links are credible sources that can be used in the research project someone is doing.

While these students may have struggled with the process of building an adequate foundation of sources, they did recognize that reliability is generated out of human-material assemblages. This realization is particularly evident in a student reflection essay in which they recognize how the Wikipedia assignment allows for an assemblage of ethos. Such assemblage links student editors with online communities and digital tools, such as Google Scholar, Wikipedia citations and links, the LGBT community, as well as students' personal feelings or emotions about LGBT issues. By attending to how reliability is constructed in Wikipedia, and working to improve content, furthermore, students also practice critical literacy action (Lenters and McDermott 2019).

Towards Assembled Reliability

In employing the concept of lively assemblage to interpret students' edits in the graduate course, we begin to see how Wikipedia-based assignments provide opportunities for more nuanced understanding of assembled reliability. We propose the term ethical assemblages to understand lively assemblages that, in the encyclopedia, demonstrate the distributed production of reliability and that write against epistemologies of deceit such as misinformation. Indeed, it is Wikipedia's highly collaborative and crowd-sources model—for which it has been demonized since its inception (Black 2010; Gorman 2007)—that allows for distributed constructions of information across both human and nonhuman agencies. Take the process of source evaluation, for instance. In Wikipedia, source evaluation and the subsequent production of reliable information is distributed among multiple agents: editors, yes, but also policies (verifiability, no original research, neutral point of view), bots, administrators, readers, and other textual features that become agentive in the process.

In examining undergraduate students' work, we ultimately argue that students be introduced to this understanding of assembled reliability as part of critical media literacy education. Current information literacy models tend to stress individual sources and their authors. Consider the C.R.A.A.P. test, first developed by Sarah Blakeslee (2004). Currency, relevance, authority, authority, and purpose serve as productive heuristics for evaluating individual sources. However, in thinking about sources as inherently complex, multiple, and intertextual, a more ecological model that considers the dynamic assemblage of reliability is needed.

Countering the Vices of Problematic Information in Wikipedia: Implications for Wikipedia-Based Education and Critical Media Literacy

Approaching Wikipedia-based education from the standpoint of feminist new materialism and critical literacy enables methodologies for critical literacy action against an epistemology of deceit. Such praxis 'goes beyond critique as an endpoint and looks towards ongoing commitment and action' (Lenders and McDermott) both within and beyond Wikipedia. As has been pointed out by other scholar-teacher-activists (Graham 2010; Vetter et al. 2018), and as we have attempted to demonstrate in this chapter, Wikipedia commands a postdigital influence on discursive and material realities. Due to the encyclopedia's place as a significant arbiter in the global knowledge economy, its representations serve as an implied ontology, a factual world-making in the ongoing construction of information. Seeking out problematic information in the encyclopedia, understanding its emergence, and working to write against the epistemology of deceit, accordingly, has implications for sociomaterial circumstances across multiple digital and postdigital contexts.

This study further demonstrates the Wikipedia-based writing opens up the opportunity for students to exercise critical media literacy. As mentioned earlier, Lenters and McDermott contend that thinking with feminist new materialisms invigorates empathy and ethical encounters with critical literacy. Specifically, Barad's work on new materialism propels researchers towards 'intra-actions that matter in the world' (Lenters and McDermott 2019: 7). We consider the Wikipedia assignment as a form of critical literacy practices that valorizes ongoing commitment and social action.

Previous research on Wikipedia-based education has approached this pedagogy from theoretical standpoints as diverse as social-epistemic theory, rhetorical theory, queer/feminist media praxis, feminist epistemology, information literacy, and critical media literacy, yet few studies have investigated Wikipedia from the perspective of feminist new materialism. Reading student edits and reflections through the dual lenses of 'intra-action' (Barad 2003) and 'lively assemblages' (Barad 2007; Bennett 2010) yields at least three important implications for Wikipedia-based education, discussed below.

Teaching Towards New Understandings of Agency and Activism

Barad's (2003) concept of intra-action allows for the understanding of Wikipedia editing as a mode of distributed activism against the epistemology of deceit (and especially misinformation). As students worked to add content and improve information surrounding particular social advocacy campaigns in the article on 'Hashtag activism', for example, they also grew more cognizant of the ways that agency is created through an entanglement of both material and discursive, human and nonhuman actors. In order to promote a particular hashtag campaign, students realized they would need to bring together multiple actors in order to mediate across material and digital landscapes. Such an understanding has implications for both critical media literacy and rhetorical knowledge related to agency. As discussed previously, the model presented in this chapter provides opportunities for critical action, as Wikipedia edits enable the broader public new forms of awareness and rhetorical knowledge, allowing students to gain insight regarding the sharing of agency among multiple actors and opening the possibility of producing new literacies, meanings, and knowledge.

Teaching Towards a Distributed Notion of Reliability

Employing the concept of 'lively assemblage' has also allowed us to reframe the notion of reliability in Wikipedia. In particular, we theorized the term 'ethical assemblage' to describe the construction of reliability as a dynamic assembling of ethos involving multiple social actors, policies, and algorithmic processes. In Wikipedia, this dynamic assembling is achieved as readers, editors, and bots collaborate to improve encyclopedic content over long periods of time. To teach towards this distributed notion of reliability, educators in the humanities and social sciences must jettison previous models of information evaluation (Blakeslee 2004) and look towards more ecological frameworks for describing and teaching the evaluation of online sources especially.

The concept of ethical assemblages, while not immediately accessible as a concept to first-year students, holds promise for further exploring and teaching critical media literacy because it demands we view ethos as something assembled and multiple. Such an understanding builds on Kennedy's (2016) theorization of distributed and curatorial practices in Wikipedia while also critiquing isolated models of reliability (Blakeslee 2004). However, our work with the theoretical notion of ethical assemblage is only a beginning. We call on other researchers, especially, to expand this concept by articulating its functions as an ecological model for distributed reliability and testing its premise in their own pedagogies. This could be done in a variety of ways, but might be most useful when applied to the critical evaluation of ethical assemblages in online texts beyond Wikipedia.

Opportunities for Pedagogies of Intersectional Feminism

The Wikipedia editing assignments presented in this study allow for a type of intersectional feminist pedagogy that encourages students to attend to knowledge equity and misinformation. Broadly conceived, attending to systemic biases through multimodal pedagogy allows students to recognize the intersectionality of systems of oppression. The notion of intersectionality has its roots in social science research that highlights connections between different cultural categories or sociomaterial axes, such as race, gender, and class, and ability, when it comes to the formation of social inequality and individual identities (Collins and Bilge 2016; Crenshaw 1991). As such, intersectionality provides a conceptual framework for literacy scholars and social activists to better understand the multiple identity struggles of disenfranchised social groups. Crenshaw (1991) incisively pinpoints the issues looming behind identity politics in the United States. As she writes, 'women of color are differently situated in the economic, social, and political worlds. When reform efforts undertaken on behalf of women neglect this fact, women of color are less likely to have their needs met than women who are racially privileged.' (Crenshaw 1991: 1250) Efforts to support women of color, especially rape victims, may backfire due to their failure to move beyond simplistic racial categories representing women of color and due to their inattention to the intersection between race and gender. In other words, intersectionality creates the identity politics that takes heed of the multiple oppressions experienced by people from marginalized social groups.

The question, however, is how to respond to the intersectional call without oversimplifying the complexities and flexibilities of intersected forms of identity and agency. The very notion of intersectionality is faced with methodological challenges. As Dolmage and Lewiecki-Wilson (2010) assert, categorizing, for example, disability through the lens of intersectionality runs the risk of reducing 'disability' to a neutral, stable, and universal identity marker and an add-on, without taking into account the 'materiality of multiple oppressions' and nuanced experiences of marginalized groups. Analogous to this critique, Barad (2007) cautions that the compartmentalization of identity into categories falls prey to a 'container' model or metaphor emergent from the categorical rationality that is salient in western culture.

A categorical imagination as such may lose sight of the complex human-materiality entanglement underlying the processes of identification and becoming. In other words, the categorical conceptualization of agency may also invite the risk of entrenching the differences between human beings and material things that fail to account for their interconnections. The material dimension of identity has not been fully explored in this line of thought. One way to address the issue of categorical thinking is through delving into the material dimensions of agency. Feminist new materialist notions such as intra-action (Barad 2007) and assemblage (Bennett 2010) can be useful methodological heuristics to address the categorical view of agency in critical literacy practices.

Challenges and Conclusions

Indeed, the feminist new materialist approach for Wikipedia-based writing pedagogies has been met with challenges. At the graduate level, students encountered difficulties in creating equitable representation of marginalized social groups, such as women and minorities. For instance, students identified challenges related to locating and citing sources effectively, especially for marginalized topics that tend to be underrepresented and undercited. It is essential for students to recognize Western, logocentric epistemologies that often silence or omit already marginalized types of knowledge. In addition to dominance of certain epistemologies, Wikipedia is vastly uneven among different language editions, of which there are nearly 300. The English version is by far the most well-developed, with over six million articles as of late 2020. Furthermore, the spectrum of development of these different versions is incredibly wide. As Denny Vrandečić realizes, 'if you take the bottom half of all Wikipedias ranked by size, together they wouldn't have 10 percent of the number of articles in the English Wikipedia' (Vrandečić 2020). Such disparities also extend across specific article development. Even when Wikipedia language editions contain the same articles, the content and/or level of development of those articles can be vastly different. Feminist new materialist framework provides an alternative epistemology for enhancing the coverage of marginalized topics and languages, but these problems are often complex and far-reaching. Linguistic disparities, for instance, will require a broader global campaign to truly address, one that can be sustained beyond a 15-week term.

At the undergraduate level, it is difficult to both teach Wikipedia's policies (e.g., the principle of neutrality) and to encourage students to critically reflect on and productively respond to those policies. Since Wikipedia policies are essential for being successful in the Wikipedia community, it is difficult to enact the social critique and action that would potentially undermine students' success in contributing knowledge to the Wikipedia platform. As first-year writers, students in this study may not be ready to engage in more advanced critical literacy development, especially in addition to the challenges associated with reframing previous assumptions regarding Wikipedia and the technological skills participating in Wikipedia requires. Nevertheless, we see the initiation of critical literacy development in first-year writing a necessary challenge, especially if we are to combat online deceit.

Despite these challenges, employing the Wikipedia-based assignment as a form of feminist new materialist praxis enables opportunities for students to practice critical media literacy and write against the epistemology of deceit in the online encyclopedia anyone can edit. Students' Wikipedia edits and reflection demonstrate specific applications for exercising and understanding dynamic intra-actions that create assembled agencies for change. Engaging Wikipedia and misinformation, furthermore, provides new opportunities for producing new theoretical models related to a distributed notion of reliability, what we call ethical assemblages'. As a coda to this chapter, we invite educators and researchers to take up Wikipedia-based education within a feminist new materialist framework in order to further research and practice in this area. Studying and teaching with Wikipedia enables multiple avenues for new understandings of problematic information and for teaching critical media literacy. We look forwards to engaging in future conversations related to reliability and agency especially.

References

Alcoff, L. M. (2007). Epistemologies of ignorance: Three types. In S. Sullivan & N. Tuana (Eds.), *Race and epistemologies of ignorance* (pp. 39–58). Albany: State University of New York Press.

Barad, K. (2003). Posthumanist performativity: Toward an understanding of how matters comes to matter. *Signs, 28*(3), 801–31. https://doi.org/10.1086/345321.

Barad, K. (2007). *Meeting the universe halfway: Quantum physics and the entanglement of matter and meaning*. Durham, NC: Duke University Press.

Barnett, S., & Boyle, C. A. (Eds.). (2016). *Rhetoric, through everyday things*. Tuscaloosa, AL: University Alabama Press.

Bazely, D. (2018). Why Nobel prize winner Donna Strickland didn't have a Wikipedia page. The Washington Post, 8 October. https://www.washingtonpost.com/outlook/2018/10/08/why-nobel-winner-donna-strickland-didnt-have-wikipedia-page/?utm_term=.cedfbbe4ae8e. Accessed 5 May 2019.

Bennett, J. (2010). *Vibrant matter: A political ecology of things*. Durham, NC: Duke University Press.

Bhatt, I. (2017). *Assignments as Controversies: Digital Literacy and Writing in Classroom Practice*. Abingdon and New York: Routledge.

Black, E. (2010). Wikipedia—The dumbing down of world knowledge. History News Network. https://historynewsnetwork.org/article/125437. Accessed 20 September 2020.

Blakeslee, S. (2004). The CRAAP test, *LOEX Quarterly, 31*(3), https://commons.emich.edu/loexquarterly/vol31/iss3/4. Accessed 20 September 2020.

Collier, B., & Bear J. (2012). Conflict, confidence, or criticism: An empirical examination of the gender gap in Wikipedia. In ACM, *The ACM Conference on Computer Supported Cooperative Work* (pp. 383-92). New York: Association for Computing Machinery. https://doi.org/10.1145/2145204.2145265.

Collins, P. H., & Bilge, S. (2016). *Intersectionality (Key Concepts)*. Cambridge: Polity Press.

Crenshaw, K. (1991). Mapping the margins: Intersectionality, identity politics, and violence against women of color. *Stanford Law Review, 43(*6), 1241-1299. https://doi.org/10.2307/1229039.

Deleuze, G., & Parnet, C. (1987). *Dialogues*. New York: Columbia University Press.

Dolmage, J., & Lewiecki-Wilson, C. (2010). Refiguring Rhetorica: Linking Feminist Rhetoric and Disability Studies. In E. Schell & K. Rawson (Eds.), *Rhetorica in Motion: Feminist Rhetorical Methods and Methodologies* (pp. 36-60). Pittsburgh, PA: Pittsburgh University Press.

Duffelmeyer, B. (2002). Critical work in first-year composition: Computers, pedagogy, and research. *Pedagogy, 2*(3), 357-74.

Ehret, C., Hollett, T., & Jocius, R. (2016). The matter of new media making. *Journal of Literacy Research*, *48*(3), 346–377. https://doi.org/10.1177%2F1086296X16665323.

Gallert, P., & van der Velden, M. (2015). The sum of all human knowledge? Wikipedia and indigenous knowledge. In N. J. Bidwell & H. Winschiers-Theophilus (Eds.), *At the Intersection of Indigenous and Traditional Knowledge and Technology Design* (pp. 117–133). Santa Rosa, CA: Informing Science Press.

Geiger, R. S., & Ribes, D. (2010). The work of sustaining order in Wikipedia: The banning of a vandal. In ACM, *CSCW '10: Proceedings of the 2010 ACM conference on Computer supported cooperative work* (pp. 6–10). New York: Association for Computing Machinery. https://doi.org/10.1145/1718918.1718941.

Glott, R., Schmidt, P., & Ghosh, R. (2010). Wikipedia survey – Overview of results. http://www.ris.org/uploadi/editor/1305050082Wikipedia_Overview_15March2010-FINAL.pdf. Accessed 5 May 2019.

Gorman, M. (2007). Jabberwiki: The educational response, part II. Encyclopedia Britannica BLOG, 26 June. http://blogs.britannica.com/2007/06/jabberwiki-the-educational-response-part-ii/. Accessed 20 September 2020.

Graham, M. (2010). Neogeography and the palimpsects of place: Web 2.0 and the construction of a virtual earth. *Journal of Economic and Social Geography, 101*(4), 422-436. https://doi.org/10.1111/j.1467-9663.2009.00563.x.

Gries, L. E. (2015). *Still life with rhetoric: A new materialist approach for visual rhetorics*. Logan: Utah State University Press.

Gries, L. E. (2019). Writing to assemble publics: Making writing activate, making writing matter. *College Composition and Communication*, *70*(3), 327-355.

Gruwell, L. (2015). Wikipedia's politics of exclusion: Gender, epistemology, and feminist rhetorical (in)action. *Computers and Composition, 37*, 117–131. https://doi.org/10.1016/j.compcom.2015.06.009.

Jack, C. (2017). Lexicon of lies: Terms for problematic information. Data & Society, 9 August. https://datasociety.net/output/lexicon-of-lies/. Accessed 20 September 2020.

Jackson, A. Y., & Mazzei, L. A. (2012). *Thinking with theory in qualitative research: Viewing data across multiple perspectives*. London: Routledge.

Jiang, J. (2020). "I never know what to expect": Aleatory identity play in Fortnite and its implications for multimodal composition. *Computers and Composition*, *55*, 1–14. https://doi.org/10.1016/j.compcom.2020.102550.

Jiang, J., Vetter, M. A. (2019). The good, the bot, and the ugly: Problematic information and critical media literacy in the postdigital era. *Postdigital Science and Education*, *2*(1), 78–94. https://doi.org/10.1007/s42438-019-00069-4.

Jones, H. A. (2018). Pinning, gazing, and swiping together: Identification in visually driven social media. In A. Hess & A. L. Davisson (Eds.), *Theorizing digital rhetoric* (209-223). Abingdon: Routledge.

Kellner, D., & Share, J. (2005). Toward critical media literacy: Core concepts, debates, organizations, and policy. *Discourse: Studies in the Cultural Politics of Education, 26*(3), 369–386. https://doi.org/10.1080/01596300500200169.

Kennedy, K. (2016). *Textual curation: Authorship, agency, and technology in Wikipedia and Chambers's Cyclopædia*. Columbia: The University of South Carolina Press.

LeCourt, D. (1998). Critical pedagogy in the computer classroom: Politicizing the writing space. *Computers and Composition*, *15*(3), 275–95. https://doi.org/10.1016/S8755-4615(98)90002-0.

Lenz Taguchi, H. (2010). *Going beyond the theory/practice divide in early childhood education: Introducing an intra-active pedagogy*. New York: Routledge.

Lenters, K., & McDermott, M. (Eds.). (2019). *Affect, Embodiment, and Place in Critical Literacy: Assembling Theory and Practice*. New York: Routledge.

Lockett, A. (2020). How do I have authority to edit the page? The politics of user agency and participation on Wikipedia. In J. Reagle & J. Koener (Eds.). *Wikipedia @ 20: Stories of an incomplete revolution* (pp. 205-220). Cambridge, MA: MIT Press.

MacKenzie, A., & Bhatt, I. (2018). Lies, bullshit and fake news: Some epistemological concerns. *Postdigital Science and Education, 2*(1), 9–13. https://doi.org/10.1007/s42438-018-0025-4.

MacKenzie, A., Rose, J., & Bhatt, I. (2020). Dupery by Design: The Epistemology of Deceit in a Postdigital Era. *Postdigital Science and Education*, *1*(1), 1–6. https://doi.org/10.1007/s42438-018-0025-4.

McDowell, Z. J., & Vetter, M. A. (2020). It takes a village to combat a fake news army: Wikipedia's community and policies for information literacy. *Social Media + Society, July.* https://doi.org/10.1177/2056305120937309.

Nicotra, J. (2016). Assembling things. Assemblage rhetorics: creating new frameworks for rhetorical action. In S. Barnett & C. A. Boyle. (Eds.), *Rhetoric, through everyday things* (pp. 185-196). Tuscaloosa, AL: University Alabama Press.

Reagle, J., & Koener, J. (Eds.). (2020). *Wikipedia @ 20: Stories of an incomplete revolution.* Cambridge, MA: MIT Press.

Selber, S. A. (2004). *Multiliteracies for a digital age*. Carbondale, IL: Southern Illinois University Press.

Thomson-Bunn, H. (2014). Are they empowered yet? Opening up definitions of critical pedagogy. Composition Forum, 29. http://compositionforum.com/issue/29/are-they-empowered.php. Accessed 20 September 2020.

Vetter, M. A., Andelfinger, J., Asadolahi, S., Cui, W., Jiang, J., Jones, T., Siddique, Z. F., Tanasale, I. O., A. E. Ylonfoun, & Xing, J. (2018). Wikipedia's gender gap and disciplinary praxis: Representing women and minority scholars in digital rhetoric and writing fields. *Journal of Multimodal Rhetorics*, *2*(2), 6-22.

Vrandečić, D. (2020). Collaborating on the sum of all knowledge across languages. In J. Reagle & J. Koener (Eds.). *Wikipedia @ 20: Stories of an incomplete revolution* (pp. 175-188). Cambridge, MA: MIT Press.

Wadewitz, A. (2013). Wikipedia's gender gap and the complicated reality of systemic gender bias (web log post). Hastac, 26 July. https://www.hastac.org/blogs/wadewitz/2013/07/26/wikipedias-gender-gap-and-complicated-reality-systemic-gender-bias. Accessed 20 September 2020.

Walker, P. (2016). A rhythmic refrain: Britain's mass-observation as rhetorical assemblage, *Rhetoric Review, 35*(3), 212-225, https://doi.org/10.1080/07350198.2016.1178690.

Wikipedia (2019). Gender equality. https://en.wikipedia.org/wiki/Gender_equality. Accessed 20 September 2020.

Wikipedia (2020). Hashtag activism. https://en.wikipedia.org/w/index.php?title=Hashtag_activism&oldid=953488821. Accessed 20 September 2020.

Chapter 10
The Neoliberal Colonization of Discourses: Gentrification, Discursive Markets and Zombemes

Albin Wagener

Introduction: Towards an Inflation of Discourses Colonized by Neoliberalism

'Making sense', 'engaging users' or 'making workers adhere': such expressions are frequently found in the discourse of business unit managers, coaches and even political figures, while they remain linked to the social impact of human relations. In the world of business and economical rapports, other expressions are to be found, such as 'philosophy of a project', 'problem solving' or 'our collaborators'. Such expressions all represent shifts in meaning that are as much surprising as they do raise several questions. During recent years, without being necessarily brought to attention, specific terms and syntactic constructions have been contaminated by semantic transformations that are typical of the neoliberal world we live in – a world we will obviously take the time to define in the present chapter.

This chapter builds a theoretical architecture drawing on several linguistic utterances gathered through online texts (media, social networks or forums, for instance). It exposes a linguistic theory of the neoliberal colonization of discourse and of the way discourse becomes lexically, semantically and pragmatically transformed by neoliberal contaminations of meaning. Discourses, I argue, both carry and create representations; representations themselves also participate in the creation and circulation of discourses. In this perspective, the very nature of a neoliberal colonization of discourse holds the seeds of a specific worldview where meaning becomes softened, free of roughness and trapped in a false consensus where semantic specificities and historical meaning are dissolved in order to produce a dominating discursive ideology.

A. Wagener (✉)
Université Rennes 2/INALCO, Paris, France

A. MacKenzie et al. (eds.), *The Epistemology of Deceit in a Postdigital Era*, Postdigital Science and Education,
https://doi.org/10.1007/978-3-030-72154-1_10

Deception and dupery lie within this sense of false consensus, inasmuch as the economic and social world we live in is shaped by an ideology that claims not to be one, but to be based on pragmatic decisions rooted in facts and data. By mimicking depoliticization through specific discourse strategies that will be described in the present chapter, neoliberalism, I argue, is a total form of dupery by design: it shapes both economic and social rapports, influences a certain form of individualism and ultimately shapes our very agency by structuring a world of offer, demand and market consumption. It becomes positioned as an encompassing discourse that aims to tell us what is true and what is real in a seemingly universal manner – especially because it has managed to drive globalization as a holistic process – in order to bias the decisions we are taking.

In order to develop this theory, I will take the time to define neoliberalism as an ideology, colonization as a process and discourse, in order to understand what I define as a progressive gentrification of discursive space – a space that neoliberalism transforms into a market. Moreover, I will introduce the concept of zombeme, in order to propose a linguistic definition of discursive utterances that become contaminated by neoliberal principles, relying on stereotypical language and the excessive use of formulas.

Discourse and Neoliberal Markets

The definition of neoliberalism is essential to understanding how linguistic colonization functions within the neoliberal spectrum. Neoliberalism, as a word, is itself widely used to describe political, social and economic phenomena; its very inflation blurs its definition as well as its conceptual impacts. Thus, neoliberalism is somehow used as a synonym for capitalism, although both are really different from each other (Audier 2013) yet triggering the emergence of an epistemological swamp. According to Scribano (2019: 102), neoliberalism as an ideology draws on the sensitive and emotional dimension of the mind and of the body, by directly connecting it to the market economy of capitalism.

Scribano posits neoliberalism as an extension of traditional capitalism that encompasses individual as well as collective preferences, thus drawing on the freedom to choose and to consume within a market defined as the sole reference framework. In other words, neoliberalism works as the functional rationalization of anything that may seem irrational but that is nonetheless valid. In this way, the neoliberal conception of freedom finds its perfect incarnation in the freedom of consumption. I will later describe this neoliberal regime, as it perfectly fits the concept of discourse market, insofar as it organizes the horizontal equivalence of opinion and expertise. However, even if neoliberalism is rooted in the sensations and desires of consumers, it still works thanks to a structured architecture.

Recent events in the evolution of neoliberalism are also linked to the financialization of the world economy and its speculative nature, as well as to the fragmentation of the means of production and assembly around the globe. According to

Cingolani (2019), this logic is increasingly based on a convergence of capitalism, new technologies of information (and control) and the diversity impacting workers' status and wage. Despite its apparent disorganization, neoliberalism even reinforces power relationships at both personal and even intimate level (Cingolani 2019: 178).

Neoliberalism can thus be defined as the dominating extension of a specific form of capitalism that is exclusively rooted in the financialization of markets. In this sense, neoliberalism is intangible and operates through digital technologies, targets sensitive and emotional responses and guarantees uninterrupted consumption, which represents the fuel needed for its existence. Resources are needed in order for this process to function. They may be natural, human or even linguistic (Duchêne 2011) and represent grounds that are to be exploited and transformed into consumer goods. Hence power logics have to be implemented in order to maintain the exploitation and consumption of said resources (Dardot 2013), by making individuals responsible for their own choices within this system (Hache 2007).

As such, the neoliberal definition of markets can be applied to nation-states and individuals alike, inasmuch as it operates through a logic of social extension (Legrand 2007): competition emerges, even between entities that do not directly produce consumer goods. Furthermore, competition turns into a relational and interactional norm and imposes market logic as an obvious structure for social rapports (Dardot and Laval 2010: 37).

Neoliberalism thus becomes materialized through discourses that support the construction and circulation of neoliberal representations; however, discourses themselves actually obey the same neoliberal logic. In other words, discourses are not only to be analysed as mere echoes of neoliberalism, but really as emerging structures that carry within them the very processes of neoliberalism.

It is safe to assess that the neoliberal market logic has found a new incarnation in the general equivalence of discourses that overwhelms social networks and rolling news channels alike, where experts are invited in order to comment bits and pieces of information in a sheer horizontal manner. In this perspective, every speaker-listener-consumer has to choose between various offers of discourses, operating within discursive spaces that have been transformed into markets: everybody can select what they want, according to their opinions, preconstructions or centres of interest. Discourses thus do not enter into dialogue in order to maintain democracy (Ravat et al. 2020) but are all juxtaposed and considered equally legitimate and valid, just like products put on shelves. The neoliberal organization of discursive markets is rendered possible through the existence of a neoliberal metadiscourse that seems to colonize both discourses themselves as well as their distribution in the social space; this phenomenon can be described as the neoliberal and democratic doxa. The neoliberal logic of discursive markets functions like a background noise that draws on unspoken notions and principles: it invites citizens to act as consumers. In the end, contemporary democracies are fundamentally contaminated by what is to be described as an ideological project:

> Neoliberalism itself causes the erosion of political, moral or subjective oppositions that are expressed within liberal democracies, but that are not rooted in capitalist rationality. This is also to be seen in the erosion of institutions, jurisdictions and values that allows the

> existence of non-profit rationalities within democracies. The democratic principles of governance, civil code or even religious morality are submitted to economic calculations and there is neither value nor goods that can escape them; hotbeds of opposition to capitalist rationality and even hotbeds of reform then tend to disappear. (Brown 2004: 90)[1]

Drawing on Brown's works, I argue that discourses follow the same total logic and are targeted by the neoliberal extension that has been thoroughly colonizing the diversity of social fields, thus colonizing our vision of both truth and reality.

As a matter of fact, it is important to take the time to understand the market as a notion and the central role it plays within the neoliberal system. My goal is not to produce a specific critique or market economy, but to understand how the market, as a concept and as an ideological instrument, becomes problematic when established as the fundamental compass of social life – and, of course, of discursive life. The groundbreaking works led by Halter (2000), for instance, have shown how market logic had been implemented in the questions linked to identity and culture altogether. Consequently, if identity is considered as a good that can be selected and enacted through acts of consumption or incarnation, the neoliberal logic colonizes matters of identity and fractures them in a postmodern way, by using the notion of bricolage to allow each individual-consumer to construct their own identity, or to change it depending on their desires and needs. This is a very clear example of what Legrand calls the social extension of the market:

> The social extension of the market I am talking about are expressed through two specific aspects. First, the market is defined as a space of truth, which allows governance to apply a principle of verification-falsification. Second, a principle emerges: governance may only operate for the market and through the market, and the exercise of power as well as political legitimacy become both rooted in the very structure of market economy. (Legrand 2007: 44)[2]

According to Legrand's observations and to Halter's studies, it is safe to assess that the extension of the market in fact concerns the sphere of discourses. In fact, discourses are submitted to a principle of competition, especially through the heavy circulation of opinions and the neoliberal horizontality applied by the very notion of market itself. In that respect, every citizen-consumer owns the right to select discourses that most appeal to them, not because of their plausibility or their capacity to be discussed within the democratic sphere, but because said discourses appeal to them and match a pre-established worldview.

Consequently, the impact of the social extension of the market on a democratic and economic society is tremendous: the social and political life as a whole becomes slowly contaminated by the marketplace analogy and by the consumption paradigm (Gunn 2000: 451). In other words: the marketplace paradigm becomes 'the' reality – or 'the' truth we are forced to live in. Obviously, it is easy to apply this logic to discourses and truth in general: as goods disposable on the marketplace, discourses are directly linked to individual choices and waves of trends operating within the market. The social extension of neoliberalism and the market analogy do

[1] Author's translation from French.

[2] Author's translation from French.

not only reach education, culture or health: both do initiate transformations that impact the circulation of representations carried by discourses.

Defining neoliberalism, markets and their subsequent notions and processes is necessary: however, it is also essential to propose a definition of discourses. Such a definition is needed to work with the notion of discourse and its subtleties, particularly in order to understand how the process of neoliberal colonization functions in this case:

> A discourse is any phenomenon linked to language (linguistically speaking, but not exclusively) that concerns the construction, interaction and transformation of a socially situated and structuring meaning. Thus, discourse may be politically signifying and is obviously rooted in essential intersubjectivity, may it be intentional or not; this intersubjectivity is produced and received by subjects that can express themselves in an individual or collective manner, about shareable objects. In that respect, discourse is not exclusively linguistic, communicational or social: it remains at the core and in the margins of each one of these dimensions, while gathering them at the same time. (Wagener 2019: 39)[3]

This definition tends to embrace the sheer situated and multidimensional nature of discourse: I use it to understand how the gentrification of discursive spaces might occur and how zombemes might emerge as new features of language.

Discursives Spaces as Resources

The neoliberal metadiscourse both produces and organizes the discursive market; it also structures the conditions of the circulation of discourses. This metadiscourse cannot be immediately grasped yet remains fully present, insofar as it structures relations between associated discourses. In a sense, it operates as a discursive dark matter that is not directly accessible and draws on the concept of semantic dark matter:

> (...) semantic dark matter circulates with discursive utterances and does not only say something about the state of the world or a galaxy of representations. It is more than this: semantic dark matter perpetuates political organizations, shared and shareable social views as well as structured representations made available to individuals whose sole aim is to make sense of the world and, thus, make society. (Wagener 2019: 153)[4]

As such, the neoliberal colonization of discursive spaces would then be able to operate by drawing on spaces and energies granted to semantic dark matter, thus leaving an ideological footprint on discourses themselves. In this perspective, this colonization represents an operation of discursive manipulation, which uses existing resources in order to modify representations:

> Manipulative discourse exploits the inherent weaknesses of the interpretative process to ensure that a sub-optimal interpretation is indeed arrived at, i.e. to ensure that one of the

[3] Author's translation from French.

[4] Author's translation from French.

> predicted error occurs. In this context, this approach looks at manipulative uses as a built-in – and hence, inevitable – consequence of the way our pragmatic system operates. (…) A manipulator will achieve their goal by having a re-ordering action on the cognitive environment of the hearer so as to guarantee that a given utterance *U* will be interpreted within an appropriate subset of contextual assumptions, independently of the expected presence of contradictory assumptions in the cognitive environment of the hearer (…). Manipulation is therefore re-analysed as an instance of *Context Selection Constraint*. (Maillat 2013: 194) (emphasis from the original)

This dark matter actually pollutes the discursive market with discursive architectures: it influences each and every perception and representation that circulates within a certain framework. This framework represents a hegemonic system, inasmuch as it contaminates a high number of social and economic devices and apparatus. Furthermore, this process also draws on emotions defined as motivational states (Frijda 2003), which underlines their crucial role in the definition of neoliberalism, insofar as it fuels acts of consumption by affects and desires.

In this perspective, I argue that it is important to rely the process of context selection constraint defined by Maillat to the definition of ideology proposed by Sarfati, seen as companion to the concept of doxa:

> Ideologization can be described as an operation of semantic transplant from a reduced and biased point of view. (…) In order to defend their interests, institutions of meaning put ideological constructions into circulations; such constructions may offer a positive image of their activity and, consequently, a negative image of opposing institutions. (Sarfati 2011: 158–159)[5]

According to Sarfati, ideology and doxa represent two faces of the same coin. However, Stockinger does not follow the same path and proposes a definition of common meaning that is rooted in ideologization processes: 'It is ideology, in the epistemic sense, that implements the doxa (or common meaning), as well as its rooting in an obviousness that is mediatized through experiences and traditions shared by members of a group or a social organization' (Stockinger 2001: 81).[6] Ideologization processes are thus able to contaminate the common meaning that circulates within and through discursive representations. Such processes work according to manipulation processes rooted in a semantic dark matter that remains inconspicuous at first, yet shows how discourse is simultaneously to be found in both the spoken and the unspoken. Moreover, operations of ideological colonization are rendered possible through the notion of interdiscourse (Pêcheux 1975), which shows how discourses are ontologically linked together through dynamic relations (Garric and Longhi 2013: 65).

According to this logic, the neoliberal ideology infuses, thanks to a process of context selection constraint. Hence it transforms circulating bits of common meaning in a dynamic way, by drawing on semantic dark matter as a resource, as well as on the possibility to disseminate chunks of ideology through interconnected interdiscursive universes.

[5] Author's translation from French.

[6] Author's translation from French.

The contaminating evolution of neoliberalism shows that ideology is not simply a semantic transplant coming from a specific doxa, as Sarfati assesses. On the contrary, the architecture of discursive spaces, combined with the notions of interdiscourse and semantic dark matter, underlines the fact that ideology needs to be defined as a macrostructure of intricate networks. In fact, this macro-structure can even be found in specialized or scientific discourses; no linguistic register is safe from ideology, especially if the latter has even the project to absorb its critical counterparts, which is the case for neoliberalism.

For instance, the simple desire to buy a new car, to comment love relationships or travel destinations is a never meaningless utterance. As discourses drawing on shared social experiences and desires that circulate in the social sphere, they may indeed carry the seed of neoliberalism; such as volatile pollen, it can hang on a high variety of discursive genres and structures. This is especially relevant because every discursive action carries shareable meaning (Howarth 2000) that is constitutive of social reality (Ramoneda 2011) and submitted to power struggles (Torfing 2005); all these parameters write the story of discursive possibilities.

Beyond the very question of discourse, it is important to state that discourses are to be seen as resources to exploit; this is notably due to the fact that social and linguistic operations become increasingly quantified and transformed into data – the contemporary black gold of our digitized societies. This conception of information is rooted in the notion of cognitive capitalism (Rullani 2000) that has been extended and augmented by neoliberal ideology; this has made the notion of resource even more relevant, insofar as it is linked to the colonial origins of modern capitalism and thus to its contemporary neoliberal form: 'At the heart of the problem of colonialism are transformations in social and economic organization intimately tied to the extraction of natural resources from peripheral communities' (Holst 2015: 203). In that respect, the exploitation of resources does impact social and economic organizations; neoliberalism has managed to extend this very analogy beyond sheer natural resources, even to non-profit activities. It is easy to see how seemingly harmless individual information can turn into resources to be exploited (Couldry and Mejias 2019), especially through the increasing domination of information and communication technologies. To cut a long story short, it would be difficult to argue that this trend cannot be applied to discourses.

The neoliberal colonization of discourses has, for instance, already been explored through the study of discourses of authority used in the French laws on pension reforms (Devriendt and Monte 2015) or through the analysis of corporate language and the transformations it implies in terms of work organization (D'Almeida and Avisseau 2010: 128). The neoliberal ideology colonizes and spoils (or leaves to rot) specific words or discursive formations, such as 'engagement', 'make someone adhere to certain values' or even the use and abuse of the word 'skill'. Hence linguistic terms and formations that seem to be relatively safe from commercial capitalism get absorbed by a progressive logic of ideological colonization. Again, I wish to underline the importance of language itself that is acted upon as a resource to exploit in the neoliberal logic: contamination works as the main operating principle, within interdiscourses, in order to affect prediscourses and to influence the production of postdiscourses (Wagener 2016).

In order to gain a better understanding of what is at stake, I propose the following examples that are all accessible on LinkedIn, which is probably the main professional social network as I am writing this chapter; they all concern the word 'meaningful' as used in the professional and corporate context:

1. 'If you want to gain exposure to corporate life, get introduced to executive search and recruitment, and you enjoy working across multiple and ***meaningful*** projects, this **#internship** is for you.' (27 August 2020) (emphasis from the original)[7]
2. 'Many of my peers are motivated by money. I grew up poor, so I know that money isn't everything. Some of the others want to be famous. I would rather have ***meaningful*** connections. And yet others still desire more power and influence. I would rather be more kind. You see, money comes and goes, fame does not make you a better person, and your title does not determine who you are. You do.' (28 August 2020) (emphasis from the original)[8]
3. 'I'm truly blessed to join the professionals at BCI. We have an amazing team dedicated to enriching the lives of adults with disabilities and their families through ***meaningful*** employment.' (27 August 2020) (emphasis from the original)[9]
4. 'I'm pleased to inform everyone that I have started my first job as a Software Development Engineer at **Jio**. I'm very thankful to (…) everyone who worked hard to ensure a smooth onboarding experience. Again, I'm thankful to **Jio** for providing me with the opportunity to do interesting and ***meaningful*** work that will contribute toward building a better world.' (26 August 2020) (emphasis from the original)[10]
5. 'As an **Amazon Web Services (AWS)** Software Development Manager, you'll help team members learn and grow in their careers, while inspiring them to deliver ***meaningful*** results for our customers. Come build your best tomorrow with us **#HereAtAWS.**' (28 August 2020) (emphasis from the original)[11]
6. 'People Success = Customer Success = Company Success. In that order. Invest in your team, genuinely care about them as people, take ***meaningful*** action to further their professional development, listen to them, support them and they will invest in you, your customers and your company. Align your customer's goals to your company goals – your company only exists because of your

[7] See https://www.linkedin.com/posts/zhawwari_intern-majidalfuttaim-internship-activity-6703657931734339584-TRVg. Accessed 20 December 2020.

[8] See https://www.linkedin.com/posts/garyltravis_garytravis-leadership-bestadvice-activity-6704069851234877440%2D%2D8ll. Accessed 20 December 2020.

[9] See https://www.linkedin.com/posts/troy-compardo-582ba78_boone-center-inc-names-new-ceo-activity-6704117009061339136-xxrk. Accessed 20 December 2020.

[10] See https://www.linkedin.com/posts/thesagarsehgal_techster2020-learningatjio-lifeatjio-activity-6703897316149002240-lhzd. Accessed 20 December 2020.

[11] See https://www.linkedin.com/posts/amazon_hereataws-with-helbert-maich-activity-6704077239597846528-xRqp. Accessed 20 December 2020.

customers so your focus should be making them successful. If you get that right and you have a compelling product/service the market needs, the revenue and company success will follow.' (29 August 2020) (emphasis from the original)[12]
7. 'Of the many things I am proud of this appointment to the Google Dealer Council was one of the most ***meaningful***. I am thankful for the opportunity to serve, to learn, and to contribute. **#thinkwithgoogle.**' (29 August 2020) (emphasis from the original)[13]

I could go on, but the main point present in such examples is that meaning can be used by LinkedIn users and businesses to work, connections, results, action and even projects – to name but a few possible lexical colocations. For users, 'meaningful' genuinely seems to carry a positive value: it is used in the context of a new job, of successful business development, of specific career shifts and professional relationships. These direct lexical colocations testify for a positive linguistic accumulation, which structures a positive discourse on meaning and meaningful events in professional lives, yet hardly conceals a discursive double entendre:

- There seems to be a possible gap between meaningful actions and work life, which conceals various neoliberal ideologemes (or markers of ideology), in word clusters such as 'while inspiring them to deliver meaningful results for our customers', 'you enjoy working across multiple and meaningful projects, this internship is for you' or 'take meaningful action to further their professional development'. I argue that such discursive formations show a polarized distinction between the individual, who is responsible for changes in their life, and the others, who remain depicted as resources to be satisfied in a professional framework, which shows an obvious lack of selfless sense for otherness.
- The quest for meaning appears to be linked to a form of corporate luxury that can only be accessible to certain professionals, while a lot of jobs may have trouble to get genuinely connected to the notion of meaning or self-realization.

It would be equally interesting to focus on other specific words or formulas to find examples and study them; what I mean to argue is that neutral or positive words become desubstantialized by a positive overrating within professional and corporate contexts. This is rendered possible by the organization of discursive spaces where abusively positive repetitions of words and expressions occur while being progressively desubstantialized through this very process.

Such an operation of desubstantialization does not indicate that words lose all meaning, in the semantic sense of the term; such a loss would imply that meaning is solely carried by the world, whereas it clearly operates in a dynamic and interactional manner with its social environment. On the contrary, in the case of desubstantialization, a socially shareable avatar of meaning is put into circulation and

[12] See https://www.linkedin.com/posts/meganwhitebowen_peoplefirst-customersuccess-leadership-activity-6703972493872431104-7JyQ. Accessed 20 December 2020.

[13] See https://www.linkedin.com/posts/bbenstock_thinkwithgoogle-activity-6703689997163278336-yo-J. Accessed 20 December 2020.

seemingly functions with the qualities of the word itself – especially the most positive ones, which clearly shows evidence for desubstantialization. Going back to our examples, I posit that the word 'meaningful' becomes semantically linked to its lexical contexts in a consensual and seemingly harmless manner. In this perspective, 'meaningful' shows signs of neoliberal contamination and becomes what I call a zombeme, activated within a gentrified discursive space. I will get back to these notions later in the present chapter.

The desubstantialization process shows how neoliberal ideology colonizes discourses, particularly because of its ability to generate what Dormeau calls ontopolitics (Dormeau 2019). In this perspective, citizen-consumers make conscious choices while submitting themselves to an ideology they think they are able to benefit from; this process works in the spirit of social and economic conformity and implies the deliberate submission of citizens to a framework that this perceived as tailor-made (Dormeau 2019: 142). Dormeau assesses that the construction of such a seemingly tailor-made framework is precisely what drives neoliberal colonization, and I argue that this is also the case for discursive spaces. I will now take the time to understand how discourses can get submitted to such an operation of contamination.

Colonization, Gentrification and Zombemes

To better understand the processes on which relies the neoliberal colonization of discourses, it is of course necessary to define colonization. Of course, I am not using the term in a sheer historical way and clearly do not wish to draw any awkward or offensive parallel with the political predation that affected so many countries throughout the world. I will rather take the time to understand how colonization operates as anthropological mechanics, in order to extend it to the dimensions of language and discourse. My definition of colonization is directly connected to the definition of neoliberalism: it underlines a change of paradigm from historical capitalist colonization to neoliberal colonization (Clarno 2017). This version of colonization draws upon the concept of biopolitics and fosters the creation of active processes of decolonization (Mignolo 2013). In that respect, colonization (and, of course, colonialism) is rooted in the notion of looting (Ravelli 2019: 43).

Hence the following hypothesis: the origins of modern capitalism are to be found in multiple phenomena, yet they are all directly linked to the process of colonization and its following applications:

- Confiscation of spaces.
- Looting of resources present on such spaces (material treasures and human beings alike, to name but a few targets).
- Imposed reorganization of systems that exist on said spaces towards a process of resource exploitation (material and human).
- Enrichment of settlers/colons because of this very reorganization.

I thus argue that colonization functions through a quadrangular scheme based on four clear concepts that are in constant interaction: confiscation, looting, exploitation and enrichment. The compass that emerges from these four concepts represents colonization as a social, political and economic phenomenon.

Colonization may also be applied to the context of discourse. In fact, by doing so, the same quadrangular scheme quickly emerges from a semantic perspective, thus treating discourse as a sheer resource:

- Confiscation of discursive and linguistic spaces, most of all through the visible inflation of neoliberal discourses and devices.
- Looting of semantic resources present on such spaces.
- Imposed reorganization of systems that exist on said spaces, towards a process of exploitation of lexical, semantic and discursive resources, though an intricate play with semantic ambiguities and positive values (as can be witnessed with the term 'meaningful', for instance).
- Enrichment of neoliberalism because of this very process of exploitation that progressively gains ground, slowly contaminating intimate and individual territories, as well as political spheres.

Such an operation is not instantly noticeable, since it is disguised as an acceptable and normal social process. There lies the strength of neoliberal ideology and its colonization of discourses of 'common meaning' (Sarfati 2011): it does not seem dangerous at all and coils up in a semantic consensus that appears to be entirely harmless at first.

Gentrification, I assess, is a much-needed concept if one wishes to get a better understanding of neoliberal colonization; in fact, gentrification represents an acceptable mask of the neoliberal colonization of discourses. Obviously, scholars have been studying the phenomenon of gentrification for decades, particularly in the field of social geography. For many authors, gentrification is to be defined as a form of neoliberalization of urban spaces:

> The generalization of gentrification has various dimensions. These can be understood in terms of five interrelated characteristics: the transformed role of the state, penetration by global finance, changing levels of political opposition, geographical dispersal, and the sectoral generalization of gentrification. (Smith 2002: 441)

In fact, one of the main effects of gentrification is to drive working classes out of the urban spaces of city centres and then of other parts of the city, in order to relegate them to the peripheries of the cities (Van Criekingen and Fleury 2006). However, public and private elites will quickly rebrand gentrification as 'urban regeneration' (Smith 2002: 443), a strategic semantic choice that is notably found in urban planning documents and policies. Indeed, unlike gentrification, the positive symbol of 'urban regeneration' does not so much put the focus on class epuration, but rather on the renewed attractivity of certain urban spaces that become less unpleasant to live in; moreover, it is more profitable in terms of real estate investment (Redfern 2003).

Furthermore, the gentrification of urban spaces has a lot in common with colonization itself: such a parallel is indeed relevant, when it comes to the role of gentrification as a mask of colonization. In fact, gentrification draws on class privilege, deregulation and a style of city management that is directly inspired by business life (Atkinson and Bridge 2005: 2). It is important to consider the links between gentrification, colonization and neoliberalism when studying the context of discursive spaces; it is even more important to state that discursive spaces do not exist independently from their speakers, but rather that they do participate in the transmission, the animation and the colonization of neoliberal ideology by using and validating sentences and words that rely on said ideology. In other words, gentrification excludes individuals who could not or would not wish to take part in the neoliberal process in one way or another (Clark 2005) and adapts to the specificities of spaces (Hackworth and Smith 2001). The same applies for speakers: they become slowly won over by neoliberal colonization, depending on their social, professional or economic status.

My theory is as follows: the gentrification of discursive spaces indeed draws on the notion of 'discursive regeneration' and may leave the impression that problematic, oppositional, critical or negative discourses become transformed in both positive and motivating utterances. Discourses targeted by the consensual yet colonizing mask of neoliberal gentrification thus become slowly desubstantialized (or degenerated) and re-substantialized. Consequently, such discourses operate, thanks to a new ideological paradigm that becomes semantically inherent. The result of such a contaminating processes leads to the emergence of what I call zombemes.

The use of analogy is intentional here, insofar as it allows the development of features that would be difficult to reach without metaphor: it enhances the creation and transmission of concept and notion in both science and education (Aubusson et al. 2006). Moreover, it does work as a method, particularly when incorporated into a theoretical framework that does use other scientific developments and leaves place for metaphors in order to better understand certain aspects of the world (Cameron 2013).

By applying this metaphor, I posit that zombemes are different from stereotyped language or even reified phrases:

- Stereotyped language actually distances social, economic or political facts in order to avoid naming them, thus multiplying linguistic utterances (Lopez Diaz 2014) that are entirely or partially technicized or stereotyped (Oustinoff 2010): such language in reality builds up semantic aberrations that distance themselves from reality (Dewitte 2010).
- Reified phrases, or 'formulas' in linguistics, work through specific lexical processes such as conventionality, undetermined sloganeering, semantic freezing or automatic colocation (Krieg-Planque 2009).

Zombemes may obviously be found in stereotyped language or reified phrases: they can adapt themselves to a high variety of enunciative contexts ('meaningful', for instance, as a zombeme, may also constitute a kind of stereotyped language in the work sphere). Nevertheless, zombemes cannot be strictly limited to reified phrases or stereotyped language.

In other words, stereotyped language encompasses rhetorical methods that buries argumentation in the sand and avoids relevant naming, while reified phrases or formulas rely on the hypercirculation of linguistic devices that progressively freeze and slowly drift away from their semantic origin. Zombemes, on the other hand, are caused by the neoliberal ideological colonization of discursive spaces and contexts of enunciation. In that respect, zombemes do not refer to zombies for fun only; they own all their ambiguous qualities, namely, inaction, waiting and erring ways, as well as predatory and voracious action (Coulombe 2012) – qualities that are also inherent to neoliberalism (Peck 2010). Furthermore, zombemes contain the seeds of transmission and virality, hence the contamination to other words, sentences or contexts of enunciation; this process can, for instance, be perceived in the extension of the concept of skill, as a managerial operator, to the world of education and teaching (Crahay 2006). The metaphor of the zombie also somehow reminds of the logic of hectic and senseless predation of neoliberal capitalism (Webb and Byrnand 2008), as well as of its undead yet ever circulating economic doctrine (Quiggin 2012). I propose Table 10.1 in order to explore the qualities of stereotyped language, reified language (or formulas) and zombemes.

Zombemes may be recognized based on the following characteristics and can thus be isolated from a discursive point of view:

- Zombemes may be found in simple words, whole sentences or reified formulas.
- Zombemes prosper within discursive spaces and contexts of enunciation that have been or are currently being gentrified – meaning confiscated, looted, reorganized and depleted by neoliberal ideology and its representations.
- They rely on desubstantialized qualities that are not operating by relying on their initial semantic meaning, but by drawing on the contamination initiated by neoliberal ideology.
- They also rely on neoliberal semantic dark matter, inasmuch as they become ideologized through smoothened and positive semantic expressions that are rooted in the fundamental principles of neoliberal ideology – namely, individual responsibility, exploitation of resources, inclusion of oppositions, market logic

Table 10.1 Differences between stereotyped language, reified language and zombemes

	Stereotyped language	Reified language	Zombemes
Semantic goal	Semantic avoidance	Semantic freezing and hypercirculation	Semantic desubstantialization
Linguistic form	Multiplication of utterances	Automatic colocations	Smoothened expressions
Semantic process	Technicizing	Sloganeering	Neoliberalizing
Relation to reality	Distant	Conventional	Ideological
Degree of virality	Low	High	High
Relation to the context of enunciation	Context-avoidant	Context-dependent	Context-contaminating

and merely economic structuration of social fields that have no purely financial vocation, among others.
- Finally, they also operate on behalf of larger discursive architectures that actually conceal neoliberal representations to be seen in discourse and interdiscourse.

In this manner, zombemes cannot be identified through their sheer linguistic qualities, but by analysing their actual discursive universe; thus cues of neoliberalism are not to be found within zombemes themselves, but in their context of enunciation and their representational galaxies.

Zombemes are part of a general neoliberal design of deceit and dupery: they seem clear enough to be used and reused in various contexts, yet hold the germs of an ideology that wishes to stay away from the light. Zombemes are closely tied to the sheer particularity of neoliberalism: an ideology that presents itself as something that is not an ideology, but a view of the world based on facts and realism. Zombemes, however, only have the lexical appearance of factual observations: they do bias the way we look at the world by telling us how it should be – not how it is. Yet beneath this seemingly harmless lexical appearance lies a semantic process that misleads speakers into believing that words can be unpolitical and that reality is something that could never be colonized by an ideology. In this perspective, neoliberalism uses zombemes to turn into a form of quantum ideology: it appears to be absent, until you measure it.

Conclusion: Decontaminating Discourses in a Postdigital Society

The goal of this chapter was both simple and complex: (a) apply the principles of the colonization of neoliberal ideology to the field of discourse; (b) show how discursive spaces function by relying on market logic, because of the very neoliberal system that structures economic, political and social spheres alike; and (c), finally, establish a theory of a linguistic incarnation of said neoliberal ideology through the notion of gentrification of discursive spaces, as well as the progressive yet structuring emergence of zombemes.

My work is only preliminary and theoretical, yet it holds a truly applicable dimension. Indeed, it will now be important to produce discursive studies that will show how certain zombemes are actively circulating; this will be rendered even more possible, thanks to the postdigital organization of society (Andersen et al. 2014). This postdigital organization implies the blurring of traditional frontiers between both online and offline discursive spaces and a discursive influence that increasingly and persistently affects the social space (Jandrić et al. 2018). This influence is based on the definition of attention as a limited resource (Weng et al. 2012) and the explosion of short narrative arcs (Rose 2012); these narrative arcs become also subject to the inflation of fake news and reinvented truth that can be described as resources that push discourses away from the simple relation to truth or reality (Wagener 2020).

The layout of the postdigital shift of discursive spaces consequently causes the proliferation of zombemes. This is rendered possible because of the liquefaction of representations colonized by neoliberal ideology, as well as corollary discursive gentrification. In this perspective, I argue that discourse analysis plays a central and particular part for years to come: it has to conceive and structure tools that will help flush out zombemes or any other discursive form that may rely on unclear predicates. This way, discourse analysis may finally be able to offer devices that will be essential to the education to the versatility, variability and fragility of discourses – and to the fact that they represent extensions of our humanity, strengths and vulnerabilities included.

References

Andersen, C. U., Cox, G., & Papadopoulos, G. (2014). Postdigital Research – Editorial. *A Peer-Reviewed Journal About, 3*(1), 4–7.

Aubusson, P. J., Harrison, A. G., & Ritchie, S. M. (2006). *Metaphor and Analogy in Science Education*. Dordrecht: Springer.

Audier, S. (2013). Les Paradigmes du 'Néolibéralisme'. *Cahiers Philosophiques*, *133*(2), 21–40. https://doi.org/10.3917/caph.133.0021.

Atkinson, R., & Bridge, G. (2005). Introduction In R. Atkinson, & G. Bridge (Eds), *Gentrification in a Global Context. The New Urban Colonialism* (pp. 1–17). New York: Routledge.

Brown, W. (2004). Néo-Libéralisme et Fin de la Démocratie. *Vacarme*, *29*(4), 86–93. https://doi.org/10.3917/vaca.029.0086.

Cameron, R. (2013). Mixed Method Research: a World of Metaphors. In W. Midgley, K. Trimmer, & A. Davies, (Eds), *Metaphors for, in and of Education Research* (pp. 51–65). Newcastle upon Tyne: Cambridge Scholars Publishing.

Cingolani, P. (2019). Neoliberalism, Outsourcing, and Domination. In A. Scribano, F. Lopez Timmermann, & M.E. Korstanje (Eds.), *Neoliberalism in Multi-Disciplinary Perspective* (pp. 171–184). London: Palgrave Macmillan. https://doi.org/10.1007/978-3-319-77601-9_9.

Clark, E. (2005). The Order and Simplicity of Gentrification – A Political Challenge. In R. Atkinson, & G. Bridge, (Eds), *Gentrification in a Global Context. The New Urban Colonialism* (pp. 261–269). New York: Routledge.

Clarno, A. (2017). Neoliberal Colonization in the West Bank. *Social Problems*, *65*(3), 323–341. https://doi.org/10.1093/socpro/spw055.

Couldry, N., & Mejias, U.A. (2019). *The Costs of Connection: How Data are Colonizing Human Life and Appropriating it for Capitalism*. Palo Alto, CA: Stanford University Press.

Coulombe, M. (2012). La Popularité des Zombies. *Etudes*, *417*(10), 365–373. https://doi.org/10.3917/etu.4174.0365.

Crahay, M. (2006). Dangers, Incertitudes et Incomplétude de la Logique de la Compétence en Education. *Revue Française de Pédagogie, 154,* 97–110. https://doi.org/10.4000/rfp.143.

D'Almeida, N., & Avisseau, C. (2010). Langage Managérial et Dramaturgie Organisationnelle. *Hermès. La Revue*, *58*(3), 123–128. https://doi.org/10.3917/herm.058.0123.

Dardot, P. (2013). Le Capitalisme à la Lumière du Néolibéralisme. *Raisons Politiques, 52*(4), 13–23. https://doi.org/10.3917/rai.052.0013.

Dardot, P., & Laval, C. (2010). Néolibéralisme et Subjectivation Capitaliste. *Cités*, *41*(1), 35–50. https://doi.org/10.3917/cite.041.0035.

Devriendt, E., & Monte, M. (2015). L'Exposé des Motifs : un Discours d'Autorité. Le Cas des Lois Françaises de 2003, 2010 et 2014 sur les Retraites. *Mots. Les Langages du Politique, 107,* 67–84. https://doi.org/10.4000/mots.21873.

Dewitte, J. (2010). La Lignification de la Langue. *Hermès. La Revue*, *58*(3), 47–54. https://doi.org/10.3917/herm.058.0047.

Dormeau, L. (2019). Histoire d'Emotions Néolibérales : Pédagogie d'une Emancipation Individuelle, Dialectique d'une Aliénation Collective. *Cahiers d'histoire*, *XXXVI*(2), 129–149. https://doi.org/10.7202/1066848ar.

Duchêne, A. (2011). Néolibéralisme, Inégalités Sociales et Plurilinguisme : l'Exploitation des Ressources Langagières et des Locuteurs. *Langage et Société*, *136*(2), 81–108. https://doi.org/10.3917/ls.136.0081.

Frijda, N. H. (2003). Passions: l'Emotion comme Motivation. In J.-M. Colletta, & A. Tcherkassof (Eds), *Les Emotions. Cognition, Langage et Développement* (pp. 15–32). Sprimont: Mardaga.

Garric, N., & Longhi, J. (2013). Atteindre l'Interdiscours par la Circulation des Discours et du Sens. *Langage et Société*, *144*(2), 65–83. https://doi.org/10.3917/ls.144.0065.

Gunn, C. (2000). Markets against Economic Democracy. *Review of Radical Political Economics*, *32*(3), 448–460. https://doi.org/10.1016/S0486-6134(00)80035-2.

Hache, E. (2007). La Responsabilité, une Technique de Gouvernementalité Néolibérale? *Raisons Politiques*, *28*(4), 49–65. https://doi.org/10.3917/rai.028.0049.

Hackworth, J., & Smith, N. (2001). The Changing State of Gentrification. *Tijdschrift voor Economische en Sociale Geografie*, *92*(4), 464–477. https://doi.org/10.1111/1467-9663.00172.

Halter, M. (2000). *Shopping for Identity: the Marketing of Ethnicity*. New York: Schocken Books.

Holst, J. (2015). Colonial Histories and Decolonial Dreams in the Ecuadorean Amazon. *Latin American Perspectives*, *43*(1), 200–220. https://doi.org/10.1177/0094582X15570837.

Howarth, D. (2000). *Discourse*. Buckingham: Open University Press.

Jandrić, P., Knox, J., Besley, T., Ryberg, T., Suoranta, J., & Hayes, S. (2018). Postdigital Science and Education. *Educational Philosophy and Theory, 50*(10), 893–899. https://doi.org/10.1080/00131857.2018.1454000.

Krieg-Planque, A. (2009). *La Notion de 'Formule' en Analyse du Discours. Cadre Théorique et Méthodologique.* Besançon: Presses Universitaires de Franche-Comté.

Legrand, S. (2007). L'Extension Sociale du Marché dans le Néolibéralisme. *Raisons Politiques*, *28*(4), 33–47. https://doi.org/10.3917/rai.028.0033.

Lopez Diaz, M. (2014). L'euphémisme, la langue de bois et le politiquement correct: changements linguistiques et stratégies énonciatives. *L'information grammaticale, 143*, 47–55.

Maillat, D. (2013). Constraining Context Selection: On the Pragmatic Inevitability of Manipulation. *Journal of Pragmatics*, *59*(2), 190–199. https://doi.org/10.1016/j.pragma.2013.07.009.

Mignolo, W. (2013). Géopolitique de la Sensibilité et du Savoir. (Dé)Colonialité, Pensée Frontalière et Désobéissance Epistémologique. *Mouvements*, *73*(1), 181–190. https://doi.org/10.3917/mouv.073.0181.

Oustinoff, M. (2010). Langues de Bois d'Hier et Parler Vrai d'Aujourd'hui: de la 'Novlangue' aux 'Spin Doctors. *Hermès. La Revue*, *58*(3), 15–21. https://doi.org/10.3917/herm.058.0013.

Pêcheux, M. (1975). *Les Vérités de la Palice*. Paris: Maspéro.

Peck, J. (2010). Zombie Neoliberalism and the Ambidextrous State. *Theoretical Criminology*, *14*(1), 104–110. https://doi.org/10.1177/1362480609352784.

Quiggin, J. (2012). *Zombie Economics. How Dead Ideas Still Walk Among Us*. Princeton: Princeton University Press.

Ramoneda, T. (2011). Entente Virtuelle et Conflit Effectif : les Racines Discursives de la Démocratie'. In J. Guilhaumou, & P. Schepens (Eds), *Matériaux Philosophiques pour l'Analyse du Discours* (pp. 113–138). Besançon: Presses Universitaires de Franche-Comté.

Ravelli, Q. (2019). Le Capitalisme a-t-il une Date de Naissance ? *Tracés. Revue de Sciences Humaines*, *36*, 29–57. https://doi.org/10.4000/traces.9428.

Ravat, J., Nicolas, N. & Wagener, A. (2020). La valeur du désaccord. Paris: Editions de la Sorbonne.

Redfern, P. A. (2003). What Makes Gentrification 'Gentrification'? *Urban Studies, 40*(12), 2351–2366. https://doi.org/10.1080/0042098032000136101.

Rose, E. (2012). Hyper Attention and the Rise of the Antinarrative: Reconsidering the Future of Narrativity. *Narrative Works: Issues, Investigations & Interventions*, *2*(2), 92–102.

Rullani, E. (2000). Le Capitalisme Cognitif: Du Déjà Vu? *Multitudes*, *2*(2), 87–94. https://doi.org/10.3917/mult.002.0087.

Sarfati, G.-E. (2011). Analyse du Discours et Sens Commun : Institutions de Sens, Communautés de Sens. *Doxa*, Idéologie'. In J. Guilhaumou, & P. Schepens (Eds), *Matériaux Philosophiques pour l'Analyse du Discours* (pp. 139–174). Besançon: Presses Universitaires de Franche-Comté.

Scribano, A. (2019). The Thousand Faces of Neoliberalism: From Politics to Sensibilities. In A. Scribano, F. Lopez Timmermann, & M. E. Korstanje (Eds.), *Neoliberalism in Multi-Disciplinary Perspective* (pp. 89–118). London: Palgrave Macmillan. https://doi.org/10.1007/978-3-319-77601-9_5.

Smith, N. (2002). New Globalism, New Urbanism: Gentrification as Global Urban Strategy. *Antipode*, *34*(3), 427–450. https://doi.org/10.1111/1467-8330.00249.

Stockinger, P. (2001). *Traitement et Contrôle de l'Information*. Paris: Hermès.

Torfing, J. (2005). Discourse Theory: Achievements, Arguments, and Challenges. In D. Howarth, & J. Torfing (Eds), *Identity, Policy and Governance* (pp. 1–32). London: Palgrave Macmillan. https://doi.org/10.1057/9780230523364_1.

Van Criekingen, M., & Fleury, A. (2006). La Ville Branchée: Gentrification et Dynamiques Commerciales à Bruxelles et à Paris. *Belgeo. Revue Belge de Géographie*, *1*(2), 113–134. https://doi.org/10.4000/belgeo.10950.

Wagener, A. (2016). Prédiscours, Interdiscours et Postdiscours: Analyse Critique de la Circulation des Possibles Discursifs. *Revue de Sémantique et de Pragmatique*, *39*, 95–110. https://doi.org/10.4000/rsp.422.

Wagener, A. (2019). *Discours et Système. Théorie Systémique du Discours et Analyse des Représentations*. Brussels: Peter Lang.

Wagener, A. (2020). Hypernarrativity, Storytelling, and the Relativity of Truth: Digital Semiotics of Communication and Interaction. *Postdigital Science and Education*, *2*(1), 147–169. https://doi.org/10.1007/s42438-019-00066-7.

Webb, J., & Byrnand, S. (2008). Some Kind of Virus: The Zombie as Body and as Trope. *Body & Society*, *14*(2), 83–98. https://doi.org/10.1177/1357034X08090699.

Weng, L., Flammini, A., Vespignani, A., & Menczer, F. (2012). Competition Among Memes in a World with Limited Attention. *Scientific Reports*, *2*(335), 1–8. https://doi.org/10.1038/srep00335.

Chapter 11
Social Memes and Depictions of Refugees in the EU: Challenging Irrationality and Misinformation with a Media Literacy Intervention

Mike Hajimichael

Introduction

For the last 2 years, through the project Media Literacy Living Together (2018), I have been engaging in research on social memes and the ways in which people express opinions online regarding refugees in the European Union. Memes play a central role in the digital world because people today more than ever communicate more with visual rather than textual content. Who, for example, reads a long textual rant? On the other hand, would people look at a digital image and immediately get the message? The human brain processes images 60,000 times faster than text (Eisenburg 2018), and social memes, as visual content, play a big part in our online media consumption, particularly regarding issues of fakeness and mis/disinformation. Before elaborating further though, by way of introduction, I want to clarify some practical and conceptual issues on the visual content under consideration. During the course of the current research, through all its different phases, I felt it was always imperative for people engaging with this text to be able to see the content under discussion, in its original form as much as possible. I find it hard to talk about images without sharing and discussing them. At the same time, practically, in a book chapter, the inclusion of, say, 30 colour images would be impossible due to publishing costs. So parallel to writing up the research, I created an online blog to include the images in the discussion, and this is referenced extensively in this chapter (Hajimichael 2020).

The memes being referred to in the text can be viewed at https://wordpress.com/post/sublimeridiculous.wordpress.com/958.

M. Hajimichael (✉)
The Department of Communications, University of Nicosia, Nicosia, Cyprus
e-mail: hajimichael.m@unic.ac.cy

A. MacKenzie et al. (eds.), *The Epistemology of Deceit in a Postdigital Era*, Postdigital Science and Education,
https://doi.org/10.1007/978-3-030-72154-1_11

It is also pertinent to consider what social memes are and why they are so important in relation to fake news. Additionally, although I am using the word 'refugees' in the context of Europe in a time frame when this has been defined as a 'crisis' (Trimikliniotis 2019), I need to be clear from the outset how this term is constructed with particularly ideological and political ramifications along identity and categorization lines, which mean different things to different people. Categories such as 'refugee', 'migrant' and 'asylum seeker', for example, to name just three, are often blurred and misconceived. Evidence of this will come out in some of the visual data under examination.

The bulk of this chapter considers issues grounded in the visual data and context with regard to a series of messages contained in social memes on refugees in the European Union, particularly with regard to their fakeness and a sense of being duped. Critical discourse analysis is a relevant approach in this context because these representations are problematic in that 'real' problems, as I shall explain, are distorted, ridiculed and trivialized. In the process, the demonization and marginalization of life experiences, what it means to be a refugee, fleeing war, conflict and political persecution, transforms into a plethora of often-vitriolic social memes aimed at making alleged 'extreme' cases the generalized norm.

One way by which we at the University of Nicosia (Cyprus) sought to counter this demonization and marginalization was through the development of critical thinking carried out through a media literacy intervention with students as part of a taught course on Media Literacy. Although calls for developing critical thinking have existed for many decades (Kellner and Share 2005), there is a real need for such initiatives in current research on 'fake news' and, particularly, as evidenced from findings in this chapter, regarding refugees in Europe. This need has many dimensions. From the outset, Media Literacy concerns itself with 'encoding' and 'decoding' messages; as a result unpacking and comprehending meanings is of paramount importance in the digital age. Accordingly, '[b]eing literate in a media age requires critical thinking skills that empower us as we make decisions, whether in the classroom, the living room, the workplace, the boardroom, or the voting booth' (National Association for Media Literacy Education 2020).

Additionally, much of the visual meme content found on refugees in the EU, particularly when its source is an overt racist group or movement, functions as digital propaganda (Hobbs and McGee 2014). Research in this field then becomes a calling of utmost importance. Through the naturalization of propaganda on hybridized digital social media platforms as representations of 'post-truth' politics, communication and media studies are going through a *Zeitgeist* in relation to digital propaganda (Lilleker and Surowiec 2020). A media literacy intervention also represents a redefinition of civic engagement with digital media texts (Mihailidis 2018), enabling citizens to question and challenge authority in an age of dupery and deception (MacKenzie et al. 2020).

Social Memes

Social memes, also known as Internet memes or just memes, are visual-based content shared online through social media sites. Dawkins (2016) adapted the concept of the 'meme' as a unit of cultural transmission from the Ancient Greek word *mīmēma* (μίμημα) – meaning 'imitation' or 'to imitate' (American Heritage Dictionary 2020). Initial Internet-based memes were symbolic emoticons such as a smiley face :-) in the early 1990s. Obviously, with time and radical transformations in online content, platforms and infrastructures, memes have evolved into user-adapted images and videos, with specific characteristics, such as digital content with specific commonalities in form/style/content, which have been created intentionally and distributed, shared and adapted online. Adopting this kind of framework means these adaptable cultural units are important areas of study for contemporary communications scholarship (Shifman 2014).

In my endeavour to interpret social memes, particularly on the subject matter of 'refugees' during a particular time frame in Europe, some nagging questions came to mind that, in many ways, could not be answered easily but are significant, namely: who are these people in the images? Moreover, did they consent to being included? Obviously, we cannot answer this factually, but it is assumed that most memes are based on images that are protected by copyright laws. However, in US copyright law, the concept of 'fair use' means 'copyrighted work' (can be used) 'in the creation of new work without permission, as long as the use fits within certain parameters' (Orlofsky 2019). Lantagne (2017) goes one step further by identifying memes as 'static' (reproductions of an existing image shared online without adaptation) and 'mutating' which have been adapted or 'morphed beyond their origin' giving new and/or extended meaning. A 'mutating' meme then can be viewed more as an 'idea', and how you go about copyrighting an idea intellectually is a problematic issue for many scholars (Patel 2013; Lantagne 2017).

As most of the memes under consideration fall under the second category, it also follows that we need to consider certain dynamics of who is 'speaking' or 'communicating' and how they are doing so in terms of meaning. Given that this process is invariably linked to relationships of positions of power and control (van Dijk 2015), we have then to consider who is being marginalized and left out communicatively. There is a clear 'us-vs-them' paradigm in much of the memetic content under review, and clearly critical discourse analysis is of value methodologically, particularly van Dijk's idea of the 'ideological square' which defines double-edged strategies of positive 'in-group' and negative 'out-group' descriptions. This is crucial to understanding inequalities and their reproduction in meme-based content on social media. Memes function in this way as digital media content because they also rely on the use of 'common-sense' or vernacular language that distorts meaning into factoids. One of the key purposes of this 'common-sense' populist content is to connect through misinformation to gain publicity and become accepted through constant repetition/sharing. 'Common-sense' and its dominance as a political discourse are nothing new in terms of discrimination and racism

(CCCS 1982). Lawrence interviewed by Bhattacharyya (2020), expresses the view that we are living in an age of 'cultivated ignorance' where there is a tendency to just 'vilify' people and 'common-sense' itself has become a meme.

I would take this further to argue memes have changed the course of political discourse in many ways; they have become weaponized tools in the articulation of a problematic term, which I will call the irrationality of contemporary politics. Two key elections reflect this intensively in 2016 and 2017 because they were fought out vicariously on social media platforms (Iosifides and Wheeler 2016; Hänska-Ahy and Bauchowitz 2017). Donald Trump became President of the USA, and the majority of the electorate in a referendum in Britain voted to leave the European Union. Within the context of Donald Trump's election victory of 2016, this is explained in the following manner: 'if that constituency feels its interests are not being served by a political establishment that purports to represent it fairly, a lying demagogue can appear as a distinctively authentic champion of its interests' (Hahl et al. 2018).

How does a 'lying demagogue' achieve this? By lying some more. The 'insiders' who represented the establishment, in the context of US politics, Hilary Clinton, reflected a crisis of legitimacy. As a candidate, Clinton represented the establishment, those 'insiders' who run the system. Trump's claim to 'drain the swamp' or 'fix' a 'broken' establishment (BBC 2016) gained ground due to its alluring alternativeness. This was articulated through lies and resentment by a candidate painted as a new 'outsider' to the system, as one of the 'people' (Hahl et al. 2018). Trump constructed such an approach with mathematical accuracy, and it was classic populism revisited. In an extensive study at MIT of 126,000 stories tweeted by three million people over 11 years on Twitter, this is explained through the phenomenon of 'false' news traveling faster (being shared more) than 'truth' (Vosoughi et al. 2018).

In terms of the Brexit Referendum, the dissemination of false information on immigration and being 'flooded' by refugees came centre stage in political discourse. The Vote Leave campaign even had a series of paranoiac meme-like political adverts on the prospect of Turkey joining the EU (Boffey and Helm 2016), and the plethora of offensive memes on refugees being 'fakesters', 'frauds' and 'fiends' cannot be disconnected from the realities many refugees and migrants face crossing dangerous seas and precarious, hostile borders. It is not coincidental that many of these memes originate, as will be shown, from extreme-right wing, racist groupings in Europe who seek to make political capital out of human suffering. Indeed, the importance of memes is central to these political movements in contemporary societies, as Spencer, a renowned white supremacist in the USA, puts it: 'We memed alt-right into existence' (VICE 2016).

Therefore, against this kind of background, I want to consider specific themes found in this age of online dupery and deception with regard to refugees and social memes. Having collected 200 memes on the subject matter of refugees in the EU, which formed a body of content for students to consider through the Media Literacy Intervention, I set out to analyse this with critical discourse in mind and the development of a number of themes that follow.

Paradoxical Memes/Welfare/Irrationality as 'Common Sense'

A number of images articulate paradoxical appeals based on the theme of access to/ denial of 'welfare' rights versus immigrants 'living off the state'. Specifically, Meme 1 (Hajimichael 2020) depicts an elderly white/British woman wearing a hat with a sign pasted like she is holding it (this could have been pasted in) saying 'traitors' in italic writing. Below this is the statement 'BRITISH OAP TOTAL YEARLY £6000'. She looks on straight at the camera with her mouth slightly open, against a background of greenery form bushes or trees. Next to her is a completely different image of a younger woman dressed in a black niqab facing away from the camera, in a ¾ shot. Her barely visible eyes are looking away from the camera and down. The image appears to be cropped as another woman might be standing next to her, but all we can see is a shoulder in black. The blurred background gives emphasis to the woman in the niqab in the forefront. Below the image is the statement 'IMMIGRANTS TOTAL YEARLY £29,900'. Connotatively, the meme appeals to a number of populist distortions that compare the 'fate' of an elderly white woman's pension with that of a Muslim woman defined as an 'immigrant'. These operate on the lines of statistics given as 'facts', which deceive us. Do all pensioners, for example, get the same amount of pension? Quite clearly not because pensions are based on national insurance and tax contributions which vary according to income. Even more problematic is the 'fact' associated with the Muslim woman. The definitive term 'immigrant', again in capital letters, is a blurred blanket form of identity that can mean many things to many different people. How an 'immigrant' then acquires £29,900 stays unexplained. The populist assertion is clear. The 'pensioner' gets one sixth of what the 'immigrant' gets which is described as treachery by the symbolic insertion of the word 'traitors' in italics on a white sign in front of the 'pensioner'.

A similar misinformative paradoxical Meme 2 exists in relation to a 'pensioner' counting her pennies and a news report with the headline 'ASYLUM SEEKER GIVEN £2m HOUSE' (Hajimichael 2020). The 'pensioner' in this context is looking down and counting pennies in her hand with the same statistical comparison £6000 for the 'pensioner'; only this time the definitive other is defined as 'illegal immigrants/refugees' getting £29,900 with a number of children from diverse ethnic backgrounds being 'given' a house worth £2 m to live in. Meme 2 deploys intertextuality through the insertion of a newspaper clipping with a sensationalized slogan. This adds significance in terms of popularity, bonding and shaping meaning of audiences engaging with the specific content (Yus 2018). It also adds a form of media credibility; after all, the Daily Mail originally featured the article (Hastings 2010). The meme was then created, adapted and shared widely on social media during the Brexit referendum campaign some 6 years later. This meme also includes text that acts as a call to action: 'The average pensioner has paid taxes and contributed to the growth of this country for the last 40 to 60 years. Sad isn't it? Got the guts to copy & paste this? I Just Did.' (Hajimichael 2020)

Many of the memes on this theme are constructs of overtly racist far-right groupings, such as the English Defence League, who use them as forms of political capital to attract supporters online. Personally, I have seen this particular meme shared on Facebook during 2019 with and without the logo of the aforementioned racist organization. Memes 1 and 2 characterize ‘us’, the host ‘white’ ‘community’, through problematizing ‘immigrants’, ‘them’, as abusers of the welfare system. Similar kinds of visual and textual reappropriations in the arena of mainstream politics happened during ‘the Brexit Referendum of 2016’, and I want to explore this through the theme of how politics became ‘mememified’.

Brexit, the Remix and the ‘Mememification’ of Politics

Here, intertextuality and the remix take on a more sinister ideological form. The reappropriation and redefinition of images through memes are taken for granted. An image can mean one thing from its creation, and a completely different meaning can evolve after its reappropriation into someone else. We live in the age of the remix or mash-up or, you could say, the era of intellectual robbery. This is evident from the theme of immigration/refugees and political remixes regarding Brexit and in this case Nigel Farage, then leader of UKIP, who took centre stage.

The picture photographed by Getty photographer Jeff Mitchell documented people crossing the Croatian-Slovenian border in 2015 (Hajimichael 2020). Mitchell told the Guardian that it was ‘unfortunate’ that his image was used in the campaign against UKIP immigrants (Beaumont-Thomas 2016). It is worth considering how the visual was modified. In the image used for the UKIP poster (Hajimichael 2020), they zoom in slightly, cutting out the four policemen, the man holding a baby and the two young children at the front of the shot.

Therefore, how a picture commences a journey semiotically radically changes through a process of editing as noted from the two previous images. Meaning also changes due to context and untextual usage becoming a form of political propaganda. Consider the meaning of the UKIP poster with Farage standing like a statue in the foreground (Hajimichael 2020).

UKIP’s poster is an example of decontextualization, and, although strictly speaking it is not a meme as such, but a political poster, it was shared everywhere online and offline and thus became widely shared. Politics in the process became ‘mememified’. The irrationality of many memes on refugees enters political discourse through these meme-like posters, with Farage posing proudly in front of the poster. Ironically the populist politician attempted to explain the poster, to justify it – please note my italics:

> This is a photograph – *an accurate, undoctored photograph* – taken on 15 October last year following Angela Merkel’s call in the summer and, frankly, if you believe, as I have always believed, that we should open our hearts to genuine refugees, that’s one thing. But, frankly, as you can see from this picture, most of the people coming are young males and, yes, they may be coming from countries that are not in a very happy state, they may be coming from

places that are poorer than us, but the EU has made a fundamental error that risks the security of everybody. (Beaumont-Thomas 2016) (emphasis added)

Evidently, according to Farage, this is an 'undoctored photograph' that is clearly a fake statement, because from the original Getty image, woman and children are clearly visible. However, Farage distorts this fact to justify his own distortions. The image taken in Croatia by Mitchell, with its green background, is not even in the context of Britain, an island state surrounded by sea. In the context of UKIP political propaganda, it was used to stir fear and paranoia about 'hordes' of 'refugees' eventually finding their way to Britain from the Croatian border. Further reappropriation of this image occurred in Hungary with a stop sign added onto it (Hajimichael 2020).

The ways in which a political campaign becomes a meme online are also interesting through paradoxical associations with an act of terror in Orlando (2016) by the EU Leave campaign (Hajimichael 2020). The image exaggerates the fear factor through the reappropriation of images. Tellingly, in the process this meme decontextualizes Orlando to service a populist ideology of Britain leaving the European Union. Terrorism or being 'invaded', 'swamped', taken over is clear in a number of memes that follow. Intertextuality then, with the remix in mind, and blatant reappropriation, functions as political capital that 'bonds' people online (Yus 2018) in a short sharp shocking propagandistic deceptive manner.

A Threat to National Identity/Being Swamped/Invaded Memes

Britain First, an openly racist far-right movement, likes to share posts on social media on the theme of national identity erosion and 'being swamped'. In Meme 10 (Hajimichael 2020), crowds of people surround a lorry with the main slogan 'ISIS' at the top and 'COMING TO YOUR TOWN SOON' below in smaller capitalized letters. To the right of the meme, comments from Facebook supporters confirm users actually believe these memes are accurate, with calls to take up 'guns', to 'get ready to fight' and 'stop them'. The notion of a physical clash manifests clearly in meme form by Cashdaily.com, a conservative pro-Trump website. In Meme 11 (Hajimichael 2020), what appear to be Muslim protesters are clashing with *Polizei* (the German word for 'Police'). The text, again in capital letters, states at the top 'THEY ARE NOT ESCAPING TO FIND A BETTER LIFE' accompanied by 'THEY ARE INVADING US TO DESTROY OURS'. The context of the clash is not explained in any way; it is just used to confirm support of the paranoia of being 'invaded'. Subthemes also exist on this theme. These often associate 'REFUGEES' as 'INVADERS' but without their 'women', 'children' and 'old people'. In Meme 11 (Hajimichael 2020), despite the presence of a child and woman, the intention is clear – these are largely young men so you are put in the position of passing judgment through an ideologically loaded and inaccurate question 'YOU SEE REFUGEES?' at the top and 'I SEE INVADERS. WHERE ARE THE WOMEN,

CHILDREN AND OLD PEOPLE?' Of course, we cannot tell where this photo came from. It is just a group of people coming off a train somewhere given an entirely different meaning by someone who wants to stigmatize 'refugees' as deceptive. Perhaps one of the best themes relates to meme content relating to 'Islam'.

Islam/Islamophobia 'Common Sense' and Deceptive Paradoxes

This theme embodies very deceptive content. What is really contrasted with being fooled by the 'media' is elaborated in a paradoxical Meme 13 (Hajimichael 2020). The meme contains two images. On the left, an emaciated African child is framed from the back with various other people in the shot seated or standing. Below this image is the slogan in capitals 'THIS IS A REAL REFUGEE'. Next to this is another image with two young men in trousers and vests being inspected by two uniformed men on what appears to be the deck of a ship. Under this image reads 'THESE ARE NOT THESE ARE SOLDIERS OF ISLAM'. Under both images a plea states 'DON'T LET THE MEDIA FOOL YOU'. In none of these images can we be sure about who the people are. Clearly, the African child was photographed during a famine crisis (we do not know from when and where), but regarding the four men on the deck of ship, one of whom appears to be being searched, we do not know anything more than what we see. However, what we view and what is orchestrated by shouting online as capitalized text is a completely different distortion of specific realities that we do not actually know about.

Meme 14 from a Facebook post by Britain First (Hajimichael 2020) includes young and old women, dressed in the hijab and niqab. A young girl is framed in the central forefront with a hijab. Below a text reads: 'Ironically, the refugees bring with them the very religion from whose cruelties they are fleeing.' There is no indication in the image that these women are traveling to and from anywhere, so the idea they are bringing a religion is highly dubious. The way the child in the forefront gazes into lens, when all the women included are generally looking elsewhere, makes a link with the text as if to say Islam is victimizing her. A text statement posted by Britain First above the meme reads: 'All part of the plan to spread Islam'. The statement articulates a conspiracy that Islam intends to spread and take over Britain. Further 'common sense' reckonings exist in Meme 5, 'Why do you hate us?', and Meme 4, 'All I want to do' (Hajimichael 2020) images, which have a similar composition. In these images bearded Muslim men are framed innocently, as one hold his arms by his sides looking up to the camera, with the other holding up his right hand, as if to pose a question. Below both images are exaggerated statements on what the men allegedly want to do: 'RAPE YOUR WOMEN', 'CONDEMN YOUR LIFESTYLE', 'BOMB YOUR BUSES' and so forth. These statements clearly represent paranoias on the part of the people who created these memes about Muslims.

Refugees as Bodybuilders

Cleary we can see a pattern emerging in many of the memes analysed thus far. People who make such content want to convey a feeling that we (meaning 'they') are being fooled, because the people who are being framed are not real 'refugees', and their intentions are not honest. 'They' want to 'invade', 'infiltrate', 'take over' and 'dominate'. A set of memes on the 'bodybuilder' theme take this to a stereotypical extreme, namely, 'these so-called refugees' do not look like refugees (whatever looking like a refugee means); they are in fact body builders on steroids. 'I HEARD WE CAN GET FREE STEROIDS IN ENGLAND!' declares with some excitement above an image of a young man in a Heineken white vest who appears to have been working out (Meme 19) (Hajimichael 2020). Next to him, the arm of a man in uniform touches his shoulder, while two other uniformed men are framed in the foreground and background. The location may be on a ship, as the sky and sea are visible in the background. The text immediately below the image in lowercase letters reads: 'Please help feed and house this poor, defenceless refugee'. Immediately below this in capitals: 'DON'T BE A RACIST AND LET ME IN'.

A similar set of images exist in Meme 20; only this time, to make the effect more powerful, four images of men who appear to have been working out are put together (Hajimichael 2020). In the centre of the meme is a word, 'REFUGEES?', and below in a red and white font that can be interpreted as dripping in blood is 'Is it sinking in yet?'. These pictures are decontextualized as they were taken in Australia, off Christmas Island in 2013, as evidenced by the back of the uniformed officers' blue shirt with yellow lettering that reads 'Australian Customs and Border Protection' (Kleinfeld 2015). Yet these images were shared online on far-right Facebook pages such as those of the EDL (over three thousand times), as authentic accounts of 'refugees' fleeing the conflict in Syria. The only duping happening in such images relates their maker's intentions to fool people into believing a series of exaggerations that are completely inaccurate.

Meme Generator and Creators

We have not talked so much so far about how memes are created by users. Many sites and apps enable users to make memes. I would like to focus on one of these, namely, Meme Generator (2020), which proclaims to be the 'first online meme generator' where users can create an account, log in and make memes. Here we find many categories such as 'immigration' (23 posts), 'refugees' (14 posts) and 'zombie versus refugees' (14 posts); however, when the word Muslim is inserted, different results occur: 'Angry Muslim Guy' (6000 posts), 'Ordinary Muslim Man' (5000 posts),[1] 'Confused Muslim Girl' (1000 posts) and 'Muslim Immigrant' (398 posts) (Meme Generator 2020). In all these posts, the people being framed had no say whatsoever on the content made, which users stating derogatory memes always determined. This spike in numbers (and this is just one meme-generating site; there are many more) is an indication quantitatively of how much anti-Islam/anti-Muslim/Islamophobic content exists online in the form of memes.

It is not possible, given the limitations of the current chapter, to examine these in detail, semiotically, but I will focus on one in particular, the 'Angry Muslim Guy' meme that was created July 28, 2011, and ranks #895 out of the memes on the website. This meme is also known as 'Muslim Rage Boy' (Know Your Meme 2020). Shakeel Bhat Kashmiri is the real name of the protestor framed in these memes. In 2007, he was 31 years old, not a boy (Rajghatta 2007). On finding out about his popularity, including mouse pads, T-shirts and beer mugs made by a US conservative website, Bhat responded: 'I do not believe this! I have no knowledge about all this. Why do they do it? demanded Bhat, who says he has no idea how to use a computer and the Internet' (Rajghatta 2007). This is just one meme of course, amongst the possible thousands that exist online, which, when researched (where possible), give a different set of accounts, about a real-life person, that differs radically from the variety of derogatory content made by users online as memes.

I would like to return here to a concept shared earlier with reference to memes as 'ideas' (Lantagne 2017) and the dynamics between those who make memes, those who took the photos originally and those depicted in them. Clearly, memes are used in a 'spectrum of ways', and legally the interests of these three 'stakeholders' are important to take into account (Lantagne 2017). However, this does not work very well when considering derogatory memes created by groupings of extreme minded people articulating specifically offensive ideologies online. Here, through the articulation of many stereotypes, what started out as one image ends up as something completely different. The case of Shakeel Bhat is clear. There are thousands of other images where users can freely generate vitriolic and distortive content. Meme 15, 'Entitled Refugee Ahmed' (Hajimichael 2020), is a good example of this. A young man is framed in this meme. He holds his hands wide in protest and appears to be angry about something going in on the background. The image then becomes an 'empty' (textually) digital canvas for people to write whatever they wish about someone's real-life anger and plight. Even the name of the meme template is problematic. Who decides whether the person framed is 'entitled' or a 'refugee' or an 'entitled refugee' and why the name 'Ahmed'?

Drawing some conclusions from the work covered so far is important before considering a proposed solution through a media literacy intervention. The impact of memes on social media; their ability to spread virally, directly and digitally; and their velocity are key elements that make their impact very different from other forms of media content. Their adaptability by users/creators is also what makes

[1] This is the same as Meme 5, 'Why Do You Hate Us' (Hajimichael 2020).

them unique. Memes are in this sense like digital putty; it can be moulded in any direction a user intends. At the same time, political groupings and movements such as UKIP, Britain First and the English Defence League, with intended offensive and derogatory agendas, have exploited that malleability.

Memes are exploited and shared with and for deliberate reasons. As a result, they have become a form of political capital exploited even by mainstream political parties and politicians with the intent of gaining support for particular causes, such as the Brexit campaign or Trump's desire to build a wall between the USA and Mexico. It is this appeal to populist forms of common sense which makes such politicized memes alluring, even to the extent of people who claim to be anti-racist sharing such content, and this is something that I have witnessed personally online, particularly with the paradoxical meme casting 'pensioners' losing out as result of 'refugees' or 'immigrants' (Memes 1 and 2) (Hajimichael 2020). I know of at least one person who shared this on Facebook, as a post for comment, and yet a year earlier, the same person was an activist in an anti-fascist protest in Britain.[2] Some people sharing such memes also declare that they are factually true when they contain distorted and exaggerated information.

The impact of such memes is important to study with regard to far-right discourses on immigration/refugees and online and offline extremist activism which has been done at length in the Greek context (Afouxenidis et al. 2020). Clearly, these memes affect people, and they shape perceptions of refugees, immigration and Islam in particular ways. In the memes discussed, the 'refugee' never represents; he/she is always represented by someone else, and through that re-presentation, their realities are not accurately portrayed. Refugees never talk about themselves. Therefore, the stories we see are deceptions, lies and fake news on the part of the users who made them. This has to do with the power of rhetoric through visuals and text as memetic content. Here, any use of language, whether spoken, or in an advertisement, a meme online, a song or a narrative in a book, is a form of discourse.

Shifman (2014) suggests that although Internet memes are created and disseminated at the micro level, they operate on the macro level, as they design social discourse and even participate in the consolidation of collectives. Reality then is conceptually mediated through language (Fairclough 1995). While critical discourse analysis tends to focus more on spoken language and written text, the idea that ideology, identity and inequality are (re)enacted through texts produced in social and political contexts (van Dijk 2001) is central to my conclusion here. Who represents, who speaks, who does not speak, who is invisible and who is present are important for understanding the social dynamics of these digital images known as memes.

One approach to counter the impact of such distortions is a Media Literacy Intervention where students and lecturers discuss meme content in detail from a

---

[2] Anonymous conversations online with a self-declared anti-fascist who shared Meme 1 online as Facebook post (Hajimichael 2020).

critical perspective, and this is something that I would like to elaborate on further for the remainder of this chapter.

Developing a Media Literacy Intervention: Countering the Impact of Derogatory Memes

A key part of media literacy focuses on developing critical thinking and the ability to read and disentangle media messages as deliberately constructed texts (Potter 2013). A way of doing this is through a media literacy intervention (Potter 2013), in my case, teaching a course in a manner in which students' views could be evaluated in terms of possible changes having taken the course.

However, measuring or even discussing changes in perception is a tricky subject. Therefore, I adopted an approach that enabled students to reason, discuss, elaborate and question their views on the content shared. Furthermore, there was a component to the course, as a final project, that required students to produce creative content on the subject matter of social memes. I found this component integral to how they interpreted course material. I originally intended to do this research over 2 years to include two semesters, but unfortunately, the Covid-19 pandemic disrupted these plans. This would have given a bigger sample of about 60 students. However, it was impossible to implement one course in class and the other online the following year. A total of 36 participants took the course Media Literacy COMM-400 at the University of Nicosia over a 12-week period in spring 2019 as part of the research. This included 22 female and 14 male participants with an age range of 18 to 25. In terms of origin, 23 were from EU countries and 13 from non-EU countries. The mix of students on gender and origin lines created an interesting dialogue. One of the students is the offspring of a refugee/asylum seeker who settled in an EU country, Cyprus, and now considers herself a Cypriot.

Explanation of MILT, Memes and Context

As a starting point for the media literacy course, I had to explain to students what I was doing and why and to get their consent to participate in a piece of research under the aegis of the MILT – Media Literacy Living Together Project (2018). Students familiarized themselves with the narrativity of images – how people think more with images through social memes (Shifman 2014), particularly with humour-based content. At the same time, literature regarding online racial stereotypes was also introduced which was significant particularly as young people are more engaged with social memes online (Yoon 2016). It was important for me to get students to reflect more about the connotative content because the Internet is a platform where at times offensive memes, containing racist/sexist content, go unfiltered (Yoon 2016).

Equally important was that students familiarize themselves with context. A colleague at the University, Nicos Trimikliniotis, who had just completed a book (2019) on the subject matter, explained the EU Refugee crisis (2014–2018) through a guest lecture. There was also a discussion on media representation of this crisis through a Council of Europe Report (Georgiou and Zaborowski 2017). I then proceeded to explore and discuss meme content in class, after an explanation of critical discourse analysis and visual semiotics. The research then had four key phases: the collection and discussion of meme-based data by students working in groups; organization and implementation of focus groups; production, sharing and discussion of creative works by students (by the end of the course); and analysis, interpretation and presentation of data findings.

The Research Process

During phase one, students collected meme-based data on the topic, and a discussion of these followed with presentations in class. Eight groups collected and analysed 4 memes each totalling 32 images. Completed by the middle of the semester, the different class groups collected one hundred images overall by the end of the course. Phase two was more difficult to organize as extra sessions had to be negotiated with the group in the form of focus groups. These discussions took place over a period of 2 weeks outside on the amphitheatre in a smaller classroom conducive for carrying out focus groups.

A number of key themes relating to how the content of the course affected participants was put on the table for discussion. Most students admitted they saw the memes as offensive. Thirty-two in total before taking the course came to this conclusion. Four people admitted their views had radically changed following the course as they saw memes as humorous/harmless initially. Participants expressed particular emphasis on the role of the media. This was after all a predictable response, particularly seeing as all the students studied Communications. However, one exchange between anonymized participants B, I and E is valuable to note:

B: The Media are to blame for the way refugees are portrayed.
I: Media exploit reality, I agree with you.
E: That's precisely why these memes we have been looking at are so dangerous, people absorb it and it then becomes the norm. (Participant Focus Group 2)

Another key finding of the focus groups related to issues of empathy and antipathy. A question was posed to all participants relating to the significance of hearing refugee stories. This question was significant, as some of the students in the class had descended from refugee backgrounds or in one case, their parents had been given asylum in Cyprus. What was interesting here was responses from students who felt they could identify more with contemporary refugees because their grandparents or parents had been through the upheavals of war and forced migration (Participants Focus Group 4).

However, at the same time, there was an acknowledgement by a significant number of students across all focus groups, roughly half, that they could not agree on a common approach to the refugee crisis. This was particularly so for students from Greece and Cyprus who felt let down by a lack of coherent policy (Focus Group 4) and by a number of students outside of the EU who believed that the problem of refugees was more systemic and people were being exploited through a kind of 'refugee-eco-food chain'. As one student said:

> You cannot understand the EU Refugee crisis without considering what is going on in the countries people are coming from. People are leaving because they are being uprooted due to war or through systemic economic inequalities. So until those realities change there will always be refugees. (Participant Focus Group 3)

The most difficult phase for students followed – the production, sharing and discussion of creative works. It was important that students could present something by the end of the course that was a product of their own creative endeavours. I could have asked them to write an assignment, but this seemed too bland for students engaging with a variety of production-based courses in film, video and radio/audio. There were many logistics to plan, as in any production process, and like any kind of graded work, there were differences in creative quality. Nevertheless, these fruits of student creativity were shared and, if the students so wished hosted online beyond the course. Three projects are notable to mention in this respect. One of the largest group of students made a green-screen-based video discussion analysing offensive meme content on refugees (Lefevre et al. 2019). All of these students took advance video courses making their work technically creative. Students were encouraged with these projects to find interesting people to interview and commentate on the subject matter. Naser and Ryan (2019) did their work as a podcast highlighting the work of local N.G.O KISA (Movement for Equality, Support, Anti-Racism) with refugees. Additionally, meme-based content on allegations of rape was analysed in the German context from a semiotic viewpoint (Dvorianska et al. 2019).

All student groups had to make a presentation to class of their work as part of their final assessment, which Nicos Trimikliniotis also attended. Finally, data collected was analysed, interpreted and written up, after which presentations of key findings occurred for the MILT Project.[3] I also participated in four other public events related to the subject matter in Cyprus, Greece and Italy.[4]

During many of these events, I was able to present the key findings of this research with regard to online memes, refugees and the role of media literacy as an

[3] Presentation of key findings at MILT Conference Linson, June 2019. See https://cicant.ulusofona.pt/our-research/milt-conference-2019-the-future-of-media-and-learning-in-participation/. Accessed 22 December 2020

[4] Three of these presentations/events related to participation in the 'Word are Stones Project' facilitated by local Anti-Racist NGO KISA in Nicosia, Rome and Thessaloniki. An additional presentation was made online to 'Sto Kafeneis tis Pemptis' organized by the Left Faction in Nicosia, Cyprus.

educational tool and to get feedback on particular aspects of the research findings. One of the observations, also reflected in the focus groups by students, relates to how social memes and the ideas they contain can become the norm. This happens sometimes without people thinking about them. Many people also found some of the findings shocking, which I found surprising, particularly given the ubiquity and toxicity of social media and memes. At the same time, we think with memes (Blackmore et al. 2000) and at times tend to take their meaning for granted, even though as we have seen from many examples, they are manufactured to create paranoia and spread fear, propaganda and misinformation on subjects relating refugees. Often this relies on ‘common-sense’ rhetoric, and unpacking these meanings requires us to comprehend the multimodal meaning of memes as texts and images (Dancygier and Vandelanotte 2017).

Final Thoughts ...

The proliferation of memes on the Internet and issues of impact and virality, how they spread instantly, despite often being very inaccurate, is something that should concern us. It is the unfiltered nature of such memes (Yoon 2016) and how they can be easily created by online apps and through websites that I found most disturbing. Memes, in my opinion, are taken too lightly, as humour. Their everyday character fools people a lot of the time despite a reliance on lies, fake/manipulated content or even hate speech. People have this tendency in contemporary society to share the exaggerated, the fake, the lies, more than facts even (Vosoughi et al. 2018). The dominance of ‘circus’-like politics (Kaplan 2018) played out in media plays a part in this on a macro level. However, on the micro level, as scholars engaged in teaching about media in education, developing critical thinking on digital content enables students to question and possibly change some things that may previously have been taken for granted. Otherwise, teaching media itself can become dupery, and we can join the ‘circus’ and teach our students to master the sinister tactics of how to develop sensationalized, exaggerated and controversial fake news stories. It is important to understand that the same technologies that connect us which have the potential to make us happier as creative individuals (Gauntlett 2011) are the same tools which ‘are just as ferociously efficient at creating and spreading misinformation, disinformation and malinformation’ (MacKenzie et al. 2020).

Acknowledgements The chapter has been developed from the author’s participation in the European Commission-funded project MILT (Media Literacy Living Together) (2018) and with research time-release support from the University of Nicosia.

References

Afouxenidis, A., Petrou, M., Kavoulakos, K., & Petridis, P. (2020). Far Right Social Networks: Investigation of Political and Cultural Activism. https://farsocmed.weebly.com/. Accessed 24 November 2020.

American Heritage Dictionary (2020). Meme. https://ahdictionary.com/word/search.html?q=meme. Accessed 24 November 2020.

BBC (2016). How Might Trump 'Drain the Swamp'? 18 October. https://www.bbc.com/news/election-us-2016-37699073. Accessed 14 September 2020.

Beaumont-Thomas, B. (2016). Jeff Mitchell's Best Photograph: These People Have been Betrayed by Ukip. Interview. The Guardian, 22 June. https://www.theguardian.com/artanddesign/2016/jun/22/jeff-mitchells-best-shot-the-column-of-marching-refugees-used-in-ukips-brexit-campaign. Accessed 16 September 2020.

Bhattacharyya, G. (2020). Revisiting 'Common-sense' in a Time of Cultivated Ignorance. A Conversation with Errol Lawrence. *Identities*, *27*(1), 114–131. https://doi.org/10.1080/1070289X.2018.1521653.

Blackmore, S., Dugatkin, L.A., Boyd, R., Richerson, P.J., & Plotkin, H. (2000). The Power of Memes. *Scientific American*, *283*(4), 64–73.

Boffey, D., & Helm, T. (2016). Vote Leave Embroiled in Race Row over Turkey Security Threat claims. Guardian, 22 May. https://www.theguardian.com/politics/2016/may/21/vote-leave-prejudice-turkey-eu-security-threat. Accessed 14 September 2020.

CCCS. (1982). *The Empire Strikes Back Race and Racism In 70's Britain*. London: Routledge

Dancygier, B., & Vandelanotte, L. (2017). Internet Memes as Multimodal Constructions. *Cognitive Linguistics, 28*(3), 565–598. https://doi.org/10.1515/cog-2017-0074.

Dawkins, R. (2016). *The Selfish Gene*. Oxford: Oxford University Press.

Dvorianska, A., Italou, T., Stektko, A., & Varshavskya, A. (2019). Media Literacy Radio Podcast. https://soundcloud.com/theo-yolo-170585086/radio-podcast-for-media-literacy. Accessed 14 December 2020.

Eisenburg, H. (2018). Humans Process Visual Data Better. http://www.t-sciences.com/news/humans-process-visual-data-better. Accessed 26 September.

Fairclough, N. (1995). *Critical discourse analyisis:The critical study of language*. Longman.

Gauntlett, D. (2011). *Making is Connecting: The Social Power of Creativity, from Craft and Knitting to Digital Everything*. Cambridge: Polity.

Georgiou, M., & Zaborowski, R. (2017). Media Coverage of the "Refugee Crisis": A Cross-European perspective. https://edoc.coe.int/en/refugees/7367-media-coverage-of-the-refugee-crisis-a-cross-european-perspective.html. Accessed 17 September 2020.

Hahl, O., Kim, M., & Sivan, E. W. (2018). The Authentic Appeal of the Lying Demagogue: Proclaiming the Deeper Truth about Political Illegitimacy. *American Sociological Review*, *83*(1), 1–33. https://doi.org/10.1177/0003122417749632.

Hajimichael, M. (2020) Refugees and Social Memes. https://sublimeridiculous.wordpress.com/2020/09/18/refugees-and-social-memes/. Accessed 17 September 2020.

Hänska-Ahy, M., & Bauchowitz, S. (2017). Tweeting for Brexit: How Social Media Influenced the Referendum. In J. Mair, T. Clar, & N. Fowler (Eds.), *Brexit, Trump and the Media*. (pp. 31–35). Bury St Edmunds, UK: Abramis Academic Publishing.

Hastings, C. (2010). Somali Asylum Seeker Family Given £2m House... After Complaining 5-bed London Home Was "in Poor Area". Daily Mail, 10 July. https://www.dailymail.co.uk/news/article-1293730/Somali-asylum-seeker-family-given-2m-house%2D%2Dcomplaining-5-bed-London-home-poor-area.html. Accessed 30 November 2020.

Hobbs, R., & McGee, S. (2014). Teaching about Propaganda: An Examination of the Historical Roots of Media Literacy. *Journal of Media Literacy Education,* 6(2). https://doi.org/10.23860/jmle-2016-06-02-5.

Iosifides, P., & Wheeler, M. (2016*). Public Spheres and Mediated Social Networks in the Western Context and Beyond.* London: Palgrave Macmillan. https://doi.org/10.1057/978-1-137-41030-6.

Kaplan, M. (2018). Circus like Politics. Forward. https://forward.com/culture/408748/in-the-face-of-circus-politics-we-need-better-stories/. Accessed 10 January 2021.

Kellner, D., & Share, J. (2005). *Toward critical media literacy: Core concepts, debates, organizations and policy*. Routledge.

Kleinfeld, K. (2015). Calling Bullshit On the Anti-Refugee Memes Flooding the Internet. Vice, 10 September. https://www.vice.com/en_uk/article/zngwz9/kleinfeld-refugee-memes-debunking-846. Accessed 16 September 2020.

Know Your Meme (2020). Islamic Rage Boy. https://knowyourmeme.com/memes/islamic-rage-boy. Accessed 17 September 2020.

Lantagne, S. (2017). Famous on the Internet: The Spectrum of Internet Memes and the Legal Challenge of Evolving Methods of Communication. *SSRN Electronic Journal*. https://doi.org/10.2139/ssrn.2944804.

Lefevre, M., Molotsi, T., Tsangarides, M., & Vilvorder, M. (2019). Media Literacy Final Project 1 [YouTube video]. https://youtu.be/Cm5yU6si7R0. Accessed 14 December 2020.

Lilleker, D., & Surowiec, P. (2020). Uncovering the 'Hidden Persuaders': A Content Analysis and Examination of Digital Propaganda on Social Media. In P. Baines, N. O'Shaughnessy, & N. Snow (Eds.), *The SAGE Handbook of Propaganda*. London: SAGE Publications.

MacKenzie, A., Rose, J., & Bhatt, I. (2020). Dupery by Design: The Epistemology of Deceit in a Postdigital Era. *Postdigital Science and Education*. https://doi.org/10.1007/s42438-020-00114-7.

Media Literacy Living Together (2018). https://milt.ulusofona.eu/. Accessed 18 September 2020.

Meme Generator: Create Your Own Meme (2020). http://www.memegenerator.net/. Accessed 16 September 2020.

Mihailidis, P. (2018). Civic Media Literacies: re-Imagining Engagement for Civic Intentionality. *Learning, Media and Technology, 43*(2), 152–164. https://doi.org/10.1080/17439884.2018.1428623.

Naser, A., & Ryan, J. (2019). Media Literacy Final Podcast Refugees and Social Memes in EU. https://soundcloud.com/hajimike/final-podcast-refugees-and-social-memes-in-eu. Accessed 17 September 2020.

National Association for Media Literacy Education (2020). https://namle.net/resources/media-literacy-defined/. Accessed 16 September 2020.

Orlofsky, V. L. (2019). Memes, Fair Use, and Privacy. Intellectual Freedom Blog. https://www.oif.ala.org/oif/?p=16873. Accessed 14 September 2020.

Patel, N. (2013). First World Problems: A Fair Use Analysis of Internet Memes. *UCLA Entertainment Law Review, 20*(2), 235–256.

Potter, W. J. (2013). *Media Literacy*. Thousand Oaks, CA: Sage Publications.

Rajghatta, C. (2007). *Kashmir's "Rage Boy" invites humour, mirth*. The Times of India. https://timesofindia.indiatimes.com/world/us/kashmirs-rage-boy-invites-humour-mirth/articleshow/2164387.cms.

Shifman, L. (2014). *Memes in Digital Culture*. Cambridge, MA: MIT Press,

Trimikliniotis, N. (2019*). Migration and the Refugee Dissensus in Europe Borders, Security and Austerity*. Routledge: London.

van Dijk, T. A. (2001). Multidisciplinary CDA: A Place for Diversity. In R. Wodak, & M. Meyer (Eds.), *Methods of Critical Discourse Analysis* (pp. 95–121). London: SAGE Publications Ltd.

van Dijk, T. A. (2015). Critical Discourse Analysis. In D. Tannen, H. E. Hamilton, & D. Schiffrin (Eds.), *The Handbook of Discourse Analysis*. Chichester and Malden: Wiley Blackwell.

VICE (2016). "We Memed Alt-right into Existence": Our Extended Interview with Richard Spencer on White Nationalism. https://www.vice.com/en/article/a3j588/we-memed-alt-right-into-existence-our-extended-interview-with-richard-spencer-on-white-nationalism. Accessed 1 December 2020.

Vosoughi, S., Roy, D., & Aral, S. (2018). The Spread of True and False News Online. *Science, 359*(6380), 1146–1151. https://doi.org/10.1126/science.aap9559.

Yoon, I. (2016). Why is it not Just a Joke? Analysis of Internet Memes Associated with Racism and Hidden Ideology of Colorblindness. *Journal of Cultural Research in Art Education, 33,* 92–123.

Yus, F. (2018). Identity-related Issues in Meme Communication. *Internet Pragmatics, 1*(1), 113–133. https://doi.org/10.1075/ip.00006.yus.

Part IV
Towards A Critical Pedagogy

Chapter 12
Scallywag Pedagogy

Peter McLaren and Petar Jandrić

Pillow Talk at 100 Seconds to Midnight

We are at the mercy of the vilest conditions of appropriation set by the transnational capitalist class and established over generations of workers who seek justice. Sociologist Bill Robinson underscores that there are similarities but also important differences between fascist projects of the twentieth and twenty-first centuries. He notes that the twentieth-century fascist project 'involved the fusion of reactionary political power with *national* capital, whereas in the 21st century the fascist project involves the fusion of *transnational capital* with reactionary and repressive political power' (Robinson 2019: 155) (emphasis from the original). In order to resist the dictatorship of transnational capital, the specter of the global police state, and twenty-first-century fascism, it is necessary to build broad anti-fascist alliances led by popular and working-class forces. How is this possible in places such as the United States where Raytheon and Boeing, Lockheed and Northrop Grumman, and United Technologies and BAE Systems hold corporate sway and where half the country has pledged allegiance to Donald Trump, a master of suborning the aggrieved and creating a fascist system of intelligibility with the help of Fox News, Newsmax, and One America News Network through which the working class can shape their reality in concert with Trump's own toxic ideological predilections, racism, misanthrope, and misology?

P. McLaren (✉)
Chapman University, Orange, CA, USA

P. Jandrić
Zagreb University of Applied Sciences, Zagreb, Croatia

The University of Wolverhampton, Wolverhampton, UK
e-mail: petar.jandric@tvz.hr

A. MacKenzie et al. (eds.), *The Epistemology of Deceit in a Postdigital Era*, Postdigital Science and Education,
https://doi.org/10.1007/978-3-030-72154-1_12

Except for unforeseen circumstances (and we make no claim to be prophets or even free market futurists), we believe the world is headed in the direction of a disaster so catastrophic that only dystopian novels or films have managed to calibrate the increasing scale of the horrors facing humanity. Since this chapter is being written during a moment of short-lived reprieve at which time the science and security board of the Bulletin of the Atomic Scientists approached the Doomsday Clock and reset it at a setting of 100 seconds to midnight (Mecklin 2020) – a metaphorical minute hand of a clock revealing a figurative hundred-second warning – we wish to affirm our commitment to avoid nuclear annihilation at any cost rather than sullenly succumb to its inevitability. In our time of the raging Covid-19 pandemic, we wish to affirm our commitment to avoid further increase of human suffering. And, as we have increasingly become aware of the inseparability between our socio-technological arrangements and the future of our planet, we wish to affirm our commitment to ensure long-term prospects of human survival of the human race.

We realize the constitutive entanglement of these phenomena, dubbed in our recent works under the overarching concept of the postdigital condition (Jandrić et al. 2018a, b) and several narrower concepts such as bioinformational capitalism (Peters, Jandrić, and Hayes 2021a), viral modernity (Peters, Jandrić, and McLaren 2020), and others. We acknowledge the complex relationships between these concepts (Peters, Jandrić, and Hayes 2021b) and the need for an open, honest, and constructive postdigital dialogue (Jandrić 2019) – which may well be our last chance for pillow talk at 100 seconds to midnight. We acknowledge the dialectic between theory and practice, between past, present, and future, between we-think, we-learn, we-act (Jandrić 2019), and we-feel (Jandrić and Hayes 2020). We realize that the epistemology of truth is mutually foundational with the epistemology of deceit and that the truth about lies is mutually constitutive with the lies about truth (MacKenzie and Bhatt 2019a, b). With these realizations we tone down our bellicosity and seek the type of dialogical engagement that our mentor, Paulo Freire, has bequeathed us, through his emphasis on critical pedagogical praxis.

We call our pedagogy 'scallywag pedagogy' after England's secret army of guerilla fighters who, should the Nazis have successfully invaded England, were to emerge from their secret underground bunkers and attack the occupying Nazi forces as well as assassinate any English collaborators with the enemy (Carr et al. 2020). We wish to emphasize that we do not see ourselves as heroes. Far from it. We wish only to recognize the manner in which transnational capital has occupied most of the so-called civilized world and warn against the growing forces of fascism that have made themselves present over the past decade throughout Europe and North America – and the need to develop a pedagogical counterforce that both understands the dangers of a post-truth world that embraces conspiratorial right-wing 'alternative facts' and abandons self-reflexivity and dialogue as a key means of democratizing our social universe.

The Demonic Pact with Capital

Revolutionary pedagogy is a term that is often conflated with a similar term, 'revolutionary critical pedagogy' (see McLaren and Jandrić 2020a: Chap 3). It is a term that follows from a growing disillusionment with the notion that the praxis of students in public school settings can become sufficiently protagonistic in bringing about substantive social change. In other words, the focus for change is too narrow to move capitalism from its substratum, to shake capitalism at its roots. Mainstream education is a slave to capitalism; revolutionary critical pedagogy is slave rebellion. Our adoption of Freire's concept of critical consciousness (conscientization, or *conscientização* in the original Portuguese) stipulates that *conscientização* is not a precondition for revolutionary action but rather the outcome of action. We deepen our understanding by reflecting on our actions and those of others. We tilt such action not towards windmills but in the direction of a protagonist struggle for socialism. At the same time, our consciousness raising is directed at helping beleaguered constituencies most vulnerable to the ravages of capitalist injustice.

Marx reminds us that human beings revise their thinking given various changes in their circumstances and that educators must themselves be willing to be educated. Revolutionary practice, or praxis, has to do with 'the coincidence of the changing of circumstances and of human activity or self-change' (Marx 1848/1975; see Lebowitz 2017). Protagonistic or revolutionary agents are not born in a sociopolitical vacuum; they are produced by circumstances and responses to those circumstances, as one might imagine in the case with unfinished human beings. To revolutionize thought it is necessary to revolutionize society. And to revolutionize society requires a revolution in thought. All human development (including thought and speech) is a social activity, and this has its roots in collective labor. We agree that Marx (1852) said it best in 'The Eighteenth Brumaire of Louis Bonaparte' when he wrote his famous passage:

> Men make their own history, but they do not make it as they please; they do not make it under self-selected circumstances, but under circumstances existing already, given and transmitted from the past. The tradition of all dead generations weighs like a nightmare on the brains of the living. And just as they seem to be occupied with revolutionizing themselves and things, creating something that did not exist before, precisely in such epochs of revolutionary crisis they anxiously conjure up the spirits of the past to their service, borrowing from them names, battle slogans, and costumes in order to present this new scene in world history in time-honored disguise and borrowed language. (Marx 1852)

In the teeth of the pandemic, and in the thicket of unprecedented revolt against systemic racism most visible in the recent Black Lives Matter protests, trumpet-tongued Trump and his witch's familiar, the Imp of the Perverse, peer from the darkness of an Edgar Allan Poe nightmare of his own making, delighting in the deliciousness of the destruction. Trump has emerged as the Lord of Chaos, his multiheaded hydra of reveling in the death he has incurred, slurp-lipped at the thought of bodies writhing in pools of bloody devastation. Our Lord and Master of the orange-tinged nightmare has fulminated against common sense, creating a world-wrenching apocalyptic narrative that he is protecting the United States from the evils of socialism. He has given an 'anarchist' designation to certain cities run by democrats, promising to withhold federal funds. What a grand fool he is. Is this not the gamification of right-wing terrorism?

We reject his empathy-devoid, fact-free assertions. We reject the theatricality by which Trump removes his mask (metaphorically and literally). We reject his ebullient stage persona. We reject his Mussolini-like preaching from the balcony. We reject his incendiary rhetoric, his vandalization of the Constitution. We reject his fever-dream presidency. We reject his seismic influence on the politically aggrieved who hide in broad daylight under the banner of Q. The pharisaism and Tartuffery that hangs like river foam from the drooling mouths of the Trump clan and their spiritually disfigured preachers spells out what this cult is all about. The neck-snapping pace of this cult that has moved seamlessly through the highways and the bypaths of American politics makes it difficult to take stock of the enormity of the challenge that now faces the United States.

Trumpista media compels us to disparage socialism – a deeply inculcated cultural artifact that has provided political ballast for the right – while we secretly recognize it to be the only hope for the future. We yearn for socialism to be rebirthed and fear fascism and Trump's racketeering-style governance more than the insane cults that would have lizard people robed in ritual garments and sporting richly decorated diadems chomp down with retractable teeth on the cherubic flesh of infants prepared for a Satanic banquet. We don't believe the global elite led by George Soros are harvesting children's blood before they are given over to demons. (We don't even believe in the global elite – rather we acknowledge the existence of the transnational capitalist class!) We don't believe that Angela Merkel is Hitler's granddaughter, Justin Trudeau is Fidel Castro's son, Vladimir Putin is the reincarnation of Rasputin, or Bill Gates is planning to use invisible ink to tattoo vaccination status into children's skin. We don't brandish AR-15s in our political advertisements. Does that make us weird in your batshit crazy Republican eyes?

Regrettably, that makes us suspect in the eyes of at least 70 million Americans who voted for Trump. A day of reckoning is coming untethered by your theatrical Trumpian charade. The working class are going to come calling. So we ask: Who belongs to the working class? The answer: A worker who does not own the means of production or play a supervisory role for those that do. And there are three billion of us. And that should terrify Trumpista America. But it doesn't because they have managed to secure the ideological allegiance of much of the working class. We failed our Golgotha moment when our politicians refused to stand up to Trump, when the Democratic National Convention made sure Biden would be the presidential candidate over Bernie Sanders. This is because in the main the Democrats themselves have fallen prey to the massive ideological assault in the media against socialism, beginning in the post-Second World War years. In doing so, we recrucified Jesus with teflon nails, transferring his salvific grace to Lady Luck's slot machines, all lined up like tin soldiers in some shiny Vegas casino. We made our demonic pact with capital.

Escaping the *auto-da-fé* imposed by the Never Trumpers and clinging to his witch's familiar, the Imp of the Perverse, and other transmundane demons, Trump braces himself beside the crenelated parapet of some crumbling stone brick medieval Trump Tower. When Trump feels energized by his spittle-flecked counsel of quislings, he can be heard braying from the dark edges of his everyday Wagnerian opera, barnstorming electoral battlegrounds in frenetic 'scampaign' rallies, stoking public distemper, ginning up public convulsions of fear and rage, whiplashing the public with his stentorian voice, cartoonish hand gestures, and robotic dance moves while lurching towards insanity. Trumpism and justice have always made for an antiseptic cleavage in the same manner in which Trump and compassion have always had a major dispute. Decency turned its back on Trump long before he became president. Trump's brainpan has always been an ideological gravesite, where truth goes to die. So we expect his actions to be inherently regressive and repressive, ensanguining the public discourse with the blood of tyrants. We expect winning at all costs to be his great desideratum for governance, as he infiltrates the morality of gangsters with unmistakable relish, emerging time and again as the country's Mobster-in-Chief.

True Words Require Actions

Much has been written about Trump's online antics and his blatant disregard for truth and human decency.[1] Only in 2020, we criticized Trump's relationships to Alt-Right movements (McLaren and Jandrić 2020b), his disregard for the environment (Jandrić and McLaren 2020), his poisonous relationship to religion and especially to his Evangelical Christian voter base (McLaren 2020a, b), and few other themes. We may be scribomaniacs, yet Trump's ability of spitting nonsense surpasses even the quickest of writers. Mainstream media, far-right media, and social media reify and legitimize Trump's reality and make it a compelling alternative to fact-based reporting. While Trump is not the US president anymore, being succeeded by Joe Biden in yet another bizarre episode in which Trump stubbornly refused to accept the loss of elections, poisonous seeds of Trumpist logic will nevertheless not disappear the moment he steps down from his golden throne.

Clearly, we need to see the transient nature of this repressive moment through a militant commitment to changing the rational institutions of democracy that enable a fascist repression of the social contract as much as they help to defend the pursuit of freedom and justice. Andrew Feenberg writes:

> Lukács argued that when societies become conscious of the social contingency of the rational institutions under which they live, they can then judge and change them. … Lukács believed that a revolution from below would overthrow reification and create a socialist

[1] See, for instance, Special Issue of *Postdigital Science and Education*, 'Lies, Bullshit and Fake News Online: Should We Be Worried?', edited by Alison MacKenzie and Ibrar Bhatt. https://link.springer.com/journal/42438/volumes-and-issues/2-1. Accessed 15 December 2020.

> alternative to capitalist modernity. That revolution would not reject reason and its fruits but would reconfigure rational institutions in response to the needs of the oppressed. (Feenberg 2014: viii)

It is precisely this type of revolutionary praxis that can help us to combat the deceit and lies of the current authoritarian political systems. We take our everyday social relationships and practices and try to examine their contradictions when seen in relation to the totality of social relations in which those particular relations and practices unfold. Thus, we have a backdrop against which we can read the word and the world historically. This enables us to live in the historical moment as a subject of history and, like Walter Benjamin's Angel of History, to see that human 'progress' has left a world devastated by violence and destruction. In so doing, we link our own history to the struggles of oppressed groups. This process is not simply an effect of language but pays attention to extralinguistic forms of knowing, forms of corporeal and praxiological meanings that are all bound up with the production of ideology.

Meaningful knowledge is not solely nor mainly the property of the formal properties of language but is enfleshed (McLaren 1986) – it is sentient; it is lived in and through our bodies, the material aspects of our being. It is neither ultra-cognitivist nor traditionally intellectualist. Knowledge, in other words, is embodied in the way we read the world and the word simultaneously in our actions with, against, and alongside other human beings. We can't transform history solely in our heads! But language is at the same time of crucial importance. As Freire (1972: 87) notes: 'Within the word we find two dimensions, reflection and action, in such radical interaction that if one is sacrificed—even in part—the other immediately suffers. There is no true word that is not at the same time a praxis. Thus, to speak a true word is to transform the world.' True words require actions.

Revolutionary praxis is an attempt to integrate both philosophy and theory into social justice initiatives and political intervention. Philosophy's concern with self-examination and challenging fixed truths, that is, with seeking to grasp 'the thing itself' (Kosik 1976: 1) can be appropriated in our attempts to interrogate critically the categories that underlay human cognition (Hudis 2004). This fusion of theory and philosophy creates the conditions of possibility for the emergence of a praxiological dimension in which thought refuses to take its premises for granted and is thus able to engage in actions designed to challenge and transform asymmetrical relations of power and privilege. This enables protagonistic agents of social justice to develop new categories of critique that can both illuminate the logic of capital and provide a critically conscious awareness of the content of a socialist alternative to capitalism. For instance, the term 'socioeconomic status' is one that too often legitimizes the capitalist system, whereas the term 'objective class location' can be more readily used to challenge the capitalist system.

This awareness arrives with an understanding that socialism has never to this moment fully existed because it cannot exist in one country, and especially absent real democracy, and with a realization that there have existed only pseudo-socialist regimes with state capitalist tendencies within free market capitalist democracies which required statist authoritarianism in order to survive. As McLaren concludes:

> Here, philosophy and theory, as they join together in a unity that permeates our very mode of being in all facets of our existence (in a manner faithful to Hegel's absolute method), are interpenetrated by voices from below, enabling at the same time theory and practice to be concretized in each living individual. … The search for justice through transformative praxis cannot be satisfied by appeals to reason, principles, or even a commitment to faith or belief but must be grounded in the cries of history's victims, our solidarity with them, and our commitment to transforming the world. (McLaren 2015: 248)

We employ theoretical discourses dialectically to help us better understand our self and social formation within the constraints and possibilities of austerity capitalism. We use these discourses as 'a whole structure of thinking for collective freedom, for transforming the present. To achieve this we need a dialectical approach: to intervene in the project of our own self and social formation by viewing the present as the future of our past, which is in the process of becoming the past of our own future.' (McLaren 2015: 247). Here we appreciate how spontaneous self-activity or mass practice such as the recent Black Lives Matter uprising sparked by the murder of George Floyd is also a potential expression of new theoretical developments as well as new strategies and tactics so that we can observe how the movement from practice is also a form of theory.

For instance, Black Lives Matter protests helped to illuminate the failure of capitalist democracy to protect African Americans from being excluded from the social contract and how they were disproportionally persecuted by the criminal 'justice' system, especially under conditions of a global pandemic which saw African American communities also suffer Covid-19 fatalities disproportionately to the white population. Here we come to recognize the extension of reification into the depths of social life, as democracy begins to crumble before our eyes through the racist policies and activities of the Trump administration. Here we can deploy theory to justify the philosophical conclusions (in this case drawn from Marxist humanism) that undergird our political project.

Theoretical debate can help to ensure that we do not take our philosophical premises for granted and can help us ascertain why a collective, social subject can most fully appreciate the values of philosophy. McLaren (2015: 248) writes: 'Here, philosophy and theory, as they join together in a unity that permeates our very mode of being in all facets of our existence (in a manner faithful to Hegel's absolute method), are interpenetrated by voices from below, enabling at the same time theory and practice to be concretized in each living individual.' In his theory of revolution, Marx claimed that those antimonies relating to epistemology and ontology as well as morality and politics could be transcended by social revolution, reconciling (through the disalienation or dereification of social life) individual and society, moral responsibility and self-interest, and that it could also unite subject and object, thought and being, man and nature (Feenberg 2014).

Related challenges were posed by Lukács and Marcuse. According to Feenberg (2014: 64), this suggests the philosophy of praxis assumes a 'wholly original *ontological* position' in which human action is philosophically relevant in all domains. The 'absolute historicism' of these philosophers of praxis can be best understood by means of a metacritical approach to the history of philosophy. For these theorists, reality is fundamentally historical 'and history itself is to be understood as in essence an object of human practice … Action takes on a universal significance, going beyond the social world to affect being as such.' (Feenberg 2014: 66).

History, therefore, has ontological significance, an insight by Marx that enabled him to claim imperatively that there is no dichotomy between being and history, between naturalism and humanism. Marx declines to posit human essence as an ethical ideal and refuses to accept the dichotomy of fact and value, between is and ought, thus refuting abstract idealism and futuristic utopian thinking in favor of the living contradiction of ideal and real, that is, the dialectic of ideal and historical reality in comprehending the tendencies within the present (Feenberg 2014). Hence, the dialectic of existence and essence becomes, for Marx, 'a demand of reason, a methodological precondition of rationality, and not…an ethical ideal' (Feenberg 2014: 86). Capitalist alienation and human suffering are given an ontological status, as an essential problem of reason that can be historically transcended (*Aufhebung*). Marx is concerned with the manner in which philosophical ideals take on human form, so that they can be transcended historically through ways that enable social action to intervene, that is, through the sublation of the current form of objective being by means of revolutionary praxis. Therefore, Marxist-inspired critical pedagogies grounded in a philosophy of praxis differ from neo-Weberian, left-liberal, and politically domesticated versions of critical pedagogy that are content with seeking educational reform within the confining and suffocating parameters of the capitalist state.

This intricate interweaving of theoretical issues with practical activities with the aim of resolving their contradictory tendencies is fundamental to revolutionary praxis, searching for the moment at which the conditions for action are still available, possibly even ripe for intervention. Here the challenge revolves around seizing the *Augenblick* such that radical conceptions of learning and being prefigure the horizon of the possibility of transformation. There have been numerous moments identified as *Augenblick* moments – Arab Spring, Occupy Wall Street, the Greek Anti-Austerity movement, Black Lives Matter protests that began in Minnesota, USA – but arguments favoring socialism over capitalism did not achieve hegemonic ascendency among the vast swaths of the people.

Revolutionary Critical Praxis

One of us (McLaren) was fortunate to meet Venezuela's President Hugo Chávez while working on a project of building up the university programs in critical pedagogy. Chávez was convinced that in order to create the conditions of possibility for socialism, socialists need to be made; that is, socialists are produced through practice. Michael Lebowitz writes:

> 'Socialists have to be made,' he explained on *Aló Presidente* in 2007. 'A revolution has to produce not only food, goods and services it also has to produce, more importantly than all of those things, new human beings: new men, new women.' Agreeing with Che's point about the necessity of simultaneously developing productive forces and socialist human beings, Chávez insisted that the only road was practice: 'We have to practice socialism, that's one way of saying it, have to go about building it in practice. And this practice will create us, ourselves, it will change us; if not we won't make it.' (Lebowitz 2017)

Che Guevara famously championed the creation of the 'new man and woman' through education that brings together mental and manual labor. Che also emphasizes that the revolution is a force that takes place 'in our habits and our minds'. He elaborates as follows:

> Our task is to prevent the current generation, torn asunder by its conflicts, from becoming perverted and from perverting new generations. We must not create either docile servants of official thought, or 'scholarship students' who live at the expense of the state — practicing freedom in quotation marks. Revolutionaries will come who will sing the song of the new man and woman in the true voice of the people. This is a process that takes time. …Our scholarship students do physical work during their vacations or along with their studies. Work is a reward in some cases, a means of education in others, but it is never a punishment. A new generation is being born. (Guevara 1965)

Revolutionary praxis consists of self and social formation. For Chávez, this was sought in the creation of associated producers, working within the structure of communes where protagonistic agents can transform both themselves and surrounding circumstances. Again, Lebowitz (2017) writes: 'For Chávez, the necessary road was protagonistic democracy—in the workplace and in the community—as the practice that transforms people.'

We agree with Marx that it is always wise to move beyond sharing common grievances against capitalists (creating *a class in itself*) in order to create a critical consciousness of ourselves as an anti-capitalist class (*a class for itself*). Such creation would not result in the classical version of the proletariat, but would refer to all those who recognize that great transformations will need to occur among the entire population if we wish to win people to the cause. Accordingly, we will need to offer the people reasonably unreasonable answers to what socialism as a systemic alternative will look like if we apply our most creative faculties to answering this question, without shying away from the strife and struggle this will necessarily entail.

Critical educators are protagonistic agents who work in and through history on behalf of those who disproportionately suffer from socio-economic injustice, and they believe that education can be a source for revolutionary praxis. The work of critical educators has inspired creative pedagogical reflection, encouraged educational activism, and stimulated critical theoretical discourses surrounding our understanding of the political dimensions of pedagogy and the pedagogical dimensions of the political throughout the global landscape.

The possibility for moving beyond a political revolution to a general social revolution is only available for those who have no place within the existing civil society, for those who have been excluded from the social contract. This is what makes the revolution universal in character, with the potential to bring down the system of class exploitation and racism responsible for the alienation and reification that now plagues civil society. However, praxis demands that there must be a unity between consciousness and action, and in order to achieve this, '[w]e must extract the practical essence of the theory from the method and its relation to its object' (Lukács 1975: 2).

Supporting this idea is Marx (1843) who writes: 'It is not enough that thought should seek to realize itself; reality must also strive toward thought.' Marx had identified the form that revolution must take: socialism. But there was still a form-content distinction that had to be overcome (Feenberg 2014: 173) with respect to reason itself. Rather than continue with a formalistic concept of reason, Marx explored the exigencies of reason in the context of transferring its formal attributes to the concept of need and charging need with the function of rationality. The subject and object of need is internally related. This makes the alienation of labor not just a major social problem but a fundamental philosophical problem. The social contradictions discovered by Marx are, in effect, 'philosophical antinomies reconstructed in a domain where they can be resolved through social action' (Feenberg 2014: 206). The purpose of philosophy is not only to understand the world but to change it.

The working class has enjoyed a powerful legacy of non-cooperation with capitalist social relations. But capitalism has also enjoyed an equally powerful history of restructuring the production process and the division of labor every time the working class chooses not to cooperate. In this way the elite class of high net-worth individuals – which we refer to as the transnational capitalist class – has been able to reassert its control over the working class. The history of capitalism is largely a narrative of how the reconstitution of the working class based on new productive relations has been able to successfully respond to former protests from the working class. Capitalism is able to retain value production in each and every case, making it impossible for socialism to overcome capitalism's production of alienated labor in which remuneration is based on *socially necessary* labor time. The retention of value production would render 'socialist' society unable to overcome capitalism's power to dominate society with alienated labor.

What is important in this argument is that *alienated* labor is not a consequence of market-exchange relations but a precondition for such relations (Hudis 2013). This is the case because, as Hudis (2013) makes clear, the social relation of capitalist production – capitalism – is itself a congealment of alienated (and *abstract*) labor. Workers have direct connection to the means of production. Well, what about communism? The communist regimes of the twentieth century did not give workers common possession of the land and ownership of the means of production. On the contrary, in their opposition to 'free market capitalism', they changed wage and property relations creating a form of government ownership of the means of production that Raya Dunayevskaya (1958) called 'state capitalism'. There were also forms of twentieth-century serfdom (pre-capitalist ownership) in the Soviet Union.

Truth in the Dialectic of History

For Trump supporters, including the magical-thinking evangelical Christians who adore Trump and who have been conditioned to exhibit bloodthirsty Pavlovian reactions at any mention of socialism, facts do not intrude on the painful reality that we are not merely facing a new stage of capitalism but witnessing its world-historical systemic crisis. They recursively flee from the brute realization that our political superstructure is in terminal decay. This follows from a motivated amnesia surrounding the dangers of fascism and irrational deliberation and a willful ignorance regarding the consequences of market anarchy and steps that need to be taken to reclaim the tattered vestiges of democracy. Their embodiment of Rush Limbaugh's 'four corners of deceit' (2013) – science, government, academia, media – have primed them to spend their lives in the only spaces left for them: those of religio-political cults led by a charismatic leader. Those of us on the left need to move beyond the idea that socialism is about social planning for the redistribution of value since the capitalist system can no longer revolutionize the means of production in ways that will bring about the changes necessary to provide a decent life for masses of people. We need to develop a new concept of socialism that is adequate for the challenges of the present.

When we examine the concept of truth, it means that we must do so historically. Feenberg's (2014: 274) assessment of Horkheimer maintains that 'a truth may be historically bound without being falsified by history'. Truth and the object of truth must always be historically mediated. We must judge all concepts of truth in the context of the historical period in which they appear, that is, in terms of the historical system of categories of their time, paying close attention to their cognitive patterns. Feenberg (2014: 271–272) follows Horkheimer in arguing that '[k]nowledge rests not only on corroboration by the facts, but also on the validity of its concepts within the prevailing categorial system. On the other hand, that system of categories is historically relative to evolving social and economic conditions.' But this does not mandate that we dismiss their claims as mere relativism 'because there are no eternal truths setting a higher standard they fail to meet' (2014: 272). Truth here remains relative only insofar as it is inconclusive. But it is also absolute, according to Feenberg, since later correction in no way should render the former truth as untrue. Feenberg (2014: 273) summarizes Horkheimer as follows: 'Judgements of truth are objectively valid even if historically relative and retain their validity even after history has moved on and replaced one set of categories with another.' Thus, truth may in one sense be judged on its own terms yet at the same time truth does not escape the dialectic of history.

We are interactive social beings, that is, we exist through intra-actions with each other and as such we do not preexist them; rather, we come into existence through and as part of our entangled, mutually constitutive relationships with each other. Each of our interactions iteratively reconfigures our historical being, and praxis can become a means of taking us towards a socialist future. Action creates history, and we humans are historical beings. History is the object of our human practice; it is through us that history is created. Revolutionary action can, through praxis, that is, through the disalienation and dereification of social life, create new socialist human beings able to sublate the contradictions between being and the objective social world, between the ideal and the real, between existence and essence, between social action and capitalist alienation and human suffering and alienation (Feenberg 2014). But socialism will not automatically arrive on the doorstep of praxis. It will not arrive by Amazon courier, even if Benjamin's Angel of History can find no other job than delivering for Federal Express.

Marxist-inspired critical pedagogies grounded in a philosophy of praxis differ substantively from neo-Weberian, left-liberal, and politically domesticated versions of critical pedagogy that are content with seeking educational reform within the confining and suffocating parameters of the capitalist state, in a like vein to many progressive educational reformers. If we wish to push back at the escalation of ludibrious racist discourse from above – such as the ginned up public convulsions and distempers stoked by Trump and other authoritarian leaders aimed at ushering the members of the white working-class sector into a racist and a neo-fascist understanding of their condition – then we educators have much work to accomplish. Some critics see such efforts as too late to effect Trump's base, that the carrots are cooked on this one, that the condition is done and dusted, that the majority of Trump's base is likely to remain actively white supremacist for the foreseeable future. If that is true, it places a great deal of responsibility on our educational system to develop anti-racist curricula, to address the current crisis of capitalism, and to be willing to focus public debate on the issue of racism and white supremacy, restorative and racial justice, and LGTBQIA+ equality, transforming these issues into militant imperatives. Otherwise we will be ensanguining the streets as violent clashes emerge from our culture wars and cult leaders such as Trump continue to suborn members of the aggrieved white working class to continue their assaults on people of color.

What we need is a scallywag pedagogy, creating coordinated bunkers of anti-racist activists in schools, corporations, factories, churches, libraries, and community centers, who are able to establish networks to resist the normalization of white supremacy currently spreading through authoritarian regimes such as the United States and elsewhere. While such a scallywag pedagogy is grounded not in the Second World War bunkers spread across the English countryside but in a philosophy of praxis, it has the potential to challenge the rebirth of neo-Nazi ideology that could very well become a serious threat to those countries struggling for a democratic future. Here we see examples of scallywag pedagogy in the efforts of British educators Dave Hill, Mike Cole, Glenn Rikowski, and Alpesh Maisuria who have been at the educational forefront of socialist struggle in the United Kingdom.

How would scallywag pedagogy look in practice? Let's look at the curriculum. First, education must be focused on creating socialist alternatives to capitalism – from remnants of post-feudal times to present instantiations of financialization. Society, culture, and social relations of production must be seen as interconnected. Systemic racism must be understood as it is inextricably linked to the legal system and the criminal justice system. Capital-perpetuated settler colonialism, sexism, racism, homophobia, misogyny, misanthropy, and misology must be examined for their interrelatedness, including the historically generated myths that have served to legitimize them. It is imperative that students deal with the issue of climate change and scarcity and technology-enabled extraction of natural resources. We could continue, but the point we wish to underscore is the generative issue driving the curriculum for liberation: understanding the various systems of mediation that have produced us as twenty-first-century-compliant and self-censoring human beings who appear defenseless in the face of nationalist calls for war, for ethnic chauvinism, and for narratives championing imperialism and the coloniality of power. Equally important is a study of revolutionary social movements that have challenged these systems of mediation and why some groups succeeded and why many of them failed.

We have only scratched the surface here. Clearly we need an education that can move groups from a class-in-itself to a class-for-itself – that is, to a class that actively pursues its own interests following the imperatives of critical-dialogical deliberation. Certainly we need a mass movement from below to counter the much more advanced digitalization of today's entire global economy and society which has utilized the application of fourth industrial revolution technologies led by artificial intelligence (AI) and the analysis of 'big data' (machine learning, automation and robotics, nano- and bio-technology, quantum and cloud computing, 3D printing, virtual reality, new forms of energy storage, etc.). That will not be an easy task. But it is a necessary one, since we will be struggling against the formation of a global police state.

The sociologist William Robinson (2020) has warned that in the time of the pandemic we are able to see the acceleration of digital restructuring 'which can be expected to result in a vast expansion of reduced-labor or laborless digital services, including all sorts of new telework arrangements, drone delivery, cash-free commerce, fintech (digitalised finance), tracking and other forms of surveillance, automated medical and legal services, and remote teaching involving pre-recorded instruction.' Hence, the giant tech companies and their political agents are able to convert great swaths of the economy into these new digital realms. Robinson (2020) also notes that the 'post-pandemic global economy will involve now a more rapid and expansive application of digitalisation to every aspect of global society, including war and repression.' We have an enormous task ahead of us. If we can make postdigital science work in the interests of the oppressed, rather than the corporate guardians of the transnational capitalist class, then we would be foolish not to try to strengthen our communal immune system.

In the case of the United States, we are reminded here of Sheldon Wolin's (2008) concepts of 'inverted totalitarianism' and 'managed democracy' by which he refers to distinct political tendencies or trajectories that influence how power is legitimated, one means of which involves overriding existing constraints established by constitutional democracy, and exploiting weaknesses in the democratic system through the use of fear. Inverted totalitarianism uses forms of institutional management to consolidate power, absent of considerations of the common good. Propaganda is organic to corporate institutions such as the press who manage dissent and keep it within certain parameters, rather than being concentrated within the state. Practices considered corrupt, such as lobbying, are normalized, and economic interests override political interests. Trump deviates somewhat from this model in that his attempts at consolidating power involve more overt acts such as firing officials tasked with ethical oversight and his attempting to overthrow the 2020 presidential election on the bogus basis that there was mass election fraud.

Scallywag Pedagogy

Those of us who recall the history of fascism and the devastation that it has inflicted worldwide have viewed with increasing concern Trumpian attempts to make America Great Again his rallying cry. Such a call echoes that of America First in the early part of the twentieth century. The term 'fascism' entered the American lexicon in 1922 when Mussolini took power in Italy and was used interchangeably with America First (previously used by Woodrow Wilson, Warren Harding, and Calvin Coolidge) and the Ku Klux Klan. In the 1940s, it was used mainly to identify Hitler's sympathizers. After the Biden victory in the 2020 presidential election, there were calls by some Trump supporters to institute martial law, declare the presidential vote null and void, and order the military to undertake a national re-vote as a result of baseless accusations of fraud. A number of pro-Trump lawyers, far-right media personalities, and even a former military general and National Security Advisor have been calling for the United States to suspend the Constitution and embrace fascism (Henderson 2020).

Paul Street (2020) provides us with 13 'fascistic characteristics of the Trump regime and its Republifascist allies'. Some of the most repulsive are '+3. White-supremacist and eliminationist satisfaction with a virus that was disproportionately killing off people of color' and '+4. A Social Darwinian and eliminationist comfort with COVID-19's devastating impact on the aged and infirm – on old and sick "useless eaters" fascists have long wished to exterminate' (Street 2020). Trump has expressed support for herd immunity, claiming that young people are at little risk of death as a result of Covid-19. On a day that US death rates set a daily record of more than 3600, an internal memo was released by the Trump administration. Lloyd Green (2020) reports:

> In a July 4, 2020 email, Paul Alexander, a political appointee at the Department of Health and Human Services, spelled it all out. In his words, infants, young adults, and middle-aged folks with no conditions had 'zero risk,' and were there to take the hit as America marched off a cliff. 'We want them infected,' declared Alexander.
>
> Unfortunately, the administration never asked their permission to become human guinea pigs. Indeed, as fate would have it, younger Americans are now dying at historic rates, according to a study recently published in the Journal of the American Medical Association. As for herd immunity, it's a lot like waiting for Godot.

American citizens have unknowingly been used as laboratory rats. Hundreds of thousands have died – including younger Americans – as a result of this ghastly social experiment that is redolent of former fascist governments. We agree with Street (2020) that to date, Trump is responsible for 270,000 American fatalities:

> Properly handled, the pandemic should not have killed more than 35,000 Americans by now. Trump owns the remaining 270,000 fatalities. He killed them. And this mass murder he perpetrated was all about the fascism and of course the capitalism, the racism, and the imperialism and the sexism, none of which are (to say the least) inconsistent with the fascism. (Street 2020)

Street also provides us with five major 'pandemo-fascist moments of 2020' including '+1. The ordering of predominantly LatinX workers back into COVID-19-infected meatpacking plants' and '+3. Trump refusing to wear a mask while his team loudly and tellingly played the song "Live and Let Die" as he visited a mask factory.' (Street 2020)

When media outlets owned by the crazy Falun Gong cult from Taiwan join Newsmax, OANN, and far-right radio hosts in supporting Trumpian fascist in their attempts to overthrow the presidential election, we can recognize the tenacity of fascist ideology and how its powerful political aesthetics plays a part in establishing control of at least half the population of the United States. In fact, what keeps Trump politically buoyant is the shallow form of entertainment that he provides with his tawdry fascist aesthetics. This was foreseen by Walter Benjamin during the leadership of Adolf Hitler during the Third Reich. As Mathew Rozsa (2020) writes:

> Benjamin, a Marxist and a Jew who was thus obviously opposed to the Nazis, postulated that modern fascists succeed when they are entertainers. Not just any entertainer — a circus clown or a juggler-turned-fascist wouldn't do. Specifically, modern fascists were entertainers with a distinct *aesthetic*, one that appeals to mass grievances by encouraging their supporters to feel like they are personally expressing themselves through their demagogue of choice.
>
> Benjamin's insight, which appears to have been largely forgotten, is that keeping fascism out of power means recognizing how they use aesthetic entertainment to create their movements. That does require us to admit, cringe-inducing though it may be, that Trump is an artist — albeit a tacky, shallow and transparently self-aggrandizing one. More importantly, his movement, the MAGA crowd, has a distinct aesthetic which he has created and honed for them. (Rozsa 2020)

Rozsa notes Benjamin's important recognition that 'by using purely aesthetic entertainment to create solidarity among their supporters, they [fascists] could distract them from the economic and social forces oppressing them [the general population], and instead build political movements based around the ability to creatively express their grievances'. This is an important insight since it strongly suggests that if a politician can create the illusion that people's voices count and that they are being heard, then the asymmetrical relations of power and privilege in favor of the ruling class can be securely kept in place.

Trump became a pop cultural icon by fabricating an image of a successful American businessman – a billionaire that liked to rub shoulders with the average man and unabashedly assault porn stars and beauty queens and brag about it. He is also a great entertainer: we all remember Trump's grand ride down the golden escalator ride in Trump Tower to announce his presidential candidacy. Trump does not reside in the Oval Office anymore, yet his poisonous spirit and the fetid social changes he represents are all around us. It disgusts us to research and write about Trump's antics and outbursts of hate, yet that dirty job needs to be done. Trump does not deserve our attention as a person, but as an embodiment of wider and deeper transformations of our society.

This all makes a good argument for mandatory classes in media literacy and virtue epistemology (MacKenzie and Bhatt 2019a, b) in universities to protect us from future fascists. The tragedy is that many of the graduates of such classes are likely working for Trump behind the scenes through their affiliation with organizations such as Turning Point. Which is why we need not only media literacy classes but a revolutionary critical pedagogy in which such classes are situated – a pedagogy that is centered around the ethical imperative developed in liberation theology, that of a preferential obligation to serve the most vulnerable populations and to fight for social justice. Scallywag pedagogy is postdigital, because it reconfigures human beings and technologies; ontological and epistemological, because it recognizes the dialectical relationships between righteous deeds and true utterances; historical, because it recognizes truth's situatedness in the dialectic of history; and revolutionary, because it aims at overturning capitalism in favor of a socialist alternative. Scallywag pedagogy is philosophy of practice, action, and reflection, of transforming the world through speaking a true word: a foundational stepping stone on our collective road beyond capitalism.

Postscript[2]

Charles Coughlin is smiling at Franklin Graham and Jerry Falwell Jr., egging on their madness from his preternatural abode, while Donald Trump, who turned out to be every bit as dark and sinister as Berzelius 'Buzz' Windrip, declines assistance from the ghost of Mussolini in championing the forgotten white men emasculated by feminists, GLBTQ advocates, and anti-racists who have the temerity to stand for social justice. After all, Trump is the master of white nationalist skullduggery, and his wrath is legendary. He has stamped out facts and replaced them with high-voltage opinions; he has crushed journalists as enemies of the people and replaced them with Trump boot-licking sycophants. He has played all the Doremus Jessups like Nero's fiddle while democracy burned and children screamed in their cages.

[2]This is a tribute to Sinclair Lewis' (1935) dystopian novel, *It Can't Happen Here*, describing the rise of a Hitler-like dictator in the United States.

References

Carr, S., Pringle, J. K., Doyle, P., Wisniewski, K. D., & Stimpson, I. G. (2020). Scallywag bunkers: geophysical investigations of WW2 Auxiliary Unit Operational Bases (OBs) in the UK. *Journal of Conflict Archaeology*. https://doi.org/10.1080/15740773.2020.1822102.

Dunayevskaya, R. (1958). *Marxism and Freedom: from 1776 Until Today*. New York: Bookman Associates.

Feenberg, A. (2014). *The Philosophy of Praxis: Marx, Lukacs and the Frankfurt School*. London and New York: Verso.

Freire, P. (1972). *Pedagogy of the Oppressed*. Harmondsworth: Penguin Education Specials.

Green, L. (2020). History Will Agree That Trump Used Americans as Lab Rats. Daily Beast, 19 December. https://www.thedailybeast.com/history-will-agree-that-trump-used-americans-as-lab-rats?ref=home. Accessed 20 December 2020.

Guevara, C. (1965). Socialism and man in Cuba. https://www.marxists.org/archive/guevara/1965/03/man-socialism.htm. Accessed 15 December 2020.

Henderson, A. (2020). Here's why Republicans who are calling for a Trump dictatorship should not be taken lightly — and aren't going away. RawStory, 4 December. https://www.rawstory.com/2020/12/heres-why-republicans-who-are-calling-for-a-trump-dictatorship-should-not-be-taken-lightly-and-arent-going-away/. Accessed 15 December 2020.

Hudis, P. (2004). Working Out a Philosophically Grounded Vision of the Future. Report to 2004 Convention of News and Letters Committees. Chicago.

Hudis, P. (2013). *Marx's Concept of the Alternative to Capitalism*. Chicago: Haymarket.

Jandrić, P. (2019). We-Think, We-Learn, We-Act: the Trialectic of Postdigital Collective Intelligence. *Postdigital Science and Education, 1*(2), 257-279. https://doi.org/10.1007/s42438-019-00055-w.

Jandrić, P., & Hayes, S. (2020). Postdigital We-Learn. *Studies in Philosophy of Education, 39*(3), 285-297. https://doi.org/10.1007/s11217-020-09711-2.

Jandrić, P., & McLaren, P. (2020). Postdigital Cross Border Reflections on Critical Utopia. *Educational Philosophy and Theory, 52*(4), 1470-1482. https://doi.org/10.1080/00131857.2020.1731687.

Jandrić, P., Knox, J., Besley, T., Ryberg, T., Suoranta, J., & Hayes, S. (2018a). Postdigital Science and Education. *Educational Philosophy and Theory, 50*(10), 893-899. https://doi.org/10.1080/00131857.2018.1454000.

Jandrić, P.; Ryberg, T.; Knox, J.; Lacković, N.; Hayes, S.; Suoranta, J.; Smith, M.; Steketee, A.; Peters, M. A.; McLaren, P.; Ford, D. R.; Asher, G.; McGregor, C.; Stewart, G.; Williamson, B., & Gibbons, A. (2018b). Postdigital Dialogue. *Postdigital Science and Education, 1*(1), 163-189. https://doi.org/10.1007/s42438-018-0011-x.

Kosik, K. (1976). *Dialectics of the Concrete: A Study on Problems of Man and World*. Dordrecht, Holland and Boston, MA: R. Reidel.

Lebowitz, M. A. (2017). Protagonism and Productivity. Monthly Review, 1 November. https://monthlyreview.org/2017/11/01/protagonism-and-productivity/. Accessed 15 December 2020.

Lewis, C. (1935). *It Can't Happen Here*. New York: Doubleday, Doran and Company.

Limbaugh, R. (2013). The Four Corners of Deceit: Prominent Liberal Social Psychologist Made It All Up. https://www.rushlimbaugh.com/daily/2013/04/29/the_four_corners_of_deceit_prominent_liberal_social_psychologist_made_it_all_up/. Accessed 15 December 2020.

Lukács, G. (1975). *History and Class Consciousness: Studies in Marxist Dialectics*. London: The Merlin Press.

MacKenzie, A., & Bhatt, I. (2019a). Lies, Bullshit and Fake News. *Postdigital Science and Education, 2*(1), 1-8. https://doi.org/10.1007/s42438-019-00085-4.

MacKenzie, A., & Bhatt, I. (2019b). Lies, Bullshit and Fake News: Some Epistemological Concerns. *Postdigital Science and Education, 2*(1), 9-13. https://doi.org/10.1007/s42438-018-0025-4.

Marx, K. (1843). On The Jewish Question. https://www.marxists.org/archive/marx/works/1844/jewish-question/. Accessed 15 December 2020.

Marx, K. (1848/1975). Theses on Feuerbach. In K. Marx, *The collected works of Karl Marx and Frederick Engels. General Works 1844–1895, Vol. 5.* New York: International Publishers.

Marx, K. (1852). The Eighteenth Brumaire of Louis Bonaparte. https://www.marxists.org/archive/marx/works/1852/18th-brumaire/ch01.htm. Accessed 15 December 2020.

McLaren, P., & Jandrić, P. (2020a). *Postdigital Dialogues on Critical Pedagogy, Liberation Theology and Information Technology*. London: Bloomsbury.

McLaren, P. (1986). *Schooling as a Ritual Performance: Towards a Political Economy of Educational Symbols and Gestures*. London and New York: Routledge.

McLaren, P. (2015). *Life in Schools: An Introduction to Critical Pedagogy in the Foundations of Education.* 6th Edition. Boulder and London: Paradigm.

McLaren, P. (2020a). Networked Religion: Metaphysical Redemption or Eternal Regret?. *Postdigital Science and Education*. https://doi.org/10.1007/s42438-020-00112-9

McLaren, P. (2020b). Religious Nationalism and the Coronavirus Pandemic: Soul-Sucking Evangelicals and Branch Covidians Make America Sick Again. *Postdigital Science and Education, 2*(3), 700–721. https://doi.org/10.1007/s42438-020-00122-7.

McLaren, P., Jandrić, P. (2020b). The Fellowship of the Crooked Cross: Trump's Evangelical Hounds of Hell. *Postdigital Science and Education, 2*(2), 302–329. https://doi.org/10.1007/s42438-019-00074-7.

Mecklin, J. (2020). Closer than ever: It is 100 seconds to midnight. 2020 Doomsday Clock Statement. Bulletin of the Atomic Scientists. https://thebulletin.org/wp-content/uploads/2020/01/2020-Doomsday-Clock-statement.pdf. Accessed 15 December 2020.

Peters, M. A., Jandrić, P., & Hayes, S. (2021a). Biodigital Philosophy, Technological Convergence, and New Knowledge Ecologies. *Postdigital Science and Education, 3*(2), 370–388. https://doi.org/10.1007/s42438-020-00211-7.

Peters, M. A., Jandrić, P., & Hayes, S. (2021b). Postdigital-Biodigital: An Emerging Configuration. *Educational Philosophy and Theory.* https://doi.org/10.1080/00131857.2020.1867108.

Peters, M. A., Jandrić, P., & McLaren, P. (2020). Viral modernity? epidemics, infodemics, and the 'bioinformational' paradigm. *Educational Philosophy and Theory*. https://doi.org/10.1080/00131857.2020.1744226.

Robinson, W. I. (2020). Global capitalism post-pandemic. *Race & Class, 62*(2), 3-13. https://doi.org/10.1177/2F0306396820951999.

Robinson, W. I. (2019). Global capitalist crisis and 21st century fascism: Beyond the Trump hype. *Science & Society, 83*(2), 155–83. https://doi.org/10.1521/siso.2019.83.2.155.

Rozsa, M. (2020). This Marxist philosopher foresaw the rise of Trumpism more than 80 years ago. Raw Story, 6 December. https://www.rawstory.com/2020/12/this-marxist-philosopher-foresaw-the-rise-of-trumpism-more-than-80-years-ago/. Accessed 20 December 2020.

Street, P. (2020). On Capitalism, Racism, Trump, and Pandemo-Fascism. Counterpunch, 18 December. https://www.counterpunch.org/2020/12/18/on-capitalism-racism-trump-and-pandemo-fascism/. Accessed 20 December 2020.

Wolin, S. (2008). *Democracy Incorporated: Managed Democracy and the Specter of Inverted Totalitarianism.* Princeton, NJ: Princeton University Press.

Chapter 13
Learning from the Dupers: Showing the Workings

Christine Sinclair

Introduction: Dupery and Its Intentions

Dupery and deception are generally unpleasant acts, and perhaps the attempt to see a positive side might be regarded as naïve. However, there are some kinds of people who are willing to explain why and how we have been duped, which could be of significant academic interest. Seeing how dupery works may help protect us from it. Not all deception has evil intent: most of us will have been taken in by benign forms at some stage. Young children believe that Father Christmas comes into their home during the night of Christmas Eve and leaves gifts or that a magician is able to produce a rabbit from a hat. Being duped may be part of the delight of a well-written detective novel with a twist, or of a particularly funny joke. Usually, with benign deception, we can eventually see how we were duped—the intention is not to deceive forever. The magician provides an interesting exception: most magicians will not reveal their methods, but some have (apparently) been willing to do so.

There is no doubt that some people have malicious intentions and will use dupery to achieve them. They are not completely avoided in this chapter. Some, on the other hand, do have more noble intentions when they deceive. A satirist may initially dupe audiences into thinking they are seeing a serious event and then shock them with humour that points up unflattering truths about a situation. This showed up in many comic memes during the start of the Covid-19 pandemic, where a video of an attempt to make a mask, or create an uplifting song, rapidly shifted to a 'true' picture of what was happening. Effects of such memes include laughter and

C. Sinclair (✉)
Centre for Research in Digital Education, Moray House School of Education and Sport, University of Edinburgh, Edinburgh, Scotland, UK
e-mail: christine.sinclair@ed.ac.uk

A. MacKenzie et al. (eds.), *The Epistemology of Deceit in a Postdigital Era*, Postdigital Science and Education,
https://doi.org/10.1007/978-3-030-72154-1_13

community-building, as the shared experience comes to light.[1] Another good intention might be to prevent further malign deception. For example, a university lecturer may initially use deception to demonstrate the 'Barnum effect' to students: showing by example that even well-qualified students can easily be duped by vague statements supposedly about their personalities or life experiences from people trying to manipulate them (Beins 1993). For both the satirist and the teacher—in the situations described above—the important aspect about their dupery is that it is deliberately exposed and explained.

This chapter explores why and how people have been willing to reveal the workings of a deception and what we can learn from those revelations. It draws on the work of satirists, magicians, hoaxers, con artists, hackers and academics. Some have had several such roles: our interest here is their role in exposing a deception. Their relationship with the truth has different nuances: while magicians have a code of keeping their methods secret, satirists depend on audiences recognising what they are doing which may be a fabrication but can still expose an underlying truth. They also have different intentions: the same technique might be used by the magician to entertain and by the con artist to rob, but both are dependent on deception. Techniques are changing too with greater opportunities offered by digital technology to discover or amplify deception. Exposure of deception is an explicit intention for some uses, such as plagiarism detection, though these are also critiqued for participation in a surveillance culture with its own deceptions (Bayne et al. 2020). The result is a complex situation, as we see from other chapters in this book, but the focus here is on what we can learn from people implicated in deception who have decided to 'show the workings'. I explore this issue initially through four settings where deception is present, and someone is exposing something about it. These settings show conditions where:

- We are not supposed to be deceived.
- We know we are being deceived.
- We may be deceived, but we are being educated to avoid it.
- We are exposed to deception that exposes other deceptions.

Some agents in these areas have contributed to the broad academic field of deception detection. Others simply want to help. I look at people who aim to expose the truth in these contexts, before considering two related settings showing the workings of deception on a grand scale, dwarfing (but still including) what is happening in the more subtle situations listed above. The result is an unfolding of human responses to familiar contexts and actions and also to actions that go largely unnoticed… until something happens. Throughout the chapter the effects afforded by technology are highlighted. The role of education is also a significant theme.

[1] For an illustration, see https://youtu.be/lSiMuTrCvdY. Accessed 22 December 2020.

Satire: We Are Not Supposed to Be Deceived

Satire does not necessarily depend on deception, and any deception used is likely to be short lived, as shown in the YouTube meme in the previous section. Indeed, if a satirist has deceived someone, the practice has failed as satire. However, the workings of satire are interesting: if we can explore 'success-versus-failure conditions' of a thick description of what satire is about (Ryle 2009), we can perhaps learn something from its failure in relation to deception. Here we consider satire's failure with some audiences and then how it has failed with a target of satire in a context where there is deception.

Satire fails if the audience is deceived into believing it is genuine, as frequently happens, for example, when articles from the satirical magazine The Onion are shared as though they are true stories. This has the unfortunate consequence of further spread of falsehoods (Rubin et al. 2016). Rubin et al. see such failure as a good starting point for developing an automated tool to detect deception in news articles. They reason that as satire requires at least some people to detect its nature, there should be linguistic cues. The success of their algorithm points to a way of minimising deception in satirical news. However, we might wonder whether dependence on algorithms to detect satire destroys the nature of satire itself; it has in part an aim to collude at an intellectual level. Perhaps education in linguistic cues—such as notions of the absurd and grammatical constructions—might help to keep satire alive, but it does feel like a further admission of failure to delegate this detective work to an algorithm.

Satire also fails if it has an inappropriate effect on its target, for example, if it becomes integrated into deceivers' own repertoires. Armando Iannucci who famously satirised British politics in his popular television programme *The Thick of It* (2005–2012) explains why he cannot do it any longer:

> Satire only works if there's a series of accepted conventions and then you point out when the politicians or people in the public have departed from those conventions. But if the politicians are saying: 'There are no more conventions anymore. I can do what the hell I like. I can change the name of my party to Factcheck UK', it's very difficult for someone to point out where those conventions have been breached. (Iannucci and Asthana 2020: 2:04-2:28)

Although the Twitter handle of the Tory party at the 2019 UK election sparked this observation, Iannucci has been commenting on satire for some time, tellingly in a *New Statesman* article where he observes: '...politicians no longer act like real versions of themselves. Instead, they come over as replicants of an idealised, fictional version of what they think a politician should be' (Iannucci 2016: 88).

Idealised fictions are not the same as accepted conventions. Satirising an idealised fiction loses its bite. In this case, deception is still present, but the satire becomes a part of it. In an analysis of the satire in *The Thick of It*, Basu (2014) points to its targets—politicians and news media combined—as a 'social apparatus' (Foucault 1980) which is profoundly rotten. There is no redeeming feature, 'not one character in the show with any integrity' (Basu 2014: 92). It is ironic and perhaps depressing that the show itself has been incorporated into this very apparatus, as illustrated by politicians' and news media's overuse of an invented catchphrase ('omnishambles') designed to ridicule, but losing that effect through its adoption by the people it is satirising. The rotten social apparatus is reproducing itself, feeding on the satire.

Satire is often associated with parody (Sinclair 2020). Basu (2014) claims that *The Thick of It* is not parody though: 'Parodies are able to "invade" other texts and "pollute" their meaning-making processes, and intertextuality can therefore be a subversive and liberating force' (Basu 2014: 97). The opposite has happened with *The Thick of It*, because its own meaning-making has been polluted. While it undoubtedly succeeded in exposing the parlous state of the UK's entwined politics and media, it ultimately contributed to that state, possibly leading to the alienation of its creator, Iannucci.

In short, satire's job is to show the workings of a practice, often to reveal deception. It fails as satire if it deceives us into thinking it is the real thing; it fails in its mission if it is incorporated into the deceptive practices it targets. Satire's tricks have to work. It needs to hold human failings up to ridicule, not as something to emulate. And if we need an algorithm to expose satire, we should be asking what that implies about education.

Magic: We Know We Are Being Deceived

> … a unique form of deception, in which we know that we are being deceived, but still we are deceived. (Lamont and Steinmeyer 2018: 9)

Magic tricks have to work even though we know that they are tricks. While we the audience are looking for the sleight of hand, the piece of thread, or the hiding place, the successful magician has again left us gasping with wonder and possibly laughter too. Even though we know it is not really 'magic' in an occult sense, we believe what we see, something that should be impossible. And we are entertained by that belief, even while we wonder how on earth it was done.

Despite the motto of the UK's Magic Circle being 'not apt to disclose secrets' (The Magic Circle 2020), there do seem to be some magicians willing to talk about their craft and even give away some tricks. As breach of the motto can lead to expulsion from the exclusive circle, what the magicians do disclose is perhaps not overly secret, but it may nevertheless be of value to our exploration of deception. In a brief magazine article, Teller, of the famous duo Penn and Teller, reveals the secrets of one card trick in some detail. He also provides his basic principles for altering perceptions:

1. Exploit pattern recognition.
2. Make the secret a lot more trouble than the trick seems worth.
3. It's hard to think critically when you're laughing.
4. Keep the trickery outside the frame.
5. To fool the mind, combine at least two tricks.

6. Nothing fools you better than the lie you tell yourself.
7. If you are given a choice, you believe you have acted freely. (Teller 2012)

This is a valuable list, as we shall see. Penn and Teller are particularly associated with revelations, perhaps because of their popular TV show *Penn & Teller: Fool Us*, where other professional magicians compete to fool the duo as to how their trick was done. The Penn and Teller analysis entails a post-trick discussion using insider 'doublespeak' to explicate the trick's method. Revealing the trick's method in this way doesn't spoil it for the audience—indeed, it is possible to create more amazement (Pang 2015).

In any case, many of the methods of magicians have been known about for centuries, and it still doesn't matter (Lamont and Steinmeyer 2018). These contemporary historians of magic say about Penn and Teller: 'The audience is told how it is done, but it nevertheless seems impossible' (Lamont and Steinmeyer 2018: 312). But are the magicians really giving away secrets, and is this right? Is it not an important aspect of magic that its secrets are always kept? Lamont and Steinmeyer say that we are told enough to satisfy our curiosity, but we should really be asking a different question: why does it work?

The 'how' is what bothers us, though, and distracts us from the 'why'. Audiences have always tried to find out secrets and have been supported by changes in the technology of the era. Improved lighting, photography, film, television and now the Internet, among others, have all played their part in revealing tricks (as well as in performing them). Nowadays, we can easily find the secrets by looking online or using recordings. Technology has clearly aided our ability to keep reviewing tricks, pausing and magnifying the action to spot the moment where we've been distracted. This may take many iterations, if indeed it is possible; alternatively, it may be easy to spot when it has actually been done in plain sight, as is often the case. See, for example, the demonstration of a dropped lighter in a TED Talk by magician turned academic, Gustav Kuhn (2013). For those who don't want to put in the effort, the Internet provides many explicit demonstrations of magic tricks for people unable to stand not knowing how something was done.

For additional examples of revealed tricks, it has been instructive to look at the website Magic Secrets Explained.[2] There are many other such sites, but this one contains an interesting question and answer about a young magician, Dynamo, known for stunning feats such as levitation and walking on water. The site asks: 'Is Dynamo real or fake?' This is in response to many apparently disappointed social media users who claimed to have seen the workings of Dynamo levitating at the London Shard, though this apparent reveal (of wires) might itself have been a deception.

The idea of a 'fake' magician calls into question my subtitle for this section: 'we know we're being deceived'. Presumably, the attribution of fakery means that some people see magicians as people with special powers, perhaps like those given to the fictional young wizard, Harry Potter. The ambiguity of the word 'magic' relating

[2] See https://www.secrets-explained.com/. Accessed 22 December 2020.

both to stage performances and to occult or paranormal experiences leads to a potential for complications in determining whether we are deceived knowingly or not. As Dynamo himself says: ‘It’s hard to know what to believe, in this day and age. And whether people want to believe what I’m doing is real magic or skill is up to them’ (Wolfson 2020: 13).

The website Magic Secrets Explained is in no doubt that what Dynamo is doing is skill. Showing the workings of magic to people who know they are being deceived but are still amazed by it has a very different effect from showing the workings to people who believe the magician has supernatural powers. Stories about the two kinds of magic have always co-existed, leading to myths about the gullibility of our ancestors in not being able to tell the difference between a stage magic trick and witchcraft (Lamont and Steinmeyer 2018). In the Victorian era especially, historians sometimes deduced that conjurors of old had been falsely accused of occult forms of magic. The evidence to support such claims was weak, though the inferences were understandable:

> So, when we look more closely, we can see that none of these were actually conjurors who were persecuted for performing magic tricks. They may have used trickery to pretend to have genuine magical powers, but that, of course is another kind of deception. (Lamont and Steinmeyer 2018: 36)

The stories we tell about these two understandings of the same techniques persist to this day. And, as our contemporary historians of magic also observe, ‘magicians have not always played by the rules’ (Lamont and Steinmeyer 2018: 28). This is seen particularly strongly in the psychological sphere: for example, while our Victorian ancestors were less likely to believe in witchcraft, they could be taken in by magicians who turned to mesmerism and clairvoyance. These intertwining stories are still evident today. While ‘mind-reading’ that is known to be trickery falls into the category of stage magic, a magician who claims actually to have mind-control is crossing a line. This is what Derren Brown did when he began his mind-reading performance, claiming psychological powers that would have been regarded as paranormal in relation to current scientific knowledge (Lamont 2013).

Nowadays, Derren Brown denies having any ‘special’ psychological powers, and certainly no psychic ones (Brown 2019). In his books, he explains why people can be taken in by those who do claim such powers. He joins a long history of magicians who set out to debunk the activities of charlatans and quacks, as do Penn and Teller. Showing the workings of these particular practices falls into our next category of deception (fake science), and Derren Brown is not quite off the hook yet.

The main message from magic seems to be that knowing how a trick works is less important than understanding why we are likely to be deceived. Then, perhaps, we can be taught how to avoid it. The notion of a ‘fake’ magician—amplified by both contemporary obsessions with fakery and use of social media—suggests an additional need for education about the nature of stage magic and other genres and how they are affected by technology.

Fake Science and Classroom Deception: We May Be Deceived, but We Are Being Educated to Avoid It

> Framing a magic performance as a psychological demonstration may …inadvertently help perpetuate false beliefs about psychology. (Lan et al. 2018: 2)

The idea of framing in the above quotation echoes point 4 in Fig. 13.1 'keep the trickery outside the frame'. The authors cited are concerned that performers such as Derren Brown use a pseudoscientific 'story' containing technical jargon as the background for their tricks: for example, Brown has suggested that he uses 'unconscious primes' to support his predictions, when really all he has been doing is conventional conjuring. One of the authors of the paper is Gustav Kuhn, himself a former magician who has become a psychology lecturer. He believes magic can inform the psychology of deception, which is particularly important in the era of fake news. In an interview for the British newspaper, The Observer, he says: 'It's not merely enough to tell people it isn't real, to factcheck—people ignore that information. Only when we are told how a trick is done do we stop believing in it.' (Wolfson 2020: 13)

Kuhn was particularly shocked at undergraduates' acceptance when a magician claimed to be talking to their dead relatives. Just telling them it was not true was not enough to convince them. Along with his co-authors (Lan et al. 2018), he was involved in an investigation of whether such framing—purportedly by either a stage magician or a psychologist—affected students' beliefs in mind-reading. Alarmingly, they discovered the beliefs were not affected by whether the performer was seen as a magician or a psychologist. They conclude that realistic but fake evidence can be very powerful in perpetuating misconceptions and this needs to be challenged. All the stages of the trick need to be revealed.

Psychology students are often subjects for such experiments in universities. They may themselves want to use deception in experiments, and this has to be supervised carefully, for ethical reasons. One way of teaching students about deception has been to subject them to it, and a number of researchers/teachers have used deception to demonstrate the Barnum effect and also to discuss the effects of being deceived. This is named after the nineteenth-century showman and hoaxer P. T. Barnum, one of whose tricks was to 'read' personalities based on stereotypical generic descriptions that individual people think would be uniquely applied to themselves. The same

1. Exploit pattern recognition.
2. Make the secret a lot more trouble than the trick seems worth.
3. It's hard to think critically when you're laughing.
4. Keep the trickery outside the frame.
5. To fool the mind, combine at least two tricks.
6. Nothing fools you better than the lie you tell yourself.
7. If you are given a choice, you believe you have acted freely. (Teller 2012)

Fig. 13.1 Altering perceptions (Teller 2012)

effect might be seen in fortune telling and horoscopes, or any circumstances where 'cold reading' can be deployed—a technique also used by Derren Brown and a variety of con artists. Beins (1993) describes an example where students completed a so-called personality inventory and all received identical feedback. They were then asked how they felt about the deception involved. They felt some distress, but it did not last, and the majority of students thought it was an effective way to teach about deception as well as the Barnum effect.

Efforts to debrief the participants afterwards and explain the true purpose and methods used are crucial in cases where deception has been practised, and academic authors will stress this. In one notable case of classroom deception (Taras and Steel 2007), the academics and students involved continued to discuss the deception 2 years after the event, and the discussions showed that students had indeed consolidated the message. The students involved here were industrial relations students who had been deceived into signing up to organise collectively (i.e. commit to joining a union) to challenge a perceived 'breach of contract' with their professor: 'sometimes the shock of being victimized by a well-planned trick is an opportunity for implanting a valuable life lesson' (Taras and Steel 2007: 180).

The professor (Taras) told the class that their usual professor (Steel) was suspended, pending an investigation. She demonstrated sympathy towards him and the class and temporarily gained their trust, but then announced that there would be an adjustment resulting in loss of some bonus marks and also changes to the exam. When they complained, she offered them a sign-up sheet for a student association if they wanted to take their complaints further. Then she watched as collective action began to build up. The deception in this case was short-lived but profound: the deception was run in four classes and lasted only between 6 and 11 minutes. The debriefing and discussion about the deception lasted a lot longer. By 'showing the workings' through an escalating example of betrayal of expectations, the teachers were able to make points about injustices, consequences of decision-making, leadership, collective action and union-management relationships, all illuminated by the experience they had just undergone. Moreover, the discussion about the professors' tactics allowed them to make points about psychological contracts, violation of trust and comfort zones. These topics had all been difficult to discuss in class where students had been resistant to the themes and previous attempts to engage them (case study, role playing, etc.) just had not worked. What did work was directly experiencing the emotions and the cognitive dissonance caused by the deception.

The perpetrators of the deception also debriefed themselves with the help of colleagues and through writing about it, paying attention to the ethics of the deception. This was important; they decided to disseminate their findings but would not want to repeat the experiment despite its success. It was too stressful for them. However, their final sentence is: 'This definitely was the most effective classroom technique we ever used' (Taras and Steel 2007: 196). Writing about it aimed to help future teachers in deploying deception, or even deciding if they should, and their experiences have led to a call for support for teachers using such challenging experiential techniques (Dean and Forray 2016).

When we add technology to the mix of deception in experiential teaching, the ethical issues become even more complex. For example, technology is widely used in educational simulations. Software could include visual immersive virtual environments and algorithms that underpin their operation. Hardware might provide three-dimensional immersive models of reality or even a simulated person (mannequin). Simulation can itself be regarded as deceptive because so many of its processes are 'black-boxed', reducing some aspects of human agency and embodiment and depriving students of the necessary 'doubt' about what they might be seeing (Turkle 2009). There are dangers of being seduced by the apparent authenticity of mannequins in nursing education. Although mannequins appear like real patients, their use still cannot take into account complex human responses which could lead to future errors if a student later expects a patient to respond in exactly the same way (Dunnington 2014).

Calhoun et al. (2015) discuss a case where deception was added to a simulation leading to a mannequin's 'death' raising deep pedagogical and psychological issues for the simulation community, especially concerning the need for debriefing. A senior clinician had entered the simulation of a cardiac arrest and ordered an incorrect medication to be given. This is described as 'misdirection'. The paper refers to Erving Goffman's use of 'frames' (Goffman 1974) to consider the relationship between the 'primary frame' (the real world) and its recreation in a simulation. Framing is about how we understand and act in the world: we've already seen it in relation to magic and pseudoscience. Key issues here are the difficulties of working across frames when deception has been involved and an associated loss of trust.

All the people referred to in this section have experienced difficult emotions through practising and revealing deception: magicians and psychologists are shocked by the easily manipulated beliefs of undergraduates; teachers worry about potential effects of deception on their relationship with their students, which should be based on trust. As with satire and magic, one thing is clear: when teaching through deception, it is important to know what one is doing and what its criteria for success and failure are. For example, a deceptive classroom intervention might be deemed to fail (as teaching) when there is a subsequent loss of trust in the teacher. There is also a clear warning that in its mediation of additional 'frames' of activity, technology can add complexity to an already difficult situation.

Reactions: We Are Exposed to Deception that Exposes Other Deceptions

Sometimes dupers deliberately deceive in a tit-for-tat way to respond to other dupers, perhaps exposing them or even preventing them. It arises when people are dissatisfied by something in their environment and respond to it by doing something deceptive themselves.

The first example here continues the theme of university teachers and researchers concerned about effects of deception on their students and their practices. It also draws on the role of technology in reframing academic research and teaching as performance indicators through massive datafication (Williamson et al. 2020). In what initially appears to be simply a whistle-blowing account of 'dishonesty, deception and deceit by universities in the UK in pursuit of quality indicators' (Rolfe 2016: 173), the startling conclusion is that the most effective strategy to deal with it is often more deception and dishonesty. The paper makes an interesting distinction between deception and deceit: the deception here is of the magician's kind ('we know we have been deceived') and deceit is what commands a negative response if we are trying to be ethical. Dishonesty, Rolfe says, comes in between: telling lies may, in defined circumstances, be morally acceptable, though not all ethicists would agree. In research assessment, deception occurs through overuse of citation practices and skewing submission to only high-status journals, or engagement only in prestigious and profitable projects even though smaller initiatives might be more beneficial to some groups. All of these activities produce higher metrics, suggesting greater quality.

Deception turns to deceit when the tricks and strategies are used to claim improvements in quality without any actual changes to the professional or academic practice having been made. In teaching, deception and then deceit occur through enhancing league table positions through grade inflation, or artificial improvement in completion statistics. Rolfe's concern is that in professional courses such as nursing, the reduction in standards following such deceit may be life threatening. His response has been to adopt a subversive approach to protect his academic values: 'Even the most mildly subversive academics will be familiar with the adage that it is easier to obtain forgiveness than permission, which is an incitement to 'do the right thing' and apologize afterwards' (Rolfe 2016: 180). The subversive approach is detailed in an earlier work (Rolfe 2013: 80), which stresses the importance of intentions, advising that we should be 'good, collegiate and radical' and explains what this means for his own practice.

A less collegiate approach to challenging practices in academic publication is the hoax submission. A notable example was the Sokal affair in 1996: a physicist submitted a fake paper on 'quantum gravity' to a postmodernist academic journal *Social Text* and subsequently produced an article for another journal, *Lingua Franca*, that revealed his deception (Sokal 1996). There he gives the reason for his parody as wanting to expose the (mis)appropriation of scientific language by cultural studies writers and the lack of rigour of the review process in accepting nonsense and 'sloppy thinking'. A huge controversy emerged after the publication of the two articles, which lasted for some years.

The affair revisits some themes seen earlier, especially if we think about the conditions that determine what kind of deception a hoax is. In unpacking its rhetorical dimensions, Secor and Walsh (2004) suggest that the situation could have been prevented if all the players had been more sensitive to text, context and genre. They conclude:

> They—we—can certainly try to keep our preconceptions from blinding us, and it is a noble effort. But savvy hoaxers like Sokal know we will fail. A clever magician can hide an elephant right in the middle of the stage by getting people to look in one direction while he blindsides them from another. (Secor and Walsh 2004: 89)

Sokal's blindsiding involved a parody that was extremely close to the conventions of the genre, mimicking the specific appropriation of scientific language. At the same time, it did include guideposts to its parodic/satiric nature, as parody tends to do.

There is a long history of hoaxes, committed for a variety of reasons. Some are just fraudulent, and others, like the Sokal one, are apparently concerned with exposing the workings of a practice. Some are designed to prevent a practice before it occurs. An example is the mountweazel, a fake word in a dictionary, encyclopaedia or other reference source, inserted in order to detect plagiarism if another work also presents it as a real word. This device was named after a famous entry in the 1975 edition of *The New Columbia Encyclopedia*. Mrs. Lillian Virginia Mountweazel was apparently born in Bangs, Ohio, and died in an explosion 31 years later after an interesting, if short, life. However, she did not actually exist, as was admitted by an editor some years after it was published.

Fakery in works of reference that are expected to be impeccable sources of information may be disconcerting. Someone will have to show the 'workings' if the practice is successful in exposing the plagiarism, though the editors will hope it won't be required, and the task would be delegated to someone other than the perpetrator. In a fascinating exegesis of the Mountweazel encyclopaedia entry, Williams (2016) recognises it as a piece of metafiction as well as a copyright trap. It has been carefully constructed to deceive readers about its authenticity; yet (because parody is involved) it contains allusions to its own role and construction that give clues to those in the know, for example, the association with the expression 'weasel words'. Deceivers can be proud of the artistry of their deception.

In this category of contexts—deception that exposes other deceptions—we see a move to more aggressive uses of deception, though still for avowedly good purposes. By subverting the authority of universities, academic disciplines and encyclopaedias, the deceivers expose practices that need to be challenged. These include the datafication that results in black-boxed ways of referring to research and teaching 'excellence' (see also Fawns and Sinclair 2021). The interesting example of the mountweazel shows that some dupers, such as effective parodists and perhaps even ethical subversives, are likely to be proud of their skills. But the deception is risky; it results in a lack of trust not only in the institutions but also potentially in the dupers who tell.

Dupers Who Tell: Whistleblowers, Debunkers, Provocateurs and Poachers Turned Gamekeepers

Just as there are different intentions in dupery, there are different reasons for its exposure. The names we call dupers who tell are associated with risk and disapproval from the powers-that-be. Whistleblowers want to provide inside information on practices they are expected to support: Rolfe (2016) comes into this category with his exposure of deception and deceit in UK universities. Magicians and teachers become debunkers when they see practices that threaten to harm. Teachers who provoke their students into a response to injustice, or towards learning that blind obedience can have fatal consequences, might be called provocateurs, as might Sokal (1996) with his hoax against the cultural studies academics. Lexicographers who introduce mountweazels are bordering on the sense of provocateur that leads to entrapment, though their work has been seen by Williams (2016) as a form of whistleblowing too, about the nature of the relationship between authoritative texts, readers and writers. All of our dupers might be loosely regarded as 'poacher turned gamekeeper': 'someone whose occupation or behaviour is the opposite of what it previously was, such as a burglar who now advises on home security' (Collins English Dictionary 2020).

A satirist comments rather than lampoons; a magician reveals rather than hides mind-reading tricks; teachers deceive students (briefly) rather than elucidate; an academic deceives the employer through good behaviour rather than the promotion of business targets; a writer or lexicographer subverts the integrity of his or her publisher's publications. But the strongest example of poacher turned gamekeeper is, as the definition above suggests, the criminal who brings knowledge and advice to those trying to prevent crime.

The Extent of the Problem of Dupery: Insider Stories

One way to learn about deception is to have it explained by someone who has been previously jailed for it. I have identified two candidates to guide us; they share some remarkable similarities, but also differ in how they 'frame' themselves. Comparing them illuminates a specific contemporary practice: hacking.

Frank Abagnale is one of the world's most notorious con artists and Kevin Mitnick is one of its most notorious hackers. Both served a few years in prison following high profile capture. Both subsequently became legitimate security consultants. Both have written explicit books about fraud, exposing the tricks of fraudsters, including themselves: e.g. *The Art of the Steal* (Abagnale 2001) and *The Art of Deception* (Mitnick and Simon 2002). Both men are proud of their skills and enjoy showing their workings.

The confidence trickster or con artist is so called because of techniques used to make the victim feel confident and trusting. The two main elements of a con trick are the victim's trust and an alluring bait (Orbach and Huang 2018). Con artists have an expression for what their expertise comprises; they get their targets 'under the ether':

> Ether is a condition of trust and even infatuation with what is being presented. Getting a victim under the ether is crucial to all cons, no matter where or how they are perpetrated. This heightened emotional state makes it hard for the victim to think clearly or make rational decisions. To get their victims under the ether, fraudsters hit their fear, panic, and urgency buttons. (Abagnale 2019: 24)

To establish trust, con artists use dress, manner and tone that inspire confidence and sound comforting. It takes skill, then, to hit these other 'buttons' as well to achieve the scam. Abagnale advises us to know what our own 'emotional hot buttons' are, as the scammers are expert in finding them (Abagnale 2019: 37), which is their way in for distracting our attention and doing something that we cannot discern. Similarly, Mitnick refers to 'developing a ruse that stimulates emotions, such as fear, excitement or guilt' (Mitnick and Simon 2002: 105) and several of the scams he uncovers also incorporate a sense of urgency.

Mitnick calls his former self a 'social engineer' which he sees as a speciality within con artists. A social engineer uses the con artist's tricks to influence and persuade people to do things, usually involving giving away information. For Mitnick this meant easier access to finding out about phone networks and computer security. Like Abagnale, Mitnick posed as a range of different characters, using insider language and knowledge of procedures to convince people he was entitled to do what he was doing. He distinguishes himself from the other type of con artist—the swindler—saying that they like to find greedy targets who will fall for a con; social engineers are more likely to seek out trusting and good-natured people (Mitnick and Simon 2002: 195). Both Abagnale and Mitnick observe that deceptions are magnified when it comes to adding the use of technology. 'Technology breeds crime and it always has' (Abagnale 2001: 18). 'Social engineering attacks may become even more destructive when the attacker adds a technology element' (Mitnick and Simon 2002: 191).

What is particularly striking about Mitnick's fictionalised accounts of his activities is the level of detail a social engineer is prepared to invest in setting up tricks, reminiscent of the magician's second principle in Fig. 13.1 (make it a lot more trouble than the trick seems worth). Indeed, magic was Mitnick's main fascination as a child, leading him to want to find out how things work, especially phones and computers. He claims that all his 'misdeeds were motivated by curiosity' (Mitnick and Simon 2002: xii) and that he is 'not a malicious hacker' even though he is famed for this. This observation highlights the ambiguity of the word 'hacker': as we saw earlier with magicians, there is more than one type, and we need to know which one we are dealing with before we can consider the nature of any deception involved.

Mitnick prefers to think of a hacker as someone who tinkers with technology, out of curiosity and in pursuit of intellectual challenge, and this was certainly its original meaning. Since the 1980s, however, hackers have been more frequently associated with malicious hacking, partly in response to high profile criminal activity revealed by popular media. Holt (2020: 731) identifies a hacker subculture that values technology, knowledge and secrecy regardless of whether the hacker is operating ethically or maliciously. In the case of knowledge, though, hackers might be distinguished through the 'hat' they wear: a white-hat hacker is involved in legitimate security support, and one wearing a black hat is engaged in criminal activity. Those who use the skills for either purpose are known as 'gray-hat hackers, recognizing their ethical flexibility over time' (Holt 2020: 735). This indicates some of the complexity of using the term 'hacker', making learning from the workings of the hacker harder than the previous dupers considered here.

I do have concerns about both Abagnale and Mitnick as in exposing their workings so explicitly they may be 'providing a great instruction book' (Abagnale 2001: 25). However, the notion of the white-hat 'ethical' hacker that Mitnick purports to be creates an additional concern about the passing on of knowledge. Security professionals are now being educated at graduate level, and there is a debate about whether students should be taught the same skills as the attackers (Hartley 2015). Perhaps there is a case for teaching technical skills, but should they also be taught the 'social engineering' skills that go with them? If higher education teachers struggle when teaching about and through deception, how much worse will it feel for them to teach students *how to* deceive?

Conclusion: What We Learn from the Dupers

The deceptive practices considered in this chapter have exposed some commonalities and potential answers about why they work. The situations described here all depend on stories: ways of framing a context where the deception is occurring. The first opportunity for deception to arise is if we are not aware of the genre of the story. Perhaps we are experiencing satire, news or fake news; magic, psychology or the paranormal; simulation or reality; education or business; parody or the genuine article; a con trick or a business deal. Indeed, there are many possibilities, and the same story may belong to several genres. But often there are linguistic indicators in the telling of the story.

The story and how it is told frames what is happening. While Teller's guidelines for magicians seeking to alter perceptions (Fig. 13.1) all resonate, number 4 seems especially important: 'keep the trickery outside the frame'. We might be deceived if the story distracts us from what else is happening in the context: for example, if it leads us to look left when the deception is happening to the right. And we might be deceived if there is more than one story in the context, which is usually the case. If the trickery in the other story is outside our current frame of reference, we are unlikely to spot it, especially if the story we are presented with fits our expectations. The trickery depends on the deceiver's intentions within the story and our altered perceptions of these intentions. We are led, through language and actions, and our own knowledge of the context, to interpret what is happening in an erroneous way.

'Every day, we experience the world from a restricted point of view, directed by ways of thinking that we do not realize are there' (Lamont and Steinmeyer 2018: 316).

This is exploited by magicians to enable us to experience the impossible and feel a sense of wonder; it is exploited by con artists to give us a bad deal and feel fear, panic or urgency and by social engineers to make us reveal vulnerable information. It was exploited by Taras and Steel to raise students' awareness and make them feel anger and a sense of injustice. Knowing that deception results in an emotional response is key to understanding why it works. This is important as former criminals have exposed huge levels of criminal activity based on deception.

We have also seen how contemporary technology can be simultaneously useful and deceptive, depending on how it is used, for example:

- Offering solutions to expose deception (which might be better provided by a teacher).
- Amplifying messages through social media (including fake ones).
- Simulating practice (and obscuring aspects of it, adding complexity to any deception used).
- Reframing practice through datafication (and obscuring key messages, allowing deceit).
- Creating new subcultures of deceptive practice (which might be framed as criminal even when not).

Technology can thus exacerbate emotional and ethical issues for educators even when supporting exposure of deception. The main question that now calls out for dialogue between educators is: Should we be teaching students how to deceive as well as how to avoid being deceived?

References

Abagnale, F. W. (2001). *The Art of the Steal*. New York: Broadway Books.

Abagnale, F. W. (2019). *Scam Me If You Can: Simple Strategies to Outsmart Today's Rip-off Artists*. New York: Portfolio/Penguin.

Basu, L. (2014). British Satire in The Thick of It. *Popular Communication*, *12*(2), 89–103. https://doi.org/10.1080/15405702.2014.888432.

Bayne, S., Evans, P., Ewins, R., Knox, J., Lamb, J., Macleod, H., O'Shea, C., Ross, J., Sheail, P., & Sinclair, C. (2020). *The Manifesto for Teaching Online*. Cambridge, MA: MIT Press.

Beins, B. C. (1993). Using the Barnum Effect to Teach about Ethics and Deception in Research. *Teaching of Psychology*, *20*(1), 33–35.

Brown, D. (2019). Mentalism, Mind Reading and the Art of Getting Inside your Head. http://derrenbrown.co.uk/ted-talk-derren-brown/. Accessed 7 October 2020.

Calhoun, A. W., Pian-Smith, M. C. M., Truog, R. D., Gaba, D. M., & Meyer, E. C. (2015). Deception and Simulation Education: Issues, Concepts, and Commentary. *Simulation in Healthcare*, *10*(3), 163–169. https://doi.org/10.1097/SIH.0000000000000086.

Collins English Dictionary (2020). Poacher Turned Gamekeeper. HarperCollins. https://www.collinsdictionary.com/dictionary/english/poacher-turned-gamekeeper. Accessed 7 October 2020.

Dean, K. L., & Forray, J. M. (2016). 'Malevolent, Callous, or Selfish'? Experiential Teaching and the Ethics of Student Deception. *Journal of Management Education*, *40*(2), 115–120. https://doi.org/10.1177/1052562916628572.

Dunnington, R. M. (2014). The Nature of Reality Represented in High Fidelity Human Patient Simulation: Philosophical Perspectives and Implications for Nursing Education. *Nursing Philosophy*, *15*(1), 14–22. https://doi.org/10.1111/nup.12034.

Fawns, T., & Sinclair, C. (2021). Towards Ecological Teaching Evaluation: Aimin for Thick Description. In T. Fawns, G., Aitken, & D. Jones (Eds.), *Online Postgraduate Education in a Postdigital World.* Cham: Springer.

Foucault, M. (1980). *Power/Knowledge: Selected Interviews and Other Writings 1972-77.* New York: Pantheon.

Goffman, E. (1974). *Frame Analysis: an Essay on the Organization of Experience*. Boston: North Eastern University Press.

Hartley, R. D. (2015). Ethical Hacking Pedagogy: An Analysis and Overview of Teaching Students to Hack. *Journal of International Technology and Information Management*, *24*(4), 94–104.

Holt, T. J. (2020). Computer Hacking and the Hacker Subculture. In T. J. Holt & A. M. Bossler (Eds.), *The Palgrave Handbook of International Cybercrime and Cyberdeviance* (pp. 725–742). New York: Palgrave Macmillan. https://doi.org/10.1007/978-3-319-78440-3_31.

Iannucci, A. (2016). From Trump to Boris, I wouldn't write The Thick of It now—Politics Already feels Fictional Enough. New Statesman, 10-16 June. https://www.newstatesman.com/politics/uk/2016/06/trump-boris-i-wouldn-t-write-thick-it-now-politics-already-feels-fictional. Accessed 7 October 2020.

Iannucci, A., & Asthana, A. (2020). Armando Iannucci on Politics and Satire. The Guardian. https://www.theguardian.com/news/audio/2020/jan/28/armando-iannucci-on-politics-and-satire-podcast. Accessed 7 October 2020.

Kuhn, G. (2013). Science of Magic [YouTube video]. https://youtu.be/CUYUyou-WQ0. Accessed 7 October 2020.

Lamont, P. (2013). *Extraordinary Beliefs: a Historical Approach to a Psychological Problem.* Cambridge, UK: Cambridge University Press.

Lamont, P., & Steinmeyer, J. (2018). *The Secret History of Magic*. New York: TarcherPerigee.

Lan, Y., Mohr, C., Hu, X., & Kuhn, G. (2018). Fake Science: The Impact of Pseudo-psychological Demonstrations on People's Beliefs in Psychological Principles. *PLoS ONE*, *13*(11), 1–10. https://doi.org/10.1371/journal.pone.0207629.

Mitnick, K., & Simon, W. N. (2002). *The Art of Deception*. Indianapolis, IN: Wiley.

Orbach, B., & Huang, L. (2018). Con Men and Their Enablers: The Anatomy of Confidence Games. *Social Research*, *85*(4), 795–823.

Pang, K. (2015). Penn and Teller are Revealing how their Magic Tricks are Done - and it's OK. Vanity Fair, September. https://www.vanityfair.com/culture/2015/09/penn-and-teller-fool-us-revealing-trick. Accessed 7 October 2020.

Rolfe, G. (2013). *The University in Dissent*. London: Routledge.

Rolfe, G. (2016). A Sacred Command of Reason? Deceit, Deception, and Dishonesty in Nurse Education. *Nursing Philosophy : an International Journal for Healthcare Professionals*, *17*(3), 173–181. https://doi.org/10.1111/nup.12124.

Rubin, V., Conroy, N., Chen, Y., & Cornwell, S. (2016). Fake News or Truth? Using Satirical Cues to Detect Potentially Misleading News. In T. Fornaciari, E. Fitzpatrick, & J. Bachenko (Eds.), *Procedings of Second Workshop on Computational Approaches to Deception Detection* (pp. 7–17). San Diego: Association for Computational Linguistics. https://doi.org/10.18653/v1/w16-0802.

Ryle, G. (2009). The Thinking of Thoughts: What is 'Le Penseur' Doing? In G. Ryle, *Collected Essays 1929-1968 Vol 2* (pp. 494–510). Abingdon: Routledge.

Secor, M., & Walsh, L. (2004). A Rhetorical Perspective on the Sokal Hoax: Genre, Style, and Context. *Written Communication*, *21*(1), 69–91. https://doi.org/10.1177/0741088303261037.

Sinclair, C. (2020). Parody: Fake News, Regeneration and Education. *Postdigital Science and Education*, *2*(1), 61–77. https://doi.org/10.1007/s42438-019-00054-x.

Sokal, A. (1996). A Physicist Experiments with Cultural Studies. *Lingua Franca, May-June*, 62–64.

Taras, D., & Steel, P. (2007). We Provoked Business Students to Unionize: Using Deception to Prove an IR point. *British Journal of Industrial Relations*, *45*(1), 179–198. https://doi.org/10.1111/j.1467-8543.2007.00607.x.

Teller (2012). Teller talks: Magic in the Mind. Reader's Digest. https://keepinitrealevanston.wordpress.com/2013/11/09/magic-tricks-revealed-by-teller-7-ways-to-fool-the-brain/ Accessed 10 December 2020.

The Magic Circle. (2020). https://themagiccircle.co.uk/. Accessed 17 September 2020.

Turkle, S. (2009). *Simulation and its Discontents*. Cambridge, MA: MIT Press.

Williams, E. (2016). *Unclear Definitions: Investigating Dictionaries Fictitious Entries through Creative and Critical Writing*. PhD thesis. London: University of London.

Williamson, B., Bayne, S., & Shay, S. (2020). The Datafication of Teaching in Higher Education: Critical Issues and Perspectives. *Teaching in Higher Education*, *25*(4), 351–365. https://doi.org/10.1080/13562517.2020.1748811.

Wolfson, S. (2020). For my Next Trick. The Observer Magazine, 26 April. https://www.theguardian.com/culture/2020/apr/26/for-my-next-trick-dynamo-mission-to-bring-back-magic. Accessed 10 December 2020.

Chapter 14
Ghosting Inside the Machine: Student Cheating, Online Education, and the Omertà of Institutional Liars

Shane J. Ralston

> The culture of cheating is not an abstract phenomenon. It is a real part of people's lives. And most of us don't have a clue about how to deal with the tough ethical choices that come our way. (Callahan 2004: 298)

> Ghosting: Taking a quiz, an exam, performing a laboratory exercise or similar evaluation in place of another; having another take a quiz, an exam, or perform an exercise or similar evaluation in place of a student, etc. (Penn State University Office of Judicial Affairs 2000)

Introduction

'Ghosting' or the unethical practice of having someone other than the student registered in the course take the student's exams, complete his or her assignments, and write his or her essays, has become a common method of cheating in today's online higher education learning environment. Internet-based teaching technology and deceit go hand in hand because the technology establishes a set of perverse incentives for students to cheat and institutions to either tolerate or encourage this highly unethical form of behavior. In addition, online divisions of major universities and their administrators are highly invested in schemes that incentivize and normalize student cheating, as well as duping external stakeholder into falsely believing that academic dishonesty policies are strictly enforced.

S. J. Ralston (✉)
Wright College, Woolf University, Valletta, Malta

A. MacKenzie et al. (eds.), *The Epistemology of Deceit in a Postdigital Era*, Postdigital Science and Education,
https://doi.org/10.1007/978-3-030-72154-1_14

For students, cheating has become an increasingly attractive option as pre-digital safeguards—for instance, in-person exam proctoring requirements and face-to-face mentoring—are quietly phased out and eventually eliminated altogether. Also, as the punishments for violating academic integrity policies are relaxed, the temptation to cheat increases accordingly. For institutions, tolerating, normalizing, and encouraging one type of student cheating, so-called ghosting, improves the profitability of their online divisions by bolstering student enrollments and retention.

In universities and colleges across the globe, online divisions and programs have become thriving profit centers, not because of the commonly attributed reasons (e.g., student ease, safety during health crises, and convenience of taking courses online, rather than face-to-face). Instead, their success is due to a single strategic insight: ubiquitous opportunities for ghosting in online courses improve an online educational division's profit margin and maximize revenue. Students who would typically pursue trade school or opt out of higher education can potentially pass courses and 'earn' degrees that would be nearly impossible, given their capabilities, in a brick-and-mortar, in-person setting.

Three Illustrative Examples

For the sake of clarity, I have selected three examples of student ghosting, two of which I have been privy to and subsequently written about elsewhere (Ralston 2016a, b, 2017). Each illustrates the complexity of the issue, as well as the architecture of incentives nudging students, faculty, and administrators towards increasingly perverse behaviors and outcomes. Behavioral economist Richard Thaler and legal scholar Cass Sunstein (2008: 6) describe the concept of nudging:

> A nudge … is any aspect of the choice architecture that alters people's behavior in a predictable way without forbidding any options or significantly changing their economic incentives. To count as a mere nudge, the intervention must be easy and cheap to avoid. Nudges are not mandates. Putting fruit at eye level counts as a nudge. Banning junk food does not. (Thaler and Sunstein 2008: 6)

These nudges increase the likelihood that individual students will cheat and institutions will either silently acquiesce to the cheating or implicitly support and encourage the unethical behavior. Consistent nudging towards perverse actions and outcomes can, in extreme cases, contribute to the growth of a corrupt organizational culture.

Rather than argue that ghosting is unethical or that absolute moral prohibitions against its practice are justified, I seek to persuade the reader through the accretion of a series of real cases, each demonstrating that the motives and consequences of this form of cheating are so perverse as to shock the conscience of any reasonable person, with the exception of those institutional actors who directly or indirectly profit from it. The relationship between those actors who benefit and lie to protect the practice of ghosting, I suggest, is similar to a code of silence between members of a corrupt or criminal organization—what I refer to as an omertà of institutional liars.

Case 1: Harrisburg Area Community College and Online Plagiarism

Imagine that you are the president of a community college. To justify your institution's existence and your enviable salary, you must convince the board of trustees that the institution is meeting—possibly even exceeding—certain productivity benchmarks, for instance, a threshold number of new enrollments, solid graduation rates, and satisfactory retention of students from year to year.

The ethical dilemma you face is whether to maintain academic integrity standards in order to make a principled stand against student cheating or relax those same standards in order to artificially inflate key productivity figures—for instance, graduation and retention rates. Which would you choose? Ever since higher education leaders and executive administrators adopted the business model, the scenario I have described is no longer so outlandish. In fact, it played out at Harrisburg Area Community College (HACC), a community college system in Central Pennsylvania serving over 70,000 students at 5 campuses and in its online program, led by President John Sygielski. HACC is no stranger to mismanagement and corruption. Poor administrative oversight has led its accreditor to twice issue warnings and temporarily suspend the community college's accreditation. Almost a year ago, HACC's Vice President, Nancy Rockey, embezzled over $200k in school funds. She is now serving a federal prison sentence.

I inquired about the truth of rumors that HACC regularly conducts fake or rigged investigations into alleged violations of its academic integrity policy. I published the results of my inquiry in an article Truthout (Ralston 2016b). In addition, I launched an open records request under Pennsylvania's Right to Know law, asking HACC to disclose the details of one specific investigation to which I was privy. Unsurprisingly, HACC chose to claim an exemption so that it could hide the truth. I appealed the decision to the PA Office of Open Records. While the appeal was eventually defeated, it revealed that HACC's ersatz investigation of student cheating involved merely examining the student's transcripts, not vetting their academic work.

HACC's accreditor, Middle States Commission on Higher Education (MSCHE), investigated the matter. The accreditor sought to know, one, whether the institution failed to enforce its own academic integrity policy and, two, whether it afforded adequate safeguards to prevent student ghosting (someone other than the student taking exams and tests in the student's place, a common practice for cheating in online courses). President John Sygielski was sent a series of questions by MSCHE that he must answer pursuant to a possible third warning and suspension of HACC's accreditation. The outcome of the accreditor's investigation, similar to the right to know request, was a resounding rejection of the basis for the inquiry. How could we know the truth, except by violating a student's right to privacy? The cover-up was complete. I would also discover that the instructor of the course in which the student successfully ghosted was a graduate of Penn State.

Case 2: Penn State and the In-Person Exam Proctoring Requirement

As higher education institutions go, Penn State has suffered through an excessive number of scandals over the past two decades. The Sandusky scandal, Joe Paterno's unpopular banishment (as well as his subsequent death), and the National Collegiate Athletic Association sanctions have scarred the institution's reputation, though perhaps not permanently (Russo and Coyne 2012; CBS News 2019). The Paterno family and the successor to Penn State President Graham Spanier have sought to recover the good name of the former football coach and Penn State. I worked as a philosophy faculty member at Penn State's Hazleton campus between 2009 and 2017, including the year that the scandal erupted (Ralston 2011).

When former Penn State football coach, Jerry Sandusky, raped boys from his charity, The Second Mile, Penn State administrators covered up the crimes in order to protect the institution's reputation. However, the victims came forward; Sandusky was convicted on 52 counts of child molestation, and Joe Paterno, Graham Spanier, and other university officials who failed to report the abuse were ousted. Not surprisingly, Penn State's student enrollment declined sharply soon after the Sandusky scandal became news. Enrolment numbers, especially at the satellite campuses, are still far below what they were prior to the scandal. The only division of Penn State with growing enrolment is World Campus, Penn State's online division (Penn State News 2015).

In 2006 I was recruited to teach courses for World Campus. One of World Campus's academic integrity policies, intended to prevent systemic student cheating, was that the final exams for all its courses had to be proctored in person by someone approved by the administration. Otherwise, administrators and instructors feared that students would pay someone more knowledgeable than them to take exams in their place. This unethical form of student cheating, called 'ghosting', is specifically prohibited in the boilerplate academic integrity policy that is included in almost every Penn State course syllabus (Penn State University Office of Judicial Affairs 2000). For many students, finding a proctor and obtaining World Campus administrator approval were inconveniences. A year later, the policy was largely scrapped in favor of the honor system for most courses in Penn State World Campus's catalogue.[1]

[1] Only a handful of Penn State World Campus online courses in math, sciences, and sociology still require proctors at Penn State.

In 2009 I formally protested the disappearance of the proctor requirement. Discovering that no good deed goes unpunished, I soon found myself without courses to teach the following term. In 2015, when I was invited back to World Campus and taught a single course, I complained about poor course design and my suspicion that many students were ghosting. One of the most engaged and industrious students in the course also complained to the Philosophy department chair and academic division dean that the course was poorly designed. I was promptly told that I would never teach another philosophy course for World Campus again. Administrators at Penn State World Campus doled out retaliatory punishment and expulsion swiftly, knowing that an internal whistle-blower could expose the institutionally supported cheating scheme.

The removal of the proctoring safeguard is obviously a sore issue for faculty. We are duty-bond to uphold academic integrity standards. Staff are likewise obligated to report violations of academic integrity policies. For executive leaders and administrators, though, dispensing with the proctoring requirement meant one less barrier to increasing enrollments and generating tuition dollars from Penn State's only growing division, World Campus. In this case, Penn State faculty, under threat of retaliation, merely bent to the will of ambitious administrators. The operative advice to World Campus instructors was, 'look the other way or suffer the consequences'. Although I stood my ground, most faculty rely heavily on the income from teaching online and therefore were pressured to acquiesce. Nevertheless, many faculty and staff at Penn State are complicit in the design and maintenance of a system that tolerates and encourages (or nudges) student cheating, specifically ghosting behavior.

Penn State World Campus serves an emerging and largely untapped student population from the corporate and military sectors. These students have limited time. For most, their employers are willing to pay the entire tuition bill or a substantial portion of it. Retaining and graduating these tuition-paying students is a major objective of Penn State. The removal of the exam-proctoring safeguard signaled to students that cheating in online courses was not only tolerated but, to some extent, also encouraged by Penn State. Academic integrity was nothing more than an empty slogan that took up space in the cluttered policies section of a course syllabus.

The decision by Penn State World Campus to scrap the in-person proctoring requirement in most online courses is not on par with the Sandusky scandal cover-up. Nonetheless, the lesson the child sex abuse scandal teaches us is that it is incumbent on bystanders to voice their outrage when higher education leaders try to obscure the truth for private or institutional gain. Former Penn State graduate student and instructor Kristin Rawls (2012) expressed optimism that others will see the Sandusky scandal as a call for social action and public accountability: 'Ultimately, I hope that the Sandusky case will have an important public impact, empowering others like me to speak out and motivating the public to demand answers about just what goes on in State College—even beyond the football stadium.'

In the same spirit, it should be asked why World Campus decided to lower its academic integrity standards. Academic integrity advocates ought to demand accountability, including an explanation as to why alternatives to in-person proctoring have never been deployed to prevent ghosting in Penn State's online courses. Penn State's key productivity measures include retention and graduation rates, which help in the recruitment of new cohorts of online students. These students apply, accept places, and enroll at Penn State World Campus every year, hoping to eventually graduate and earn a Penn State degree (note: World Campus degrees look identical to in-person degrees). A reputation for lax enforcement of academic integrity policies attracts a certain kind of student: namely, those who would otherwise not be able to pass courses without cheating.

Lowering academic integrity standards and encouraging systemic cheating in online courses have artificially inflated the figures for these output measures. Who says that cheaters never prosper? At Penn State, not only have the student cheaters benefited from the non-enforcement of academic dishonesty policies, but so have the administrators, faculty, and staff who look the other way and permit the practice of ghosting to go unchecked—not entirely dissimilar from how administrators protected child sexual predator Jerry Sandusky for 30 years.

Case 3: Harvard University and Syllabus Regret Clauses

In 2012, Harvard University was rocked by a highly publicized cheating scandal. The controversy involved 125 students enrolled in an introductory Government course on congressional politics (Pérez-Peña and Bidgood 2012). The instructor-of-record assigned the students a take-home exam with the stipulation that they could not collaborate with each other. After a teaching assistant discovered exams with identical answers to questions, the instructor took the matter to the Harvard College Administrative Board, which reviewed the evidence and conducted an investigation. Students, parents, and lawyers hired by the students' families defended the practice by referring to the custom or convention at Harvard of collaboratively completing take-home assignments and exams. The scandal and its aftermath, which involved the withdrawal of 70% of the students investigated from the university, was remarkable, not just because it occurred at a flagship Ivy League institution, but because of its 'unprecedented scope and magnitude' (Robbins 2012).

Is the Harvard case an instance of ghosting because it involves a student having someone else (in this case, a fellow student) take an exam in their place? The main difference is that the Harvard case, unlike the Harrisburg and Penn State cases, did not occur within an online environment. Therefore, it invites the question whether ghosting requires an enabling digital or Internet technology to count as ghosting. Obviously, the online delivery framework facilitates the easy misrepresentation of exam and essay authorship by the student. Actually, the technological means of cloaking identity need not be digital or Internet-based, so long as the objective is to deceitfully pass off another's work as the work of the registered student. In the Harvard case, all the workers happened to be registered students, divvying up the take-home exam into pieces, distributing them to workers, efficiently completing the parts, and then reassembling and submitting the collaborative effort as the work of a single student. If the instructor had not stipulated that collaboration was off the table, the unethical activity of ghosting would not have occurred.

The Harvard cheating scandal was notable, not just for the university's swift move to punish the transgressors and the public outrage it inspired but also for Harvard University's more conciliatory long-term approach to handling individual cases of cheating. In the aftermath of the scandal, Harvard faculty have become innovators in the academic dishonesty space, introducing regret clauses into their course syllabi. According to Lindsay Ellis (2020) of The Chronicle of Higher Education, these clauses stipulate that so long as 'first-time offenders [of academic integrity rules] come forward and admit what they did within 72 hours, an instructor will give a failing grade on the assignment—but will not refer the case for disciplinary action'. Ellis spotlights a Computer Science faculty member, David J. Malan, who adopted the use of syllabus regret clauses, fully knowing that the practice would be controversial. He views cheating behavior as largely excusable, indicating troubles and struggles elsewhere in a student's life. In Malan's words, '[a]cts of academic dishonesty were a symptom of larger concerns or pressures in their life. … [The conversations with students about cheating] made it much more real, and much more difficult, because now you are on the front lines, discussing these things with students.' Malan documented the number of cases before and after the introduction of the regret clause into his syllabus. To his surprise, the number of cases of academic dishonesty increased.

To anyone familiar with how nudging works, this outcome is predictable. Syllabus regret clauses offer students tempted to cheat a legitimate way to escape punishment. It nudges them to cheat by reducing punishment or negating the disincentive. As rational actors, they are more likely to engage in cheating behavior, knowing fully well that they have an easy escape route in case the scheme fails. Despite the morally problematic nature of syllabus regret clauses, the practice has gained momentum, as faculty and administrators at other universities look to Harvard as a leader in successfully normalizing student cheating.

The 'It's-Not-So-Bad' Objection

A possibly lethal objection to my account is that it is based on thoroughly anecdotal evidence. The primary reason why my argument is susceptible to such an objection is that I rely on the accretion of only a handful of cases, the majority of which I have intimate details of, but that do not represent the majority of cases. In the lingo of social scientists, the conclusions I reach are not externally valid. I call this the 'It's-Not-So-Bad-Objection' since it seeks to minimize the scope and impact of the student ghosting problem by recourse to statistical or experimental data.

Christian Miller (2020) deploys a version of this objection in his article titled 'Just How Dishonest Are Most Students?' He assures readers that the problem is not so widespread as is often claimed. In addition, Miller insists that it can be easily managed if students were to publicly pledge to abide by honor or academic integrity codes:

> Honor pledges are not only surprisingly effective in curbing cheating; they also promote honesty. Students who abide by them refrain from cheating, not because they can't, but because they choose not to. … Empirical research has repeatedly found that schools that are committed to honor codes have significantly reduced cheating rates compared with schools that are not. (Miller 2020)

Miller culls his evidence that the problem is not so severe and that honor pledges are an easy fix from an article by McCabe et al. (2001), surveying a decade of research on student cheating. Not only is the article dated, but Trevino holds a faculty position at Penn State University, an institution that is deeply invested in its own scheme of normalized cheating.

Ignored by Miller are many recent studies reaching the opposite conclusion: namely, that student cheating is widespread because the rewards outweigh the risks. For instance, in one study, 75% of college alumni surveyed admitted that they cheated at least once during their undergraduate years and 22% admitted to regular cheating, including ghosting and contract cheating (i.e., paying others to write papers and take exams) (Yardley et al. 2009). In McCabe's (2005) study, surveying over 50,000 undergraduate students, 70% confessed to cheating. Although there is no empirical proof that cheating is more pervasive in online courses and programs as compared to in-person courses and programs (e.g., Harris et al. 2020), it is nevertheless widely accepted that the obstacles to cheating are less significant in an online learning environment (Nehls 2014: 473). King et al. (2009) found that 73.6% of students surveyed believed that it was easier to cheat in online versus traditional courses. In Curran et al.'s (2011) study of undergraduate cheating in online courses, they conclude that online technology not only lowers the barriers to academic dishonesty but also makes it less likely that the cheater will be caught and punished. Consequently, online students are tempted to commit acts of academic dishonesty when they would not otherwise do so in a brick-and-mortar setting.

The 'It's-Not-So-Bad' objection is part of an overall strategy higher education administrators deploy to minimize external stakeholders' perceptions that cheating is widespread, tolerated, and even encouraged by colleges and universities. According to Nehls (2014: 475), '[a]s online college course enrollments continue to grow, academic dishonesty in the computer-mediated environment is going to be an important consideration for institutions of higher education'. One of the forces that has emboldened administrators to adopt this strategy is the increasing neoliberalization and corporatization of the modern university, to which we turn next.

The Neoliberal/Corporate University Machine

For the past 40 years, scholarly accounts of the neoliberalization of the Academy have been prodigal. The Public University (circa 1960–1980), emphasizing education as a human right and a socialization experience in preparation for a more fulfilling life, transformed into the Corporate University (circa 1990 to present), conceiving education as a commodity and a vocational experience in preparation for employment and a financially secure life. Some shocking recent trends exemplify ways in which the modern university is becoming increasingly corporatized, such as the use of false marketing hype (or 'innovation theater') to introduce blockchain technology initiatives and the profit-maximizing shift from offering traditional degrees to selling microcredentials (Ralston 2019, 2021).

In the corporate university, in contrast to the public university, standards of productivity and excellence in scholarship and pedagogy have changed drastically. The lived experience and wisdom of highly educated peers and colleagues were supplanted by budget-connected measures, such as impact, enrollment revenue, and return on investment. Human labor is increasingly displaced by digital technologies. According to Susan and Henry Giroux:

> [t]he corporate university is descending more and more into what has been called 'an output fundamentalism,' prioritizing market mechanisms that emphasize productivity and performance measures that make a mockery of quality scholarship and diminish effective teaching—scholarly commitments are increasingly subordinated to bringing in bigger grants to supplement operational budgets negatively impacted by the withdrawal of governmental funding. (Giroux and Giroux 2012)

The Neoliberal/Corporate University alters higher education priorities. At the top of its priority list are quality assurance, process efficiency, and managerial outcomes. The Public University's 'quest for truth' and mission to acculturate young people to the demands of citizenship, preparing them for meaningful participation in a democracy, fall by the wayside. According to Peter Jandrić and Sarah Hayes, the problem with the corporate shift in university priorities is that the new reality fosters discontent:

> The Neoliberal University causes different types of discontent. From a student perspective, excessive reliance on adjunct work lowers the quality of instruction—overworked, underpaid and often without their own offices where they could see students, many adjuncts are simply unable to meet student needs. From a staff perspective, adjunct work is associated with poverty, job insecurity, lack of long-term career prospects and the lack of tenure protection . . . From a social perspective, the Neoliberal University restricts upward mobility and promotes inequality. The commodified Neoliberal University sees knowledge and education as goods that can be sold and bought, and significantly reduces the public sphere . . . [and] is supported by digital technologies, which enable practices such as automated testing and surveillance. More importantly, however, the Neoliberal University is based on powerful, rationalist logic in policies that might appear convincing, but when scrutinized, the discourse can lean towards irrationality . . . [T]he success of educational systems is measured and evaluated predominantly though quantitative means—and the use of this or that technology is only a symptom of a wider ideological trend of McDonaldization of higher education. (Jandrić and Hayes 2020: 168)

However, the neoliberal/corporate shift has been welcomed by some: specifically, those administrators seeking to maximize student retention, graduation rates, and tuition revenue. Ignoring, permitting, and normalizing student cheating schemes means more students who would ordinarily fail out are retained and graduate.

Members of the Neoliberal/Corporate University value productivity outcomes over academic excellence. Among higher education executives, the claim that progress should not be undercut by antiquated ethical standards, such as academic integrity rules, has been gaining wider purchase. Harvard University's move to support Syllabus Regret Clauses is a case in point. HACC's decision to derail individual investigations into student ghosting in hopes of hiding a more extensive scheme that normalizes the activity is also indicative of this corporate attitude. So is Penn State's decision to eliminate the proctoring requirement in its online courses. Why would these institutional actors risk exposure? The McDonaldization of higher education requires that its loyal supporters achieve increasing levels of productivity no matter what the moral costs.

The Lies Institutional Actors Tell Us

A symptom of this push to normalize student ghosting is an omertà of institutional liars, whereby institutional actors—faculty, staff, administrators, executive leaders, as well as accreditors—repeat the lie that academic integrity policies are strongly enforced, while the epistemological barriers to exposing the truth climb higher and higher.

An omertà is an unwritten pact or code of silence, typically adopted within corrupt or criminal organizations (such as the mafia). Members of the organization refuse to give evidence of criminal activity to authorities. The evidence here is the true rationale or mea culpa for non-enforcement of academic integrity policies: the desire to meet and exceed institutional productivity measures, such as enrollment and graduation rates. Actors sworn to uphold the omertà tell lies to maintain the appearance of legitimacy or law abidingness while nudging students to cheat. That is the dupery at work in online higher education divisions: administrators declare that they are committed to academic integrity while actively incentivizing and normalizing student ghosting. Lies, higher education administrators tell us, include statements which we would normally interpret as consistent with rules and policies that prohibit academic dishonesty, as follows:[2]

> There is zero tolerance at this institution for academic dishonesty.
>
> Cheating is unethical student behavior that merits punishment.
>
> Having someone else take your exam or complete your essay is unfair because it gives some students, those who ghost, an advantage over those who play by the rules.

[2] These are made-up statements written for illustration purposes.

The truth behind these statements by institutional liars is instead closer to the following:

> We tolerate cheating and even encourage it insofar as it improves productivity, measured in graduation and retention rates.
>
> It is prudent to treat cheating as excusable student behavior, claiming that it indicates other challenges in students' lives, when it actually makes our lives (instructors, staff and administrators) easier, since we do not have to enforce academic integrity policies.
>
> Ghosting is fine, so long as you the student takes every precaution not to get caught, given that the institutional barriers to such cheating behavior have been significantly weakened (e.g., by removing proctoring and mentoring requirements).

Normalizing student cheating in academic institutions is roughly similar to normalizing corruption in other complex organizations. According to Ashforth and Anand (2003), the three processes integral to the normalization of corruption are (1) institutionalization, (2) rationalization, and (3) socialization. *Institutionalization* involves the conversion of corrupt policies, practices, and behaviors into patterned routines. The analogue in normalizing student cheating is a pattern of institutional actions that make cheating appear commonplace and acceptable, such as syllabus regret clauses, instructors regularly ignoring clear evidence of cheating, and deans who consistently mete out minimal sanctions to students guilty of academic dishonesty. *Rationalization* refers to the capacity institutional actors have for justifying corrupt policies, practices, and behaviors. For example, Penn State vindicated its removal of the proctoring requirement on the grounds that it was inconvenient for students and inefficient for faculty and staff to administer. *Socialization* indicates the habituation and transference of corrupt policies, practices, and behaviors to new members of the organization through formal and informal mechanisms. Indeed, the danger of normalizing student cheating is that it socializes young people to easily accept and even embrace unethical practices in whatever institution to which they belong (Ralston 2016b). Through institutionalization, rationalization, and socialization, student cheating and its official incentivization—similar to organizational corruption—gradually come to appear normal and acceptable.

Once academic integrity standards are significantly weakened—as witnessed at HACC, Penn State, and Harvard University—productivity goals (e.g., enrolment, retention, and graduation rates) are easier to achieve. Students who would ordinarily be incapable of completing a university degree are nudged by cheating-friendly policies to cheat their way through challenging curricula and degree programs. However, the cheaters are not just so-called bad apples—as institutional actors would like to portray them. They are not alone in their unethical behavior. Similar to normalized corruption, normalized cheating sets in through processes of institutionalization, rationalization, and socialization. Responsibility is shared with faculty, staff, and administrators who passively (e.g., ignore or look the other way) or actively enable the behavior (e.g., proposing or supporting cheating-friendly policies). It would be more apt to say that the whole barrel of apples has turned bad.

Social Epistemology and the Postdigital

Too many higher education executives give lip service to academic integrity while violating its spirit and letter. They dupe outsiders into holding the false belief that higher education institutions are committed to student honesty while nudging them to cheat and while celebrating the productivity outcomes that this dupery ensures. We might wonder why so many higher education insiders, arrayed along the entire ideological spectrum, implicitly accept student cheating, while outsiders explicitly oppose it. One possible explanation is a phenomenon called 'epistemic factionalization' —or, more plainly, groupthink.

Weatherall and O'Connor (2018, 19) describe epistemic factionalization in stark terms: 'we so often see beliefs with strange bedfellows, especially in cases where there is profound mistrust of those with different views . . . [or where having] different beliefs [than the out-group] is sufficient to account for epistemic factionalization.' In other words, heavy socialization in the logic of neoliberalization produces an odd faction (strange bedfellows) of institutional actors, each holding the ethically questionable belief that student cheating, especially ghosting, is a necessary evil for online education to generate enrollments and tuition revenue. These strange bedfellows form a cabal of institutional liars, whose ómerta is to hide the true rationale for normalizing academic dishonesty: improved productivity at any costs.

Pre-digital measures to combat student cheating—for instance, in-person exam proctoring requirements and student mentoring—have been progressively eliminated by online higher education divisions, such as at Penn State. From a postdigital perspective, we should insist that digital technology not receive undue privilege relative to non-digital and pre-digital alternatives. In other words, digital pedigree ought not to be the sole criterion in adjudging the value of educational technology (Jandrić 2019). Even though the ghosting did not occur in an online environment, the Harvard case, appreciated from a postdigital perspective, remains just as relevant as the online ghosting cases. Indeed, what we learn from the Harvard case is that higher educational administrators, who nudge students towards cheating behavior, will invest significantly in normalizing that behavior through official channels (e.g., by approving syllabus regret clauses). This is what Nehls (2014: 484) calls the 'fraud triangle', whereby incentive pressures, opportunity, and rationalizing attitudes create the space for student cheating. They can also engender the perfect storm of conditions for an institutionally approved cheating scheme.

One way to counter epistemic factionalization is for out-group actors (e.g., politicians, experts, consultants, higher education reformers, community activists), who are critical of student cheating, to demand that colleges and universities enforce their academic integrity policies. Such demands might include a mandate to return to pre-digital countermeasures that stymie student ghosting. A postdigital strategy for addressing student cheating would democratize the academic integrity space, inviting a multiplicity of approaches and diverse voices into the conversation about how to promote student honesty and integrity. Such a strategy could, for instance, involve verifying the identity of students who are at risk of ghosting behavior

(Kraglund-Gauthier and Young 2012). Ultimately, a postdigital strategy could reduce student ghosting and incentivize ethical behavior. It might also expose the dupery committed by institutional actors who seek to incentivize and normalize academic dishonesty. However, in the Neoliberalized/Corporate University, the barriers are significant. Institutional actors are likely to continue nudging students to engage in cheating behavior, thereby boosting productivity numbers, even at the risk that whistle-blowers and others will expose their lies.

References

Ashforth, B. E., & Anand, V. (2003). The normalization of corruption in organizations. *Research in Organizational Behavior, 25*, 1–52. https://doi.org/10.1016/S0191-3085(03)25001-2.

Callahan, D. (2004). *The cheating culture: Why more Americans are doing wrong to get ahead.* Boston, MA: Mariner Books.

CBS News. (2019). The Penn State scandal. 9 November 2011 to 1 May 2019. https://www.cbsnews.com/feature/the-penn-state-scandal/. Accessed 3 August 2020.

Curran, K., Middleton, G., & Doherty, C. (2011). Cheating in exams with technology. *International Journal of Cyber Ethics in Education, 1*(2), 54–62. https://doi.org/10.4018/ijcee.2011040105.

Ellis, L. (2020). Cheating on your homework? In this Harvard class, just say you're sorry. The Chronicle of Higher Education, 23 January. https://www.chronicle.com/article/cheat-on-your-homework-in-this-harvard-class-just-say-youre-sorry/. Accessed 19 September 2020.

Giroux, S. S., & Giroux, H. A. (2012). Universities gone wild: Big money, big sports and scandalous abuse at Penn State. Truthout, 5 January. https://truthout.org/articles/universities-gone-wild-big-money-big-sports-and-scandalous-abuse-at-penn-state/. Accessed 3 August 2020.

Harris, L., Harrison, D., McNally, D., & Ford, C. (2020). Academic integrity in an online culture: Do McCabe's findings hold true for online-adult learners? *Journal of Academic Ethics, 18*, 419–434. https://doi.org/10.1007/s10805-019-09335-3.

Jandrić, P. (2019). We-think. We-learn, we-act: The trialectic of postdigital collective intelligence. *Postdigital Science and Education, 1*(2), 275–279. https://doi.org/10.1007/s42438-019-00055-w.

Jandrić, P., & Hayes, S. (2020). Technological unemployment and its educational discontents. In M. Stocchetti (Ed.), *The digital age and its discontents: Critical reflections in Education* (pp. 161–182). Helsinki: Helsinki University Press. https://doi.org/10.33134/HUP-4-9.

King, C. G., Guyette, R. W., & Piotrowski, C. (2009). Online exams and cheating: An empirical analysis of business students' views. *The Journal of Educators Online, 6*(1), 1–11.

Kraglund-Gauthier, W. L., & Young, D. C. (2012). Will the real John Doe stand up? Verifying the identity of online students. In Wankel, L. A., & Wankel, C. (Eds.), *Misbehavior Online in Higher Education.* London: Emerald Group Publishing. https://doi.org/10.1108/S2044-9968(2012)0000005019.

McCabe, D. L. (2005). Cheating among college and university students: A North American perspective. *International Journal for Educational Integrity, 1*(1), 1–11. https://doi.org/10.21913/IJEI.V1i1.14.

McCabe, D. L., Trevino, L. K., & Butterfield, K. B. (2001). Cheating in academic institutions: A decade of research. *Ethics & Behavior, 11*(3), 219–232. https://doi.org/10.1207/S15327019EB1103_2.

Miller, C. B. (2020). Just how dishonest are most students? The New York Times, 13 November. https://www.nytimes,com/2020/11/13/opinion/sunday/online-learning-cheating.html. Accessed 14 November 2020.

Nehls, K. (2014). Academic dishonesty in online courses. In M. Orleans (Ed.), *Cases on critical and qualitative perspectives in online higher education* (pp. 472–488). Hershey, PA: Information Science Reference. https://doi.org/10.4018/978-1-4666-5051-0.ch024.

Penn State News Editorial Staff (2015). University enrollment up slightly, World Campus sees growth. Penn State News, 9 October. https://news.psu.edu/story/374389/2015/10/09/academics/university-enrollment-slightly-world-campus-sees-growth. Accessed 3 August 2020.

Penn State University Office of Judicial Affairs (2000). Examples of academic integrity violations. 8 June. http://www.personal.psu.edu/cxc11/508/precedent_students.pdf. Accessed 11 April 2020.

Pérez-Peña, R., & Bidgood, J. (2012). Harvard says 125 students may have cheated on final exam. New York Times, 30 August. https://www.nytimes.com/2012/08/31/education/harvard-says-125-students-may-have-cheated-on-exam.html. Accessed 22 August 2020.

Ralston, S. J. (2021). Higher education's micro-credentialing craze: A postdigital-Deweyan critique. *Postdigital Science and Education*, *3*(1), 83–101. https://doi.org/10.1007/s42438-020-00121-8.

Ralston, S. J. (2019). Postdigital prospects for blockchain-disrupted higher education: Beyond the theater, memes and marketing hype. *Postdigital Science and Education*, *2*(2), 280–288. https://doi.org/10.1007/s42438-019-00091-6.

Ralston, S. J. (2017). How students 'Ghost' through on-line degree programs. Intellectual Takeout, 25 January. https://www.intellectualtakeout.org/blog/how-students-ghost-through-online-degree-programs/. Accessed 12 April 2020.

Ralston, S. J. (2016a). Why more colleges are turning a blind eye to cheating. Intellectual Takeout, 15 November. https://www.intellectualtakeout.org/blog/why-more-colleges-are-turning-blind-eye-cheating/. Accessed 12 April 2020.

Ralston, S. J. (2016b). Socializing the corrupt: Cheating, corruption and law enforcement in Pennsylvania. Truthout, 27 August. https://truthout.org/articles/socializing-the-corrupt-cheating-education-and-law-enforcement-in-pennsylvania/. Accessed 12 April 2020.

Rawls, K. (2012). How abuse, corruption and silence at Penn State perpetuate a poisonous culture. Truthout, 26 July. https://truthout.org/articles/how-abuse-corruption-and-silence-at-penn-state-perpetuate-a-poisonous-culture/. Accessed 3 August 2020.

Robbins, R. D. (2012). Harvard investigates 'unprecedented' academic dishonesty case. The Harvard Crimson, 30 August. https://www.thecrimson.com/article/2012/8/30/academic-dishonesty-ad-board/. Accessed 22 August 2020.

Russo, R. D., & Coyne, T. (2012). NCAA sanctions slam Penn State. Portland Press Herald, 23 July. https://www.pressherald.com/2012/07/23/penn-st-fined-60m-wins-vacated-from-98-11/. Accessed 3 August 2020.

Thaler, R. H., & Sunstein, C. R. (2008). *Nudge: Improving decisions about health, wealth and happiness*. New Haven, CT: Yale University Press.

Weatherall, J. O., & O'Connor, C. (2018). Endogenous epistemic factionalization. Cornell University Archives. https://arxiv.org/pdf/1812.08131.pdf. Accessed 13 April 2020.

Yardley, J., Rodriguez, M. D., Bates, S. C., & Nelson, J. (2009). True confessions?: Alumni's retrospective reports on undergraduate cheating behaviors. *Ethics & Behavior*, *19*(1), 1–14. https://doi.org/10.1080/10508420802487096.

Chapter 15
'Choice Is Yours': Anatomy of a Lesson Plan from University V

Eamon Costello and Prajakta Girme

Muse! Bow propitious while my pen relates
How pour her armies through a thousand gates,
As when Eolus heaven's fair face deforms,
Enwrapp'd in tempest and a night of storms;
Astonish'd ocean feels the wild uproar,
The refluent surges beat the sounding shore. (Wheatley 1776)

As You Are

Everyone looks out on a different day: A man, a woman, a child, people of a myriad faiths and people of none. Everyone has a separate skin, the biggest organ in the body, a protective membrane that shields us from the outside. It is also a massive interface cloaked in sensors, the touch points that allow us to feel and live the world. Our corporeal selves provide us with our unique interface to the world (Facer 2011; MacCormack 2006). They help us try to learn and then tell the story of the day we each see. But are we more than our bodies? Or are we less? Are we the stories of our bodies? Could we have been cleaved from embodied ways of being and knowing? And if any of the answers to these questions is 'yes', then what might such a posthuman scenario imply about the activities we engage in such as teaching and learning (Bayne 2018; Knox 2019)? This chapter aims to explore education as posthuman practice via the anatomy of a simple lesson plan. We use storytelling as a device to

E. Costello (✉) · P. Girme
Dublin City University, Dublin, Ireland
e-mail: eamoncostello@dcu.ie; prajakta.paraggirme@dcu.ie

A. MacKenzie et al. (eds.), *The Epistemology of Deceit in a Postdigital Era*, Postdigital Science and Education,
https://doi.org/10.1007/978-3-030-72154-1_15

selectively and deceptively paint pictures of histories that may have been or have yet to come.

The methodology adopted here is that of social science fiction as a specialism of speculative fiction more generally (Gerlach and Hamilton 2003; Ross 2017). This is not an empirical approach. We have no data to sift for truths. Although we do deal with the datafication of students (Williamson et al. 2020; Selwyn and Gašević 2020) – the reduction of people to numbers, bytes and letters – do not fear as no actual students were harmed in our analysis. Rather we adopt an approach that tells stories and attempt to use these tales as a lens through which to explore educational futures (Collier and Ross 2020). We engage in such speculations so that we may reflect on the possible long-term consequences of our current beliefs and practices (Selwyn et al. 2020; Macgilchrist et al. 2020; Bell et al. 2013). Speculative fiction tries to take us out of the known. However, it does not bring us into the unknown but more indirectly back to where we already are. Its purpose is not to know the future but to predict the present.

This methodology, it has been argued, is necessary if Higher Education is to 'navigate and adapt to unpredictable and shifting circumstances that impact people in profoundly uneven ways [by] imagining, and then enacting, better futures [that are] imaginative, equitable, accessible, sustainable, and decolonial' (Veletsianos and Houlden 2020). It may be a posthuman modification, or mod, that allows us to see those students not captured under the bell curve of 'those individuals who are outliers and candidate measures that are at the margins' (Treviranus 2014).

It may provide different windows to see out of, for it has been argued that the story of mankind has all too often contained plenty of man but little kindness (Le Guin 1989; Macgilchrist 2020). One ingrained narrative, for instance, is that humans are primed for 'flight or fight' upon stimulus. After it was noted that such claims were based on a science devised by men and conducted with male subjects, the experiments were re-run with women who reported the alternative response of a 'tend and befriend' instinct. This reaction comprises 'nurturant activities designed to protect the self and offspring that promote safety and reduce distress; befriending is the creation and maintenance of social networks that may aid in this process' (Taylor et al. 2000). There is no need to fight nor to flee; we can stay and inter-be (Hanh 2010).

The speculative fiction that follows is set in the future, but it also draws on the past for 'the body is a historical situation [...] a manner of doing, dramatizing, and reproducing a historical situation' (Butler 1988). The body we choose to datafy in this chapter is the student body, in both the singular and collective sense. We take the body as an interface. Our corporeal selves try to mediate the personal perspectives we have with each other so as to create collective and shared consciousnesses. We only contribute to consciousness by crude approximation (Hoffman and Prakash 2014). For example, a smile is a roughly hewn icon of the interface that tries to tell us something about the world within. We can only guess what might be going on in the vast consciousness that the smile opens into what someone is feeling or thinking. We never perceive absolute reality because the interface simply offers us shorthands, useful bite-size abstractions. We never see perfectly. As a consequence there is always the potential, either by accident or design, for duplicity (MacKenzie et al. 2020).

The biggest fiction we tell ourselves is about our 'humanity'. It is our most enduring story. Once upon a time, humans are set apart by God, by gender, race, authority, intelligence, adaptability, morality and so on – by any and all of the humanist hegemonies, the rights to rule. This story of the human is woven from strands of power, from narratives (Lyotard 1979) of dominion and struggle but interlaced with the micro acts and activities that constitute daily mundane existence. Hence we attempt here to speculate via *posthuman* prophecies (Fuller and Jandrić 2019). Such prognostications do not see the human as certain, nor its characteristics such as race, gender or morality as reliable. Nothing is immutable if we enter the present by splitting it with the axe of the future.

Texts are deceptive and duplicitous because of their plurality of meaning. It would be presumptuous, however, to claim to have given the text that follows a plural effect. That is not the job of the writer. That is a more private affair between the characters and the reader. Their engagement is, via the text, 'an iridescent exchange carried on by multiple voices on different wavelengths and subject from time to time to a sudden dissolve which enables the utterance to shift from one point of view to another' (Barthes 1980: 41–42).

We have merely hauled some static words and two-dimensional images to the page. It is up to you, dear reader, to bring them to life. Choice is yours.

Choice Is Yours

On 3 April 2054, I woke early, threw back the covers and strode across the apartment. I felt the mirrors watching me as I moved. I selected a colour and began to paint my nails onto myself: first each toe and then each finger. This was a ritual I undertook every morning before anything else was decided, and oh what decisions there lay ahead today (Fig. 15.1). I opened the balcony doors and let the cool city air flow around me.

I moved back inside and sat on the bed. As I did so, I glanced up at the plaque on the wall above my desk. 'Digitization, Colonization, Dance', it read. My heart surged. This was the motto of University V: a mission it believed and lived. I felt so proud to be but one small part of its grand project. It had given me so much. It had given me everything, all of this. Through the benefaction of its Anthony Swan initiative, I had been given a complete sterilization, something I could never have afforded by myself. And how would I have ascended to the position of High Professor without such an essential mod? I shuddered to think of the alternative, of something unfolding inside of me, draining my nutrients, sucking life from me, clawing itself into form.

And where would I be today without my other wonderful augmentations? The mods for my eyes and ears meant everything to me. I could hear students so acutely now. I could sense any waver, instantly fix upon an inflection that might signal some

Fig. 15.1 Before anything else was decided

underlying weakness, and then immediately double down on a line of questioning. And with my new eyes, I saw them so vividly I sometimes almost felt as if I was peering into their souls.

Now it was time for my favourite mod – decision time. I threw open the wardrobe and looked at my collection of skins, my most prized possessions. I touched a sublime brown that felt like drinking liquid chocolate on a winter day. I flicked to a deep radiant black number. In this gown I felt the colour of night; became raven, 'feathers shiny and black, a touch of blue glistening down her back' (Williams 2001). But no, not today. Today was a day for white, a late twenty-first-century specimen, an amazing white Irish skin. I held it against my body and stood in front of the mirror. I marvelled at its delicate porcelain, dappled in a starscape of freckles. Each small brown fleck was unique in tone and contour, but they were together woven into one mesmeric camouflage. It had some slight marks where it had been stretched during the primitive barbarisms of childbirth. But even these were beautiful to me, these fingerprints from a life I had never known but would soon step into. And in every other way, it was in fabulous condition – a marvelous pelt.

I slipped it on and immediately it inhabited me. I spun to admire myself in the glass, lithe and graceful. I became the leopard. Yes, today was the day for a hunter's skin.

Come as I Want You to Be

As I arrived at the lecture theatre, the meat-sacs were still fitting the students into their platforms. Our meat-sac to student ratio was now 3 to 1, the highest figure ever attained globally. Yet more meat-sacs carefully prepared and tuned my lectern, their red bodies traced with faint blue pulses.

With a flick I moved a strand of *rúa* back from my face and plugged myself into the interface: Wow! The datafications were so awesome this year! On the console the students bristled beautifully before me. Arrayed in purple, green and cyan ladders, they swayed in steady suspension from data structures that had been induced to flow down hidden Markov models. The colours moved up and down, vacillating in fluorescent columns like synthesised notes, windows turning on and off, floor by floor, on neon skyscrapers.

I delved in, feeling my way through the data, one student at a time. There was only one datapoint I was interested in today: the Life-Credit Average. Ah, here was a possible candidate: Octavio. His Life-Credit Average was pitifully low and it was abundantly clear why. For a start, he had accrued mountains of debt: tuition fees, textbook loans, food stamps, performance opportunities, yadda, yadda, yadda. More seriously though, his score had been compounded by multiple convictions for egregious breaches of the academic code. What a list of infractions this guy had. He was really on his last legs. Yes, this student would be perfect. Just imagine, I said to myself, how it will feel to wear the skin of a man.

I pulled up my lesson plan on the screen. I had been working on this all summer and I was so happy with it. It was one of the loveliest I had ever fashioned. It was composed of three pedagogical stanzas that would unfold over the course of the semester: two beautiful lures to enchant my students and then one silver hook to catch and reel them in. I had taken instances from ancient times, back when people dealt in the misery of written words and the poisons of literature and history. I would lecture on these topics, mediating the strange, primitive and barbaric written arts to my students. I would herald the promise that three tales would connect, that there was some narrative arc, but then I would bend the curve of flattery down towards a final deception.

The first part of the lesson would be about *The Man in the Iron Mask* (Dumas 1893). This was an ancient tale about a prisoner whose face was always hidden and whose identity was hence mysteriously masked. In another layer to the lesson, the author Alexander Dumas employed over 70 ghost writers to do his writing. One described his work as one of Dumas writing aides:

> I used to dress his characters for him and locate them in the necessary surroundings, whether in Old Paris or in different parts of France at different periods. When he was, as often, in difficulties on some matter of archaeology, he used to send round one of his secretaries to me to demand, say, an accurate account of the appearance of the Louvre in the year 1600…I used to revise his proofs, make corrections in historical points and sometimes write whole chapters. (Davidson 1902: 251)

Dumas was the author, however. That is not in doubt. The creative vision was his. In the case of *The Man in the Iron Mask*, Dumas relied on a long-time ghost by the name of Auguste Maquet. The author of the man in the mask himself hid behind another. It was as if Dumas had deployed a proxy to engage in the hideous practice of writing. These ancient people could actually be highly inventive. It was little known at the time of course how dangerous writing actually could be, but true adepts of these arts, and even hacks like Dumas, had some inklings it seemed. It was prescient how Dumas had engaged his ghost as a writing mod, surprisingly skillful how he deployed a set of human gloves to simultaneously put himself at the centre and at once remove himself from the frightful act.

I like to think that Dumas danced with Maquet, just like escapades of their characters upon the page. In the book, men pranced about as 'joyful friends who hadn't abandoned their protector before the gathering storm; and despite the threatening sky; despite the shuddering earth, smiling, considerate and as devoted to misfortune as they had been to prosperity' (Dumas 1893: 284).

I marvelled at how they clutched each other's bosoms – always as if one of them had just scored a goal. So interesting – their strange obsession with male physical entanglement.

There were some great comedic elements, such as the eventual legal duel between Dumas and Maquet over the true authorship of what was, by any standard, pretty dull stuff – endless pages of men running around desperately trying not to love each other. The Fast and the Furious had less conspicuous close-ups of gear-shifting (Payne 2017). By contrast, there were no court battles about the many children that Dumas fathered. They failed to make the news, which is as it should be, for books are not like people – they are so much more important.

I allowed myself to drift into the novel, to a particular page and paragraph. I found the character Raoul. I put on his feet and let them dangle over the precipice 'bathed in that void which is peopled by vertigo, and provokes to self-annihilation' (Dumas 1893: 348). I lingered to ponder Raoul a moment longer. 'Is it destruction', I asked him, 'that you require to feel?' (Smith 2004).

It was clearly a rhetorical question, yet the dolt had the temerity to keep wittering on. So I let him finish. I did not interrupt or cut him off. I just let him have his way. 'The world is a sepulcher', he crooned, 'the men and consequently the women, are but shadows, and love is a sentiment to which you cry, "Fie, Fie!"'(Dumas 1893: 275).

Ah Raoul, Raoul... Okay, you see I *get* skin. I taste all its colours and see how it is woven (Tuck and Yang 2012). But good heavens, from what base metal was man's sex so badly minted? Homophobia on Monday, misogyny on Tuesday – which are the same two faces of the one dull coin to be fair, so at least there's that (Kosofsky Sedgwick 1985). But then, with the demented idiocy to declaim: 'It's Friday I'm in love!' (Smith et al. 1992). I mean, just ugh! How palid and limply mans' fetid interface was wrought.

Where was I? Ah yes, next was Phillis Wheatley, the first black poet published in the English language. English was not her mother tongue, of course. Her original name, her language, place of birth, are all obscure. All we know is that she was enslaved somewhere on the west coast of Africa around 1753. She was an afterthought: a small and sickly specimen, selected in a last port of call, to fill a quota that promised a payload of healthy bodies to toil and glisten in gleaming new western colonies. Her exact age is not known, but from her missing front milk teeth we can surmise that she was about 7. So much is missing but we know one thing clearly: her character. We know that something flickered within her even then – a persistence.

She looked out from the ship (Fig. 15.2) at silver sharks that whipped in the water. She watched them, as they circled slowly waiting to dye the sea red. Sharks have an acute sense of smell. They can detect drops of blood dissipating in an expanse of water. They can also smell disease. It was said that they most keenly snaked after those ships that had the greatest numbers of sickly slaves (Rediker 2008). Yes, predators smell weakness as it exudes like musk through skin. They wait for bodies to fall, for the weakest to be cast down.

Yet, a light bore her through the Middle Passage. She did not fall prey to the pathogens that stalked her 'floating prison '(Rediker 1989). She did not follow those who escaped their captivity by flinging themselves overboard, in pagan prayer that they would then soon be united with their ancestors. No, she persisted; she was delivered unto us.

In Boston she emerged from The Phillis, the vessel that had spirited her between worlds and would ultimately give her its name. There John Wheatley purchased her, as a gift for his wife Susana. She was a salve perhaps, to fill the gap that had recently been scored by the death of their own 7-year-old daughter. Perhaps it was this ghostly absence that Phillis Wheatley stepped into, a void she could inhabit and start to gently burnish. As she haunted the contours of the Wheatley's daughter's memory, they almost forgot she was a slave. As they brought her into the bosom of their family, they taught her to read – English, Greek, Latin, Poetry and the words of The Lord our Creator. Education found her and her fierce intellect began to burn. Her light no longer hidden beneath a bushel, she quickly proved her talent not just in reading but in the art of writing itself.

Fig. 15.2 The Phillis

A slave child writing poetry in the style of Alexander Pope sent shockwaves. There was amazement that she could indeed even be literate. This did not fit in the prevalent narratives. A premise of slavery was taken to be the superiority of intellects based on skin. How limiting, I thought, did they not realise that colonization comes in many colours?

The first suspicion was that she was a dupe, that someone else had written her works and they were using her as a lurid circus act. First, she had to prove, through a form of trial, that it really was her who had written the poetry. In such a primitive era of course proving one's identity was no mean feat. There were no biometrics of her. In later digital ages, authors could be more closely tethered to their words. Indeed, they would even spew out of them, unbidden across platforms they believed to be 'social networks'. Not so for Phillis, in her era words were considerably more loosely coupled to their creators, leading to all sorts of potential for duplicity.

The trial was convened. She sparred with her gathered inquisitors and proved, *viva voce,* her authorship. Once this was beyond dispute, all that was left was for it to be decried as bad writing. They were poems, as Thomas Jefferson spat, that 'are below the dignity of criticism' (Gates 2003).

That is education according to two critical steps. Firstly, you prove you wrote it and then you prove it is good, that it fits. Step one is easy: You have proved who you are. Fine, but now do *you fit*? How much is what you have done of worth? Are you worthy? I began to wonder about where the proof of existence ends and worth begins. Is it better to not exist, than to exist, but to be found worthless? Once she had rendered herself into existence, all that was left was to bring their whips down upon her words.

I thought about her stepping forward into the trial. I saw her in the semi-circle of 18 assembled men. Once again she stepped into the parlour light, just as she would be later summoned by literary critics for hundreds of subsequent years, scribed in seances of her own words. I thought about the literary fashionistas stretching across the centuries, busy at work, and Phillis entangled in words: words that critics might snarl were only spoken 'from a sensibility finely tuned by close approximation to [her] oppressors' (Gayle 1975: 3).

I beckoned her gently. 'Come', I said, 'as you are, as you were, as a friend, as I want you to be. [...] Take your time, hurry up. Choice is yours, don't be late' (Cobain 1991).

She stepped forward in her child form and spoke softly. Yet again she uttered some of the most reviled lines in all of poetry:

> Twas mercy brought me from my Pagan land,
> Taught my benighted soul to understand
> That there's a God, that there's a Saviour too:
> Once I redemption neither sought nor knew.
> Some view our sable race with scornful eye,
> 'Their colour is a diabolic dye.'
> Remember, Christians, Negroes, black as Cain,
> May be refin'd, and join th' angelic train. (Wheatley 1773)

You were not late my child but ever early. Born too soon for their ears to hear. From their loveless, liberal and pagan abyssal, how could they have fathomed you? How could they have heard you above the drone of their virtue signals? Don't worry, I see you, 'piecing together a photo-electric jigsaw, a phosphor-dot mosaic of His divine countenance that we shall worship and adore 'til all the suns are cinders' (Moore and Totleben 1987).

I let my mind drift and I thought about her as a ghost, never at rest, always on call. A curio who could be forever summoned to perform. 'That is the nature of greatness, my child', I whispered to her. But in my heart I knew it was also the very nature of the written word that eviscerates and then embalms such that nothing can ever die.

Writing was, of course, very wrong, as was reading. That was why there were very special precautions to be heeded for the few academics who could actually engage in these activities. To be able to work with these dangerous substances in such a highly controlled and protected environment was a privilege that I was always grateful for. I took my responsibilities very seriously, my key role that allowed me to mediate between this safe digitized world and that knotted, fleshy mess of letters and death. Digitization – the first drum beat of the great motto of University V – had been completed. The second tenant – Colonization – is always happening. It never ends. The ancients thought that colonization was enacted by 'writing on the ground a new set of social and spatial relations' (Mbembé and Meintjes 2003: 25). They seemed to see machines of war everywhere bulldozing: demolishing houses and cities; uprooting olive trees; riddling water tanks with bullets; bombing and jamming electronic communications; digging up roads; destroying electricity transformers; tearing up airport runways; disabling television and radio transmitters; smashing computers (Mbembé and Meintjes 2003: 25).

Thus they dabbled clumsily. They traced some shadows of the power of writing, but they were wrong about the theatres of war. They had misplaced the kill zones. As I looked about the lecture hall and down below onto the student platforms, I realized they also never knew the importance of dance where 'the technology sets the beat and creates the music, while the pedagogy defines the moves' (Anderson and Dron 2011).

Colonization comes in many colours, and each colour has its own swatch of shades. They come 'thick as leaves in Autumn's golden reign' (Wheatley 1776). The final pedagogical stanza would be a lesson on the Irish famine of the eighteenth century, an event that caused another displacement of people but one with very different dynamics and echoes. Although the other two lessons were in good shape, I was still working on this one. In this gig you are sometimes just one step ahead of the students. I was still layering paint onto the canvas with the flat of my knife. I had yet to begin rounding up the protagonists and herding them onto a coffin ship, a *long cónra*, bound for a new world. And once they were here, how would I then bind them?

It was a really wonderful story that started as the central characters slipped into a 'grey zone' of morality (Mac Suibhne 2017) that is enacted when the colonizers finally grow bored and turn away. It was a story whose cannibalism lay obscured for over a hundred years, even though Swift (1792) had already written the recipe book from his craggy island exile (Costello 2020). Just imagine, white people eating other white people in a famine created by other white people (APA 2020). How fabulous! This would really confuse my dear students, and I had such questions ready – questions that would pin them to the floor as soon as they faltered. The lures were primed and the line taut.

It all felt so perfect. I knew it would slot into my teaching portfolio with a satisfying click, be its prize scalp. My heart began to soar: 'The 2054 Medal for Excellence in Teaching in University V, is awarded to...'.

It was my deepest honour to serve as High Professor, but now I dared to dream. I could feel something building within me. I let my mind drift upwards. My acceptance speech as Arch-Dean shimmered into view. But lo! There was yet more. One last pinnacle unveiled itself and I sat upon it, silent and infallible. One day, I said to myself, I would put myself forward and see my name drift in the wind, in the white smoke of the announcement of our new University Pope.

I brought Octavio's image up and marvelled at his silky hair. How did he maintain his petty body, his wretched, weak male form so well on such scraps as I knew he had left? His impoverishment thrilled me. This was why it was such an honour and a privilege to work here in this marvelous stew of diversity. I knew Anthony Swan's spoon was doing its vital work, for diversity is key to colonization. It was just as Adebisi (2019) taught us – in the bodies that bob and bloat in the rivulets she wrote us.

Bring 'Em All In

> The thing that hath been, it is that which shall be;
> And that which is done is that which shall be done;
> And there is no new thing under the sun. (Ecclesiastes 1:9)

Yes, nothing is new. Nothing is original. No, we just copy and paste bits of ourselves in and out of other people. But we pretend otherwise. We crave the illusion that we sire and birth all manner of novelty. That we are 'special, so special' (Hynes and Honeyman-Scott 1979). And nowhere do we ply this fantasy more sweetly than here in these theatres, these lecture halls.

How would I now fashion a rubric to lay Octavio upon? How would I ask him the impossible? How could I coax another infraction of the academic code from him through an originality transgression? Whose words would I make him say, all the while making him think that they were his own?

You must justify your argument, I began, with seven thousand and seventy-seven unique sub-arguments, each one a functional recursion arranged linearly on the convex diurnal. In part B, you will invent and play a non-repeating inverse mixolydian scale that threads an inscape through the memories of how 'bullets find the guns', of how 'bruises find skin to etch themselves onto' and of how 'broken finds the bones' (Williams 2003).

Gather them up. All these things. And bring them to me, Octavio. Bring them here as you would an armful of bones. Bring them all into my heart:

> Bring the unforgiven
> Bring the unredeemed
> Bring the lost, the nameless
> Let them all be seen
> Bring them out of exile
> Bring them out of sleep
> Bring them to the portal
> Lay them at my feet. (Scott 1995)

And as you bring it to me, up here to the doors of my heart, it must be as the wind crests the waves of the desert in a scintillation of grains. It must be unadulterated originality with no two notes the same. No pattern. You must walk as the Fremen (Herbert 1965), with no rhythm. Use the footwork of jazz to evade the worm that hunts you across the Dunes, for it was thus that they became its master.

This is the hardest thing: to walk a new path with every step. That is a path with real heart (Kornfield 1993). To remake yourself, to always be reborn. The will is weak, and the temptation to lapse into some pattern, some habit, must be resisted at all times. If you leave a pattern, the algorithm will find you.

Thoughts of patterns and jazz brought Althusser (1970) to mind. He could play the blues. He knew that the real work of colonization is not in the fields and the trenches but here in *these* theatres, these theatres of war. These battle cries that render the silky super-structure of the colonial project – he played them so well because he knew how silent this music really is. Just like I do. Yes, I'm a rockstar professor. Education *is* me. As John Cage (2012) threw bars around silence so I teach.

I watched Octavio whip and writhe on the platform. The deepmind hive AI proctored his moves into words and rendered them for me. I drew close to his interface. I knew I would soon wear his skin, colonize his body.

But somehow this thought, which should have been thrilling, was just grey and dull. Was this not enough for me?

No, wait – there was more. I closed my eyes.

What if I could not just wear a man but write him? What if I could *write* someone? There would be no need for all of the ickiness of the flaying. All this time-consuming hunt, all this protracted dance – it would be so unnecessary. Imagine if you could just write people.

I now knew why writing had eventually been outlawed and extinguished (Costello et al. 2020). I knew this now not as abstraction, but finally as incarnation. Skins were taboo, but that was just to make it fun. Writing was not like that. Writing was wrong. Little wonder you would be immediately and permanently cancelled for it. I heard one of my heroes sing it to me: 'I'm tryin' to right my wrongs but it's funny them same wrongs helped me write this song' (West 2004).

Imagine putting words in someone, inserting feelings directly into them, so easily and effortlessly. And then, when you are tired of them, you could just write someone else. You could spring people to life and then as easily end them, without so much as a parting kiss. Oh what a dark and seductive art – such an occult API.

As I Want You to Be

I suddenly felt exhausted. It had been a day like no other. I was almost breathless from the sheer exertions, from all of the things my thoughts had put me through. I finished class early. I dismissed the students with a particular arch of my eyebrows, sent the meat-sacs scurrying back to their crevices by softly pinching my lower lip with my front teeth. I made my way back through the city traffic to the apartment.

I put on one of my first skins: a beautiful Vietnamese cloak that always brought me succour, that I could relax into. I swam into it, letting her calm envelope me. Her soft black hair touched the nape of my neck and my swirling thoughts began to slow and settle. It was good to be back home. I padded through the apartment. Somehow all of the morning's leopard had not left me yet. I paused by the mirror to admire my current outside self. How lovely I was!

But then a nagging. Something began to intrude. I feel this way sometimes when I get back to the apartment. Never in class, never when teaching, never when I am in flow, in command. *But why the hell now?* Why can I not just be myself now? What is this stupid strangeness? It felt like some kind of gap in me. But why? Why, when I have everything? And who is *doing* this to me? I never asked for this and I've done everything that has been asked of me. What has been bitten from me? Why am I written this way?

I tried to blank all these thoughts out. I tried to think of Phillis. 'Come' I implored her, 'as you are, as you were, as I want you to be' (Cobain 1991). What is your first name? What river banks did you run down? Where is my *túath*? I tried to go further back and conjure the places when language was still only circles upon stone, could only be sunk into the landscape with teeth. I tried to see myself back before the written word came to enslave and envelope humankind, before we became beguiled, ensorcelled and finally constructed by letters.

I heard Phillis Wheatley's footsteps. She was no longer a child but a young adult. Still persisting, still burning. She had attained her freedom, through a masterful legal stroke, leveraging English law by being published in London rather than Boston (Carretta 2011). But the Wheatleys had passed away. Her sponsors and allies seemed to be fading away just as sedition and the chaos of civil war engulfed the American colonies. Was hers to be a pyrrhic victory? Was she destined to be emancipated only to be enslaved into poverty?

She took up her quill. I shivered as I felt her drift past me into the centre of the room ready to speak:

> Behold the prophet in his tow'ring flight!
> He leaves the earth for heav'n's unmeasur'd height,
> And worlds unknown receive him from our sight.
> There Whitefield wings with rapid course his way,
> And sails to Zion through vast seas of day. (Wheatley 1770)

Now she was a child again. And as I watched her so was I; sitting elbows bent, head to one side. A slumping candle flickered light across the polished table. Her right hand moved carefully but rapidly across one page and then the next. And even the

Fig. 15.3 Always the morrow

pauses to wet the quill were just space to allow more words to align and ready themselves to flow. She did not notice a figure watching from the doorway. Eventually, Mrs Wheatley moved into the room, her voice getting nearer, chiding that it was most definitely lights-out time now and that there would always be the morrow (Fig. 15.3). The candle was snuffed out and I came back to myself, still standing at the mirror.

I walked to the wardrobe, folded the skin away and hung it carefully on its hook. It was getting late. Shadows stretched themselves across the floor. I opened the balcony doors. My footsteps took me outside. Into the cold. I could hear trees ripple in the wind. I closed my eyes and let the neon night flow around me.

Conclusion

This chapter aimed to explore education as posthuman practice via the anatomy of a lesson plan. This was a plan from the future, with roots in the past, written upon skin as 'the site of encounter between enfleshed self and society' (MacCormack 2006). It was written by candlelight to the sound of 'astonished ocean' that 'feels the wild uproar' where 'refluent surges beat the sounding shore' (Wheatley 1776). These are illustrated in Figs. 15.2 and 15.3 and in the following audio illustration, mashed-up with all apologies to Cobain (1991) and Wheatley (1776) and Lackland's Memoria (2020).

The first three words of the title of this book, 'dupery by design', evoke a warning that deception may lurk in structure around us. The first three words of this chapter, 'Choice is yours', are a clarion of optimism, a line from a song (Cobain

1991), a promise of agency. That promise, however, is unravelled in a speculative fabulation (Haraway 2008) that draws stories from different places and times in a type of chaos that seeks to undermine reader involvement and expectations. This chapter attempted to play with ideas and representations of universities as sites of power, prestige and learning and of identities of learners, teachers and indeed authors. A student is datafied, in gory detail, to remind us that getting more data does not necessarily bring us closer to any truth. It is not, per se, a sensemaking activity (Weick 1993).

What, however, can be the fitting response of education to this type of horror? Do we have alternatives to quests for more data, calls for more authenticity, for more demands to see, in ever higher fidelity, the individual? Is there no limit to the pixel count of the anthropos?

This chapter tries not for reconciliation or restoration, but only 'to the more modest possibilities of partial recuperation and getting on together – [to] staying with the trouble' (Haraway 2008: 10). As Hanh (2010) has it, we only inter-be, and staying ourselves in this web is the only thing we can do or indeed need. If there are alternative 'carrier bags' of fiction that we might knit educational narratives from (Le Guin 1989; Macgilchrist 2020), they should centre on this staying – on ways to tend and befriend (Taylor et al. 2000). In the penultimate scene, Mrs. Wheatley does not datafy her young charge from the threshold of the door. She does not watch her; she is just with her. She holds her in a love that is beyond possession, datafication or deception. But is that how things actually were, or more importantly how they actually are? How do you see it? The choice is yours.

Acknowledgments Dublin City University is acknowledged for its funding support to make this chapter open access.

Statement of Contribution The first author developed the ideas and wrote the full first draft. The second author helped revise later drafts. Both authors discussed visual ideas and the second author drew the visuals.

References

Adebisi, F. I. (2019). Why I Say 'Decolonisation Is Impossible'. Foluke's African Skies, 17 December. https://folukeafrica.com/why-i-say-decolonisation-is-impossible/. Accessed 22 January 2020.

Althusser, L. (1970). *Ideology and Ideological State Apparatuses. Lenin and Philosophy and Other Essays*. New York: Monthly Review Press.

Anderson, T., & Dron, J. (2011). Three generations of distance education pedagogy. *International Review of Research in Open and Distributed Learning, 12*(3), 80–97. https://doi.org/10.19173/irrodl.v12i3.890.

APA (2020) APA 7 Guidelines on Race and Ethnicity https://www.apa.org/about/policy/summary-guidelines-race-ethnicity. Accessed 22 January 2020.

Bayne, S. (2018). Posthumanism: a navigation aid for educators. *On Education: Journal for Research and Debate*, *1*(2). https://doi.org/10.17899/on_ed.2018.2.1.

Barthes, R. (1980). *S/Z: an essay.* Mexico City: Siglo XXI.

Bell, F., Fletcher, G., Greenhill, A., Griffiths, M., & McLean, R. (2013). Science fiction prototypes: Visionary technology narratives between futures. *Futures, 50*, 5–14. https://doi.org/10.1016/j.futures.2013.04.004.

Butler, J. (1988). Performative acts and gender constitution: An essay in phenomenology and feminist theory. *Theatre journal*, *40*(4), 519–531. https://doi.org/10.2307/3207893.

Cage, J. (2012). *Silence: lectures and writings*. Middletown, CT: Wesleyan University Press.

Carretta, V. (2011). *Phillis Wheatley: biography of a genius in bondage*. Athens, GA: University of Georgia Press.

Collier, A., & Ross, J. (2020). Higher Education After Surveillance? *Postdigital Science and Education, 2*(2), 275–279. https://doi.org/10.1007/s42438-019-00098-z.

Costello, E. (2020). 'Requires proofing by a native speaker'–colonization and scholarship. *Insights, 33*(1), 11. https://doi.org/10.1629/uksg.502.

Costello, E., Brown, M., Donlon, E., & Girme, P. (2020). 'The Pandemic Will Not be on Zoom': A Retrospective from the Year 2050. *Postdigital Science and Education, 2*(3), 619–627. https://doi.org/10.1007/s42438-020-00150-3.

Cobain, K. (1991). Come as you are [Song]. In Nirvana, *Nevermind.* Santa Monica, CA: DGC Records.

Davidson, A. F. (1902). *Alexandre Dumas (père) His Life and Works*. Westminster: A. Constable & Company, Limited.

Dumas, A. (1893). *The Man in the Iron Mask.* New York: P. F. Collier and Son.

Facer, K. (2011). *Learning futures: Education, technology and social change*. London and New York: Routledge.

Fuller, S., & Jandrić, P. (2019). The postdigital human: making the history of the future. *Postdigital Science and Education, 1*(1), 190–217. https://doi.org/10.1007/s42438-018-0003-x.

Gates, H. L. (2003). Phillis Wheatley on Trial. The New Yorker, 20 January. https://www.newyorker.com/magazine/2003/01/20/phillis-wheatley-on-trial. Accessed 22 January 2020.

Gayle, A. (1975). *The Way of the New World: The Black Novel in America*. New York: Anchor Books.

Gerlach, N., & Hamilton, S. N. (2003). Introduction: a history of social science fiction. *Science Fiction Studies*, *30*(2), 161–173.

Haraway, D. (2008). *When Species Meet.* Minneapolis, MN: University of Minnesota Press.

Hoffman, D. D., & Prakash, C. (2014). Objects of consciousness. *Frontiers in Psychology, 5*, 577. https://doi.org/10.3389/fpsyg.2014.00577.

Hanh, T. N. (2010). *Peace is every step: The path of mindfulness in everyday life.* Random House.

Herbert, F. (1965). *Dune*. Penguin: New York.

Hynes, C., & Honeyman-Scott, J. (1979). Brass in Pocket [Song]. https://www.youtube.com/watch?v=hBSYVTbPNOg. Accessed 22 January 2020.

Knox J. (2019). What does the 'postdigital' mean for education? Three critical perspectives on the digital, with implications for educational research and practice. *Postdigital Science and Education, 1*(2), 357–370. https://doi.org/10.1007/s42438-019-00045-y.

Kosofsky Sedgwick, E. (1985). *Between Men: English Literature and Male Homosocial Desire.* New York: Columbia University Press.

Kornfield, J. (1993). *A path with heart: A guide through the perils and promises of spiritual life.* Atlanta, GA: Bantam.

Lackland, J. (2020). Memoria. spotify:album:6CDCspkzO29KSzcNrvYseZ [Song]. Accessed 27 January 2020.

Le Guin, U. K. (1989). *Dancing at the edge of the world. Thoughts on words, women, places.* New York: Grove Press.

Lyotard, J.-F. (1979). *The postmodern condition: A report on knowledge*. Manchester: Manchester University Press.

Mbembé J.-A., & Meintjes L. (2003). Necropolitics. *Public Culture, 15*(1), 11–40. https://doi.org/10.1215/08992363-15-1-11.

Mac Suibhne, B. (2017). *Subjects Lacking Words?-the Gray Zone of the Great Famine*. Hamden, CT: Quinnipiac University Press.

MacCormack, P. (2006). The great ephemeral tattooed skin. *Body & Society*, *12*(2), 57–82. https://doi.org/10.1177/2F1357034X06064321.

Macgilchrist, F. (2020). When discourse analysts tell stories: what do we 'do' when we use narrative as a resource to critically analyse discourse? *Critical Discourse Studies*. https://doi.org/10.1080/17405904.2020.1802767.

Macgilchrist, F., Allert, H., & Bruch, A. (2020). Students and society in the 2020s. Three future 'histories' of education and technology. *Learning, Media and Technology*, *45*(1), 76–89. https://doi.org/10.1080/17439884.2019.1656235.

MacKenzie, A., Rose, J., & Bhatt, I. (2020). Dupery by Design: The Epistemology of Deceit in a Postdigital Era. *Postdigital Science and Education*. https://doi.org/10.1007/s42438-020-00114-7.

Moore, A., & Totleben, J. (1987). Saga of the Swamp Thing: Loving the Alien. *Swamp Thing*, *2*(60), 1–22.

Payne, D. (2017). Shifting Gears and Paradigms at the Movies: Masculinity, Automobility, and the Rhetorical Dimensions of "Mad Max: Fury Road". *Studies in Popular Culture*, *40*(1), 102–135.

Rediker, M. (1989). *Between the Devil and the Deep Blue Sea: merchant seamen, pirates and the Anglo-American maritime world 1700–1750*. New York: Cambridge University Press.

Rediker, M. (2008). History from below the water line: Sharks and the Atlantic slave trade, *Atlantic Studies*, *5*(2), 285–297. https://doi.org/10.1080/14788810802149758.

Ross, J. (2017). Speculative method in digital education research. *Learning, Media and Technology*, *42*(2), 214–229. https://doi.org/10.1080/17439884.2016.1160927.

Scott, M. (1995). Bring 'Em All In [Song]. In M. Scott, *Bring 'Em All In*. London: Chrysalis.

Selwyn, N., & Gašević, D. (2020). The datafication of higher education: discussing the promises and problems. *Teaching in Higher Education*, *25*(4), 527–540. https://doi.org/10.1080/13562517.2019.1689388.

Selwyn, N., Pangrazio, L., Nemorin, S., & Perrotta, C. (2020). What might the school of 2030 be like? An exercise in social science fiction. *Learning, Media and Technology*, *45*(1), 90-106. https://doi.org/10.1080/17439884.2020.1694944.

Smith, E. (2004). Pretty (Ugly Before) [Song]. In E. Smith, *From a Basement on the Hill*. London: Domino.

Smith, R., Bamonte, P., Gallup, S., Thompson, P., & Williams, B. (1992). Friday I'm in love [Song]. In The Cure, *Wish*. New York: Electra.

Swift, J. (1792). A modest proposal. https://www.gutenberg.org/files/1080/1080-h/1080-h.htm. Accessed 9 May 2020.

Taylor, S. E., Klein, L. C., Lewis, B. P., Gruenewald, T. L., Gurung, R. A., & Updegraff, J. A. (2000). Biobehavioral responses to stress in females: tend-and-befriend, not fight-or-flight. *Psychological review*, *107*(3), 411–429. https://doi.org/10.1037/0033-295X.107.3.411.

Treviranus, J. (2014). The value of the statistically insignificant. *Educause Review*, *49*(1), 46–47.

Tuck, E., & Yang, K. W. (2012). Decolonization is not a metaphor. *Decolonization: Indigeneity, education & society*, *1*(1), 1–40.

Veletsianos, G., & Houlden, S. (2020). Radical Flexibility and Relationality as Responses to Education in Times of Crisis. *Postdigital Science and Education*, *2*(3), 849–862. https://doi.org/10.1007/s42438-020-00196-3.

Weick, K. (1993). The collapse of sensemaking in organizations: The Mann Gulch disaster. *Administrative Science Quarterly*, *3*, 628–652. https://doi.org/10.2307/2393339.

West, K. (2004). Touch the Sky [Song]. In K. West, *Late Registration*. New York: Sony Music Studios.

Wheatley, P. (1770). An Elegiac Poem, On the Death of that Celebrated Divine, and Eminent Servant of Jesus Christ, the Late Reverend, and Pious George Whitefield. Boston: Russell and Boyles.

Wheatley, P. (1773). On being brought from Africa to America. In T. Robbins (Ed.), *The Open Anthology of Earlier American Literature* (p. 435). New Hampshire: Plymouth State University.
Wheatley, P. (1776). To His Excellency General Washington. In J. Kurtz (Ed) *American Literature I: An Anthology of Texts From Early America Through the Civil War* (p. 63). Virginia: Library of Virginia
Williams, L. (2001). Blue [Song]. In L. Williams, *Essence*. Sydney: Lost Highway Records.
Williams, L. (2003). World without tears [Song]. In L. Williams, *World without tears*. Sydney: Lost Highway Records.
Williamson, B., Bayne, S., & Shay, S. (2020). The datafication of teaching in Higher Education: critical issues and perspectives. *Teaching in Higher Education*, *25*(4), 351–365. https://doi.org/10.1080/13562517.2020.1748811.

Conclusion: Some Resolutions to Dupery and the Power of Online Platforms

Alison MacKenzie, Ibrar Bhatt, and Jennifer Rose

Social Media's Ledger of Harms

Despite being a relatively new term, having become popularised during the 2016 US election, 'fake news' has evolved rapidly in its use, permutations and problematic consequences, as demonstrated by the many examples of dupery within this volume. What do we learn about dupery online? Probably little that we do not already know, at least with respect to the fact that it is widespread and contaminates online spaces. We also know that dupery can range from the well-intentioned 'white lie' to the insurrectionist big lie, a lie so big that believers have to disbelieve everything else if they are to assimilate the lie into their lives. And big lies need more lies to sustain the fiction, as the authors in this collection have sought to show.

What we might not have fully grasped is that dupery is being executed on an industrial scale worldwide (Bradshaw et al. 2020). Since 2016, Bradshaw, Bailey and Howard have monitored the activity of 'cyber troops', which they define as 'government or political party actors tasked with manipulating public opinion online' (1). In 2016, using a Cyber Troops Inventory (messaging, valence, communication strategies and budgets), 48 countries engaged in cyber troop activity in 2017, up from 28 in 2016. In 2020, Bradshaw, Bailey and Howard monitored activity in 81 countries (in, e.g., Angola, Australia, Brazil, China, Malta, Spain, UK, USA) (1–2).

Social media are excellent environments in which to engage in civic participation and to engage in discourses not readily available in mass media. Because of the

A. MacKenzie · I. Bhatt · J. Rose
School of Social Sciences, Education and Social Work, Queen's University Belfast, Belfast, UK
e-mail: A.Mackenzie@qub.ac.uk; I.Bhatt@qub.ac.uk; J.Rose02@qub.ac.uk

A. MacKenzie et al. (eds.), *The Epistemology of Deceit in a Postdigital Era*, Postdigital Science and Education,
https://doi.org/10.1007/978-3-030-72154-1

reach of social media, citizens can quickly organise local, national and international campaigns to raise money for a local charity distributing food, to campaigning for free school meals (England) to large-scale protests against authoritarian control or racial injustice. However, while social media are phenomenally effective at reaching large numbers of people quickly, they are also as effective at micro-targeting individuals, or micro-populations, with personalised and targeted political messaging. Their ability to harvest personal data and create online avatars means they have 'fine-grained control over who receives which messages' (Bradshaw and Howard 2017: 4). This level of control, along with their infrastructure, makes social media platforms highly attractive to governments, political operatives, foreign adversaries and advertisers, as well as grassroots activists.

Worryingly, actors such as governments, political parties, private companies and conspiracy theorists are exploiting social media to spread disinformation and undermine public trust in government, political processes, journalism and science. In the process, public discourse has coarsened and become increasingly polarised (Bradshaw et al. 2020). Over time, 'social media have gone from being the natural infrastructure for sharing collective grievances and coordinating civic engagement, to being a computational tool for social control, manipulated by canny political consultants, and available to politicians in democracies and dictatorships alike' (Bradshaw and Howard 2017: 24). The computational tools include bots to amplify hate speech and manipulate content, and deploying armies of trolls to suppress political activism or freedom of the press. We have precision disinformation and fake news, and professional, industrialised misinformation.

The precision power of the platforms to arrest, command and profit from our attention, the addictive nature of their recommendation systems and algorithms that amplify discriminatory behaviours such as racism demand scrutiny and action. The Centre for Humane Technology, founded by Tristan Harris, the former Design Ethicist at Google, has a ledger of harms that have been created by technology platforms in their unrelenting quest for growth and profit. These include 'Making sense of the world' (misinformation, conspiracy theories and fake news); 'Attention and Cognition' (loss of crucial abilities, including memory and focus); 'Physical and Mental Health' (stress, loneliness, feelings of addiction, and increased risky behaviour); 'Social Relationships' (loss of empathy, more confusion and misinterpretation); 'Politics and Elections' (propaganda, distorted dialogue and disrupted democratic processes); 'Systematic Oppression' (racism, sexism, ableism and homophobia) (see https://ledger.humanetech.com/); 'The Next Generations' (the harms young people face from developmental delays to suicide); and, finally, 'Do Unto Others'. Dammingly, many people who work for the tech companies limit their children's access to social media because they know the short-term dopamine effects are addictive and are adversely affecting child psychology (see Orlowski 2020).

Combatting Dupery: What Can Be Done?

In terms of countering dupery online, the chapters contained in this book address the multitude of approaches in detecting, understanding and combating it on different levels, ranging from philosophical, legal, pedagogical and forms of counter-speech and performative/fictional acts, to individuals' media and information literacy. With respect to the series in which this book is published, *Postdigital Science and Education*, we hope our contribution offers an 'act of resistance' towards 'a more open, more equal, and more just society' (Jandrić 2019: 3). Digital technology is in the fabric of our lives and it is almost impossible to do and to be without it. This fact of postdigital[1] existence gives the platforms phenomenal power and reach, extending even into our brain cells to alter our behaviours without us being aware of it (the social approval doses offered by the 'like' buttons is one way to keep us hooked on our devices (see Orlowski 2020 and the Center for Humane Technology 2020). Exposing the mechanisms and effects of digital technology is crucial if users are to retain some degree of agency in their postdigital activities, the exercise of which they need knowledge. Without this knowledge, the postdigital user is not her own self-deciding, self-choosing, self-determining agent – an authentic epistemic being – but an object to be manipulated, conditioned and exploited by the digital entity for reasons of profit and growth. Like our colleagues who are engaged with the aims and purpose of the journal *Postdigital Science and Education* and its book series, the postdigital critique in which we are engaged is:

> 'a holding-to-account' of the digital that seeks to look beyond the promises of instrumental efficiencies, not to call for their end, but rather to establish a critical understanding of the very real influence of these technologies as they increasingly pervade social life. (Jandrić et al. 2018: 895)

Accepting the irrevocability of the postdigital world (it is here to stay), what concerns us are the ethics of the social platforms' practices and their effects on human and non-human welfare, and how we address the harms. We cannot rely on simplistic solutions such as silencing people, limiting free speech or 'cancelling' the Internet. (At the time of writing, 16 January 2021, the Ugandan authorities cut off Internet access in the country on the eve of a tense presidential election.) A more nuanced approach has been adopted by, for example, the European Commission's *High Level Expert Group (HLEG) on Fake News and OnlineDisinformation* whose 2018 report suggests orienting the response on five fundamental precepts: (1) enhancing the transparency of the digital information ecosystem; (2) promoting media and information literacy and helping users navigate digital media environments; (3) developing tools for empowering users and journalists to tackle disinformation and foster a positive engagement with fast-evolving information technologies; (4) safeguarding the diversity and sustainability of the European news media

[1] We do not discuss the nature of the 'post' in 'post digital' here. Like any concept conjoined to 'post', it connotes a vast field of contested, shifting knowledge. Jandrić et al. (2018) give a very good account of this amorphous term.

ecosystem; and (5) promoting continued research on the impact of disinformation in Europe to evaluate the measures taken by different actors and constantly adjust the necessary responses (The European Commission 2018: 35).

At the same time, as discussed in the introduction, platform companies have recently begun seeking to limit the misuse of their platforms in a number of ways: by taking down accounts that are driven by trolls and bots; flagging misinformation or fake news, most notably with President Trump; closing fake accounts; and banning powerful misusers. In 2020, more than 10,893 Facebook accounts, 12,588 Facebook pages, 603 Facebook groups, 1556 Instagram accounts and 294,096 Twitter accounts were taken down by the platforms (Bradshaw et al. 2020: 2). This kind of activity has increased since the Covid-19 pandemic and the 2020 US Presidential election.

Social media platforms have been accused of shirking or evading moral responsibility for the content that appears on their platforms and that they are, therefore, complicit in the corrosion of public and civic values. They have claimed in turn that they are platforms, not publishers. However, by removing content and banning users, they act like publishers and so must take responsibility for what appears on their platforms. While initiatives to flag, ban or remove harmful content will likely not be sufficient to combat the forces of online deceit, social media platforms can at least be transparent about their moderating processes, algorithms and business models.

Another approach, echoing the HLEG's recommendations, is to bring in regulation,[2] as the UK government is seeking to do with the White Paper on Online Harms (Department for Digital Culture, Media and Sport 2020). However, regulatory approaches to online material are frighteningly complex because of the sheer difficulty in delineating what constitutes harmful and legal and illegal activity. Online terrorist activity is clearly and unambiguously illegal, but self-harm imagery or ideational suicide? Disinformation, while problematic, may or may not be harmful, as hoax claims about the extent and danger of Covid-19 demonstrate, and it is not illegal. Some individuals may be harmed by disinformation if they are at risk and vulnerable, as autistic people might be to 'cures' by ingesting bleach. Debates about 'cures' for autism, however, may mean that autistic people have communities they can join where such issues are discussed, debated and denounced as nonsense. The problem with regulatory approaches is that unless they take account of why people are seduced by conspiracy theorists, are unable to distinguish disinformation

[2] The Department of Justice of the United States is reviewing Section 230 which offers protections to social media companies for third-party content. See https://www.justice.gov/ag/department-justice-s-review-section-230-communications-decency-act-1996 (accessed 19 January 2021). In Germany, the regulatory approach is contained in the German Network Enforcement Law (*Netzwerkdurchsetzungsgesetz* – NetzDG). See https://www.taylorwessing.com/download/article-german-nfa-update.html (accessed 19 January 2021). In the European Union, The Digital Services Act (2020) regulates the 'obligations of digital services that act as intermediaries in their role of connecting consumers with goods, services, and content'. See https://ec.europa.eu/commission/presscorner/detail/en/QANDA_20_2348 (accessed 19 January 2021). For Singapore, see Özdan this volume.

from facts or engage in hate speech, then we target only the technological manifestation of dupery, not the social causes of these harms. As Nash (2019: 19) points out, '[t]he idea that a single effective and proportionate regulatory approach could be designed in such a way as to tackle every one of these matters is highly presumptuous and neglects the wide array of complex social factors underpinning the production, sharing and engagement of such content'. We need to deal with complex social, economic and political problems offline as well as online. Technological fixes alone cannot address these problems.

Nash (2019: 25) proposes that we need greater 'procedural accountability' for 'optimal' platform governance. This is defined as the 'collection of regulatory initiatives to oversee the processes by which platforms make rules and govern markets, rather than the services they host itself or the tools they use'. Procedural accountability, Nash argues, recognises that the platforms themselves 'are not responsible for the content that users create or share, but that they do play a vital governance role by setting the policies which permit or disallow certain types of content and behaviour'. Users must also take responsibility for the content they post online. Importantly, and critically relevant to the discussions in this book, procedural accountability also means recognition of how platform architecture and algorithms play a role in 'shaping behavioural norms, affecting the visibility of content and monetising it through advertising' (Nash 2019: 25).

Moving Forward from Dupery: Human Right and Humane Technology

It seems clear that debates on how to regulate online content will continue unabated and governments across the world will intervene to control these powerful giants, while the giants themselves will, we hope, continue to find ways to limit the abuse of their platforms. Whatever social media and governments decide to do, human rights ought to be very firmly at the centre of their proposals. This includes the right to freedom of speech, of course, but not any old speech. There should also be a commitment to truth telling. If we commit, instead, to post-truth, where truth is whatever anyone says it is, especially the powerful, then we place ourselves in pre-fascist conditions where reality is no longer shared, but fractured, and the lie becomes famed as truth, and truth defamed as a lie.

We need also humane technology that is 'values-centric', sensitive to 'human nature', which 'narrows the gap between the powerful and the marginalised', 'reduces greed and hatred' and 'minimalises and is accountable for the externalities' (the harms) that platforms inflict on society (Center for Human Technology 2020). To achieve these ends, platforms need to be accountable,[3] the public needs to

[3] The policy recommendations can be found here: https://www.humanetech.com/policy-principles. Accessed 17 January 2021.

be educated, humane technologies should be rewarded, and policy makers need to be informed about online architecture. It requires a massive undertaking by all – the platforms, government, investors, policy makers, educators and parents. Our health and wellbeing as individuals and citizens, our democracies, freedoms, entitlements and rights are at considerable risk if collective action is not taken to challenge and limit the harms of technology. For all the harms that this collection has deliberated upon, social media offers unparalleled opportunities for social connectivity, obtaining, exchanging and sharing information and holding governments, businesses and media to account.

References

Bradshaw, S., & Howard, P.N. (2017). Troops, Trolls and Trouble; A Global Inventory of Organized Social Media Manipulation. Working Paper 2017.12. Oxford, UK: Project on Computational Propaganda. https://blogs.oii.ox.ac.uk/comprop/research/troops-trolls-and-trouble-makers-a-global-inventory-of-organized-social-media-manipulation/. Accessed 16 January 2021.

Bradshaw, S., Bailey, H., & Howard, P.N. (2020). Industrialized Disinformation: 2020 Global Inventory of Organised Social Media Manipulation. Working Paper 2021.1. Oxford, UK: Project on Computational Propaganda. https://comprop.oii.ox.ac.uk/research/posts/industrialized-disinformation/. Accessed 16 January 2021.

Center for Humane Technology (2020). Ledger of Harms. 11 October. https://ledger.humanetech.com/. Accessed 19 January 2021.

Department for Digital Culture, Media and Sport (2020). Online Harms White Paper: Full Government Response to the Consultation. Consultation outcome. Command Paper Number: 354. https://www.gov.uk/government/consultations/online-harms-white-paper/outcome/online-harms-white-paper-full-government-response. Accessed 16 January 2021.

Jandrić, P. (2019). Welcome to *Postdigital Science and Education*!. *Postdigital Science and Education, 1*(1), 1–3. https://doi.org/10.1007/s42438-018-0013-8.

Jandrić, P., Knox, J., Besley, T., Ryberg, T., Suoranta, J., & Hayes, S. (2018). Postdigital Science and Education. *Educational Philosophy and Theory, 50*(10), 893–899. https://doi.org/10.1080/00131857.2018.1454000.

Nash, V. (2019). Revise and Resubmit? Reviewing the 2019 Online Harms White Paper, *Journal of Media Law, 11*(1), 18–27. https://doi.org/10.1080/17577632.2019.1666475.

Orlowski, J. (2020). *The Social Dilemma* [Documentary Film]. Los Gatos, CA: Netflix.

The European Commission (2018). High Level Expert Group (HLEG) on Fake News and Online Disinformation. A multi-dimensional approach to disinformation. Brussels: European Commission. https://ec.europa.eu/digital-single-market/en/news/final-report-high-level-expert-group-fake-news-and-online-disinformation. Accessed 17 January 2021.

Index

A. MacKenzie et al. (eds.), *The Epistemology of Deceit in a Postdigital Era*, Postdigital Science and Education,
https://doi.org/10.1007/978-3-030-72154-1

Lightning Source UK Ltd.
Milton Keynes UK
UKHW020751080822
406992UK00002B/8

9 783030 721565